MCSA
Windows Server® 2016

Study Guide
Exam 70-741: Networking with Windows Server 2016

Will Panek

A Wiley Brand

Senior Acquisitions Editor: Kenyon Brown
Development Editor: Kim Wimpsett
Technical Editors: Rodney R. Fournier, Chris Crayton
Production Editor: Rebecca Anderson
Copy Editor: Judy Flynn
Editorial Manager: Mary Beth Wakefield
Production Manager: Kathleen Wisor
Executive Editor: Jim Minatel
Book Designers: Judy Fung and Bill Gibson
Proofreader: Nancy Carrasco
Indexer: J & J Indexing
Project Coordinator, Cover: Brent Savage
Cover Designer: Wiley
Cover Image: ©Getty Images Inc./Jeremy Woodhouse

Copyright © 2017 by John Wiley & Sons, Inc., Indianapolis, Indiana

Published simultaneously in Canada

ISBN: 978-1-119-35933-3
ISBN: 978-1-119-35942-5 (ebk.)
ISBN: 978-1-119-35945-6 (ebk.)

Manufactured in the United States of America

For general information on our other products and services or to obtain technical support, please contact our Customer Care Department within the U.S. at (877) 762-2974, outside the U.S. at (317) 572-3993 or fax (317) 572-4002.

Wiley publishes in a variety of print and electronic formats and by print-on-demand. Some material included with standard print versions of this book may not be included in e-books or in print-on-demand. If this book refers to media such as a CD or DVD that is not included in the version you purchased, you may download this material at http://booksupport.wiley.com. For more information about Wiley products, visit www.wiley.com.

Library of Congress Control Number: 2017947568

This book is dedicated to the three ladies of my life: Crystal, Alexandria, and Paige.

Acknowledgments

I would like to thank my wife and best friend, Crystal. She is always the light at the end of my tunnel. I want to thank my two daughters, Alexandria and Paige, for all of their love and support during the writing of all my books. The three of them are my support system and I couldn't do any of this without them.

I want to thank all of my family and friends who always help me when I'm writing my books. I want to thank my brothers, Rick, Gary, and Rob. I want to thank my great friends Shaun, Jeremy, and Gene.

I would like to thank all of my friends and co-workers at StormWind Studios. I want to especially thank the team who I work with on a daily basis, and that includes Tom W, Dan Y, Corey F, Ronda, Dan J, Jessica, Dave, Tiffany, Tara, Ashley, Brittany, Doug, Mike, Vince, Desiree, Ryan, Ralph, Dan G, Tyler, Jeff B, Shayne, Patrick, Noemi, Michelle, Zachary, Colin, and the man who makes it all possible, Tom Graunke. Thanks to all of you for everything that you do. I would not have been able to complete this book without all of your help and support.

I want to thank everyone on my Sybex team, especially my development editor, Kim Wimpsett, who helped me make this the best book possible, and Rodney R. Fournier, who is the technical editor of many of my books. It's always good to have the very best technical guy backing you up. I want to thank Rebecca Anderson, who was my production editor, and Judy Flynn for being the copyeditor.

I want to also thank Chris Crayton and Nancy Carrasco for being my proofreaders. Special thanks to my acquisitions editor, Kenyon Brown, who was the lead for the entire book. Finally, I want to thank everyone else behind the scenes that helped make this book possible. It's truly an amazing thing to have so many people work on my books to help make them the very best. I can't thank you all enough for your hard work.

About the Author

 **William Panek** holds the following certifications: MCP, MCP+I, MCSA, MCSA+ Security and Messaging, MCSE-NT (3.51 & 4.0), MCSE 2000, 2003, 2012/2012 R2, MCSE+Security and Messaging, MCDBA, MCT, MCTS, MCITP, CCNA, CCDA, and CHFI. Will is also a four time and current Microsoft MVP winner.

After many successful years in the computer industry, Will decided that he could better use his talents and his personality as an instructor. He began teaching for schools such as Boston University and the University of Maryland, just to name a few. He has done consulting and training for some of the biggest government and corporate companies in the world including the United States Secret Service, Cisco, the United States Air Force, and the US Army.

In 2015, Will became a Sr. Microsoft Instructor for StormWind Studios (www.stormwindstudios.com). He currently lives in New Hampshire with his wife and two daughters. Will was also a Representative in the New Hampshire House of Representatives from 2010 to 2012. In his spare time, he likes to do blacksmithing, shooting (trap and skeet), snowmobiling, playing racquetball, and riding his Harley. Will is also a commercially rated helicopter pilot.

Contents

Table of Exercises

Introduction

This book is drawn from more than 20 years of IT experience. I have taken that experience and translated it into a Windows Server 2016 book that will help you not only prepare for the MCSA: Windows Server 2016 exams but also develop a clear understanding of how to install and configure Windows Server 2016 while avoiding all of the possible configuration pitfalls.

Many Microsoft books just explain the Windows operating system, but with *MCSA: Windows Server 2016 Complete Study Guide*, I go a step further by providing many in-depth, step-by-step procedures to support my explanations of how the operating system performs at its best.

Microsoft Windows Server 2016 is the newest version of Microsoft's server operating system software. Microsoft has taken the best of Windows Server 2003, Windows Server 2008, and Windows Server 2012 and combined them into the latest creation, Windows Server 2016.

Windows Server 2016 eliminates many of the problems that plagued the previous versions of Windows Server, and it includes a much faster boot time and shutdown. It is also easier to install and configure, and it barely stops to ask the user any questions during installation. In this book, I will show you what features are installed during the automated installation and where you can make changes if you need to be more in charge of your operating system and its features.

This book takes you through all the ins and outs of Windows Server 2016, including installation, configuration, Group Policy objects, auditing, backups, and so much more.

Windows Server 2016 has improved on Microsoft's desktop environment, made networking easier, enhanced searching capability, and improved performance—and that's only scratching the surface.

When all is said and done, this is a technical book for IT professionals who want to take Windows Server 2016 to the next step and get certified. With this book, you will not only learn Windows Server 2016 and ideally pass the exams, but you will also become a Windows Server 2016 expert.

The Microsoft Certification Program

Since the inception of its certification program, Microsoft has certified more than 2 million people. As the computer network industry continues to increase in both size and complexity, this number is sure to grow—and the need for proven ability will also increase. Certifications can help companies verify the skills of prospective employees and contractors.

The Microsoft certification tracks for Windows Server 2016 include the following:

MCSA: Windows Server 2016   The MCSA is now the lowest-level certification you can achieve with Microsoft in relation to Windows Server 2016. It requires passing three exams: 70-740, 70-741, and 70-742.

MCSE: Cloud Platform and Infrastructure   The MCSE certifications, in relation to Windows Server 2016, require that you become an MCSA first and then pass two additional exams. The additional exams will vary depending on which of the two MCSE tracks you choose. For more information, visit Microsoft's website at www.microsoft.com/learning.

How Do You Become Certified on Windows Server 2016?

Attaining Microsoft certification has always been a challenge. In the past, students have been able to acquire detailed exam information—even most of the exam questions—from online "brain dumps" and third-party "cram" books or software products. For the new generation of exams, this is simply not the case.

Microsoft has taken strong steps to protect the security and integrity of its new certification tracks. Now prospective candidates must complete a course of study that develops detailed knowledge about a wide range of topics. It supplies them with the true skills needed, derived from working with the technology being tested.

The new generations of Microsoft certification programs are heavily weighted toward hands-on skills and experience. It is recommended that candidates have troubleshooting skills acquired through hands-on experience and working knowledge.

Fortunately, if you are willing to dedicate the time and effort to learn Windows Server 2016, you can prepare yourself well for the exam by using the proper tools. By working through this book, you can successfully meet the requirements to pass the Windows Server 2016 exams.

MCSA Exam Requirements

Candidates for MCSA certification on Windows Server 2016 must pass at least the following three Windows Server 2016 exams:

- **70-740:** Installation, Storage, and computer with Windows Server 2016
- **70-741:** Networking with Windows Server 2016
- **70-742:** Identity with Windows Server 2016

For those who have a qualifying certification, they can take the Upgrading exam "Upgrading Your Skills to MCSA: Windows Server 2016" (Exam 70-743). The objectives for this exam span the three individual exams. This book covers all of the objectives for the Upgrading exam. For details about the exam, visit Microsoft's website at www.microsoft.com/learning.

Microsoft provides exam objectives to give you a general overview of possible areas of coverage on the Microsoft exams. Keep in mind, however, that exam objectives are subject to change at any time without prior notice and at Microsoft's sole discretion. Visit the Microsoft Learning website (www.microsoft.com/learning) for the most current listing of exam objectives. The published objectives and how they map to this book are listed later in this introduction.

> For a more detailed description of the Microsoft certification programs, including a list of all the exams, visit the Microsoft Learning website at: www.microsoft.com/learning.

Tips for Taking the Windows Server 2016 Exams

Here are some general tips for achieving success on your certification exam:

- Arrive early at the exam center so that you can relax and review your study materials. During this final review, you can look over tables and lists of exam-related information.

- Read the questions carefully. Do not be tempted to jump to an early conclusion. Make sure you know *exactly* what the question is asking.

- Answer all questions. If you are unsure about a question, mark it for review and come back to it at a later time.

- On simulations, do not change settings that are not directly related to the question. Also, assume the default settings if the question does not specify or imply which settings are used.

- For questions about which you're unsure, use a process of elimination to get rid of the obviously incorrect answers first. This improves your odds of selecting the correct answer when you need to make an educated guess.

Exam Registration

At the time this book was released, Microsoft exams are given using more than 1,000 Authorized VUE Testing Centers around the world. For the location of a testing center near you, go to VUE's website at www.vue.com. If you are outside of the United States and Canada, contact your local VUE registration center.

Find out the number of the exam that you want to take and then register with the VUE registration center nearest to you. At this point, you will be asked for advance payment for the exam. The exams are $165 each, and you must take them within one year of payment. You can schedule exams up to six weeks in advance or as late as one working day prior to the date of the exam. You can cancel or reschedule your exam if you contact the center at least two working days prior to the exam. Same-day registration is available in some locations, subject to space availability. Where same-day registration is available, you must register a minimum of two hours before test time.

When you schedule the exam, you will be provided with instructions regarding appointment and cancellation procedures, ID requirements, and information about the testing center location. In addition, you will receive a registration and payment confirmation letter from VUE.

Microsoft requires certification candidates to accept the terms of a nondisclosure agreement before taking certification exams.

Who Should Read This Book?

This book is intended for individuals who want to earn their MCSA: Windows Server 2016 certification.

This book will not only help anyone who is looking to pass the Microsoft exams, it will also help anyone who wants to learn the real ins and outs of the Windows Server 2016 operating system.

What's Inside?

Here is a glance at what's in each chapter:

Chapter 1: Configuring TCP/IP   In the first chapter, I show you how TCP/IP gets configured on a server and within a network. I also show you how to subnet an IPv4 network. I also show you how to work with IPv6.

Chapter 2: Configuring DNS   This chapter shows you how to install Windows Server 2016 DNS in an enterprise environment.

Chapter 3: Configuring DHCP   I take you through the advantages and benefits of using Windows Server 2016 DHCP.

Chapter 4: Implementing IP Address Management   This chapter will show you how to implement and configure Windows Server 2016 IPAM.

Chapter 5: Configuring Network Access   This chapter takes you through the different ways to create and manage network access and VPN access.

Chapter 6: Understanding File Services   You will see the different ways that you can setup and configure Windows Server 2016 file servers and tools that work with file servers.

Chapter 7: Configuring High Availability   In this chapter I will explain the advantages of using Windows Server 2016 high availability. I show you how to configure NLB and high availability.

Chapter 8: Implementing Software Defined Networking   This chapter shows you how to create and maintain a Windows Server 2016 Software Defined Network.

What's Included with the Book

This book includes many helpful items intended to prepare you for the MCSA: Windows Server 2016 certification.

Assessment Test   There is an assessment test at the conclusion of the introduction that can be used to evaluate quickly where you are with Windows Server 2016. This test should be taken prior to beginning your work in this book, and it should help you identify areas in which you are either strong or weak. Note that these questions are purposely more simple than the types of questions you may see on the exams.

Objective Map and Opening List of Objectives   Later in this introduction, I include a detailed exam objective map showing you where each of the exam objectives are covered. Each chapter also includes a list of the exam objectives that are covered.

Helpful Exercises   Throughout the book, I have included step-by-step exercises of some of the more important tasks that you should be able to perform. Some of these exercises have corresponding videos that can be downloaded from the book's website. Also, in the following section I have a recommended a home lab setup that will be helpful in completing these tasks.

Exam Essentials   The end of each chapter also includes a listing of exam essentials. These are essentially repeats of the objectives, but remember that any objective on the exam blueprint could show up on the exam.

Chapter Review Questions   Each chapter includes review questions. These are used to assess your understanding of the chapter and are taken directly from the chapter. These questions are based on the exam objectives, and they are similar in difficulty to items you might actually receive on the MCSA: Windows Server 2016 exams.

    The Sybex Interactive Online Test Bank, flashcards, videos, and glossary can be accessed at http://www.wiley.com/go/sybextestprep.

Interactive Online Learning Environment and Test Bank

The interactive online learning environment that accompanies this study guide provides a test bank with study tools to help you prepare for the certification exams and increase your chances of passing them the first time! The test bank includes the following elements:

Sample Tests   All of the questions in this book are provided, including the assessment test, which you'll find at the end of this introduction, and the chapter tests that include the review questions at the end of each chapter. In addition, there is a practice exam. Use these questions to test your knowledge of the study guide material. The online test bank runs on multiple devices.

Electronic Flashcards   One set of questions is provided in digital flashcard format (a question followed by a single correct answer). You can use the flashcards to reinforce your learning and provide last-minute test prep before the exam.

Glossary   The key terms from this book and their definitions are available as a fully searchable PDF.

Videos   Some of the exercises include corresponding videos. These videos show you how the author does the exercises. There is also a video that shows you how to set up virtualization so that you can complete the exercises within a virtualized environment. The author also has videos to help you on the Microsoft exams at www.youtube.com/c/williampanek.

Recommended Home Lab Setup

To get the most out of this book, you will want to make sure you complete the exercises throughout the chapters. To complete the exercises, you will need one of two setups. First, you can set up a machine with Windows Server 2016 and complete the labs using a regular Windows Server 2016 machine.

The second way to set up Windows Server 2016 (the way I set up Server 2016) is by using virtualization. I set up Windows Server 2016 as a virtual hard disk (VHD), and I did all the labs this way. The advantages of using virtualization are that you can always just wipe out the system and start over without losing a real server. Plus, you can set up multiple virtual servers and create a full lab environment on one machine.

I created a video for this book showing you how to set up a virtual machine and how to install Windows Server 2016 onto that virtual machine.

How to Contact Sybex/Author

Sybex strives to keep you supplied with the latest tools and information you need for your work. Please check the website at www.sybex.com/go/mcsawin2016, where I'll post additional content and updates that supplement this book should the need arise.

You can contact me by going to my website at www.willpanek.com. You can also watch free videos on Microsoft networking at www.youtube.com/c/williampanek. If you would like to follow information about Windows Server 2016 from Will Panek, please visit Twitter @AuthorWillPanek.

Certification Objectives Maps

Table I.1 provides the objective mappings for the 70-740 exam. In addition to the book chapters, you will find coverage of exam objectives in the flashcards, practice exams, and videos on the book's companion website:

```
http://www.wiley.com/WileyCDA/WileyTitle/
productCd-111885991X,miniSiteCd-SYBEX.html
```

TABLE I.1   70-741 exam objectives

Objective	Chapter
Implement Domain Name System (DNS) (15–20%)	
1.1. Install and configure DNS servers	Chapter 2
This objective may include but is not limited to: Determine DNS installation requirements; determine supported DNS deployment scenarios on Nano Server; install DNS; configure forwarders; configure Root Hints; configure delegation; implement DNS policies; implement DNS global settings using Windows PowerShell; configure Domain Name System Security Extensions (DNSSEC); configure DNS Socket Pool; configure cache locking; enable Response Rate Limiting; configure DNS-based Authentication of Named Entities (DANE); configure DNS logging; configure delegated administration; configure recursion settings; implement DNS performance tuning; configure global settings using Windows PowerShell	Chapter 2
1.2. Create and configure DNS zones and records	Chapter 2
This objective may include but is not limited to: Create primary zones; configure Active Directory integration of primary zones; create and configure secondary zones; create and configure stub zones; configure a GlobalNames zone; analyze zone-level statistics; create and configure DNS Resource Records (RR), including A, AAAA, PTR, SOA, NS, SRV, CNAME, and MX records; configure zone scavenging; configure record options, including Time To Live (TTL) and weight; configure round robin; configure secure dynamic updates; configure unknown record support; use DNS audit events and analytical (query) events for auditing and troubleshooting; configure Zone Scopes; configure records in Zone Scopes; configure policies for zones	Chapter 2
Implement DHCP (15–20%)	
2.1. Install and configure DHCP	Chapter 3
This objective may include but is not limited to: Install and configure DHCP servers; authorize a DHCP server; create and configure scopes; create and configure superscopes and multicast scopes; configure a DHCP reservation; configure DHCP options; configure DNS options from within DHCP; configure policies; configure client and server for PXE boot; configure DHCP Relay Agent; implement IPv6 addressing using DHCPv6; perform export and import of a DHCP server; perform DHCP server migration	Chapter 3
2.2. Manage and maintain DHCP	Chapter 3
This objective may include but is not limited to: Configure a lease period; back up and restore the DHCP database; configure high availability using DHCP failover; configure DHCP name protection; troubleshoot DHCP	Chapter 3

TABLE I.1 70-741 exam objectives *(continued)*

Objective	Chapter
Implement IP Address Management (IPAM) (15–20%)	
3.1. Install and configure IP Address Management (IPAM)	Chapter 4
This objective may include but is not limited to: Provision IPAM manually or by using Group Policy; configure server discovery; create and manage IP blocks and ranges; monitor utilization of IP address space; migrate existing workloads to IPAM; configure IPAM database storage using SQL Server; determine scenarios for using IPAM with System Center Virtual Machine Manager for physical and virtual IP address space management	Chapter 4
3.2. Manage DNS and DHCP using IPAM	Chapter 4
This objective may include but is not limited to: Manage DHCP server properties using IPAM; configure DHCP scopes and options; configure DHCP policies and failover; manage DNS server properties using IPAM; manage DNS zones and records; manage DNS and DHCP servers in multiple Active Directory forests; delegate administration for DNS and DHCP using role-based access control (RBAC)	Chapter 4
3.3. Audit IPAM	Chapter 4
This objective may include but is not limited to: Audit the changes performed on the DNS and DHCP servers; audit the IPAM address usage trail; audit DHCP lease events and user logon events	Chapter 4
Implement Network Connectivity and Remote Access Solutions (25–30%)	
Implement network connectivity solutions	Chapter 5
This objective may include but is not limited to: Implement Network Address Translation (NAT); configure routing	Chapter 5
Implement virtual private network (VPN) and DirectAccess solutions	Chapter 5
This objective may include but is not limited to: Implement remote access and site-to-site (S2S) VPN solutions using remote access gateway; configure different VPN protocol options; configure authentication options; configure VPN reconnect; create and configure connection profiles; determine when to use remote access VPN and site-to-site VPN and configure appropriate protocols; install and configure DirectAccess; implement server requirements; implement client configuration; troubleshoot DirectAccess	Chapter 5

Objective	Chapter
Implement Network Policy Server (NPS)	Chapter 5
This objective may include but is not limited to: Configure a RADIUS server including RADIUS proxy; configure RADIUS clients; configure NPS templates; configure RADIUS accounting; configure certificates; configure Connection Request Policies; configure network policies for VPN and wireless and wired clients; import and export NPS policies	Chapter 5

Implement Core and Distributed Network Solutions (10–15%)

Objective	Chapter
Implement IPv4 and IPv6 addressing	Chapter 1
This objective may include but is not limited to: Configure IPv4 addresses and options; determine and configure appropriate IPv6 addresses; configure IPv4 or IPv6 subnetting; implement IPv6 stateless addressing; configure interoperability between IPv4 and IPv6 by using ISATAP, 6to4, and Teredo scenarios; configure Border Gateway Protocol (BGP); configure IPv4 and IPv6 routing	Chapter 1
Implement Distributed File System (DFS) and Branch Office solutions	Chapter 6
This objective may include but is not limited to: Install and configure DFS namespaces; configure DFS replication targets; configure replication scheduling; configure Remote Differential Compression (RDC) settings; configure staging; configure fault tolerance; clone a Distributed File System Replication (DFSR) database; recover DFSR databases; optimize DFS Replication; install and configure BranchCache; implement distributed and hosted cache modes; implement BranchCache for web, file, and application servers; troubleshoot BranchCache	Chapter 6

Implement an Advanced Network Infrastructure (10–15%)

Objective	Chapter
6.1 Implement high performance network solutions	Chapter 7
This objective may include but is not limited to: Implement NIC Teaming or the Switch Embedded Teaming (SET) solution and identify when to use each; enable and configure Receive Side Scaling (RSS); enable and configure network Quality of Service (QoS) with Data Center Bridging (DCB); enable and configure SMB Direct on Remote Direct Memory Access (RDMA) enabled network adapters; enable and configure SMB Multichannel; enable and configure virtual Receive Side Scaling (vRSS) on a Virtual Machine Queue (VMQ) capable network adapter; enable and configure Virtual Machine Multi-Queue (VMMQ); enable and configure Single-Root I/O Virtualization (SR-IOV) on a supported network adapter	Chapter 7

TABLE I.1   70-741 exam objectives *(continued)*

Objective	Chapter
6.2. Determine scenarios and requirements for implementing Software Defined Networking (SDN)	Chapter 8
This objective may include but is not limited to: Determine deployment scenarios and network requirements for deploying SDN; determine requirements and scenarios for implementing Hyper-V Network Virtualization (HNV) using Network Virtualization Generic Route Encapsulation (NVGRE) encapsulation or Virtual Extensible LAN (VXLAN) encapsulation; determine scenarios for implementation of Software Load Balancer (SLB) for North-South and East-West load balancing; determine implementation scenarios for various types of Windows Server Gateways, including L3, GRE, and S2S, and their use; determine requirements and scenarios for distributed firewall policies and network security groups	Chapter 8

Exam objectives are subject to change at any time without prior notice and at Microsoft's sole discretion. Please visit Microsoft's website (www.microsoft.com/learning) for the most current listing of exam objectives.

Assessment Test

1. Which of the following subnet masks are represented with the CIDR of /27?
   A. 255.255.255.254
   B. 255.255.255.248
   C. 255.255.255.224
   D. 255.255.255.240

2. You are the network administrator for a midsize organization that has installed Windows Server 2016 onto the network. You are thinking of moving all machines to Windows 10 and IPv6. You decide to set up a test environment with four subnets. What type of IPv6 addresses do you need set up?
   A. Global addresses
   B. Link-local addresses
   C. Unique local addresses
   D. Site-local addresses

3. You are the network administrator for ABC Company. You have an IPv6 prefix of 2001:DB8:BBCC:0000::/53, and you need to set up your network so that your IPv6 addressing scheme can handle 1,000 more subnets. Which network mask would you use?
   A. /60
   B. /61
   C. /62
   D. /63

4. You assign two DNS server addresses as part of the options for a scope. Later you find a client workstation that isn't using those addresses. What's the most likely cause?
   A. The client didn't get the option information as part of its lease.
   B. The client has been manually configured with a different set of DNS servers.
   C. The client has a reserved IP address in the address pool.
   D. There's a bug in the DHCP server service.

5. Your DHCP server crashed in the middle of the day. You rebooted the server, got it running within 5 minutes, and nobody but you seemed to notice that it had gone down at all. What additional steps must you take?
   A. None. If there were no lease-renewal requests during the 5-minute period in which the DHCP server was down, none of the clients will ever know that it went down.
   B. You need to renew all the leases manually.
   C. None. The DHCP server automatically assigned new addresses to all the clients on the network transparently.
   D. You must reboot all the client machines.

6. You are the administrator for a Windows Server 2016 network that uses DHCP. You notice that your DHCP database is getting too large and you want to reduce the size of the data- base. What should you do?

    A. From the folder containing the DHCP database, run `jetpack.exe dhcp.mdb temp.mdb`.

    B. From the folder containing the DHCP database, run `shrinkpack.exe dhcp.mdb temp.mdb`.

    C. From the folder containing the DHCP database, run `jetshrink.exe dhcp.mdb temp.mdb`.

    D. From the folder containing the DHCP database, run `shrinkjet.exe dhcp.mdb temp.mdb`.

7. You are the network admin for an Active Directory domain named Stormwind.com. You have a new security policy that states that whenever possible, you should install new Nano Servers. Which server role can be deployed on a Nano Server?

    A. Active Directory Domain Services

    B. DHCP Server

    C. Network Policy and Access Services

    D. Web Server (IIS)

8. You have been asked to explain how DHCP works. What abbreviation can you explain to show how DHCP operates?

    A. DORA

    B. RODA

    C. DHRA

    D. AORD

9. You are the network administrator for a large training company. You have been asked to setup the default gateway setting using DHCP. Which option would you configure?

    A. 003 Router

    B. 006 DNS

    C. 015 DNS Domain Name

    D. 028 Broadcast Address

10. You are the network administrator for your organization. You need to view the DNS server information from the IPAM database. What PowerShell command would you use?

    A. `View-IpamDnsServer`

    B. `Get-IpamDnsServer`

    C. `View-DnsServer`

    D. `Get-DnsServer`

11. You are the administrator for StormWind Studios online training company. You need to change the IPAM discovery configuration. What PowerShell command do you use?

    A. `Get-IpamDiscovery`

    B. `Get-IpamDiscoveryDomain`

    C. `Set-IpamDiscovery`

    D. `Set-IpamDiscoveryDomain`

12. You are the network administrator for your company. You need to use a PowerShell command to configure an IP address block in IPAM. What command do you use?

A. `Set-IpamIP`

B. `Set-IpamBlock`

C. `Set-IPBlock`

D. `Set-IPAddressBlock`

13. Your network contains an Active Directory domain named Stormwind.com. Network Access Protection (NAP) is deployed to the domain. You need to create NAP event trace log files on a client computer. What should you run?

A. Register-ObjectEvent

B. Register-EngineEvent

C. tracert

D. logman

14. Your network contains an Active Directory domain named Stormwind.com. The domain contains a RADIUS server named Server1 that runs Windows Server 2016. You add a VPN server named Server2 to the network. On Server1, you create several network policies. You need to configure Server1 to accept authentication requests from Server2. Which tool should you use on Server1?

A. Set-RemoteAccessRadius

B. CMAK

C. NPS

D. Routing and Remote Access

15. You are the administrator for a large communications company. Your company uses Windows Server 2016, and your user's files are encrypted using EFS. What command-line command would you use to change or modify the EFS files?

A. Convert

B. Cipher

C. Gopher

D. Encrypt

16. You want to publish a printer to Active Directory. Where would you click in order to accomplish this task?

A. The Sharing tab

B. The Advanced tab

C. The Device Settings tab

D. The Printing Preferences button

17. You have been hired by a small company to implement new Windows Server 2016 systems. The company wants you to set up a server for users' home folder locations. What type of server would you be setting up?

   A. PDC server

   B. Web server

   C. Exchange server

   D. File server

18. In a three-node cluster set to a Node Majority quorum model, how many cluster nodes can be offline before the quorum is lost?

   A. Zero

   B. One

   C. Two

   D. Three

19. You are the administrator for a mid-size company who wants to setup and test a cluster. What PowerShell command would you use to run a validation test on a cluster?

   A. Test-Cluster

   B. Validate-Cluster

   C. Set-Cluster

   D. Add-Cluster

20. You are a network administrator for a small company that uses Hyper-V. You need to reboot your virtual machine. What PowerShell command can you use?

   A. Restart-VM

   B. Reboot-VM

   C. Shutdown-VM

   D. ShutStateOff

Answers to Assessment Test

1. C. The CIDR /27 tells you that 27 1s are turned on in the subnet mask. Twenty-seven 1s equals 11111111.11111111.11111111.11100000. This would then equal 255.255.255.224. See Chapter 1 for more information.

2. C. The unique local address can be FC00 or FD00, and it is used like the private address space of IPv4. Unique local addresses are not expected to be routable on the global Internet, but they are used for private routing within an organization. See Chapter 1 for more information.

3. D. To calculate the network mask, you need to figure out which power number (2^x) is greater than or equal to the number you need. Since we are looking for 1000, $2^{10} = 1024$. You then add the power (10) to the current network mask (53 + 10 = 63). See Chapter 1 for more information.

4. B. Manual settings override DHCP options. See Chapter 2 for more information.

5. A. When the DHCP server crashed, the scope was effectively deactivated. Deactivating a scope has no effect on the client until it needs to renew the lease. See Chapter 2 for more information.

6. A. Microsoft's jetpack.exe utility allows you to compact a JET database. Microsoft JET databases are used for WINS and DHCP databases. See Chapter 2 for more information.

7. B. One of the nice advantages of DHCP is that it is one of the only Roles that can be installed onto a Nano server. See Chapter 3 for more information.

8. A. The abbreviation that helps you remember how DHCP works is DORA. Discover, Offer, Request, and Acknowledge. See Chapter 3 for more information.

9. A. 003 Router is used to provide a list of available routers or default gateways on the same subnet. See Chapter 3 for more information.

10. B. The Get-IpamDnsServer command allows an administrator to view DNS server information from the IPAM database. See Chapter 4 for more information.

11. D. Administrators can use the Set-IpamDiscoveryDomain PowerShell command to change the IPAM discovery configuration. See Chapter 4 for more information.

12. B. Administrators can use the Set-IpamBlock PowerShell command to configure an IP address block in IPAM. See Chapter 4 for more information.

13. D. Logman creates and manages Event Trace Session and Performance logs and allows an administrator to monitor many different applications through the use of the command line. See Chapter 5 for more information.

14. C. The NPS snap-in allows you to setup RADIUS servers and which RADIUS server would accept authentication from other RADIUS servers. You can do your entire RADIUS configuration through the NPS snap-in. See Chapter 5 for more information.

15. B. Cipher is a command-line utility that allows you to configure or change EFS files and folders. See Chapter 6 for more information.

16. A. The Sharing tab contains a check box that you can use to list the printer in Active Directory. See Chapter 6 for more information.

17. D. File servers are used for storage of data, especially for users' home folders. Home folders are folder locations for your users to store data that is important and that needs to be backed up. See Chapter 6 for more information.

18. B. In a three-node cluster, only one node can be offline before the quorum is lost; a majority of the votes must be available to achieve the quorum. See Chapter 7 for more information.

19. A. Administrators would use the Test-Cluster to complete validation tests for a cluster. See Chapter 7 for more information.

20. A. The PowerShell command of Restart-VM restarts a virtual machine. See Chapter 8 for more information.

Chapter

1

Configuring TCP/IP

THE FOLLOWING 70-741 EXAM OBJECTIVES ARE COVERED IN THIS CHAPTER:

✓ **Configure IPv4 and IPv6 addressing**

- Configure IP address options
- Configure IPv4 or IPv6 subnetting
- Configure supernetting
- Configure interoperability between IPv4 and IPv6
- Configure ISATAP
- Configure Teredo

In this chapter, I will discuss the most important protocol used in a Microsoft Windows Server 2016 network: *Transmission Control Protocol/Internet Protocol (TCP/IP)*.

TCP/IP is actually two protocols bundled together: the Transmission Control Protocol (TCP) and the Internet Protocol (IP). TCP/IP is a suite of protocols developed by the US Department of Defense's Advanced Research Projects Agency in 1969.

This chapter is divided into two main topics: First I'll talk about TCP/IP version 4, and then I'll discuss TCP/IP version 6. TCP/IP version 4 is still used in Windows Server 2016, and it was the primary version of TCP/IP in all previous versions of Windows. However, TCP/IP version 6 is the latest release of TCP/IP, and it has been incorporated into Windows Server 2016.

Understanding TCP/IP

I mentioned that TCP/IP is actually two protocols bundled together: TCP and IP. These protocols sit on a four-layer TCP/IP model.

Details of the TCP/IP Model

The four layers of the TCP/IP model are as follows (see Figure 1.1):

Application Layer   The *Application layer* is where the applications that use the protocol stack reside. These applications include File Transfer Protocol (FTP), Trivial File Transfer Protocol (TFTP), Simple Mail Transfer Protocol (SMTP), and Hypertext Transfer Protocol (HTTP).

Transport Layer   The *Transport layer* is where the two Transport layer protocols reside. These are TCP and the User Datagram Protocol (UDP). TCP is a connection-oriented protocol, and delivery is guaranteed. UDP is a connectionless protocol. This means that UDP does its best job to deliver the message, but there is no guarantee.

Internet Layer   The *Internet layer* is where IP resides. *IP is a connectionless protocol that relies on the upper layer (Transport layer) for guaranteeing delivery. Address Resolution Protocol (ARP)* also resides on this layer. ARP turns an IP address into a Media Access Control (MAC) address. All upper and lower layers travel through the IP protocol.

Link Layer   The data link protocols like Ethernet and Token Ring reside in the *Link layer*. This layer is also referred to as the *Network Access layer*.

FIGURE 1.1   TCP/IP model

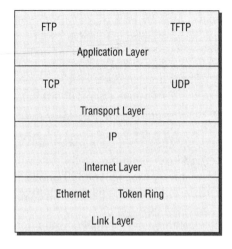

How TCP/IP Layers Communicate

When an application like FTP is called upon, the application moves down the layers and TCP is retrieved. TCP then connects itself to the IP protocol and gets released onto the network through the Link layer (see Figure 1.2). This is a connection-oriented protocol because TCP is the protocol that guarantees delivery.

FIGURE 1.2   TCP/IP process

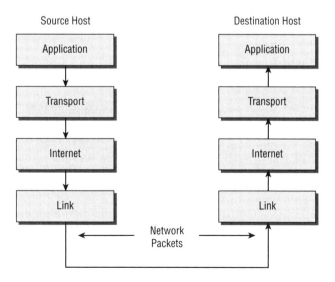

When an application like TFTP gets called, the application moves down the layers, and UDP is retrieved. UDP then connects itself to the IP protocol and gets released onto the network through the Link layer. This is a connectionless protocol because UDP does not have guaranteed delivery.

Understanding Port Numbers

TCP and UDP rely on port numbers assigned by the *Internet Assigned Numbers Authority (IANA)* to forward packets to the appropriate application process. Port numbers are 16-bit integers that are part of a message header. They identify the application software process with which the packet should be associated. For example, let's say that a client has a copy of Internet Explorer and a copy of Mail open at the same time. Both applications are sending TCP requests across the Internet to retrieve web pages and email, respectively. How does the computer know which return packets to forward to Internet Explorer and which packets to forward to Mail?

When making a connection, the client chooses a source port for the communication that is usually in the range 1024–65535 (or sometimes in the range 1–65535). This source port then communicates with a destination port of 80 or 110 on the server side. Every packet destined for Internet Explorer has a source port number of 80 in the header, and every packet destined for Mail has a source port number of 110 in the header.

Table 1.1 describes the most common port numbers (you might need to know these for the exam). You can visit www.iana.org to get the most current and complete list of port numbers. It's good to become familiar with specific port numbers because it's a benefit to be able to determine from memory the ports that, for example, allow or block specific protocols in a firewall. Allowing only port 80, for instance, does not ensure that all web traffic will be allowed. You must also allow port 443 for certain secure web traffic.

TABLE 1.1 Common port numbers

Port Number	Description
20	FTP data
21	FTP control
23	Telnet
25	Simple Mail Transfer Protocol (SMTP)
53	Domain Name System (DNS)
80	Hypertext Transfer Protocol (HTTP), Web
88	Kerberos
110	Post Office Protocol v3 (POP3)
443	Secure HTTP (HTTPS)

Simply because a port is "well known" doesn't mean that a given service must run on it. It's technically valid to run any service on any port, but doing so is usually a bad idea. For example, if you chose to run your web server on TCP port 25, clients would need to type www.example.com:25 to reach your website from most browsers.

Understanding IP Addressing

Understanding IP addressing is critical to understanding how IP works. An IP address is a numeric identifier assigned to each device on an IP network. This type of address is a logical software address that designates the device's location on the network. It isn't the physical hardware address hard-coded in the device's network interface card.

In the following sections, you will see how IP addresses are used to identify uniquely every machine on the network (MAC address).

The Hierarchical IP Addressing Scheme

An IP address consists of 32 bits of information. These bits are divided into four sections (sometimes called *octets* or *quads*) containing 1 byte (8 bits) each. There are three common methods for specifying an IP address:

- Dotted-decimal, as in 130.57.30.56
- Binary, as in 10000010.00111001.00011110.00111000
- Hexadecimal, as in 82 39 1E 38

All of these examples represent the same IP address.

The 32-bit IP address is a structured, or hierarchical, address as opposed to a flat, or nonhierarchical, address. Although IP could have used either *flat addressing* or *hierarchical addressing*, its designers elected to use the latter for a very good reason, as you will now see.

 Real World Scenario

Why Hierarchical Addressing Is Used

What's the difference between flat and hierarchical addressing? A good example of a flat addressing scheme is a US state driver's license number. There's no partitioning to it; the range of legal numbers isn't broken up in any meaningful way (say, by county of residence or date of issue). If this method had been used for IP addressing, every machine on the Internet would have needed a totally unique address, just as each driver's license number in a particular state is unique.

continued

The good news about flat addressing is that it can handle a large number of addresses in 32 bits of data, namely, 4.3 billion. A 32-bit address space with two possible values for each position—either 0 (zero) or 1 (one)—gives you 2^{32} values, which equals approximately 4.3 billion.

The bad news—and the reason flat addressing isn't used in IP—relates to routing. If every address were totally unique, every router on the Internet would need to store the address of every other machine on the Internet. It would be fair to say that this would make efficient routing impossible, even if only a fraction of the possible addresses were used.

The solution to this dilemma is to use a hierarchical addressing scheme that breaks the address space into ordered chunks. Telephone numbers are a great example of this type of addressing. The first section of a US telephone number, the area code, designates a very large area. The area code is followed by the prefix, which narrows the scope to a local calling area. The final segment, the customer number, zooms in on the specific connection. By looking at a number such as 603-766-xxxx, you can quickly determine that the number is located in the southern part of New Hampshire (area code 603) in the Portsmouth area (the 766 exchange).

IP Address Structure

IP addressing works the same way. Instead of the entire 32 bits being treated as a unique identifier, one part of the IP address is designated as the network address (or network ID) and the other part as a node address (or host ID), giving it a layered, hierarchical structure. Together, the IP address, the network address, and the node address uniquely identify a device within an IP network.

The network address—the first two sets of numbers in an IP address—uniquely identifies each network. Every machine on the same network shares that network address as part of its IP address, just as the address of every house on a street shares the same street name. In the IP address 130.57.30.56, for example, 130.57 is the network address.

The node address—the second two sets of numbers—is assigned to, and uniquely identifies, each machine in a network, just as each house on the same street has a different house number. This part of the address must be unique because it identifies a particular machine—an individual, as opposed to a network. This number can also be referred to as a *host address*. In the sample IP address 130.57.30.56, the node address is .30.56.

Understanding Network Classes

The designers of the Internet decided to create classes of networks based on network size. For the small number of networks possessing a very large number of nodes, they created the Class A network. At the other extreme is the Class C network, reserved for the numerous networks with small numbers of nodes. The class of networks in between the very large and very small ones is predictably called the Class B network.

The default subdivision of an IP address into a network and node address is determined by the class designation of your network. Table 1.2 summarizes the three classes of networks, which will be described in more detail in the following sections.

TABLE 1.2   Network address classes

Class	Mask Bits	Leading Bit Pattern	Decimal Range of First Octet of IP Address	Assignable Networks	Maximum Nodes per Network
A	8	0	1–126	126	16,777,214
B	16	10	128–191	16,384	65,534
C	24	110	192–223	2,097,152	254

> Classless Inter-Domain Routing (CIDR), explained in detail later in this chapter, has effectively done away with these class designations. You will still hear and should still know the meaning behind the class designations of addresses because they are important to understanding IP addressing. However, when you're working with IP addressing in practice, CIDR is more important to know.

To ensure efficient routing, Internet designers defined a mandate for the leading bits section of the address for each different network class. For example, because a router knows that a Class A network address always starts with a 0, it can quickly apply the default mask, if necessary, after reading only the first bit of the address. Table 1.2 illustrates how the leading bits of a network address are defined. When considering the subnet masking between network and host addresses, the number of bits to mask is important. For example, in a Class A network, 8 bits are masked, making the default subnet mask 255.0.0.0; in a Class C, 24 bits are masked, making the default subnet mask 255.255.255.0.

Some IP addresses are reserved for special purposes and shouldn't be assigned to nodes. Table 1.3 describes some of the reserved IP addresses. See RFC 3330 for others.

TABLE 1.3   Special network addresses

Address	Function
Entire IP address set to all 0s	Depending on the mask, this network (that is, the network or subnet of which you are currently a part) or this host on this network.
A routing table entry of all 0s with a mask of all 0s	Used as the default gateway entry. Any destination address masked by all 0s produces a match for the all 0s reference address. Because the mask has no 1s, this is the least desirable entry, but it will be used when no other match exists.
Network address 127	Reserved for loopback tests. Designates the local node, and it allows that node to send a test packet to itself without generating network traffic.

TABLE 1.3   Special network addresses *(continued)*

Address	Function
Node address of all 0s	Used when referencing a network without referring to any specific nodes on that network. Usually used in routing tables.
Node address of all 1s	Broadcast address for all nodes on the specified network, also known as a *directed broadcast*. For example, 128.2.255.255 means all nodes on the Class B network 128.2. Routing this broadcast is configurable on certain routers.
169.254.0.0 with a mask of 255.255.0.0	The "link-local" block used for autoconfiguration and communication between devices on a single link. Communication cannot occur across routers. Microsoft uses this block for Automatic Private IP Addressing (APIPA).
Entire IP address set to all 1s (same as 255.255.255.255) 10.0.0.0/8 172.16.0.0 to 172.31.255.255	Broadcast to all nodes on the current network; sometimes called a limited broadcast or an all-1s broadcast. *This broadcast is not routable.*
192.168.0.0/16	The private-use blocks for Classes A, B, and C. As noted in RFC 1918, the addresses in these blocks must never be allowed into the Internet, making them acceptable for simultaneous use behind NAT servers and non-Internet-connected IP networks.

In the following sections, you will look at the three network types.

Class A Networks

In a Class A network, the first byte is the network address, and the three remaining bytes are used for the node addresses. The Class A format is Network.Node.Node.Node.

For example, in the IP address 49.22.102.70, 49 is the network address, and 22.102.70 is the node address. Every machine on this particular network would have the distinctive network address of 49. Within that network, however, you could have a large number of machines.

There are 126 possible Class A network addresses. Why? The length of a Class A network address is 1 byte, and the first bit of that byte is reserved, so 7 bits in the first byte remain available for manipulation. This means that the maximum number of Class A networks is 128. (Each of the 7 bit positions that can be manipulated can be either a 0 or a 1, and this gives you a total of 2^7 positions, or 128.) But to complicate things further, it was also decided that the network address of all 0s (0000 0000) would be reserved. This means that the actual number of usable Class A network addresses is 128 minus 1, or 127. Also, 127 is a reserved number (a network address of 0 followed by all 1s [0111 1111], so you actually start with 128 addresses minus the 2 reserved, and you're left with 126 possible Class A network addresses.

Each Class A network has 3 bytes (24 bit positions) for the node address of a machine, which means that there are 2^{24}, or 16,777,216, unique combinations. Because addresses with the two patterns of all 0s and all 1s in the node bits are reserved, the actual maximum usable number of nodes for a Class A network is 2^{24} minus 2, which equals 16,777,214.

Class B Networks

In a Class B network, the first 2 bytes are assigned to the network address, and the remaining 2 bytes are used for node addresses. The format is Network.Network.Node.Node.

For example, in the IP address 130.57.30.56, the network address is 130.57, and the node address is 30.56.

The network address is 2 bytes, so there would be 2^{16} unique combinations. But the Internet designers decided that all Class B networks should start with the binary digits 10. This leaves 14 bit positions to manipulate; therefore, there are 16,384 (or 2^{14}) unique Class B networks.

This gives you an easy way to recognize Class B addresses. If the first 2 bits of the first byte can be only 10, that gives you a decimal range from 128 up to 191 in the first octet of the IP address. Remember that you can always easily recognize a Class B network by looking at its first byte, even though there are 16,384 different Class B networks. If the first octet in the address falls between 128 and 191, it is a Class B network, regardless of the value of the second octet.

A Class B network has 2 bytes to use for node addresses. This is 2^{16} minus the two patterns in the reserved-exclusive club (all 0s and all 1s in the node bits) for a total of 65,534 possible node addresses for each Class B network.

Class C Networks

The first 3 bytes of a Class C network are dedicated to the network portion of the address, with only 1 byte remaining for the node address. The format is Network.Network.Network.Node.

In the example IP address 198.21.74.102, the network address is 198.21.74, and the node address is 102.

In a Class C network, the first three bit positions are always binary 110. Three bytes, or 24 bits, minus 3 reserved positions leaves 21 positions. There are therefore 2^{21} (or 2,097,152) possible Class C networks.

The lead bit pattern of 110 equates to decimal 192 and runs through 223. Remembering our handy easy-recognition method, this means you can always spot a Class C address if the first byte is in the range 192–223, regardless of the values of the second and third bytes of the IP address.

Each unique Class C network has 1 byte to use for node addresses. This leads to 2^8, or 256, minus the two special patterns of all 0s and all 1s, for a total of 254 node addresses for each Class C network.

Class D networks, used for multicasting only, use the address range 224.0.0.0 to 239.255.255.255 and are used, as in broadcasting, as destination addresses only. Class E networks (reserved for future use at this point) cover 240.0.0.0 to 255.255.255.255. Addresses in the Class E range are considered within the experimental range.

Subnetting a Network

If an organization is large and has lots of computers or if its computers are geographically dispersed, it makes good sense to divide its colossal network into smaller ones connected by routers. These smaller networks are called *subnets*. The benefits of using subnets are as follows:

Reduced Network Traffic   We all appreciate less traffic of any kind, and so do networks. Without routers, packet traffic could choke the entire network. Most traffic will stay on the local network—only packets destined for other networks will pass through the router and to another subnet. This traffic reduction also improves overall performance.

Simplified Management   It's easier to identify and isolate network problems in a group of smaller networks connected together than within one gigantic one.

Understanding the Benefits of Subnetting

To understand one benefit of subnetting, consider a hotel or office building. Say that a hotel has 1,000 rooms with 75 rooms to a floor. You could start at the first room on the first floor and number it 1; then when you get to the first room on the second floor, you could number it 76 and keep going until you reach room 1,000. But someone looking for room 521 would have to guess on which floor that room is located. If you were to "subnet" the hotel, you would identify the first room on the first floor with the number 101 (1 = Floor 1 and 01 = Room 1), the first room on the second floor with 201, and so on. The guest looking for room 521 would go to the fifth floor and look for room 21.

An organization with a single network address (comparable to the hotel building mentioned in the sidebar "Understanding the Benefits of Subnetting") can have a subnet address for each individual physical network (comparable to a floor in the hotel building). Each subnet is still part of the shared network address, but it also has an additional identifier denoting its individual subnetwork number. This identifier is called a *subnet address*.

Subnetting solves several addressing problems:

- If an organization has several physical networks but only one IP network address, it can handle the situation by creating subnets.

- Because subnetting allows many physical networks to be grouped together, fewer entries in a routing table are required, notably reducing network overhead.

- These things combine collectively to yield greatly enhanced network efficiency.

The original designers of the Internet Protocol envisioned a small Internet with only tens of networks and hundreds of hosts. Their addressing scheme used a network address for each physical network. As you can imagine, this scheme and the unforeseen growth of the Internet created a few problems. The following are two examples:

Not Enough Addresses A single network address can be used to refer to multiple physical networks, but an organization can request individual network addresses for each one of its physical networks. If all of these requests were granted, there wouldn't be enough addresses to go around.

Gigantic Routing Tables If each router on the Internet needed to know about every physical network, routing tables would be impossibly huge. There would be an overwhelming amount of administrative overhead to maintain those tables, and the resulting physical overhead on the routers would be massive (CPU cycles, memory, disk space, and so on). Because routers exchange routing information with each other, an additional, related consequence is that a terrific overabundance of network traffic would result.

Although there's more than one way to approach these problems, the principal solution is the one that I'll cover in this book—subnetting. As you might guess, *subnetting* is the process of carving a single IP network into smaller logical subnetworks. This trick is achieved by subdividing the host portion of an IP address to create a subnet address. The actual subdivision is accomplished through the use of a subnet mask (covered later in the chapter).

In the following sections, you will see exactly how to calculate and apply subnetting.

Implementing Subnetting

Before you can implement subnetting, you need to determine your current requirements and plan on how best to implement your subnet scheme.

How to Determine Your Subnetting Requirements

Follow these guidelines to calculate the requirements of your subnet:

1. Determine the number of required network IDs: one for each subnet and one for each wide area network (WAN) connection.

2. Determine the number of required host IDs per subnet: one for each TCP/IP device, including, for example, computers, network printers, and router interfaces.

3. Based on these two data points, create the following:

   - One subnet mask for your entire network

   - A unique subnet ID for each physical segment

   - A range of host IDs for each unique subnet

How to Implement Subnetting

Subnetting is implemented by assigning a subnet address to each machine on a given physical network. For example, in Figure 1.3, each machine on subnet 1 has a subnet address of 1.

FIGURE 1.3   A sample subnet

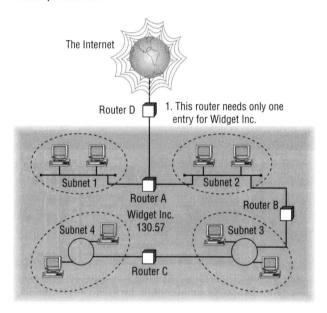

The default network portion of an IP address can't be altered without encroaching on another administrative domain's address space, unless you are assigned multiple consecutive classful addresses. To maximize the efficient use of the assigned address space, machines on a particular network share the same network address. In Figure 1.3, you can see that all of the Widget Inc. machines have a network address of 130.57. That principle is constant. In subnetting, it's the host address that's manipulated—the network address doesn't change. The subnet address scheme takes a part of the host address and recycles it as a subnet address. Bit positions are stolen from the host address to be used for the subnet identifier. Figure 1.4 shows how an IP address can be given a subnet address.

Because the Widget Inc. network is a Class B network, the first two bytes specify the network address and are shared by all machines on the network, regardless of their particular subnet. Here every machine's address on the subnet must have its third byte read 0000 0001. The fourth byte, the host address, is the unique number that identifies the actual host within that subnet. Figure 1.5 illustrates how a network address and a subnet address can be used together.

FIGURE 1.4   Network vs. host addresses

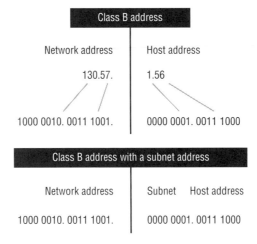

FIGURE 1.5   The network address and its subnet

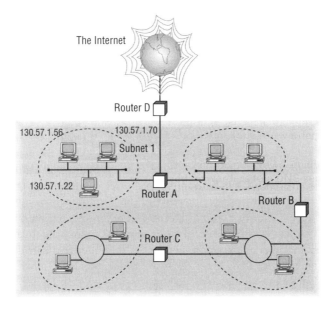

When implementing subnetting, you need some type of hardware installed onto the network. Most of us will just use a router. But if you do not want to purchase an expensive router, there is another way.

One way that you can implement subnetting is by using a Windows Server 2016 machine with multiple NIC adapters configured with routing enabled on the server. This type of router is called a *multihomed router*. This is an inexpensive way to set up a router using a Microsoft server, but it may not be the best way. Many companies specialize in routers, and these routers offer many more features and more flexibility than a multihomed router.

How to Use Subnet Masks

For the subnet address scheme to work, every machine on the network must know which part of the host address will be used as the network address. This is accomplished by assigning each machine a subnet mask.

The network administrator creates a 32-bit subnet mask comprising 1s and 0s. The 1s in the subnet mask represent the positions in the IP address that refer to the network and subnet addresses. The 0s represent the positions that refer to the host part of the address. Figure 1.6 illustrates this combination.

FIGURE 1.6 The subnet mask revealed

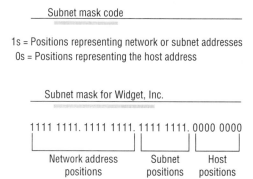

Subnet mask code

1s = Positions representing network or subnet addresses
0s = Positions representing the host address

Subnet mask for Widget, Inc.

1111 1111. 1111 1111. 1111 1111. 0000 0000

Network address positions — Subnet positions — Host positions

In the Widget Inc. example, the first two bytes of the subnet mask are 1s because Widget's network address is a Class B address, formatted as Network.Network.Node. Node. The third byte, normally assigned as part of the host address, is now used to represent the subnet address. Hence, those bit positions are represented with 1s in the subnet mask. The fourth byte is the only part of the example that represents the host address.

The subnet mask can also be expressed using the decimal equivalents of the binary patterns. The binary pattern of 1111 1111 is the same as decimal 255. Consequently, the subnet mask in the example can be denoted in two ways, as shown in Figure 1.7.

FIGURE 1.7 Different ways to represent the same mask

Subnet mask in binary: 1111 1111. 1111 1111. 1111 1111. 0000 0000
Subnet mask in decimal: 255   .   255   .   255   .   0

(The spaces in the above example are only for illustrative purposes.
The subnet mask in decimal would actually appear as 255.255.255.0.)

Not all networks need to have subnets, and therefore they don't need to use custom subnet masks. In this case, they are said to have a *default* subnet mask. This is basically the same as saying that they don't have any subnets except for the one main subnet on which the network is running. Table 1.4 shows the default subnet masks for the different classes of networks.

TABLE 1.4   Default subnet masks

Class	Format	Default Subnet Mask
A	Network.Node.Node.Node	255.0.0.0
B	Network.Network.Node.Node	255.255.0.0
C	Network.Network.Network.Node	255.255.255.0

Once the network administrator has created the subnet mask and has assigned it to each machine, the IP software applies the subnet mask to the IP address to determine its subnet address. The word *mask* carries the implied meaning of "lens" in this case; that is, the IP software looks at its IP address through the lens of its subnet mask to see its subnet address. Figure 1.8 illustrates an IP address being viewed through a subnet mask.

FIGURE 1.8   Applying the subnet mask

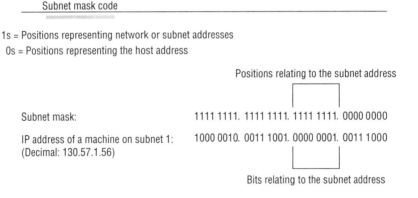

Subnet mask code

1s = Positions representing network or subnet addresses
0s = Positions representing the host address

Positions relating to the subnet address

Subnet mask: 1111 1111. 1111 1111. 1111 1111. 0000 0000

IP address of a machine on subnet 1:   1000 0010. 0011 1001. 0000 0001. 0011 1000
(Decimal: 130.57.1.56)

Bits relating to the subnet address

In this example, the IP software learns through the subnet mask that, instead of being part of the host address, the third byte of its IP address is now going to be used as a subnet address. The IP software then looks in its IP address at the bit positions that correspond to the mask, which are 0000 0001.

The final step is for the subnet bit values to be matched up with the binary numbering convention and converted to decimal. In the Widget Inc. example, the binary-to-decimal conversion is simple, as illustrated in Figure 1.9.

FIGURE 1.9   Converting the subnet mask to decimal

Binary numbering convention

Position/value: ◀── (continued)	128 64 32 16 8 4 2 1
Widget third byte:	0 0 0 0 0 0 0 1
Decimal equivalent:	0 + 1 = 1
Subnet address:	1

By using the entire third byte of a Class B address as the subnet address, it is easy to set and determine the subnet address. For example, if Widget Inc. wants to have a subnet 6, the third byte of all machines on that subnet will be 0000 0110 (decimal 6 in binary).

Using the entire third byte of a Class B network address for the subnet allows for a fair number of available subnet addresses. One byte dedicated to the subnet provides eight bit positions. Each position can be either a 1 or a 0, so the calculation is 2^8, or 256. Thus, Widget Inc. can have up to 256 total subnetworks, each with up to 254 hosts.

Although RFC 950 prohibits the use of binary all 0s and all 1s as subnet addresses, today almost all products actually permit this usage. Microsoft's TCP/IP stack allows it, as does the software in most routers (provided you enable this feature, which sometimes is not the case by default). This gives you two additional subnets. However, you should not use a subnet of 0 (all 0s) unless all the software on your network recognizes this convention.

How to Calculate the Number of Subnets

The formulas for calculating the maximum number of subnets and the maximum number of hosts per subnet are as follows:

   2 × number of masked bits in subnet mask = maximum number of subnets

   2 × number of unmasked bits in subnet mask − 2 = maximum number of hosts per subnet

In the formulas, *masked* refers to bit positions of 1, and *unmasked* refers to bit positions of 0. The downside to using an entire byte of a node address as your subnet address is that you reduce the possible number of node addresses on each subnet. As explained earlier, without a subnet, a Class B address has 65,534 unique combinations of 1s and 0s that can be used for node addresses. The question then is why would you ever want 65,534 hosts on a single physical network?

The trade-off is acceptable to most who ask themselves this question. If you use an entire byte of the node address for a subnet, you then have only 1 byte for the host addresses, leaving only 254 possible host addresses. If any of your subnets are populated with more than 254 machines, you'll have a problem. To solve it, you would then need to shorten the subnet mask, thereby lengthening the number of host bits and increasing the number of host addresses. This gives you more available host addresses on each subnet. A side effect of this solution is that it shrinks the number of possible subnets.

Figure 1.10 shows an example of using a smaller subnet address. A company called Acme Inc. expects to need a maximum of 14 subnets. In this case, Acme does not need to take an entire byte from the host address for the subnet address. To get its 14 different subnet addresses, it needs to snatch only 4 bits from the host address ($2^4 = 16$). The host portion of the address has 12 usable bits remaining ($2^{12} - 2 = 4,094$). Each of Acme's 16 subnets could then potentially have a total of 4,094 host addresses, and 4,094 machines on each subnet should be plenty.

FIGURE 1.10   An example of a smaller subnet address

Acme, Inc.

Network address: 132.8 (Class B; net.net.host.host)

Example IP address: 1000 0100. 0000 1000. 0001 0010. 0011 1100

Decimal: 132 .   8   .   18   .   60

Subnet Mask Code

1s = Positions representing network or subnet addresses
0s = Positions representing the host address

Subnet mask:
Binary: 1111 1111. 1111 1111. 1111 0000. 0000 0000
Decimal: 255 .   255 .   240 .   0
(The decimal 240 is equal to the binary 1111 0000.)

Positions relating to the subnet address

Subnet mask: 1111 1111. 1111 1111. 1111 0000. 0000 0000

IP address of an Acme machine: 1000 0100. 0000 1000. 0001 0010. 0011 1100
(Decimal: 132.8.18.60)

Bits relating to the subnet address

Binary-to-Decimal Conversions for Subnet Address

Subnet mask positions:	1	1	1	1	0	0	0	0
	↓	↓	↓	↓				
Position/value: ←(continue)	128	64	32	16	8	4	2	1
Third byte of IP address:	0	0	0	1	0	0	1	0
Decimal equivalent:					0 + 16 = 16			
Subnet address for this IP address:							16	

An Easier Way to Apply Subnetting

Now that you have the basics of how to subnet down, you'll learn an easier way. If you have learned a different way and it works for you, stick with it. It does not matter how you get to the finish line, just as long as you get there. But if you are new to subnetting, Figure 1.11 will make it easier for you.

FIGURE 1.11   Will's IPv4 subnetting chart

Subnet Mask	128	64	32	16	8	4	2	1
255	1	1	1	1	1	1	1	1
254	1	1	1	1	1	1	1	0
252	1	1	1	1	1	1	0	0
248	1	1	1	1	1	0	0	0
240	1	1	1	1	0	0	0	0
224	1	1	1	0	0	0	0	0
192	1	1	0	0	0	0	0	0
128	1	0	0	0	0	0	0	0
0	0	0	0	0	0	0	0	0

0 = HOSTS   **1** = SUBNETS   **Will Panek's Chart**

		Power		Subnets		Hosts
2	×	2	=	4	−2	2
2	×	3	=	8	−2	6
2	×	4	=	16	−2	14
2	×	5	=	32	−2	30
2	×	6	=	64	−2	62
2	×	7	=	128	−2	126
2	×	8	=	256	−2	254
2	×	9	=	512	−2	510
2	×	10	=	1024	−2	1022
2	×	11	=	2048	−2	2046
2	×	12	=	4096	−2	4094
2	×	13	=	8192	−2	8190
2	×	14	=	16384	−2	16382
2	×	15	=	32768	−2	32766

This chart may look intimidating, but it's really simple to use once you have done it a few times.

Remember that, on this chart, 1s equal subnets and 0s equal hosts. If you get this confused, you will get wrong answers in the following exercises.

Watch the Hosts column on the lower end of the chart. This represents the number of addresses available to you after the two reserved addresses have been removed. The following exercises provide some examples.

SUBNET MASK EXERCISE 1.1

Class C, 10 Hosts per Subnet

You have a Class C address, and you require 10 hosts per subnet.

1. Write down the following:

    255.255.255.____

    The blank is the number you need to fill in.

2. Look under the Hosts column and choose the first number that is larger than 10 (the number of hosts per subnet you need). You should have come up with 14.

3. Move across the page and look at the number in the Power column. The power number is 4.

4. Go to the top of the chart and look for the row with exactly four 0s (hosts). Find the number at the beginning of the row.

The number at the beginning of the row is 240. That's your answer. The subnet mask should be 255.255.255.240.

SUBNET MASK EXERCISE 1.2

Class C, 20 Hosts per Subnet

You have a Class C address, and you need 20 hosts per subnet.

1. Write down the following:

    255.255.255.___

2. Look under the Hosts column and find the first number that covers 20. (This should be 30.)

3. Go across to the power number (5).

4. Go to the top part of the chart and find the row with exactly five 0s from right to left.

The number at the beginning of the row is 224. Your answer should be 255.255.255.224.

SUBNET MASK EXERCISE 1.3

Class C, Five Subnets

Now you have a Class C address, and you need five subnets. Remember that subnets are represented by 1s in the chart.

1.   Write down the following:

     255.255.255.___

2.   Look under the Subnets column and find the first number that covers 5. (This should be 8.)

3.   Go across to the power number. (This should be 3.)

4.   Go to the top part of the chart and find out which row has exactly three 1s (remember, 1s are for subnets) from left to right.

Your answer should be 255.255.255.224.

SUBNET MASK EXERCISE 1.4

Class B, 1,500 Hosts per Subnet

This one is a bit harder. You have a Class B address, and you need 1,500 hosts per subnet. Because you have a Class B address, you need to fill in the third octet of numbers. The fourth octet contains eight 0s.

1.   Write down the following:

     255.255.___.0

2.   Look at the Hosts column and find the first number that covers 1,500. (This should be 2,046.)

3.   Go across and find the power number. (This should be 11.)

4.   Remember, you already have eight 0s in the last octet. So, you need only three more. Find the row with three 0s.

You should come up with an answer of 255.255.248.0. This actually breaks down to 11111111.11111111.11111000.00000000, and that's how you got the 11 zeros.

SUBNET MASK EXERCISE 1.5

Class B, 3,500 Hosts per Subnet

You have a Class B address, and you need 3,500 hosts per subnet.

1.   Write down the following:

     255.255.___.0

2. Look at the Hosts column and find the first number that covers 3,500. (This should be 4,094.)

3. Go across and find the power number. (This should be 12.)

4. Remember, you already have eight 0s in the last octet, so you need only four more. Count for four zeros from right to left.

You should come up with an answer of 255.255.240.0. Again, this actually breaks down to 11111111.11111111.11110000.00000000, and that's how you got the 12 zeros.

 If you get a question that gives you both the hosts and the subnets, always figure out the larger number first. Then, depending on the mask you have decided to use, make sure that the lower number is also correct with that mask.

Now try some more subnet mask exercises using the data that follows:

Class B address	Class B address
1,000 hosts per subnet	25 subnets
Class C address	Class B address
45 hosts per subnet	4,000 hosts per subnet
192.168.0.0	Class B address
10 subnets	2,000 hosts per subnet
	25 subnets

Here are the answers. If any of your answers are wrong, follow the previous examples and try to work through them again.

Class B address	Class B address
1,000 hosts per subnet 255.255.252.0	25 subnets 255.255.248.0
Class C address	Class B address
45 hosts per subnet 255.255.255.192	4,000 hosts per subnet 255.255.240.0
192.168.0.0	Class B address
10 subnets 255.255.255.240	2,000 hosts per subnet
	25 subnets 255.255.248.0

Applying Subnetting the Traditional Way

Sometimes subnetting can be confusing. After all, it can be quite difficult to remember all of those numbers. You can step back a minute and take a look at the primary classes of networks and how to subnet each one. Let's start with Class C because it uses only 8 bits for the node address, so it's the easiest to calculate. In the following sections, I will explain how to subnet the various types of networks.

Subnetting Class C

If you recall, a Class C network uses the first 3 bytes (24 bits) to define the network address. This leaves you 1 byte (8 bits) with which to address hosts. So if you want to create subnets, your options are limited because of the small number of bits available.

If you break down your subnets into chunks smaller than the default Class C, then figuring out the subnet mask, network number, broadcast address, and router address can be confusing. To build a sturdy base for subnetting, study the following techniques for determining these special values for each subnet, but also learn and use the more efficient technique presented in the later section "Quickly Identifying Subnet Characteristics Using CIDR" and the earlier section "An Easier Way to Apply Subnetting." Table 1.5 summarizes how you can break down a Class C network into one, two, four, or eight smaller subnets, and it gives you the subnet masks, network numbers, broadcast addresses, and router addresses. The first three bytes have simply been designated x.y.z. (Note that the table assumes you can use the all-0s and all-1s subnets too.)

TABLE 1.5   Setting up Class C subnets

Number of Desired Subnets	Subnet Mask	Network Number	Router Address	Broadcast Address	Remaining Number of IP Addresses
1	255.255.255.0	x.y.z.0	x.y.z.1	x.y.z.255	253
2	255.255.255.128	x.y.z.0	x.y.z.1	x.y.z.127	125
	255.255.255.128	x.y.z.128	x.y.z.129	x.y.z.255	125
4	255.255.255.192	x.y.z.0	x.y.z.1	x.y.z.63	61
	255.255.255.192	x.y.z.64	x.y.z.65	x.y.z.127	61
	255.255.255.192	x.y.z.128	x.y.z.129	x.y.z.191	61
	255.255.255.192	x.y.z.192	x.y.z.193	x.y.z.255	61
8	255.255.255.224	x.y.z.0	x.y.z.1	x.y.z.31	29

Number of Desired Subnets	Subnet Mask	Network Number	Router Address	Broadcast Address	Remaining Number of IP Addresses
	255.255.255.224	x.y.z.32	x.y.z.33	x.y.z.63	29
	255.255.255.224	x.y.z.64	x.y.z.65	x.y.z.95	29
	255.255.255.224	x.y.z.96	x.y.z.97	x.y.z.127	29
	255.255.255.224	x.y.z.128	x.y.z.129	x.y.z.159	29
	255.255.255.224	x.y.z.160	x.y.z.161	x.y.z.191	29
	255.255.255.224	x.y.z.192	x.y.z.193	x.y.z.223	29
	255.255.255.224	x.y.z.224	x.y.z.225	x.y.z.255	29

For example, suppose you want to chop up a Class C network, 200.211.192.*x*, into two subnets. As you can see in the table, you'd use a subnet mask of 255.255.255.128 for each subnet. The first subnet would have the network number 200.211.192.0, router address 200.211.192.1, and broadcast address 200.211.192.127. You could assign IP addresses 200.211.192.2 through 200.211.192.126—that's 125 additional different IP addresses.

Heavily subnetting a network results in the loss of a progressively greater percentage of addresses to the network number, broadcast address, and router address.

The second subnet would have the network number 200.211.192.128, router address 200.211.192.129, and broadcast address 200.211.192.255.

Why It's Best to Use Routers That Support Subnet 0

When subnetting a Class C network using the method in Table 1.5, if you use the $2^x - 2$ calculation, the subnet 128 in the table doesn't make sense. It turns out that there's a legitimate and popular reason to do it this way, however.

- Remember that using subnet 0 is not allowed according to the RFC standards, but by using it you can subnet your Class C network with a subnet mask of 128. This uses only 1 bit, and according to your calculator $2^1 - 2 = 0$, giving you zero subnets.

- By using routers that support subnet 0, you can assign 1–126 for hosts and 129–254 for hosts, as stated in the table. This saves a bunch of addresses! If you were to stick to the method defined by the RFC standards, the best you could gain is a subnet mask of 192 (2 bits), which allows you only two subnets ($2^2 - 2 = 2$).

Determining the Subnet Numbers for a Class C Subnet

The first subnet always has a 0 in the interesting octet. In the example, it would be 200.211.192.0, the same as the original nonsubnetted network address. To determine the subnet numbers for the additional subnets, first you have to determine the incremental value:

1. Begin with the octet that has an interesting value (other than 0 or 255) in the subnet mask. Then subtract the interesting value from 256. The result is the incremental value.

If again you use the network 200.211.192.x and a mask of 255.255.255.192, the example yields the following equation: 256 − 192 = 64. Thus, 64 is your incremental value in the interesting octet—the fourth octet in this case. Why the fourth octet? That's the octet with the interesting value, 192, in the mask.

2. To determine the second subnet number, add the incremental value to the 0 in the fourth octet of the first subnet.

In the example, it would be 200.211.192.64.

3. To determine the third subnet number, add the incremental value to the interesting octet of the second subnet number.

In the example, it would be 200.211.192.128.

4. Keep adding the incremental value in this fashion until you reach the actual subnet mask number.

For example, 0 + 64 = 64, so your second subnet is 64. And 64 + 64 is 128, so your third subnet is 128. And 128 + 64 is 192, so your fourth subnet is 192. Because 192 is the subnet mask, this is your last subnet. If you tried to add 64 again, you'd come up with 256, an unusable octet value, which is always where you end up when you've gone too far. This means your valid subnets are 0, 64, 128, and 192 (total of 4 subnets on your network).

The numbers between the subnets are your valid host and broadcast addresses. For example, the following are valid hosts for two of the subnets in a Class C network with a subnet mask of 192:

▪ The valid hosts for subnet 64 are in the range 65–126, which gives you 62 hosts per subnet.

(You can't use 127 as a host because that would mean your host bits would be all 1s. The all-1s format is reserved as the broadcast address for that subnet.)

▪ The valid hosts for subnet 128 are in the range 129–190, with a broadcast address of 191.

As you can see, this solution wastes a few addresses—six more than not subnetting at all, to be exact. In a Class C network, this should not be hard to justify. The 255.255.255.128 subnet mask is an even better solution if you need only two subnets and expect to need close to 126 host addresses per subnet.

Calculating Values for an Eight-Subnet Class C Network

What happens if you need eight subnets in your Class C network?

By using the calculation of $2x$, where x is the number of subnet bits, you would need 3 subnet bits to get eight subnets ($2^3 = 8$). What are the valid subnets, and what are the valid hosts of each subnet? Let's figure it out.

11100000 is 224 in binary, and it would be the interesting value in the fourth octet of the subnet mask. This must be the same on all workstations.

NOTE   You're likely to see test questions that ask you to identify the problem with a given configuration. If a workstation has the wrong subnet mask, the router could "think" that the workstation is on a different subnet than it actually is. When that happens, the misguided router won't forward packets to the workstation in question. Similarly, if the mask is incorrectly specified in the workstation's configuration, that workstation will observe the mask and send packets to the default gateway when it shouldn't.

To figure out the valid subnets, subtract the interesting octet value from 256 (256 – 224 = 32), so 32 is your incremental value for the fourth octet. Of course, the 0 subnet is your first subnet, as always. The other subnets would be 32, 64, 96, 128, 160, 192, and 224. The valid hosts are the numbers between the subnet numbers, except the numbers that equal all 1s in the host bits. These numbers would be 31, 63, 95, 127, 159, 191, 223, and 255. Remember that using all 1s in the host bits is reserved for the broadcast address of each subnet.

The valid subnets, hosts, and broadcasts are as follows:

Subnet	Hosts	Broadcast
0	1–30	31
32	33–62	63
64	65–94	95
96	97–126	127
128	129–158	159
160	161–190	191
192	193–222	223
224	225–254	255

You can add one more bit to the subnet mask just for fun. You were using 3 bits, which gave you 224. By adding the next bit, the mask now becomes 240 (11110000).

By using 4 bits for the subnet mask, you get 16 subnets because $2^4 = 16$. This subnet mask also gives you only 4 bits for the host addresses, or $2^4 - 2 = 14$ hosts per subnet. As you can see, the number of hosts per subnet gets reduced rather quickly for each host bit that gets reallocated for subnet use.

The first valid subnet for subnet 240 is 0, as always. Because 256 – 240 = 16, your remaining subnets are then 16, 32, 48, 64, 80, 96, 112, 128, 144, 160, 176, 192, 208, 224, and 240. Remember that the actual interesting octet value also represents the last valid subnet, so 240 is the last valid subnet number. The valid hosts are the numbers between the subnets, except for the numbers that are all 1s—the broadcast address for the subnet.

Table 1.6 shows the numbers in the interesting (fourth) octet for a Class C network with eight subnets.

TABLE 1.6   Fourth octet addresses for a Class C network with eight subnets

Subnet	Hosts	Broadcast
0	1–14	15
16	17–30	31
32	33–46	47
48	49–62	63
64	65–78	79
80	81–94	95
96	97–110	111
112	113–126	127
128	129–142	143
144	145–158	159
160	161–174	175
176	177–190	191
192	193–206	207
208	209–222	223
224	225–238	239
240	241–254	255

Subnetting Class B

Because a Class B network has 16 bits for host addresses, you have plenty of available bits to play with when figuring out a subnet mask. Remember that you have to start with the left-most bit and work toward the right. For example, a Class B network would look like x.y.0.0, with the default mask of 255.255.0.0. Using the default mask would give you one network with 65,534 hosts.

The default mask in binary is 11111111.11111111.00000000.00000000. The 1s represent the corresponding network bits in the IP address, and the 0s represent the host bits. When you're creating a subnet mask, the leftmost bit(s) will be borrowed from the host bits (0s will be turned into 1s) to become the subnet mask. You then use the remaining bits that are still set to 0 for host addresses.

If you use only 1 bit to create a subnet mask, you have a mask of 255.255.128.0. If you use 2 bits, you have a mask of 255.255.192.0, or 11111111.11111111.11000000.00000000.

As with subnetting a Class C address, you now have three parts of the IP address: the network address, the subnet address, and the host address. You figure out the subnet mask numbers the same way as you did with a Class C network (see the previous section, "Calculating Values for an Eight-Subnet Class C Network"), but you'll end up with a lot more hosts per subnet.

There are four subnets, because $2^2 = 4$. The valid third-octet values for the subnets are 0, 64, 128, and 192 (256 − 192 = 64, so the incremental value of the third octet is 64). However, there are 14 bits (0s) left over for host addressing. This gives you 16,382 hosts per subnet ($2^{14} - 2 = 16,382$).

The valid subnets and hosts are as follows:

Subnet	Hosts	Broadcast
x.y.0.0	x.y.0.1 through x.y. 63.254	x.y.63.255
x.y.64.0	x.y.64.1 through x.y.127.254	x.y.127.255
x.y.128.0	x.y.128.1 through x.y.191.254	x.y.191.255
x.y.192.0	x.y.192.1 through x.y.255.254	x.y.255.255

You can add another bit to the subnet mask, making it 11111111.11111111.11100000 .00000000, or 255.255.224.0. This gives you eight subnets ($2^3 = 8$) and 8,190 hosts. The valid subnets are 0, 32, 64, 96, 128, 160, 192, and 224 (256 − 224 = 32). The subnets, valid hosts, and broadcasts are listed here:

Subnet	Hosts	Broadcast
x.y.0.0	x.y.0.1 through x.y.31.254	x.y.31.255
x.y.32.0	x.y.32.1 through x.y.63.254	x.y.63.255
x.y.64.0	x.y.64.1 through x.y.95.254	x.y.95.255
x.y.96.0	x.y.96.1 through x.y.127.254	x.y.127.255
x.y.128.0	x.y.128.1 through x.y.159.254	x.y.159.255
x.y.160.0	x.y.160.1 through x.y.191.254	x.y.191.255
x.y.192.0	x.y.192.1 through x.y.223.254	x.y.223.255
x.y.224.0	x.y.224.1 through x.y.255.254	x.y.255.255

The following are the breakdowns for a 9-bit mask and a 14-bit mask:

- If you use 9 bits for the mask, it gives you 512 subnets (2^9). With only 7 bits for hosts, you still have 126 hosts per subnet ($2^7 - 2 = 126$). The mask looks like this:

    11111111.11111111.11111111.10000000, or 255.255.255.128

- If you use 14 bits for the subnet mask, you get 16,384 subnets (2^{14}) but only two hosts per subnet ($2^2 - 2 = 2$). The subnet mask would look like this:

    11111111.11111111.11111111.11111100, or 255.255.255.252

 Real World Scenario

Subnet Mask Use in an ISP

You may be wondering why you would use a 14-bit subnet mask with a Class B address. This approach is actually very common. Let's say you have a Class B network and use a subnet mask of 255.255.255.0. You'd have 256 subnets and 254 hosts per subnet. Imagine also that you are an Internet service provider (ISP) and have a network with many WAN links, a different one between you and each customer. Typically, you'd have a direct connection between each site. Each of these links must be on its own subnet or network. There will be two hosts on these subnets—one address for each router port. If you used the mask described earlier (255.255.255.0), you would waste 252 host addresses per subnet. But by using the 255.255.255.252 subnet mask, you have more subnets available, which means more customers—each subnet with only two hosts, which is the maximum allowed on a point-to-point circuit.

You can use the 255.255.255.252 subnet mask only if you are running a routing algorithm such as Enhanced Interior Gateway Routing Protocol (EIGRP) or Open Shortest Path First (OSPF). These routing protocols allow what is called *Variable Length Subnet Masking (VLSM)*. VLSM allows you to run the 255.255.255.252 subnet mask on your interfaces to the WANs and run 255.255.255.0 on your router interfaces in your local area network (LAN) using the same classful network address for all subnets. It works because these routing protocols transmit the subnet mask information in the update packets that they send to the other routers. Classful routing protocols, such as RIP version 1, don't transmit the subnet mask and therefore cannot employ VLSM.

Subnetting Class A

Class A networks have even more bits available than Class B and Class C networks. A default Class A network subnet mask is only 8 bits, or 255.0.0.0, giving you a whopping 24 bits for hosts to play with. Knowing which hosts and subnets are valid is a lot more complicated than it was for either Class B or Class C networks.

If you use a mask of 11111111.11111111.00000000.00000000, or 255.255.0.0, you'll have 8 bits for subnets, or 256 subnets (2^8). This leaves 16 bits for hosts, or 65,534 hosts per subnet ($2^{16} - 2 = 65534$).

If you split the 24 bits evenly between subnets and hosts, you would give each one 12 bits. The mask would look like this: 11111111.11111111.11110000.00000000, or 255.255.240.0. How many valid subnets and hosts would you have? The answer is 4,096 subnets each with 4,094 hosts ($2^{12} - 2 = 4,094$).

The second octet will be somewhere between 0 and 255. However, you will need to figure out the third octet. Because the third octet has a 240 mask, you get 16 ($256 - 240 = 16$) as your incremental value in the third octet. The third octet must start with 0 for the first subnet, the second subnet will have 16 in the third octet, and so on. This means that some of your valid subnets are as follows (not in order):

Subnet	Hosts	Broadcast
x.0-255.0.0	x.0-255.0.1 through x.0-255.15.254	x.0-255.15.255
x.0-255.16.0	x.0-255.16.1 through x.0-255.31.254	x.0-255.31.255
x.0-255.32.0	x.0-255.32.1 through x.0-255.47.254	x.0-255.47.255
x.0-255.48.0	x.0-255.48.1 through x.0-255.63.254	x.0-255.63.255

They go on in this way for the remaining third-octet values through 224 in the subnet column.

Working with Classless Inter-Domain Routing

Microsoft uses an alternate way to write address ranges, called *Classless Inter-Domain Routing* (*CIDR*; pronounced "cider"). CIDR is a shorthand version of the subnet mask. For example, an address of 131.107.2.0 with a subnet mask of 255.255.255.0 is listed in CIDR as 131.107.2.0/24 because the subnet mask contains 24 1s. An address listed as 141.10.32.0/19 would have a subnet mask of 255.255.224.0, or 19 1s (the default subnet mask for Class B plus 3 bits). This is the nomenclature used in all Microsoft exams (see Figure 1.12).

FIGURE 1.12   Subnet mask represented by 1s

Subnet mask in binary: 1111 1111. 1111 1111. 1111 1111. 0000 0000

Subnet mask in decimal: 255   .   255   .   255   .   0

(The spaces in the above example are only for illustrative purposes.
The subnet mask in decimal would actually appear as 255.255.255.0.)

Let's say an Internet company has assigned you the following Class C address and CIDR number: 192.168.10.0/24. This represents the Class C address of 192.168.10.0 and a subnet mask of 255.255.255.0.

Again, CIDR represents the number of 1s turned on in a subnet mask. For example, a CIDR number of /16 stands for 255.255.0.0 (11111111.11111111.00000000.00000000).

The following is a list of all of the CIDR numbers (starting with a Class A default subnet mask) and their corresponding subnet masks:

CIDR	Mask	CIDR	Mask	CIDR	Mask
/8	255.0.0.0	/17	255.255.128.0	/25	255.255.255.128
/9	255.128.0.0	/18	255.255.192.0	/26	255.255.255.192
/10	255.192.0.0	/19	255.255.224.0	/27	255.255.255.224
/11	255.224.0.0	/20	255.255.240.0	/28	255.255.255.240
/12	255.240.0.0	/21	255.255.248.0	/29	255.255.255.248
/13	255.248.0.0	/22	255.255.252.0	/30	255.255.255.252
/14	255.252.0.0	/23	255.255.254.0	/31	255.255.255.254
/15	255.254.0.0	/24	255.255.255.0	/32	255.255.255.255
/16	255.255.0.0				

Quickly Identifying Subnet Characteristics Using CIDR

Given the limited time you have to dispatch questions in the structured environment of a Microsoft certification exam, every shortcut to coming up with the correct answer is a plus. The following method, using CIDR notation, can shave minutes off the time it takes you to complete a single question. Since you already understand the underlying binary technology at the heart of subnetting, you can use the following shortcuts, one for each address class, to come up with the correct answer without working in binary.

Identifying Class C Subnet Characteristics

Consider the host address 192.168.10.50/27. The following steps flesh out the details of the subnet of which this address is a member:

1. Obtain the CIDR-notation prefix length for the address by converting the dotted-decimal mask to CIDR notation.

   In this case, /27 corresponds to a mask of 255.255.255.224. Practice converting between these notations until it becomes second nature.

2. Using the closest multiple of 8 that is greater than or equal to the prefix length, compute the interesting octet (the octet that increases from one subnet to the next in increments other than 1 or 0). Divide this multiple by 8. The result is a number corresponding to the octet that is interesting.

   In this case, the next multiple of 8 greater than 27 is 32. Dividing 32 by 8 produces the number 4, pointing to the fourth octet as the interesting one.

3. To compute the incremental value in the interesting octet, subtract the prefix length from the next higher multiple of 8, which in this case is 32. The result (32 – 27) is 5. Raise 2 to the computed value ($2^5 = 32$). The result is the incremental value of the interesting octet.

4. Recall the value of the interesting octet from the original address (50 in this case). Starting with 0, increment by the incremental value until the value is exceeded. The values then are 0, 32, 64, and so on.

5. The subnet in question extends from the increment that is immediately less than or equal to the address's interesting octet value to the address immediately before the next increment. In this example, 192.168.10.50/27 belongs to the subnet 192.168.10.32, and this subnet extends to the address immediately preceding 192.168.10.64, which is its broadcast address, 192.168.10.63.

    Note that if the interesting octet is not the fourth octet, all octets after the interesting octet must be set to 0 for the subnet address.

6. The usable range of addresses for the subnet in question extends from one higher than the subnet address to one less than the broadcast address, making the range for the subnet in question 192.168.10.33 through 192.168.10.62. As you can see, 192.168.10.50/27 definitely falls within the subnet 192.168.10.32/27.

Identifying Class B Subnet Characteristics

Using the steps in the previous section, find the subnet in which the address 172.16.76.12 with a mask of 255.255.240.0 belongs.

1. The corresponding CIDR notation prefix length is /20.

2. The next multiple of 8 that is greater than 20 is 24. 24/8 = 3. Octet 3 is interesting.

3. 24 – 20 = 4, so the incremental value is $2^4 = 16$.

4. The increments in the third octet are 0, 16, 32, 48, 64, 80, and so on.

5. The increments of 64 and 80 bracket the address's third-octet value of 76, making the subnet in question 172.16.64.0, after setting all octets after the interesting octet to 0. This subnet's broadcast address is 172.16.79.255, which comes right before the next subnet address of 172.16.80.0.

6. The usable address range then extends from 172.16.64.1 through 172.16.79.254.

Identifying Class A Subnet Characteristics

Try it one more time with 10.6.127.255/14. Combine some of the related steps if possible:

1. The prefix length is 14. The next multiple of 8 that is greater than or equal to 14 is 16. 16/8 = 2, so the second octet is interesting.

2. 16 – 14 = 2, so the incremental value in the second octet is $2^2 = 4$.

3. The corresponding second-octet value of 6 in the address falls between the 4 and 8 increments. This means that the subnet in question is 10.4.0.0 (setting octets after the second one to 0) and its broadcast address is 10.7.255.255.

4. The usable address range is from 10.4.0.1 through 10.7.255.254.

Determining Quantities of Subnets and Hosts

The general technique described in the previous sections is also useful when trying to determine the total number of subnets and hosts produced by a given mask with respect to the default mask of the class of address in question.

For example, consider the Class B address 172.16.0.0 with a subnet mask of 255.255.254.0.

This is a prefix length of 23 bits. When you subtract the default prefix length for a Class B address of 16 from 23, you get the value 7. Raising 2 to the 7th power results in the value 128, which is the number of subnets you get when you subnet a Class B address with the 255.255.254.0 mask.

Determining the number of hosts available in each of these 128 subnets is simple because you always subtract the prefix length that the subnet mask produces, 23 in this example, from the value 32, which represents the total number of bits in any IP address. The difference, 9, represents the remaining number of 0s, or host bits, in the subnet mask. Raising 2 to this value produces the total possible number of host IDs per subnet that this subnet mask allows. Remember to subtract 2 from this result to account for the subnet and broadcast addresses for each subnet. This gives you the actual number of usable host IDs per subnet. In this case, this value is $2^9 - 2 = 510$.

Repeated practice with this technique will reduce your time to obtain the desired answer to mere seconds, leaving time for the more challenging tasks in each question. You have a wealth of examples and scenarios in this chapter, as well as in the review questions, on which to try your technique and build your trust in this faster method.

Supernetting

Let's take a look at a different type of subnetting. Class B addresses give you 65,534 addresses, but let's say that you have 1,000 users. Would you really need a Class B address? Not if you use supernetting.

Supernetting allows you to have two or more blocks of contiguous subnetwork addresses. So what does that actually mean? Class C addresses give you 254 usable addresses. So if you needed 1,000 users, you could set up supernetting of 4 Class C addresses that are contiguous.

Example:
192.168.16.0
192.168.17.0
192.168.18.0
192.168.19.0

When you set up supernetting for a Class C, you would use a Class B subnet mask. When you set up supernetting for a Class B, you would use a Class A subnet mask. This allows you to use multiple classes to get a larger number of hosts without taking up an entire class.

So the subnet mask for the above example would be 255.255.252.0 or /22. The reason we used this subnet mask is because a 252 subnet mask allows for 4 subnets. Each of the above Class C numbers would equal one subnet on this network.

Understanding IPv6

Internet Protocol version 6 (IPv6) is the first major revamping of IP since RFC 791 was accepted in 1981. Yes, the operation of IP has improved, and there have been a few bells and whistles added (such as NAT, for example), but the basic structure is still being used as it was originally intended. IPv6 has actually been available to use in Microsoft operating systems since NT 4.0, but it always had to be manually enabled. Windows Vista was the first Microsoft operating system to have it enabled by default. It is also enabled by default in Windows 7, Windows 10, Windows Server 2008, Windows Server 2008 R2, and Windows Server 2016, and it probably will be in all Microsoft operating systems from this point on.

TCP and UDP—as well as the IP applications, such as HTTP, FTP, SNMP, and the rest—are still being used in IPv4. So, you might ask, why change to the new version? What does IPv6 bring to your networking infrastructure? What is the structure of an IPv6 address? How is it implemented and used within Windows Server 2016? I'll answer all of those questions and more in the following sections.

IPv6 History and Need

In the late 1970s, as the IP specifications were being put together, the vision of the interconnected devices was limited compared to what we actually have today. To get an idea of the growth of the Internet, take a look at Hobbes' Internet Timeline in RFC 2235 (www.faqs .org/rfcs/rfc2235.html). As you can see, in 1984, the number of hosts finally surpassed 1,000—two years after TCP and IP were introduced. With 32 bits of addressing available in IPv4, it handled the 1,000+ hosts just fine. And even with the number of hosts breaking the 10,000 mark in 1987 and then 100,000 in 1989, there were still plenty of IP addresses to go around. But when the number of hosts exceeded 2 million in 1992 and 3 million in 1994, concern in the industry started to build. So in 1994, a working group was formed to come up with a solution to the quickly dwindling usable address availability in the IPv4 space. Internet Protocol next generation (IPng) was started.

Have you heard of IP address depletion being a problem today? Probably not as much. When the working group realized that it could not have IPv6 standardized before the available addresses might run out, they developed and standardized *Network Address Translation (NAT)* as an interim solution. NAT, or more specifically an implementation of NAT called *Port Address Translation (PAT)*, took care of a big portion of the problem.

NAT works very well, but it does have some limitations, including issues of peer-to-peer applications with their IPv4 addresses embedded in the data, issues of end-to-end traceability, and issues of overlapping addresses when two networks merge. Because all devices in an IPv6 network will have a unique address and no network address translation will take place, the global addressing concept of IPv4 will be brought back (the address put on by the source device will stay all the way to the destination). Thus, with the new-and-improved functionality of IPv6, the drawbacks of NAT and the limitations of IPv4 will be eliminated.

New and Improved IPv6 Concepts

Several elements of the IPv4 protocol could use some enhancements. Fortunately, IPv6 incorporates those enhancements as well as new features directly into the protocol specification to provide better and additional functionality.

The following list includes new concepts and new implementations of old concepts in IPv6:

- Larger address space (128-bit vs. 32-bit).

- Autoconfiguration of Internet-accessible addresses with or without DHCP. (Without DHCP, it's called *stateless autoconfiguration.*)

- More efficient IP header (fewer fields and no checksum).

- Fixed-length IP header (the IPv4 header is variable length) with extension headers beyond the standard fixed length to provide enhancements.

- Built-in IP mobility and security. (Although available in IPv4, the IPv6 implementation is a much better implementation.)

- Built-in transition schemes to allow integration of the IPv4 and IPv6 spaces.

- ARP broadcast messages replaced with multicast request.

Here are more details about these features:

128-Bit Address Space   The new 128-bit address space will provide unique addresses for the foreseeable future. Although I would like to say that we will never use up all of the addresses, history may prove me wrong. The number of unique addresses in the IPv6 space is 2^{128}, or 3.4×10^{38}, addresses. How big is that number? It's enough for toasters and refrigerators (and maybe even cars) to all have their own addresses.

As a point of reference, the nearest black hole to Earth is 1,600 light years away. If you were to stack 4mm BB pellets from here to the nearest black hole and back, you would need 1.51×10^{22} BBs. This means you could uniquely address each BB from Earth to the black hole and back and still have quite a few addresses left over.

Another way to look at it is that the IPv6 address space is big enough to provide more than 1 million addresses per square inch of the surface area of the earth (oceans included).

Autoconfiguration and Stateless Autoconfiguration   Autoconfiguration is another added/ improved feature of IPv6. We've used DHCP for a while to assign IP addresses to client machines. You should even remember that APIPA can be used to assign addresses automatically to Microsoft DHCP client machines in the absence of a DHCP server. The problem with APIPA is that it confines communication between machines to a local LAN (no default gateway). What if a client machine could ask whether there was a router on the LAN and what network it was on? If the client machine knew that, it could not only assign itself an address, it could also choose the appropriate network and default gateway. The stateless autoconfiguration functionality of IPv6 allows the clients to do this.

Improved IPv6 Header   The IPv6 header is more efficient than the IPv4 header because it is fixed length (with extensions possible) and has only a few fields. The IPv6 header consists of a total of 40 bytes:

32 bytes   Source and destination IPv6 addresses

8 bytes   Version field, traffic class field, flow label field, payload length field, next header field, and hop limit field

You don't have to waste your time with a checksum validation anymore, and you don't have to include the length of the IP header (it's fixed in IPv6; the IP header is variable length in IPv4, so the length must be included as a field).

IPv6 Mobility   IPv6 is only a replacement of the OSI layer 3 component, so you'll continue to use the TCP (and UDP) components as they currently exist. IPv6 addresses a TCP issue, though. Specifically, TCP is connection oriented, meaning that you establish an end-to-end communication path with sequencing and acknowledgments before you ever send any data, and then you have to acknowledge all of the pieces of data sent. You do this through a combination of an IP address, port number, and port type (socket).

If the source IP address changes, the TCP connection may be disrupted. But then how often does this happen? Well, it happens more and more often because more people are walking around with a wireless laptop or a wireless Voice over IP (VoIP) telephone. IPv6 mobility establishes a TCP connection with a home address and, when changing networks, it continues to communicate with the original endpoint from a care-of address as it changes LANs, which sends all traffic back through the home address. The handing off of network addresses does not disrupt the TCP connection state (the original TCP port number and address remain intact).

Improved Security   Unlike IPv4, IPv6 has security built in. *Internet Protocol Security (IPsec)* is a component used today to authenticate and encrypt secure tunnels from a source to a destination. This can be from the client to the server or between gateways. IPv4 lets you do this by enhancing IP header functionality (basically adding a second IP header while encrypting everything behind it). In IPv6, you add this as standard functionality by using extension headers. Extension headers are inserted into the packet only if they are needed. Each header has a "next header" field, which identifies the next piece of information. The extension headers currently identified for IPv6 are Hop-By-Hop Options, Routing, Fragment, Destination Options, Authentication, and Encapsulating Security Payload. The Authentication header and the Encapsulating Security Payload header are the IPsec-specific control headers.

IPv4 to IPv6 Interoperability   Several mechanisms in IPv6 make the IPv4-to-IPv6 transition easy.

- A simple dual-stack implementation where both IPv4 and IPv6 are installed and used is certainly an option. In most situations (so far), this doesn't work so well because most of us aren't connected to an IPv6 network and our Internet connection is not IPv6 even if we're using IPv6 internally. Therefore, Microsoft includes other mechanisms that can be used in several different circumstances.

- *Intra-Site Automatic Tunnel Addressing Protocol (ISATAP)* is an automatic tunneling mechanism used to connect an IPv6 network to an IPv4 address space (not using NAT). ISATAP treats the IPv4 space as one big logical link connection space.

- *6to4* is a mechanism used to transition to IPv4. This method, like ISATAP, treats the IPv4 address space as a logical link layer with each IPv6 space in transition using a 6to4 router to create endpoints using the IPv4 space as a point-to-point connection (kind of like a WAN, eh?). 6to4 implementations still do not work well through a NAT, although a 6to4 implementation using an Application layer gateway (ALG) is certainly doable.

- *Teredo* is a mechanism that allows users behind a NAT to access the IPv6 space by tunneling IPv6 packets in UDP.

Pseudo-interfaces are used in these mechanisms to create a usable interface for the operating system. Another interesting feature of IPv6 is that addresses are assigned to interfaces (or pseudo-interfaces), not simply to the end node. Your Windows Server 2016 will have several unique IPv6 addresses assigned.

New Broadcast Methods   IPv6 has moved away from using broadcasting. The three types of packets used in IPv6 are unicast, multicast, and anycast. IPv6 clients then must use one of these types to get the MAC address of the next Ethernet hop (default gateway). IPv6 makes use of multicasting for this along with the new functionality called *neighbor discovery*. Not only does ARP utilize new functionality, but ICMP (also a layer 3 protocol) has been redone and is now known as ICMP6. *ICMP6* is used for messaging (packet too large, time exceeded, and so on) as it was in IPv4, but now it's also used for the messaging of IPv6 mobility. ICMP6 echo request and ICMP6 echo reply are still used for ping.

IPv6 Addressing Concepts

You need to consider several concepts when using IPv6 addressing. For starters, the format of the address has changed. Three types of addresses are used in IPv6, with some predefined values within the address space. You need to get used to seeing these addresses and be able to identify their uses.

IPv6 Address Format

For the design of IPv4 addresses, you present addresses as octets or the decimal (base 10) representation of 8 bits. Four octets add up to the 32 bits required. IPv6 expands the address space to 128 bits, and the representation is for the most part shown in hexadecimal (a notation used to represent 8 bits using the values 0–9 and A–F). Figure 1.13 compares IPv4 to IPv6.

A full IPv6 address looks like this example:

2001:0DB8:0000:0000:1234:0000:A9FE:133E

FIGURE 1.13 IPv4/IPv6 comparison

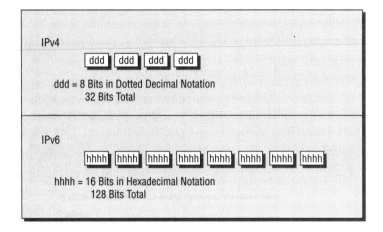

You can tell the implementation of DNS will make life a lot easier even for those who like to ping the address in lieu of the name. Fortunately, DNS already has the ability to handle IPv6 addresses with the use of an AAAA record. (*A* is short for *alias*.) An A record in IPv4's addressing space is 32 bits, so an AAAA record, or four *A*s, is 128 bits. The Windows Server 2016 DNS server handles the AAAA and the reverse pointer (PTR) records for IPv6.

IPv6 Address Shortcuts

There are several shortcuts for writing an IPv6 address. These are described in the following list:

- :0: stands for :0000:.

- You can omit preceding 0s in any 16-bit word. For example, :DB8: and :0DB8: are equivalent.

- :: is a variable standing for enough zeros to round out the address to 128 bits. :: can be used only once in an address.

You can use these shortcuts to represent the example address 2001:0DB8:0000:0000: 1234:0000:A9FE:133E, as shown here:

- Compress :0000: into :0::
  2001:0DB8:0000:0000:1234:0:A9FE:133E

- Eliminate preceding zeros:
  2001:DB8:0000:0000:1234:0:A9FE:133E

- Use the special variable shortcut for multiple 0s:
  2001:DB8::1234:0:A9FE:133E

You now also use prefix notation or slash notation when discussing IPv6 networks. For example, the network of the previous address can be represented as 2001:DB8:0000:0000: 0000:0000:0000:0000. This can also be expressed as 2001:DB8:: /32. The /32 indicates 32 bits of network, and 2001:DB8: is 32 bits of network.

IPv6 Address Assignment

So, do you subnet IPv6? The answer depends on your definition of subnetting. If you are given 32 bits of network from your ISP, you have 96 bits with which to work. If you use some of the 96 bits to route within your network infrastructure, then you are subnetting. In this context, you do subnet IPv6. However, given the huge number of bits you have available, you will no longer need to implement VLSM. For example, Microsoft has a network space of 2001:4898:: /32. That gives the administrators a space of 96 bits (2^{96} = 79,228,162, 514,264,337,593,543,950,336 unique addresses using all 96 bits) with which to work.

You can let Windows Server 2016 dynamically/automatically assign its IPv6 address, or you can still assign it manually (see Figure 1.14). With dynamic/automatic assignment, the IPv6 address is assigned either by a DHCPv6 server or by the Windows Server 2016 machine. If no DHCPv6 server is configured, the Windows Server 2016 machine can query the local LAN segment to find a router with a configured IPv6 interface. If so, the server will assign itself an address on the same IPv6 network as the router interface and set its default gateway to the router interface's IPv6 address. Figure 1.14 shows that you have the same dynamic and manual choices as you do in IPv4; however, the input values for IPv6 must conform to the new format.

FIGURE 1.14   TCP/IPv6 Properties window

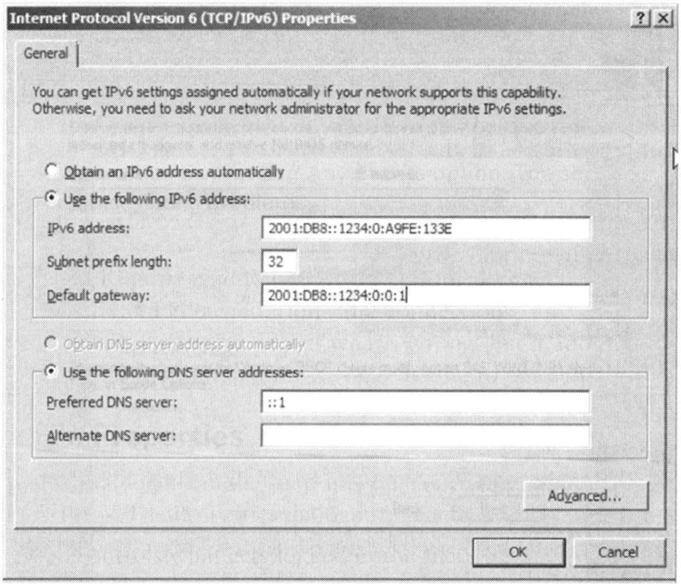

To see your configured IP addresses (IPv4 and IPv6), you can still use the ipconfig command. For example, I have configured a static IPv4 address and an IPv6 address on my server. The IPv6 address is the same as the one used in the earlier IPv6 example address. Figure 1.15 shows the result of this command on Windows Server 2016 for my server.

FIGURE 1.15   IPv6 configuration as seen from the command prompt

```
Administrator: C:\Windows\system32\cmd.exe                        _|□| ×|
Ethernet adapter Local Area Connection:

   Connection-specific DNS Suffix  . :
   Description . . . . . . . . . . . : Intel 21140-Based PCI Fast Ethernet Adapt
er (Emulated)
   Physical Address. . . . . . . . . : 00-03-FF-11-02-CD
   DHCP Enabled. . . . . . . . . . . : No
   Autoconfiguration Enabled . . . . : Yes
   IPv6 Address. . . . . . . . . . . : 2001:db8::1234:0:a9fe:133e(Preferred)
   Link-local IPv6 Address . . . . . : fe80::a425:ab9d:7da4:ccba%10(Preferred)
   IPv4 Address. . . . . . . . . . . : 192.168.1.200(Preferred)
   Subnet Mask . . . . . . . . . . . : 255.255.255.0
   Default Gateway . . . . . . . . . : 2001:db8::1234:0:0:1
                                       0.0.0.0
                                       192.168.1.1
   DNS Servers . . . . . . . . . . . : ::1
                                       192.168.1.1
   NetBIOS over Tcpip. . . . . . . . : Enabled
```

IPv6 Address Types

As stated earlier, there are three types of addresses in IPv6: anycast, unicast, and multicast. A description of each of these types of IPv6 addresses follows.

> Note the absence of the broadcast type, which is included in IPv4. You can't use broadcasts in IPv6; they've been replaced with multicasts.

Anycast Addresses   Anycast addresses are not really new. The concept of anycast existed in IPv4 but was not widely used. An *anycast address* is an IPv6 address assigned to multiple devices (usually different devices). When an anycast packet is sent, it is delivered to one of the devices, usually the closest one.

Unicast Addresses   A *unicast packet* uniquely identifies an interface of an IPv6 device. The interface can be a virtual interface or pseudo-interface or a real (physical) interface.

Unicast addresses come in several types, as described in the following list:

Global Unicast Address   As of this writing, the global unicast address space is defined as 2000:: /3. The 2001::/32 networks are the IPv6 addresses currently being issued to business entities. As mentioned, Microsoft has been allocated 2001:4898:: /32. A Microsoft DHCPv6 server would be set up with scopes (ranges of addresses to be assigned) within this address space. There are some special addresses and address formats that you will see in use as well. You'll find most example addresses listed as 2001:DB8:: /32; this space has been reserved for documentation. Do you remember the loopback address in IPv4, 127.0.0.1? In IPv6 the loopback address is ::1 (or 0:0:0:0:0:0:0:0001). You may also see an address with dotted-decimal used. A dual-stack Windows Server 2016 machine may also show you FE80::5EFE:192.168.1.200. This address form is used in an integration/migration model of IPv6 (or if you just can't leave the dotted-decimal era, I suppose).

Link-Local Address   Link-local addresses are defined as FE80:: /10. If you refer to Figure 1.15 showing the `ipconfig` command, you will see the link-local IPv6 address as fe80::a425:ab9d:7da4:ccba. The last 8 bytes (64 bits) are random to ensure a high probability of randomness for the link-local address. The link-local address is to be used on a single link (network segment) and should never be routed.

There is another form of the local-link IPv6 address called the *Extended User Interface 64-bit (EUI-64)* format. This is derived by using the MAC address of the physical interface and inserting an FFFE between the third and fourth bytes of the MAC. The first byte is also made 02 (this sets the universal/local, or U/L, bit to 1 as defined in IEEE 802 frame specification). Again looking at Figure 1.15, the EUI-64 address would take the physical (MAC) address 00-03-FF-11-02-CD and make the link-local IPv6 address FE80::0203:FFFF:FE11:02CD. (I've left the preceding zeros in the link-local IPv6 address to make it easier for you to pick out the MAC address with the FFFE inserted.)

AnonymousAddress   Microsoft Server 2016 uses the random address by default instead of EUI-64. The random value is called the *AnonymousAddress* in Microsoft Server 2016. It can be modified to allow the use of EUI-64.

Unique Local Address   The *unique local address* can be Fc00 or FD00, and it is used like the private address space of IPv4. RFC 4193 describes unique local addresses. They are not expected to be routable on the global Internet. They are used for private routing within an organization.

Multicast Address   *Multicast addresses* are one-to-many communication packets. Multicast packets are identifiable by their first byte (most significant byte, leftmost byte, leftmost 2 nibbles, leftmost 8 bits, and so on). A multicast address is defined as FF00::/8.

In the second byte shown (the 00 of FF00), the second 0 is what's called the *scope*. Interface-local is 01, and link-local is 02. FF01:: is an interface-local multicast.

There are several well-known (already defined) multicast addresses. For example, if you want to send a packet to all nodes in the link-local scope, you send the packet to FF02::1 (also shown as FF02:0:0:0:0:0:0:1). The all-routers multicast address is FF02::2.

You can also use multicasting to get the logical link layer address (MAC address) of a device with which you are trying to communicate. Instead of using the ARP mechanism of IPv4, IPv6 uses the ICMPv6 neighbor solicitation (NS) and neighbor advertisement (NA) messages. The NS and NA ICMPv6 messages are all part of the new *Neighbor Discovery Protocol (NDP)*. This new ICMPv6 functionality also includes router solicitation and router advertisements as well as redirect messages (similar to the IPv4 redirect functionality).

Table 1.7 outlines the IPv6 address space known prefixes and some well-known addresses.

Unicast vs. Anycast

Unicast and anycast addresses look the same and may be indistinguishable from each other; it just depends on how many devices have the same address. If only one device has a globally unique IPv6 address, it's a unicast address. If more than one device has the same address, it's an anycast address. Both unicast and anycast are considered one-to-one communication, although you could say that anycast is one-to-"one of many."

TABLE 1.7   IPv6 address space known prefixes and addresses

Address Prefix	Scope of Use
2000:: /3	Global unicast space prefix
FE80:: /10	Link-local address prefix
FC00:: /7	Unique local unicast prefix
FD00:: /8	Unique local unicast prefix
FF00:: /8	Multicast prefix
2001:DB8:: /32	Global unicast prefix used for documentation
::1	Reserved local loopback address
2001:0000: /32	Teredo prefix (discussed later in this chapter)
2002:: /16	6to4 prefix

IPv6 Integration/Migration

It's time to get into the mind-set of integrating IPv6 into your existing infrastructure with the longer goal of migrating to IPv6. In other words, this is not going to be an "OK, Friday the Internet is changing over" rollout. You have to bring about the change as a controlled implementation. It could easily take three to five years before a solid migration occurs and probably longer. I think the migration will take slightly less time than getting the world to migrate to the metric system on the overall timeline. The process of integration/migration consists of several mechanisms.

Dual Stack   Simply running both IPv4 and IPv6 on the same network, utilizing the IPv4 address space for devices using only IPv4 addresses and utilizing the IPv6 address space for devices using IPv6 addresses

Tunneling   Using an encapsulation scheme for transporting one address space inside another

Address Translation   Using a higher-level application to change one address type (IPv4 or IPv6) to the other transparently so that end devices are unaware one address space is talking to another

I elaborate on these three mechanisms in the following sections.

IPv6 Dual Stack

The default implementation in Windows Server 2016 is an enabled IPv6 configuration along with IPv4; this is dual stack. The implementation can be dual IP layer or dual TCP/IP stack. Windows Server 2016 uses the dual IP layer implementation (see Figure 1.16). When an application queries a DNS server to resolve a hostname to an IP address, the DNS server may respond with an IPv4 address or an IPv6 address. If the DNS server responds with both, Windows Server 2016 will prefer the IPv6 address. Windows Server 2016 can use both IPv4 and IPv6 addresses as necessary for network communication. When looking at the output of the `ipconfig` command, you will see both address spaces displayed.

FIGURE 1.16   IPv6 dual IP layer diagram

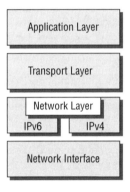

IPv6 Tunneling

Windows Server 2016 includes several tunneling mechanisms for tunneling IPv6 through the IPv4 address space. They include the following:

- Intra-Site Automatic Tunnel Addressing Protocol (ISATAP), which is used for unicast IPv6 communication across an IPv4 infrastructure. ISATAP is enabled by default in Windows Server 2016.

- 6to4, which is used for unicast IPv6 communication across an IPv4 infrastructure.

- Teredo, which is used for unicast IPv6 communication with an IPv4 NAT implementation across an IPv4 infrastructure.

With multiple tunneling protocols available and enabled by default, you might ask, what's the difference, and why is one used over the others? They all allow you to tunnel IPv6 packets through the IPv4 address space (a really cool thing if you're trying to integrate/migrate). Here are the details of these tunneling mechanisms:

ISATAP *Intra-Site Automatic Tunnel Addressing Protocol (ISATAP)* is the automatic tunnel addressing protocol providing IPv6 addresses based on the IPv4 address of the end interface (node). The IPv6 address is automatically configured on the local device, and the dual stack machine can use either its IPv4 or IPv6 address to communicate on the local network (within the local network infrastructure). ISATAP can use the neighbor discovery mechanism to determine the router ID and network prefix where the device is located, thus making intra-site communication possible even in a routed infrastructure.

The format of an ISATAP address is as follows:

[64 bits of prefix] [32 bits indicating ISATAP] [32 bits IPv4 address]

The center 32 bits indicating ISATAP are actually 0000:5EFE (when using private IPv4 addresses). The ISATAP address of the example Windows Server 2016 machine using the link-local IPv6 address is FE80::5EFE:192.168.1.200. Each node participating in the ISATAP infrastructure must support ISATAP. If you're routing through an IPv4 cloud, a border router (a router transitioning from an IPv6 to IPv4 space) must support ISATAP. Windows Server 2016 can be configured as a border router, and it will forward ISATAP packets. ISATAP is experimental and is defined in RFC 4214.

6to4   *6to4* specifies a procedure for IPv6 networks to communicate with each other through an IPv4 space without the IPv6 nodes having to know what's happening. The IPv6 nodes do not need to be dual stacked to make this happen. The border router is the device responsible for knowing about the IPv6-to-IPv4 transition. The IPv6 packets are encapsulated at the border router (and decapsulated at the other end or on the way back). There is an assigned prefix for the 6to4 implementation: 2002:: /16. 6to4 is defined in RFC 3056.

Teredo   *Teredo* (named after a kind of shipworm that drills holes in the wood of ships) is a protocol designed to allow IPv6 addresses to be available to hosts through one or more layers of NAT. Teredo uses a process of tunneling packets through the IPv4 space using UDP. The Teredo service encapsulates the IPv6 data within a UDP segment (packet) and uses IPv4 addressing to get through the IPv4 cloud. Having layer 4 (Transport layer) available to use as translation functionality is what gives you the ability to be behind a NAT. Teredo provides host-to-host communication and dynamic addressing for IPv6 nodes (dual stack), allowing the nodes to have access to resources in an IPv6 network and the IPv6 devices to have access to the IPv6 devices that have only connectivity to the IPv4 space (like home users who have an IPv6-enabled operating system connecting to IPv6 resources while their home ISP has only IPv4 capabilities). Teredo is defined in RFC 4380.

In Windows Server 2016, an IPv4 Teredo server is identified and configured (using the `netsh` command interface). The Teredo server provides connectivity resources (address) to the Teredo client (the node that has access to the IPv4 Internet and needs access to an IPv6 network/Internet). A Teredo relay is a component used by the IPv6 router to receive traffic destined for Teredo clients and forward the traffic appropriately. The defined prefix for a Teredo address is 2001:0000:: /32. Teredo does add overhead like all the other implementations discussed. It is generally accepted that you should use the simplest model available. However, in the process of integration/migration for most of us behind a NAT, Teredo will be the process to choose.

From Windows Server 2016, use the `ipconfig /all` command to view the default configurations including IPv4 and IPv6. You may notice a notation that I didn't discuss, the percent sign at the end of the IPv6 address (see Figure 1.17). The number after the percent sign is the virtual interface identifier used by Windows Server 2016.

FIGURE 1.17   IPv6 interface identifier for `ipconfig` display

```
Link-local IPv6 Address . . . . . : fe80::a425:ab9d:7da4:ccba%10
```

Useful IPv6 Information Commands

You can use numerous commands to view, verify, and configure the network parameters of Windows Server 2016. Specifically, you can use the `netsh` command set and the `route` command set as well as the standard `ping` and `tracert` functions.

Use the `netsh` command interface (as well as the provided dialog boxes, if you want) to examine and configure IPv6 functionality. The `netsh` command issued from the command interpreter changes into a network shell (`netsh`) where you can configure and view both IPv4 and IPv6 components.

Don't forget to use the ever-popular `route print` command to see the Windows Server 2016 routing tables (IPv4 and IPv6). The other diagnostic commands are still available for IPv4 as well as IPv6. In previous versions of Microsoft operating systems, `ping` was the IPv4 command, and `ping6` was the IPv6 command. This has changed in Windows Server 2016; `ping` works for both IPv4 and IPv6 to test layer 3 connectivity to remote devices. The IPv4 `tracert` command was `tracert6` for IPv6. The command is now `tracert` for both IPv4 and IPv6, and it will show you every layer 3 (IP) hop from source to destination. (This assumes that all of the administrators from here to there want you to see the hops and are not blocking ICMP. It also assumes that there are no IP tunnels, which your packets are traversing; you won't see the router hops in the tunnel either.)

Overall, the consortium of people developing the Internet and the Internet Protocol have tried to make all of the changes to communication infrastructures easy to implement. (This is a daunting task with the many vendors and various infrastructures currently in place.) The goal is not to daze and confuse administrators; it's designed to provide maximum flexibility with the greatest functionality. IPv6 is going to provide the needed layer 3 (Network layer, global addressing layer, logical addressing layer…call it what you like) functionality for the foreseeable future.

Subnetting with IPv6

Subnetting with IPv6 is a lot like subnetting with IPv4. You need to know how many bits you are going to use for the network mask to subnet it correctly.

For example, let's say you have an IPv6 prefix of 2001:DB8:BBCC:0000::/53 and you need to set up your network so that your IPv6 addressing scheme can handle 1,500 more subnets. How would you figure this out?

When determining any number of hosts or subnets, the calculation is 2 to the power (2^x). The first power number that is greater than or equal to the number you need is the power number that you add to the current network mask. Thus, in the previous question, to get to 1,500 subnets, you would need to determine which 2^x is the first one that is greater than or equal to 1,500. If you calculate your powers correctly, 2^{11} ($2^{11} = 2,048$) is the first one that is greater than or equal to 1,500. So, you would add the power of 11 to the /53 in the previous address, and you would now use /64 as your network mask. Table 1.8 shows you some of the power numbers for the power of 2.

TABLE 1.8 Powers of 2

Power	Equals
2^2	4
2^3	8
2^4	16
2^5	32
2^6	64
2^7	128
2^8	256
2^9	512
2^{10}	1,024
2^{11}	2,048
2^{12}	4,096

Summary

Why TCP/IP is the primary protocol in use today is one of the important topics covered in this chapter. You also learned that the 32-bit IPv4 address is a structured and hierarchical one that is used to identify uniquely every machine on a network. You learned how to determine available IP addresses and implement subnetting. In addition, you learned how the new layer 3 IPv6 protocol is implemented, including the structure of the IPv6 address. Finally, I discussed the new functionality included in IPv6 addressing as well as several Windows Server 2016 integration/migration implementations.

Exam Essentials

Understand what subnetting is and when to use it. If an organization is large and has many computers or if its computers are geographically dispersed, it's sensible to divide its large network into smaller ones connected by routers. These smaller networks are called *subnets*. Subnetting is the process of carving a single IP network into smaller, logical subnetworks.

Understand subnet masks.   For the subnet address scheme to work, every machine on the network must know which part of the host address will be used as the subnet address. The network administrator creates a 32-bit subnet mask consisting of 1s and 0s. The 1s in the subnet mask represent the positions that refer to the network or subnet addresses. The 0s represent the positions that refer to the host portion of the address.

Understand IPv6.   Understand the structure of an IPv6 address and how it's displayed. Know the shortcuts and rules (such as for displaying 0s) for writing IPv6 addresses. Know the integration/migration components for IPv6 included in Windows Server 2016, including tunneling and dual stack.

Review Questions

1. You are the network administrator for ABC Company. You have an IPv6 prefix of 2001:DB8:BBCC:0000::/53, and you need to set up your network so that your IPv6 addressing scheme can handle 1,000 more subnets. Which network mask would you use?

    A. /60

    B. /61

    C. /62

    D. /63

    E. /64

2. You are the network administrator for Stellacon Corporation. Stellacon has a Windows Server 2016 machine that needs to be able to communicate with all computers on the internal network. Stellacon has decided to add 15 new segments to its IPv6 network. How would you configure the IPv6 so that the server can communicate with all the segments?

    A. Configure the IPv6 address as fd00::2b0:e0ff:dee9:4143/8.

    B. Configure the IPv6 address as fe80::2b0:e0ff:dee9:4143/32.

    C. Configure the IPv6 address as ff80::2b0:e0ff:dee9:4143/64.

    D. Configure the IPv6 address as fe80::2b0:e0ff:dee9:4143/64.

3. You are the network administrator for a mid-size organization that has installed Windows Server 2016 onto the network. You are thinking of moving all machines to Windows 10 and IPv6. You decide to set up a test environment with four subnets. What type of IPv6 addresses do you need to set up?

    A. Global addresses

    B. Link-local addresses

    C. Unique local addresses

    D. Site-local addresses

4. You have a large IP-routed network using the address 137.25.0.0; it is composed of 20 subnets, with a maximum of 300 hosts on each subnet. Your company continues on a merger-and-acquisitions spree, and your manager has told you to prepare for an increase to 50 subnets with some containing more than 600 hosts. Using the existing network address, which of the following subnet masks would work for the requirement set by your manager?

    A. 255.255.252.0

    B. 255.255.254.0

    C. 255.255.248.0

    D. 255.255.240.0

5. Your company is growing dramatically via acquisitions of other companies. As the network administrator, you need to keep up with the changes because they affect the workstations and you need to support them. When you started, there were 15 locations connected via routers, and now there are 25. As new companies are acquired, they are migrated to Windows Server 2016 and brought into the same domain as another site. Management says that they are going to acquire at least 10 more companies in the next two years. The engineers have also told you that they are redesigning the company's Class B address into an IP addressing scheme that will support these requirements and that there will never be more than 1,000 network devices on any subnet. What is the appropriate subnet mask to support this network when the changes are completed?

   A. 255.255.252.0

   B. 255.255.248.0

   C. 255.255.255.0

   D. 255.255.255.128

6. You work for a small printing company that has 75 workstations. Most of them run standard office applications such as word processing, spreadsheet, and accounting programs. Fifteen of the workstations are constantly processing huge graphics files and then sending print jobs to industrial-sized laser printers. The performance of the network has always been an issue, but you have never addressed it. You have now migrated your network to Windows 10 and Windows Server 2016 and have decided to take advantage of the routing capability built into Windows Server 2016. You choose the appropriate server and place two NICs in the machine, but you realize that you have only one network address, 201.102.34.0, which you obtained years ago. How should you subnet this address to segment the bandwidth hogs from the rest of the network while giving everyone access to the entire network?

   A. 255.255.255.192

   B. 255.255.255.224

   C. 255.255.255.252

   D. 255.255.255.240

7. You work for Carpathian Worldwide Enterprises, which has more than 50 administrative and manufacturing locations around the world. The size of these organizations varies greatly, with the number of computers per location ranging from 15 to slightly fewer than 1,000. The sales operations use more than 1,000 facilities, each of which contains 2 to 5 computers. Carpathian is also in merger talks with another large organization. If the merger materializes as planned, you will have to accommodate another 100 manufacturing and administrative locations, each with a maximum of 600 computers, as well as 2,000 additional sales facilities. You don't have any numbers for the future growth of the company, but you are told to keep growth in mind. You decide to implement a private addressing plan for the entire organization. More than half of your routers don't support Variable Length Subnet Masking. Which subnet masks would work for this situation? (Choose all that apply.)

   A. 255.255.224.0

   B. 255.255.240.0

   C. 255.255.248.0

   D. 255.255.252.0

   E. 255.255.254.0

8. Which of the following subnet masks are represented with the CIDR of /27?

    A. 255.255.255.254

    B. 255.255.255.248

    C. 255.255.255.224

    D. 255.255.255.240

9. You have 3,500 client computers on a single subnet. You need to select a subnet mask that will support all the client computers. You need to minimize the number of unused addresses. Which subnet mask should you choose?

    A. 255.255.248.0

    B. 255.255.254.0

    C. 255.255.240.0

    D. 255.255.252.0

10. You ask one of your technicians to get the IPv6 address of a new Windows Server 2016 machine, and she hands you a note with FE80::0203:FFFF:FE11:2CD on it. What can you tell from this address? (Choose two.)

    A. This is a globally unique IPv6 address.

    B. This is a link-local IPv6 address.

    C. This is a multicast IPv6 address.

    D. In EUI-64 format, you can see the MAC address of the node.

    E. In EUI-64 format, you can see the IPv4 address of the node.

Chapter

2

Configuring DNS

THE FOLLOWING 70-741 EXAM OBJECTIVES ARE COVERED IN THIS CHAPTER:

✓ **Install and configure DNS servers**

■ This objective may include but is not limited to: Determine DNS installation requirements; determine supported DNS deployment scenarios on Nano Server; install DNS; configure forwarders; configure Root Hints; configure delegation; implement DNS policies; implement DNS global settings using Windows PowerShell; configure Domain Name System Security Extensions (DNSSEC); configure DNS Socket Pool; configure cache locking; enable Response Rate Limiting; configure DNS-based Authentication of Named Entities (DANE); configure DNS logging; configure delegated administration; configure recursion settings; implement DNS performance tuning; configure global settings using Windows PowerShell.

✓ **Create and configure DNS zones and records**

■ This objective may include but is not limited to: Create primary zones; configure Active Directory integration of primary zones; create and configure secondary zones; create and configure stub zones; configure a GlobalNames zone; analyze zone-level statistics; create and configure DNS Resource Records (RR), including A, AAAA, PTR, SOA, NS, SRV, CNAME, and MX records; configure zone scavenging; configure record options, including Time To Live (TTL) and weight; configure round robin; configure secure dynamic updates; configure unknown record support; use DNS audit events and analytical (query) events for auditing and troubleshooting; configure Zone Scopes; configure records in Zone Scopes; configure policies for zones.

The Domain Name System (DNS) is one of the most important networking services that you can put on your network, and it's also one of the key topics that you'll need to understand if you plan to take any of the Microsoft Windows Server 2016 exams.

By the end of this chapter, you should have a deeper understanding of how DNS works, how to set it up properly, how to configure DNS, proper management of the DNS server, and how to troubleshoot DNS issues quickly and easily in Microsoft Windows Server 2016.

Introducing DNS

The *Domain Name System (DNS)* is a service that allows you to resolve a hostname to an Internet Protocol (IP) address. One of the inherent complexities of operating in networked environments is working with multiple protocols and network addresses. Owing largely to the tremendous rise in the popularity of the Internet, however, most environments have transitioned to use *Transmission Control Protocol/Internet Protocol (TCP/IP)* as their primary networking protocol. Microsoft is no exception when it comes to supporting TCP/IP in its workstation and server products. All current versions of Microsoft's operating systems support TCP/IP, as do most other modern operating systems.

An easy way to understand DNS is to think about making a telephone call. If you wanted to call Microsoft and did not know the phone number, you could call information, tell the operator the name (Microsoft), and get the telephone number. You would then make the call. Now think about trying to connect to Server1. You don't know the TCP/IP number (the computer's telephone number), so your computer asks DNS (information) for the number of Server1. DNS returns the number, and your system makes the connection (call). DNS is your network's 411, or information, and it returns the TCP/IP data for your network.

TCP/IP is actually a collection of different technologies (protocols and services) that allow computers to function together on a single, large, and heterogeneous network. Some of the major advantages of this protocol include widespread support for hardware, software, and network devices; reliance on a system of standards; and scalability. TCP handles tasks such as sequenced acknowledgments. IP involves many jobs, such as logical subnet assignment and routing.

The Form of an IP Address

To understand DNS, you must first understand how TCP/IP addresses are formed. Because DNS is strictly on a network to support TCP/IP, understanding the basics of TCP/IP is extremely important.

An *IP address* is a logical number that uniquely identifies a computer on a TCP/IP network. TCP/IP allows a computer packet to reach the correct host. Windows Server 2016 works with two versions of TCP/IP: IPv4 and IPv6. An IPv4 address takes the form of four octets (eight binary bits), each of which is represented by a decimal number between 0 and 255. The four numbers are separated by decimal points. For example, all of the following are valid IP addresses:

- 128.45.23.17
- 230.212.43.100
- 10.1.1.1

The dotted-decimal notation was created to make it easier for users to deal with IP addresses, but this idea did not go far enough. As a result, another abstraction layer was developed, which used names to represent the dotted decimal notation—the domain name. For example, the IP address 11000000 10101000 00000001 00010101 maps to 192.168.1.21, which in turn might map to server1.company.org, which is how the computer's address is usually presented to the user or application.

As stated earlier, IPv4 addresses are made up of octets, or the decimal (base 10) representation of 8 bits. It takes four octets to add up to the 32 bits required. IPv6 expands the address space to 128 bits. The address is usually represented in hexadecimal notation as follows:

```
2001:0DB8:0000:0000:1234:0000:A9FE:133E
```

You can tell that the implementation of DNS would make life a lot easier for everyone, even those of us who like to use alphanumeric values. (For example, some of us enjoy pinging the address in lieu of the name.) Fortunately, DNS already has the ability to handle IPv6 addresses using an AAAA record. An A record in IPv4's addressing space is 32 bits, and an AAAA record (4 As) in IPv6's is 128 bits.

Nowadays, most computer users are quite familiar with navigating to DNS-based resources, such as www.microsoft.com. To resolve these "friendly" names to TCP/IP addresses that the network stack can use, you need a method for mapping them. Originally, ASCII flat files (often called *HOSTS files*, as shown in Figure 2.1) were used for this purpose. In some cases, they are still used today in small networks, and they can be useful in helping to troubleshoot name resolution problems.

As the number of machines and network devices grew, it became unwieldy for administrators to manage all of the manual updates required to enter new mappings to a master HOSTS file and distribute it. Clearly, a better system was needed.

FIGURE 2.1 HOSTS file

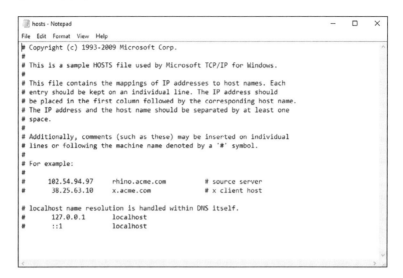

As you can see from the sample HOSTS file in Figure 2.1, you can conduct a quick test of the email server's name resolution as follows:

1. Open the HOSTS file: C:\Windows\Systems32\drivers\etc.

2. Add the IP-address-to-hostname mapping.

3. Try to ping the server using the hostname to verify that you can reach it using an easy-to-remember name.

Following these steps should drive home the concept of DNS for you because you can see it working to make your life easier. Now you don't have to remember 10.0.0.10; you only need to remember exchange03. However, you can also see how this method can become unwieldy if you have many hosts that want to use easy-to-remember names instead of IP addresses to locate resources on your network.

When dealing with large networks, users and network administrators must be able to locate the resources they require with minimal searching. Users don't care about the actual physical or logical network address of the machine; they just want to be able to connect to it using a simple name that they can remember.

From a network administrator's standpoint, however, each machine must have its own logical address that makes it part of the network on which it resides. Therefore, some scalable and easy-to-manage method for resolving a machine's logical name to an IP address and then to a domain name is required. DNS was created just for this purpose.

DNS is defined by a number of requests for comments (RFCs), though primarily by RFC 1034 and RFC 1035.

DNS is a hierarchically distributed database. In other words, its layers are arranged in a definite order, and its data is distributed across a wide range of machines, each of which can exert control over a portion of the database. DNS is a standard set of protocols that defines the following:

- A mechanism for querying and updating address information in the database
- A mechanism for replicating the information in the database among servers
- A schema of the database

DNS was originally developed in the early days of the Internet (called ARPAnet at the time) when it was a small network created by the Department of Defense for research purposes. Before DNS, computer names, or hostnames, were manually entered into a HOSTS file located on a centrally administered server. Each site that needed to resolve hostnames outside of its organization had to download this file. As the number of computers on the Internet grew, so did the size of this HOSTS file—and along with it the problems of its management. The need for a new system that would offer features such as scalability, decentralized administration, and support for various data types became more and more obvious. DNS, introduced in 1984, became this new system.

With DNS, the hostnames reside in a database that can be distributed among multiple servers, decreasing the load on any one server and providing the ability to administer this naming system on a per-partition basis. DNS supports hierarchical names and allows for the registration of various data types in addition to the hostname-to-IP-address mapping used in HOSTS files. Database performance is ensured through its distributed nature as well as through caching.

The DNS distributed database establishes an inverted logical tree structure called the *domain namespace*. Each node, or domain, in that space has a unique name. At the top of the tree is the root. This may not sound quite right, which is why the DNS hierarchical model is described as being an inverted tree, with the root at the top. The root is represented by the null set: "". When written, the root node is represented by a single dot (.).

Each node in the DNS can branch out to any number of nodes below it. For example, below the root node are a number of other nodes, commonly referred to as *top-level domains (TLDs)*. These are the familiar .com, .net, .org, .gov, .edu, and other such names. Table 2.1 lists some of these TLDs.

TABLE 2.1   Common top-level DNS domains

Domain Name	Type of Organization
com	Commercial (for example, stormwind.com for StormWind Training Corporation).
edu	Educational (for example, gatech.edu for the Georgia Institute of Technology).
gov	Government (for example, whitehouse.gov for the White House in Washington, D.C.).

TABLE 2.1   Common top-level DNS domains *(continued)*

Domain Name	Type of Organization
int	International organizations (for example, `nato.int` for NATO); this top-level domain is fairly rare.
mil	Military organizations (for example, `usmc.mil` for the Marine Corps); there is a separate set of root name servers for this domain.
net	Networking organizations and Internet providers (for example, `hiwaay.net` for HiWAAY Information Systems); many commercial organizations have registered names under this domain too.
org	Noncommercial organizations (for example, `fidonet.org` for FidoNet).
au	Australia
uk	United Kingdom
ca	Canada
us	United States
jp	Japan

Each of these nodes then branches out into another set of domains, and they combine to form what we refer to as *domain names*, such as `microsoft.com`. A domain name identifies the domain's position in the logical DNS hierarchy in relation to its parent domain by separating each branch of the tree with a dot. Figure 2.2 shows a few of the top-level domains, where the Microsoft domain fits, and a host called Tigger within the `microsoft.com` domain. If someone wanted to contact that host, they would use the *fully qualified domain name (FQDN)*, `tigger.microsoft.com`.

An FQDN includes the trailing dot (.) to indicate the root node, but it's commonly left off in practice.

As previously stated, one of the strengths of DNS is the ability to delegate control over portions of the DNS namespace to multiple organizations. For example, the Internet Corporation for Assigned Names and Numbers (ICANN) assigns the control over TLDs to one or more organizations. In turn, those organizations delegate portions of the DNS namespace to other organizations. For example, when you register a domain name, let's call it `example.com`, you control the DNS for the portion of the DNS namespace within `example.com`. The registrar controlling the `.com` TLD has delegated control over the `example.com` node in the DNS tree. No other node can be named `example` directly below the `.com` within the DNS database.

FIGURE 2.2   The DNS hierarchy

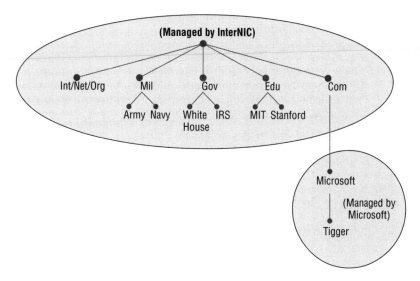

Within the portion of the domain namespace that you control (example.com), you could create host and other records (more on these later). You could also further subdivide example.com and delegate control over those divisions to other organizations or departments. These divisions are called *subdomains*. For example, you might create subdomains named for the cities in which the company has branch offices and then delegate control over those subdomains to the branch offices. The subdomains might be named losangeles.example.com, chicago.example.com, portsmouth.example.com, and so on.

Each domain (or delegated subdomain) is associated with DNS name servers. In other words, for every node in the DNS, one or more servers can give an authoritative answer to queries about that domain. At the root of the domain namespace are the root servers, which I'll cover later in the chapter.

Domain names and hostnames must contain only characters a to z, A to Z, 0 to 9, and - (hyphen). Other common and useful characters, such as the & (ampersand), / (slash), . (period), and _ (underscore) characters, are not allowed. This is in conflict with NetBIOS's naming restrictions. However, you'll find that Windows Server 2016 is smart enough to take a NetBIOS name, like Server_1, and turn it into a legal DNS name, like server1.example.com.

DNS servers work together to resolve hierarchical names. If a server already has information about a name, it simply fulfills the query for the client. Otherwise, it queries other DNS servers for the appropriate information. The system works well because it distributes the authority over separate parts of the DNS structure to specific servers. A DNS zone is a portion of the DNS namespace over which a specific DNS server has authority. (DNS zone types are discussed in detail later in this chapter.)

 There is an important distinction to make between DNS zones and Active Directory (AD) domains. Although both use hierarchical names and require name resolution, DNS zones do not map directly to AD domains.

Within a given DNS zone, resource records (RRs) contain the hosts and other database information that make up the data for the zone. For example, an RR might contain the host entry for www.example.com, pointing it to the IP address 192.168.1.10.

Understanding Servers, Clients, and Resolvers

You will need to know a few terms and concepts in order to manage a DNS server. Understanding these terms will make it easier to understand how the Windows Server 2016 DNS server works:

DNS Server Any computer providing domain name services is a *DNS name server*. No matter where the server resides in the DNS namespace, it's still a DNS name server. For example, 13 root name servers at the top of the DNS tree are responsible for delegating the TLDs. The *root servers* provide referrals to name servers for the TLDs, which in turn provides referrals to an authoritative name server for a given domain.

 The Berkeley Internet Name Domain (BIND) was originally the only software available for running the root servers on the Internet. However, a few years ago the organizations responsible for the root servers undertook an effort to diversify the software running on these important machines. Today, root servers run multiple types of name server software. BIND is still primarily on Unix-based machines, and it is also the most popular for Internet providers. None of the root servers run Windows DNS.

Any DNS server implementation supporting Service Location Resource Records (see RFC 2782) and Dynamic Updates (RFC 2136) is sufficient to provide the name service for any operating system running Windows 2003 software and newer.

DNS Client A *DNS client* is any machine that issues queries to a DNS server. The client hostname may or may not be registered in a DNS database. Clients issue DNS requests through processes called *resolvers*. You'll sometimes see the terms *client* and *resolver* used synonymously.

Resolver *Resolvers* are software processes, sometimes implemented in software libraries, which handles the actual process of finding the answers to queries for DNS data. The resolver is also built into many larger pieces of software so that external libraries don't have to be called to make and process DNS queries. Resolvers can be what you'd consider client computers or other DNS servers attempting to resolve an answer on behalf of a client (for example, Internet Explorer).

Query   A *query* is a request for information sent to a DNS server. Three types of queries can be made to a DNS server: recursive, inverse, and iterative. I'll discuss the differences between these query types in the section "DNS Queries" a bit later in the chapter.

Understanding the DNS Process

To help you understand the DNS process, I will start by covering the differences between Dynamic DNS and Non-Dynamic DNS. During this discussion, you will learn how Dynamic DNS populates the DNS database. You'll also see how to implement security for Dynamic DNS. I will then talk about the workings of different types of DNS queries. Finally, I will discuss caching and time to live (TTL). You'll learn how to determine the best setting for your organization.

Dynamic DNS and Non-Dynamic DNS

To understand Dynamic DNS and Non-Dynamic DNS, you must go back in time (here is where the TV screen always used to get wavy). Many years ago when we all worked on NT 3.51 and NT 4.0, most networks used Windows Internet Name Service (WINS) to do their TCP/IP name resolution. Windows versions 95/98 and NT 4.0 Professional were all built on the idea of using WINS. This worked out well for administrators because WINS was dynamic (which meant that once it was installed, it automatically built its own database). Back then, there was no such thing as Dynamic DNS; administrators had to enter DNS records into the server manually. This is important to know even today. If you have clients still running any of these older operating systems (95/98 or NT 4), these clients cannot use Dynamic DNS.

Now let's move forward in time to the release of Windows Server 2000. Microsoft announced that DNS was going to be the name resolution method of choice. Many administrators (me included) did not look forward to the switch. Because there was no such thing as Dynamic DNS, most administrators had nightmares about manually entering records. However, luckily for us, when Microsoft released Windows Server 2000, DNS had the ability to operate dynamically. Now when you're setting up Windows Server 2016 DNS, you can choose what type of dynamic update you would like to use, if any. Let's talk about why you would want to choose one over the other.

The *Dynamic DNS (DDNS) standard*, described in RFC 2136, allows DNS clients to update information in the DNS database files. For example, a Windows Server 2016 DHCP server can automatically tell a DDNS server which IP addresses it has assigned to what machines. Windows 2000 (and higher) and Windows 7 (and higher) DHCP clients can do this too. For security reasons, however, it's better to let the DHCP server do it. The result: IP addresses and DNS records stay in sync so that you can use DNS and DHCP together seamlessly. Because DDNS is a proposed Internet standard, you can even use the Windows Server 2016 DDNS-aware parts with Unix/Linux-based DNS servers.

Non-Dynamic DNS (NDDNS) does not automatically populate the DNS database. The client systems do not have the ability to update to DNS. If you decide to use Non-Dynamic DNS, an administrator will need to populate the DNS database manually. Non-Dynamic DNS is a reasonable choice if your organization is small to midsize and you do not want extra network traffic (clients updating to the DNS server) or if you need to enter the computer's TCP/IP information manually because of strict security measures.

Dynamic DNS has the ability to be secure, and the chances are slim that a rogue system (a computer that does not belong in your DNS database) could update to a secure DNS server. Nevertheless, some organizations have to follow stricter security measures and are not allowed to have dynamic updates.

The major downside to entering records into DNS manually occurs when the organization is using the *Dynamic Host Configuration Protocol (DHCP)*. When using DHCP, it is possible for users to end up with different TCP/IP addresses every day. This means that an administrator has to update DNS manually each day to keep it accurate.

If you choose to allow Dynamic DNS, you need to decide how you want to set it up. When setting up dynamic updates on your DNS server, you have three choices (see Figure 2.3).

FIGURE 2.3   Setting the Dynamic Updates option

None   This means your DNS server is Non-Dynamic.

Nonsecure and Secure   This means that any machine (even if it does not have a domain account) can register with DNS. Using this setting could allow rogue systems to enter records into your DNS server.

Secure Only   This means that only machines with accounts in Active Directory can register with DNS. Before DNS registers any account in its database, it checks Active Directory to make sure that account is an authorized domain computer.

How Dynamic DNS Populates the DNS Database

TCP/IP is the protocol used for network communications on a Microsoft Windows Server 2016 network. Users have two ways to receive a TCP/IP number:

- Static (administrators manually enter the TCP/IP information)
- Dynamic (using DHCP)

When an administrator sets up TCP/IP, DNS can also be configured.

Once a client gets the address of the DNS server, if that client is allowed to update with DNS, the client sends a registration to DNS or requests DHCP to send the registration. DNS then does one of two things, depending on which Dynamic Updates option is specified:

- Check with Active Directory to see if that computer has an account (Secure Only updates) and, if it does, enter the record into the database.
- Enter the record into its database (nonsecure and secure updates).

What if you have clients that cannot update DNS? Well, there is a solution—DHCP. In the DNS tab of the IPv4 Properties window, check the option labeled "Dynamically update DNS records for DHCP clients that do not request updates (for example, clients running Windows NT 4.0)," which is shown in Figure 2.4.

FIGURE 2.4   DHCP settings for DNS

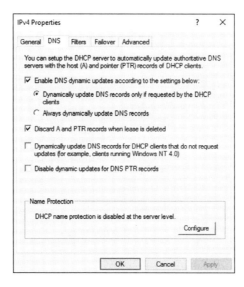

DHCP, along with Dynamic DNS clients, allows an organization to update its DNS database dynamically without the time and effort of having an administrator manually enter DNS records.

DNS Queries

As stated earlier, a client can make three types of queries to a DNS server: recursive, inverse, and iterative. Remember that the client of a DNS server can be a resolver (what you'd normally call a client) or another DNS server.

Iterative Queries

Iterative queries are the easiest to understand: A client asks the DNS server for an answer, and the server returns the best answer. This information likely comes from the server's cache. The server never sends out an additional query in response to an iterative query. If the server doesn't know the answer, it may direct the client to another server through a referral.

Recursive Queries

In a *recursive query*, the client sends a query to a name server, asking it to respond either with the requested answer or with an error message. The error states one of two things:

- The server can't come up with the right answer.

- The domain name doesn't exist.

In a recursive query, the name server isn't allowed to just refer the client to some other name server. Most resolvers use recursive queries. In addition, if your DNS server uses a forwarder, the requests sent by your server to the forwarder will be recursive queries.

Figure 2.5 shows an example of both recursive and iterative queries. In this example, a client within the Microsoft Corporation is querying its DNS server for the IP address for www.whitehouse.gov.

FIGURE 2.5   A sample DNS query

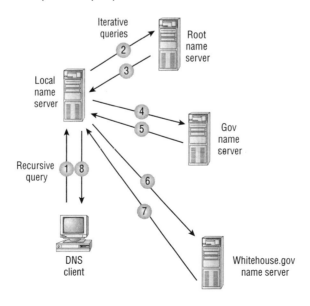

Here's what happens to resolve the request:

1. The resolver sends a recursive DNS query to its local DNS server asking for the IP address of www.whitehouse.gov. The local name server is responsible for resolving the name, and it cannot refer the resolver to another name server.

2. The local name server checks its zones, and it finds no zones corresponding to the requested domain name.

3. The root name server has authority for the root domain and will reply with the IP address of a name server for the .gov top-level domain.

4. The local name server sends an iterative query for www.whitehouse.gov to the Gov name server.

5. The Gov name server replies with the IP address of the name server servicing the whitehouse.gov domain.

6. The local name server sends an iterative query for www.whitehouse.gov to the whitehouse.gov name server.

7. The whitehouse.gov name server replies with the IP address corresponding to www.whitehouse.gov.

8. The local name server sends the IP address of www.whitehouse.gov back to the original resolver.

Inverse Queries

Inverse queries use pointer (PTR) records. Instead of supplying a name and then asking for an IP address, the client first provides the IP address and then asks for the name. Because there's no direct correlation in the DNS namespace between a domain name and its associated IP address, this search would be fruitless without the use of the in-addr.arpa domain. Nodes in the in-addr.arpa domain are named after the numbers in the dotted-octet representation of IP addresses. However, because IP addresses get more specific from left to right and domain names get less specific from left to right, the order of IP address octets must be reversed when building the in-addr.arpa tree. With this arrangement, administration of the lower limbs of the DNS in-addr.arpa tree can be given to companies as they are assigned their Class A, B, or C subnet address or delegated even further down thanks to Variable Length Subnet Masking (VLSM).

Once the domain tree is built into the DNS database, a special PTR record is added to associate the IP addresses with the corresponding hostnames. In other words, to find a hostname for the IP address 206.131.234.1, the resolver would query the DNS server for a PTR record for 1.234.131.206.in-addr.arpa. If this IP address is outside the local domain, the DNS server will start at the root and sequentially resolve the domain nodes until arriving at 234.131.206.in-addr.arpa, which would contain the PTR record for the desired host.

Caching and Time to Live

When a name server is processing a recursive query, it may be required to send out several queries to find the definitive answer. Name servers, acting as resolvers, are allowed to cache all of the received information during this process; each record contains information called *time to live (TTL)*. The TTL specifies how long the record will be held in the local cache until it must be resolved again. If a query comes in that can be satisfied by this cached data, the TTL that's returned with it equals the current amount of time left before the data is flushed.

There is also a negative cache TTL. The *negative cache TTL* is used when an authoritative server responds to a query indicating that the record queried doesn't exist, and it indicates the amount of time that this negative answer may be held. Negative caching is quite helpful in preventing repeated queries for names that don't exist.

The administrator for the DNS zone sets TTL values for the entire zone. The value can be the same across the zone, or the administrator can set a separate TTL for each RR within the zone. Client resolvers also have data caches and honor the TTL value so that they know when to flush.

Choosing Appropriate TTL Values

For zones that you administer, you can choose the TTL values for the entire zone, for negative caching, and for individual records. Choosing an appropriate TTL depends on a number of factors, including the following:

- Amount of change you anticipate for the records within the zone

- Amount of time that you can withstand an outage that might require changing an IP address

- Amount of traffic that you believe the DNS server can handle

Resolvers query the name server every time the TTL expires for a given record. A low TTL, say 60 seconds, can burden the name server, especially for popular DNS records. (DNS queries aren't particularly intensive for a server to handle, but they can add up quickly if you mistakenly use 60 seconds instead of 600 seconds for the TTL on a popular record.) Set a low TTL only when you need to respond quickly to a changing environment.

A high TTL, say 604,800 seconds (that's one week), means that if you need to make a change to the DNS record, clients might not see the change for up to a week. This consideration is especially important when making changes to the network, and it's one that's all too frequently overlooked. I can't count the number of times I've worked with clients who have recently made a DNS change to a new IP for their email or website only to ask why it's not working for some clients. The answer can be found in the TTL value. If the record is being cached, then the only thing that can solve their problem is time.

You should choose a TTL that's appropriate for your environment. Take the following factors into account:

- The amount of time that you can afford to be offline if you need to make a change to a DNS record that's being cached

- The amount of load that a low TTL will cause on the DNS server

In addition, you should plan well ahead of any major infrastructure changes and change the TTL to a lower value to lessen the effect of the downtime by reducing the amount of time that the record(s) can be cached.

Introducing DNS Database Zones

As mentioned earlier in this chapter, a DNS zone is a portion of the DNS namespace over which a specific DNS server has authority. Within a given DNS zone, there are resource records that define the hosts and other types of information that make up the database for the zone. You can choose from several different zone types. Understanding the characteristics of each will help you choose which is right for your organization.

The DNS zones discussed in this book are all Microsoft Windows Server 2012/2016 zones. Non-Windows (for example, Unix) systems set up their DNS zones differently.

In the following sections, I will discuss the different zone types and their characteristics.

Understanding Primary Zones

When you're learning about zone types, things can get a bit confusing. But it's really not difficult to understand how they work and why you would want to choose one type of zone over another. Zones are databases that store records. By choosing one zone type over another, you are basically just choosing how the database works and how it will be stored on the server.

The primary zone is responsible for maintaining all of the records for the DNS zone. It contains the primary copy of the DNS database. All record updates occur on the primary zone. You will want to create and add primary zones whenever you create a new DNS domain.

There are two types of primary zones:

- Primary zone
- Primary zone with Active Directory Integration (Active Directory DNS)

From this point forward, I refer to a primary zone with Active Directory Integration as an *Active Directory DNS*. When I use only the term *primary zone,* Active Directory is not included.

To install DNS as a primary zone, first you must install DNS using the Server Manager MMC. Once DNS is installed and running, you create a new zone and specify it as a primary zone.

The process of installing DNS and its zones will be discussed later in this chapter. In addition, there will be step-by-step exercises to walk you through how to install these components.

Primary zones have advantages and disadvantages. Knowing the characteristics of a primary zone will help you decide when you need the zone and when it fits into your organization.

Local Database

Primary DNS zones get stored locally in a file (with the suffix .dns) on the server. This allows you to store a primary zone on a domain controller or a member server. In addition, by loading DNS onto a member server, you can help a small organization conserve resources. Such an organization may not have the resources to load DNS on an Active Directory domain controller.

Unfortunately, the local database has many disadvantages:

Lack of Fault Tolerance   Think of a primary zone as a contact list on your smartphone. All of the contacts in the list are the records in your database. The problem is that if you lose your phone or the phone breaks, you lose your contact list. Until your phone gets fixed or you swap out your phone card, the contacts are unavailable.

It works the same way with a primary zone. If the server goes down or you lose the hard drive, DNS records on that machine are unreachable. An administrator can install a secondary zone (explained in the next section), and that provides temporary fault tolerance. Unfortunately, if the primary zone is down for an extended period of time, the secondary server's information will no longer be valid.

Additional Network Traffic   Let's imagine that you are looking for a contact number for John Smith. John Smith is not listed in your cell phone directory, but he is listed in your partner's cell phone. You have to contact your partner to get the listing. You cannot directly access your partner's cell contacts.

When a resolver sends a request to DNS to get the TCP/IP address for Jsmith (in this case Jsmith is a computer name) and the DNS server does not have an answer, it does not have the ability to check the other server's database directly to get an answer. Thus, it forwards the request to another DNS. When DNS servers are replicating zone databases with other DNS servers, this causes additional network traffic.

No Security   Staying with the cell phone example, let's say that you call your partner looking for John Smith's phone number. When your partner gives you the phone number over your wireless phone, someone with a scanner can pick up your conversation. Unfortunately, wireless telephone calls are not very secure.

Now a resolver asks a primary zone for the Jsmith TCP/IP address. If someone on the network has a packet sniffer, they can steal the information in the DNS packets being sent over the network. The packets are not secure unless you implement some form of secondary security. Also, the DNS server has the ability to be dynamic. A primary zone accepts all updates from DNS servers. You cannot set it to accept secure updates only.

Understanding Secondary Zones

In Windows Server 2016 DNS, you have the ability to use secondary DNS zones. Secondary zones are noneditable copies of the DNS database. You use them for *load balancing* (also referred to as *load sharing*), which is a way of managing network overloads on a single server. A secondary zone gets its database from a primary zone.

A *secondary zone* contains a database with all of the same information as the primary zone, and it can be used to resolve DNS requests. Secondary zones have the following advantages:

- A secondary zone provides fault tolerance, so if the primary zone server becomes unavailable, name resolution can still occur using the secondary zone server.

- Secondary DNS servers can also increase network performance by offloading some of the traffic that would otherwise go to the primary server.

Secondary servers are often placed within the parts of an organization that have high-speed network access. This prevents DNS queries from having to run across slow wide area network (WAN) connections. For example, if there are two remote offices within the stormwind.com organization, you may want to place a secondary DNS server in each remote office. This way, when clients require name resolution, they will contact the nearest server for this IP address information, thus preventing unnecessary WAN traffic.

 Having too many secondary zone servers can actually cause an increase in network traffic because of replication (especially if DNS changes are fairly frequent). Therefore, you should always weigh the benefits and drawbacks and properly plan for secondary zone servers.

Configure Zone Delegation

One advantage of DNS is the ability of turning a namespace into one or more zones. These zones can be replicated to each other or other DNS servers. As an administrator, you must decide when you want to break your DNS into multiple zones. When considering this option, there are a few things to think about:

- You want the management of your DNS namespace to be delegated by another location or department in your organization.

- You want to load-balance your traffic among multiple servers by turning a large zone into many smaller zones. This will help improve performance and create redundancy among your DNS servers.

- You have remote offices opening up, and you want to expand your DNS namespace.

To create a new zone delegation, you would complete the following steps:

1. Open the DNS console.

2. In the console tree, right-click the applicable subdomain and then click New Delegation.

3. Follow the instructions provided in the New Delegation Wizard to finish creating the newly delegated domain.

Understanding Active Directory Integrated DNS

Windows Server 2000 introduced *Active Directory Integrated DNS* to the world. This zone type was unique, and it was a separate choice during setup. In Windows Server 2003, this zone type became an add-on to a primary zone. In Windows Server 2016, it works the same way. After choosing to set up a primary zone, you check the box Store The Zone In Active Directory (see Figure 2.6).

FIGURE 2.6 Setting up an Active Directory Integrated zone

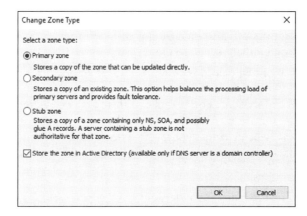

Disadvantages of Active Directory Integrated DNS

The main disadvantage of Active Directory Integrated DNS is that it has to reside on a domain controller because the DNS database is stored in Active Directory. As a result, you cannot load this zone type on a member server, and small organizations might not have the resources to set up a dedicated domain controller.

Advantages of Active Directory Integrated DNS

The advantages of using an Active Directory Integrated DNS zone well outweigh the disadvantages just discussed. The following are some of the major advantages to an Active Directory Integrated zone:

Full Fault Tolerance   Think of an Active Directory Integrated zone as a database on your server that stores contact information for all your clients. If you need to retrieve John Smith's phone number, as long as it was entered, you can look it up on the software.

If John Smith's phone number was stored only on your computer and your computer stopped working, no one could access John Smith's phone number. But since John Smith's phone number is stored in a database to which everyone has access, if your computer stops working, other users can still retrieve John Smith's phone number.

An Active Directory Integrated zone works the same way. Since the DNS database is stored in Active Directory, all Active Directory DNS servers can have access to the same data. If one server goes down or you lose a hard drive, all other Active Directory DNS servers can still retrieve DNS records.

No Additional Network Traffic   As previously discussed, an Active Directory Integrated zone is stored in Active Directory. Since all records are now stored in Active Directory, when a resolver needs a TCP/IP address for Jsmith, any Active Directory DNS server can access Jsmith's address and respond to the resolver.

When you choose an Active Directory Integrated zone, DNS zone data can be replicated automatically to other DNS servers during the normal Active Directory replication process.

DNS Security   An Active Directory Integrated zone has a few security advantages over a primary zone:

- An Active Directory Integrated zone can use secure dynamic updates.

- As explained earlier, the Dynamic DNS standard allows secure-only updates or dynamic updates, not both.

- If you choose secure updates, then only machines with accounts in Active Directory can register with DNS. Before DNS registers any account in its database, it checks Active Directory to make sure that it is an authorized domain computer.

- An Active Directory Integrated zone stores and replicates its database through Active Directory replication. Because of this, the data gets encrypted as it is sent from one DNS server to another.

Background Zone Loading   Background zone loading (discussed in more detail later in this chapter) allows an Active Directory Integrated DNS zone to load in the background. As a result, a DNS server can service client requests while the zone is still loading into memory.

Understanding Stub Zones

Stub zones work a lot like secondary zones—the database is a noneditable copy of a primary zone. The difference is that the stub zone's database contains only the information necessary (three record types) to identify the authoritative DNS servers for a zone (see Figure 2.7). You should not use stub zones to replace secondary zones, nor should you use them for redundancy and load balancing.

FIGURE 2.7   DNS stub zone type

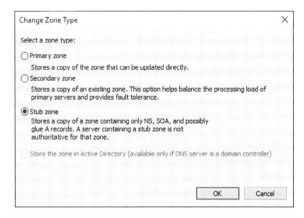

Stub zone databases contain only three record types: name server (NS), start of authority (SOA), and glue host (A) records. Understanding these records will help you on the Microsoft certification exams. Microsoft asks many questions about stub zones on all DNS-related exams.

When to Use Stub Zones

Stub zones become particularly useful in a couple of different scenarios. Consider what happens when two large companies merge: example.com and example.net. In most cases, the DNS zone information from both companies must be available to every employee. You could set up a new zone on each side that acts as a secondary for the other side's primary zone, but administrators tend to be very protective of their DNS data-bases and probably wouldn't agree to this plan.

A better solution is to add to each side a stub zone that points to the primary server on the other side. When a client in example.com (which you help administer) makes a request for a name in example.net, the stub zone on the example.com DNS server would send the client to the primary DNS server for example.net without actually resolving the name. At this point, it would be up to example.net's primary server to resolve the name.

An added benefit is that, even if the administrators over at example.net change their configuration, you won't have to do anything because the changes will automatically replicate to the stub zone, just as they would for a secondary server.

Stub zones can also be useful when you administer two domains across a slow connec-tion. Let's change the previous example a bit and assume that you have full control over example.com and example.net but they connect through a 56 Kbps line. In this case, you wouldn't necessarily mind using secondary zones because you personally administer the entire network. However, it could get messy to replicate an entire zone file across that slow line. Instead, stub zones would refer clients to the appropriate primary server at the other site.

GlobalName Zones

Earlier in this chapter, I talked about organizations using WINS to resolve NetBIOS names (also referred to as *computer names*) to TCP/IP addresses. Even today, many organizations still use WINS along with DNS for name resolution. Unfortunately, WINS is slowly becom-ing obsolete.

To help organizations move forward with an all-DNS network, Microsoft Windows Server 2016 DNS supports *GlobalName zones*. These use single-label names (DNS names that do not contain a suffix such as .com, .net, and so on). GlobalName zones are not intended to support peer-to-peer networks and workstation name resolution, and they don't support dynamic DNS updates.

GlobalName zones are designed to be used with servers. Because GlobalName zones are not dynamic, an administrator has to enter the records into the zone database manually. In most organizations, the servers have static TCP/IP addresses, and this works well with the GlobalName zone design. GlobalName zones are usually used to map single-label CNAME (alias) resource records to an FQDN.

Zone Transfers and Replication

DNS is such an important part of the network that you should not just use a single DNS server. With a single DNS server, you also have a single point of failure, and in fact, many domain registrars encourage the use of more than two name servers for a domain. Secondary servers or multiple primary Active Directory Integrated servers play an integral role in providing DNS information for an entire domain.

As previously stated, secondary DNS servers receive their zone databases through zone transfers. When you configure a secondary server for the first time, you must specify the primary server that is authoritative for the zone and will send the zone transfer. The primary server must also permit the secondary server to request the zone transfer.

Zone transfers occur in one of two ways: *full zone transfers (AXFR)* and *incremental zone transfers (IXFR)*.

When a new secondary server is configured for the first time, it receives a full zone transfer from the primary DNS server. The full zone transfer contains all of the information in the DNS database. Some DNS implementations always receive full zone transfers.

After the secondary server receives its first full zone transfer, subsequent zone transfers are incremental. The primary name server compares its zone version number with that of the secondary server, and it sends only the changes that have been made in the interim. This significantly reduces network traffic generated by zone transfers.

The secondary server typically initiates zone transfers when the refresh interval time for the zone expires or when the secondary or stub server boots. Alternatively, you can configure notify lists on the primary server that send a message to the secondary or stub servers whenever any changes to the zone database occur.

When you consider your DNS strategy, you must carefully consider the layout of your network. If you have a single domain with offices in separate cities, you want to reduce the number of zone transfers across the potentially slow or expensive WAN links, although this is becoming less of a concern because of continuous increases in bandwidth.

Active Directory Integrated zones do away with traditional zone transfers altogether. Instead, they replicate across Active Directory with all of the other AD information. This replication is secure and encrypted because it uses the Active Directory security.

How DNS Notify Works

Windows Server 2016 supports DNS Notify. *DNS Notify* is a mechanism that allows the process of initiating notifications to secondary servers when zone changes occur (RFC 1996). DNS Notify uses a push mechanism for communicating to a select set of secondary zone servers when their zone information is updated. (DNS Notify does not allow you to configure a notify list for a stub zone.)

After being notified of the changes, secondary servers can then start a pull zone transfer and update their local copies of the database.

Many different mechanisms use the push/pull relationship. Normally, one object pushes information to another, and the second object pulls the information from the first. Most applications push replication on a change value and pull it on a time value. For example, a system can push replication after 10 updates, or it can be pulled every 30 minutes.

To configure the DNS Notify process, you create a list of secondary servers to notify. List the IP address of the server in the primary master's Notify dialog box (see Figure 2.8). The Notify dialog box is located under the Zone Transfers tab, which is located in the zone Properties dialog box (see Figure 2.9).

FIGURE 2.8   DNS Notify dialog box

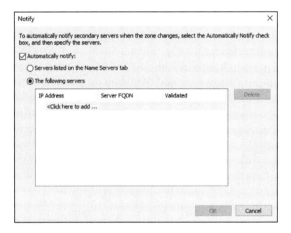

FIGURE 2.9   DNS Zone Transfers tab

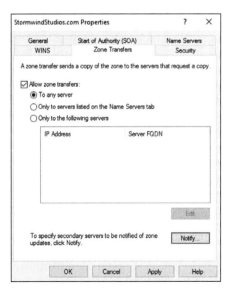

Configuring Stub Zone Transfers with Zone Replication

In the preceding section, I talked about how to configure secondary server zone transfers. What if you wanted to configure settings for stub zone transfers? This is where zone replication scope comes in.

Only Active Directory–integrated primary and stub zones can configure their replication scope. Secondary servers do not have this ability.

You can configure zone replication scope configurations in two ways. An administrator can set configuration options through the DNS snap-in or through a command-line tool called DNSCmd.

To configure zone replication scope through the DNS snap-in, follow these steps:

1. Click Start ➤ Administrative Tools ➤ DNS.

2. Right-click the zone that you want to set up.

3. Choose Properties.

4. In the Properties dialog box, click the Change button next to Replication (see Figure 2.10).

5. Choose the replication scope that fits your organization.

FIGURE 2.10   DNS zone replication scope

Advantages of DNS in Windows Server 2016

DNS in Microsoft Windows Server 2016 has some great advantages over many other versions of Microsoft DNS. Here are some of the improvements of DNS in Windows Server 2016 (some of these became available in previous versions of Windows Server):

- Background zone loading
- Support for TCP/IP version 6 (IPv6)
- Read-only domain controllers
- GlobalName zone
- DNS socket pools
- DNS cache locking
- Response Rate Limiting (RRL)
- Unknown Record Support
- IPv6 Root Hints
- DNS Security Extensions (DNSSEC)
- DNS devolution
- Record weighting
- Netmask ordering
- DnsUpdateProxy group
- DNS Policies

Background Zone Loading

If an organization had to restart a DNS server with an extremely large Active Directory Integrated DNS zones database in the past, DNS had a common problem with an Active Directory Integrated DNS zone. After the DNS restart, it could take hours for DNS data to be retrieved from Active Directory. During this time, the DNS server was unable to service any client requests.

Microsoft Windows Server 2008 DNS addressed this problem by implementing background zone loading, and Windows Server 2016 has taken it a step further. As the DNS restarts, the Active Directory zone data populates the database in the background. This allows the DNS server to service client requests for data from other zones almost immediately after a restart.

Background zone loading accomplishes this task by loading the DNS zone using separate threads. This allows a DNS server to service requests while still loading the rest of the zone. If a client sends a request to the DNS server for a computer that has not yet loaded into memory, the DNS server retrieves the data from Active Directory and updates the record.

Support for IPv6 Addresses

Over the past few years, the Internet has starting running into a problem that was not foreseen when it was first created—it started running out of TCP/IP addresses. As you probably know, when the Internet was created, it was used for government and academic purposes only. Then, seemingly overnight, it grew to be the information superhighway. Nowadays, asking someone for their email address is almost more common as asking for their phone number.

Version 4 (IPv4) was the common version of TCP/IP. The release of TCP/IP version 6 (IPv6) has solved the lack-of-IP-addresses problem. IPv4 addresses are 32 bits long, but IPv6 addresses are 128 bits in length. The longer lengths allow for a much greater number of globally unique TCP/IP addresses.

Microsoft Windows Server 2016 DNS has built-in support to accommodate both IPv4 and IPv6 address records (DNS records are explained later in this chapter). DHCP can also issue IPv6 addresses, which lets administrators allow DHCP to register the client with DNS, or the IPv6 client can register their address with the DNS server.

Support for Read-Only Domain Controllers

Windows Server 2008 introduced a new type of domain controller called the *read-only domain controller (RODC)*. This is a full copy of the Active Directory database without the ability to write to Active Directory. The RODC gives an organization the ability to install a domain controller in a location (onsite or offsite) where security is a concern.

Microsoft Windows Server 2016 DNS has implemented a type of zone to help support an RODC. A primary read-only zone allows a DNS server to receive a copy of the application partition (including ForestDNSZones and DomainDNSZones) that DNS uses. This allows DNS to support an RODC because DNS now has a full copy of all DNS zones stored in Active Directory.

A primary, read-only zone is just what it says—a read-only zone; so to make any changes to it, you have to change the primary zones located on the Active Directory Integrated DNS server.

DNS Socket Pools

If your server is running Windows Server 2016, you will be able to take advantage of DNS socket pools. *DNS socket pools* allow source port randomization to protect against DNS cache-poisoning attacks.

If you choose to use source port randomization, when the DNS service starts, the DNS server will randomly pick a source port from a pool of available sockets. This is an advantage because instead of DNS using a well-known source port when issuing queries, the DNS server uses a random port selected from the socket pool. This helps guard against attacks because a hacker must correctly access the source port of the DNS query. The socket pool is automatically enabled in DNS with the default settings.

When using the DNS socket pool, the default size of the DNS socket pool is 2,500. When configuring the socket pool, you have the ability to choose a size value from 0 to

10,000. The larger the value, the greater the protection you will have against DNS spoofing attacks. If you decide to configure your socket pool size with a zero value, only a single socket for remote DNS queries will be used.

DNS Cache Locking

Windows Server 2016 *DNS cache locking* allows cached DNS records to remain safe for the duration of the record's time to live (TTL) value. This means that the cached DNS records cannot be overwritten or changed. Because of this new DNS feature, it's tougher for hackers to perform cache-poisoning attacks against your DNS server.

DNS administrators can set how long a record will remain safe in cache. The configuration is based on a percent value. For example, if you set your cache locking value to 50 percent, then the cached records cannot be overwritten until half of the TTL has been reached. DNS cache locking is set to 100 percent by default. This means that the cached records never get overwritten.

Response Rate Limiting

Response Rate Limiting (RRL) allows an administrator to help prevent the possibility of hackers using your corporate DNS servers to initiate a denial of service attack on your corporate DNS clients.

Administrators have the ability to configure their RRL settings so that they can control how requests are responded to by DNS servers when these servers receive multiple requests by the same clients. When an administrator configures these settings, it helps prevent hackers from sending a denial of service (DoS) attack using your corporate DNS servers. When configuring RRL, an administrator can manipulate the following settings:

Responses Per Second   This setting allows administrators to set the maximum number of times the same response will be given to a client per second.

Errors Per Second   This setting allows administrators to set the maximum number of times an error response will be sent to the same client per second.

Window   This setting allows administrators to set the number of requests that are made by a client. This setting sets the number of seconds for which responses to a client will be suspended if too many requests are made.

Leak Rate   This setting allows administrators to set how often the DNS server will respond to a query during the suspended time responses. For example, if the DNS server suspends a response to a client for 20 seconds and the leak rate is 10, then the server will still respond to one query for every 10 queries sent. This will ensure that the appropriate clients get responses even when the DNS server is applying response rate limiting.

TC Rate   Administrators can set this setting to inform clients who are trying to connect using TCP when responses to the client are suspended. For example, if the TC rate is 3 and the DNS server suspends responses to a client, the server will issue a request for TCP connection for every three queries. Administrators want to set the value of the TC rate lower than the leak rate. This gives clients the option to connect using TCP before the leak rate applies.

Maximum Responses   This setting allows administrators to set the maximum number of responses a DNS server will issue to a client while responses are suspended.

White List Domains   Administrators can set the list of domains that are to be excluded from RRL settings.

White List Subnets   Administrators can set the list of subnets that are to be excluded from RRL settings.

White List Server Interfaces   Administrators can set the list of DNS server interfaces that are to be excluded from RRL settings.

Unknown Record Support

There are times when a DNS server does not recognize the RDATA format of a resource record. These resource records are known as Unknown Records.

Windows Server 2016 now supports Unknown Records (RFC 3597). This now means that administrators can add these unsupported record types into the Windows DNS server zone. Administrators can add these records using the binary on-wire supported format.

Windows caching resolvers already have the ability to support these unknown record types but DNS servers do not do any processing of these unknown records. What happens is after administrators add the unknown record types to the DNS zone, the DNS servers will respond back to the clients when queries are received.

IPv6 Root Hints

Windows Server 2016 DNS now supports root hints as published by the IANA. DNS name queries now have the ability to use IPv6 root servers for completing name resolution.

DNS Security Extensions

One major issue that you must always look at is keeping your DNS safe. Think about it: DNS is a database of computer names and IP addresses. As a hacker, if I control DNS, I can control your company. In organizations that do not support extra security like IPsec, DNS security is even more important. This is where *Domain Name System Security Extensions (DNSSEC)* can help.

Windows Server 2016 can use a suite of extensions that will help add security to DNS, and that suite is called DNSSEC, which was introduced in Windows Server 2008 R2. The DNSSEC protocol allows your DNS servers to be secure by validating DNS responses. DNSSEC secures your DNS resource records by accompanying the records with a digital signature.

To allow your DNS resource records to receive digital signatures, DNSSEC is applied to your DNS server by a procedure called *zone signing*. This process begins when a DNS resolver initiates a DNS query for a resource record in a signed DNS zone. When a response is returned, a digital signature (RRSIG) accompanies the response, and this allows the response to be verified. If the verification is successful, then the DNS resolver knows that the data has not been modified or tampered with in any way.

Once you implement a zone with DNSSEC, all of the records that are contained within that zone get individually signed. Since all of the records in the zone get individually signed, this gives administrators the ability to add, modify, or delete records without re-signing the entire zone. The only requirement is to re-sign any updated records.

DNS-based Authentication of Named Entities

Another RFC that deals with DNS security is RFC 6698. RFC 6698 explains DNS-based Authentication of Named Entities (DANE). DANE is a protocol that is based on Transport Layer Security Authentication (TLSA). The TLSA records then provide information to DNS clients telling the clients which CA server they should expect their certificate from. By knowing your CA, hackers can't corrupt your DNS cache. Man in the middle attackers can change your cache. This would then point you to their websites. DANE stops these types of attacks. DANE support is now included with Windows Server 2016.

Trust Anchors

Trust anchors are an important part of the DNSSEC process because trust anchors allow the DNS servers to validate the DNSKEY resource records. *Trust anchors* are preconfigured public keys that are linked to a DNS zone. For a DNS server to perform validation, one or more trust anchors must be configured. If you are running an Active Directory Integrated zone, trust anchors can be stored in the Active Directory Domain Services directory partition of the forest. If you decide to store the trust anchors in the directory partition, then all DNS servers that reside on a domain controller get a copy of this trust anchor. On DNS servers that reside on standalone servers, trust anchors are stored in a file called `TrustAnchors.dns`.

If your servers are running Windows Server 2016, then you can view trust anchors in the DNS Manager Console tree in the Trust Points container. You can also use Windows PowerShell or `Dnscmd.exe` to view trust anchors. Windows PowerShell is the recommended command-line method for viewing trust anchors. The following line is a PowerShell command to view the trust anchors for `Contoso.com`:

```
get-dnsservertrustanchor sec.contoso.com
```

DNSSEC Clients

Windows 7, Windows 8/8.1, Windows 10, Windows Server 2008/2008 R2, and Windows Server 2012/2016 are all DNS clients that receive a response to a DNS query, examine the response, and then evaluate whether the response has been validated by a DNS server. The DNS client itself is nonvalidating, and the DNS client relies on the local DNS server to indicate that validation was successful. If the server doesn't perform validation, then the DNS client service can be configured to return no results.

DNS Devolution

Using *DNS devolution*, if a client computer is a member of a child namespace, the client computer will be able to access resources in the parent namespace without the need to explicitly provide the fully qualified domain name of the resource. DNS devolution removes the leftmost label of the namespace to get to the parent suffix. DNS devolution allows the

DNS resolver to create the new FQDNs. DNS devolution works by appending the single-label, unqualified domain name with the parent suffix of the primary DNS suffix name.

Record Weighting

Weighting DNS records will allow an administrator to place a value on DNS SRV records. Clients will then randomly choose SRV records proportional to the weight value assigned.

Netmask Ordering

If round robin is enabled, when a client requests name resolution, the first address entered in the database is returned to the resolver, and it is then sent to the end of the list. The next time a client attempts to resolve the name, the DNS server returns the second name in the database (which is now the first name) and then sends it to the end of the list, and so on. Round robin is enabled by default.

Netmask ordering is a part of the round robin process. When an administrator configures netmask ordering, the DNS server will detect the subnet of the querying client. The DNS server will then return a host address available for the same subnet. Netmask ordering is enabled through the DNS Manager console on the Advanced tab of the server Properties dialog box.

DnsUpdateProxy Group

As mentioned previously, the DHCP server can be configured to register host (A) and pointer (PTR) resource records dynamically on behalf of DHCP clients. Because of this, the DNS server can end up with stale resources. To help solve this issue, an administrator can use the built-in security group called *DnsUpdateProxy*.

To use the DnsUpdateProxy group, an administrator must first create a dedicated user account and configure the DHCP servers with its credentials. This will protect against the creation of unsecured records. Also, when you create the dedicated user account, members of the DnsUpdateProxy group will be able to register records in zones that allow only secured dynamic updates. Multiple DHCP servers can use the same credentials of one dedicated user account.

DNS Policies

One of the newest advantages to Windows Server 2016 DNS is the ability to set up DNS Policies. Administrators can set up policies based on location, time of day, deployment types, queries, application load balancing, and more. The following are just some of the items that you can configure:

Application Load Balancing   There are many times in a corporate environment when you have multiple copies of the same application running in different locations. Application Load Balancing allows DNS to pass client requests for the same applications (even when they are in different locations) to multiple servers hosting that application. This allows DNS to give an application load balancing.

Location Based Traffic Management   Administrators can set DNS to work off of locations and help direct users to resources that are closer to their location. Administrators can set up DNS policies so that a DNS server will respond to a DNS client's query based on geographic location of the client and the IP address of the nearest requested resource.

Split Brain DNS   Another new DNS policy that an administrator can set up is the ability to have DNS split zones. Split zones allow a DNS server to respond to a client based on whether the clients are internal or external clients. Active Directory zones or standalone DNS servers can be configured as Split Brain DNS servers.

Filtering   Administrators now have the ability to set up policies to create query filters that are based on criteria that an administrator supplies. Query filters allow an administrator to set up the DNS server to send a custom response based on a specific type of DNS query and/or DNS client.

Forensics   Administrators also have the ability to set up a DNS honeypot. A honeypot allows a DNS server to redirect a malicious DNS client to an IP address that does not exist.

Time of Day Based Redirection   Administrators can set up a DNS policy to distribute application traffic between different locations. DNS will be able to do this because the policy that you set for an application will be based on the time of day. So for example, when its 1:00 p.m., a server that has a copy of the application gets all client requests, and at 7:00 p.m., a different server that has a copy of the application gets all of the client requests.

Now that you have learned about some of the new features of Windows Server 2016 DNS, let's take a look at some of the DNS record types.

Introducing DNS Record Types

No matter where your zone information is stored, you can rest assured that it contains a variety of DNS information. Although the DNS snap-in makes it unlikely that you'll ever need to edit these files by hand, it's good to know exactly what data is contained there.

As stated previously, zone files consist of a number of resource records. You need to know about several types of resource records to manage your DNS servers effectively. They are discussed in the following sections.

Part of the resource record is its class. *Classes* define the type of network for the resource record. There are three classes: Internet, Chaosnet, and Hesoid. By far, the Internet class is the most popular. In fact, it's doubtful that you'll see either Chaosnet or Hesoid classes in the wild.

The following are some of the more important resource records in a DNS database. For a complete listing of records in a Microsoft DNS database, visit Microsoft's website at https://technet.microsoft.com/en-us/library/cc958958.aspx.

Start of Authority (SOA) Records

The first record in a database file is the *start of authority (SOA) record*. The SOA defines the general parameters for the DNS zone, including the identity of the authoritative server for the zone.

The SOA appears in the following format:

```
@ IN SOA primary_mastercontact_e-mailserial_number
refresh_timeretry_timeexpiration_timetime_to_live
```

Here is a sample SOA from the domain example.com:

```
@ IN SOA win2k3r2.example.com. hostmaster.example.com. (
                    5               ; serial number
                    900             ; refresh
                    600             ; retry
                    86400           ; expire
                    3600        ) ; default TTL
```

Table 2.2 lists the attributes stored in the SOA record.

TABLE 2.2   The SOA record structure

Field	Meaning
Current zone	The current zone for the SOA. This can be represented by an @ symbol to indicate the current zone or by naming the zone itself. In the example, the current zone is example.com. The trailing dot (.com.) indicates the zone's place relative to the root of the DNS.
Class	This will almost always be the letters *IN* for the Internet class.
Type of record	The type of record follows. In this case, it's SOA.
Primary master	The primary master for the zone on which this file is maintained.
Contact email	The Internet email address for the person responsible for this domain's database file. There is no @ symbol in this contact email address because @ is a special character in zone files. The contact email address is separated by a single dot (.). So, the email address of root@example.com would be represented by root.example.com in a zone file.
Serial number	This is the "version number" of this database file. It increases each time the database file is changed.
Refresh time	The amount of time (in seconds) that a secondary server will wait between checks to its master server to see whether the database file has changed and a zone transfer should be requested.

TABLE 2.3   The SOA record structure *(continued)*

Field	Meaning
Retry time	The amount of time (in seconds) that a secondary server will wait before retrying a failed zone transfer.
Expiration time	The amount of time (in seconds) that a secondary server will spend trying to download a zone. Once this time limit expires, the old zone information will be discarded.
Time to live	The amount of time (in seconds) that another DNS server is allowed to cache any resource records from this database file. This is the value that is sent out with all query responses from this zone file when the individual resource record doesn't contain an overriding value.

Name Server Records

Name server (NS) records list the name servers for a domain. This record allows other name servers to look up names in your domain. A zone file may contain more than one name server record. The format of these records is simple:

```
example.com.    IN    NS      Hostname.example.com
```

Table 2.3 explains the attributes stored in the NS record.

TABLE 2.3   The NS record structure

Field	Meaning
Name	The domain that will be serviced by this name server. In this case I used example.com.
AddressClass	Internet (IN)
RecordType	Name server (NS)
Name Server Name	The FQDN of the server responsible for the domain

 Any domain name in the database file that is not terminated with a period will have the root domain appended to the end. For example, an entry that just has the name *sales* will be expanded by adding the root domain to the end, whereas the entry sales.example.com. won't be expanded.

Host Record

A *host record* (also called an *A record* for IPv4 and *AAAA record* for IPv6) is used to associate statically a host's name to its IP addresses. The format is pretty simple:

```
host_nameoptional_TTL IN  A  IP_Address
```

Here's an example from my DNS database:

```
www  IN  A  192.168.0.204
SMTP IN  A  192.168.3.144
```

The A or AAAA record ties a hostname (which is part of an FQDN) to a specific IP address. This makes these records suitable for use when you have devices with statically assigned IP addresses. In this case, you create these records manually using the DNS snap-in. As it turns out, if you enable DDNS, your DHCP server can create these for you. This automatic creation is what enables DDNS to work.

Notice that an optional TTL field is available for each resource record in the DNS. This value is used to set a TTL that is different from the default TTL for the domain. For example, if you wanted a 60-second TTL for the www A or AAAA record, it would look like this:

```
www 60 IN  A  192.168.0.204
```

Alias Record

Closely related to the host record is the *alias record*, or *canonical name (CNAME) record*. The syntax of an alias record is as follows:

```
aliasoptional_TTL  IN  CNAME  hostname
```

Aliases are used to point more than one DNS record toward a host for which an A record already exists. For example, if the hostname of your web server was actually chaos, you would likely have an A record such as this:

```
chaos IN A 192.168.1.10
```

Then you could make an alias or CNAME for the record so that www.example.com would point to chaos:

```
www IN CNAME chaos.example.com.
```

Note the trailing dot (.) on the end of the CNAME record. This means the root domain is not appended to the entry.

Pointer Record

A or AAAA records are probably the most visible component of the DNS database because Internet users depend on them to turn FQDNs like www.microsoft.com into the IP addresses that browsers and other components require to find Internet resources. However, the host record has a lesser-known but still important twin: the *pointer (PTR) record*. The format of a PTR record appears as follows:

```
reversed_address.in-addr.arpa. optional_TTL IN PTR targeted_domain_name
```

The A or AAAA record maps a hostname to an IP address, and the PTR record does just the opposite—mapping an IP address to a hostname through the use of the `in-addr.arpa` zone.

The PTR record is necessary because IP addresses begin with the least-specific portion first (the network) and end with the most-specific portion (the host), whereas hostnames begin with the most-specific portion at the beginning and the least-specific portion at the end.

Consider the example 192.168.1.10 with a subnet mask 255.255.255.0. The portion 192.168.1 defines the network and the final .10 defines the host, or the most-specific portion of the address. DNS is just the opposite: The hostname `www.example.com.` defines the most-specific portion, www, at the beginning and then traverses the DNS tree to the least-specific part, the dot (.), at the root of the tree.

Reverse DNS records, therefore, need to be represented in this most-specific-to-least-specific manner. The PTR record for mapping 192.168.1.10 to `www.example.com` would look like this:

```
10.1.168.192.in-addr.arpa. IN PTR www.example.com.
```

Now a DNS query for that record can follow the logical DNS hierarchy from the root of the DNS tree all the way to the most-specific portion.

Mail Exchanger Record

The *mail exchanger (MX) record* is used to specify which servers accept mail for this domain. Each MX record contains two parameters—a preference and a mail server, as shown in the following example:

```
domain IN MX preference mailserver_host
```

The MX record uses the preference value to specify which server should be used if more than one MX record is present. The preference value is a number. The lower the number, the more preferred the server. Here's an example:

```
example.com.    IN  MX  0  mail.example.com.
example.com.    IN  MX  10 backupmail.example.com.
```

In the example, `mail.example.com` is the default mail server for the domain. If that server goes down for any reason, the `backupmail.example.com` mail server is used by emailers.

Service Record

Windows Server 2016 depends on some other services, like the Lightweight Directory Access Protocol (LDAP) and Kerberos. Using a service record, which is another type of DNS record, a Windows 2000, XP, Vista, Windows 7, Windows 8 / 8.1, or Windows 10 client can query

DNS servers for the location of a domain controller. This makes it much easier (for both the client and the administrator) to manage and distribute logon traffic in large-scale networks. For this approach to work, Microsoft has to have some way to register the presence of a service in DNS. Enter the service (SRV) record.

Service (SRV) records tie together the location of a service (like a domain controller) with information about how to contact the service. SRV records provide seven items of information. Let's review an example to help clarify this powerful concept. (Table 2.4 explains the fields in the following example.)

```
ldap.tcp.example.com.  86400 IN SRV  10  100  389  hsv.example.com
ldap.tcp.example.com.  86400 IN SRV  20  100  389  msy.example.com
```

TABLE 2.4 The SRV record structure

Field	Meaning
Domain name	Domain for which this record is valid (`ldap.tcp.example.com.`).
TTL	Time to live (86,400 seconds).
Class	This field is always IN, which stands for Internet.
Record type	Type of record (SRV).
Priority	Specifies a preference, similar to the Preference field in an MX record. The SRV record with the lowest priority is used first (`10`).
Weight	Service records with equal priority are chosen according to their weight (`100`).
Port number	The port where the server is listening for this service (`389`).
Target	The FQDN of the host computer (`hsv.example.com` and `msy.example.com`).

You can define other types of service records. If your applications support them, they can query DNS to find the services they need.

Configuring DNS

In the following sections, you'll begin to learn about the actual DNS server. You will start by installing DNS. Then I will talk about different zone configuration options and what they mean. Finally, you'll complete an exercise that covers configuring Dynamic DNS, delegating zones, and manually entering records.

Installing DNS

If DNS is already installed onto your server, you can skip this exercise. But if you have not installed DNS, let's start by installing DNS. Installing DNS is an important part of running a network. Exercise 2.1 walks you through the installation of a DNS server.

 If you are using a Dynamic TCP/IP address, please change your TCP/IP number to static.

EXERCISE 2.1

Installing and Configuring the DNS Service

1. Open Server Manager.

2. On the Server Manager dashboard, click the Add Roles And Features link.

3. If a Before You Begin screen appears, click Next.

4. On the Selection type page, choose Role-Based Or Feature-Based Installation and click Next.

5. Click the Select A Server From The Server Pool radio button and choose the server under the Server Pool section. Click Next.

6. Click the DNS Server Item in the Server Role list. If a pop-up window appears telling you that you need to add additional features, click the Add Features button. Click Next to continue.

7. On the Add Features page, just click Next.

8. Click Next on the DNS Server information screen.

9. On the Confirm Installation screen, choose the Restart The Destination Server Automatically If Required check box and then click the Install button.

10. At the Installation progress screen, click Close after the DNS server is installed.

11. Close Server Manager.

Load Balancing with Round Robin

Like other DNS implementations, the Windows Server 2016 implementation of DNS supports load balancing through the use of round robin. Load balancing distributes the network load among multiple network hosts if they are available. You set up round-robin load balancing by creating multiple resource records with the same hostname but different IP addresses for multiple computers. Depending on the options that you select, the DNS server responds with the addresses of one of the host computers.

If round robin is enabled, when a client requests name resolution, the first address entered in the database is returned to the resolver and is then sent to the end of the list. The next time a client attempts to resolve the name, the DNS server returns the second name in the database (which is now the first name) and then sends it to the end of the list, and so on. Round robin is enabled by default.

Configuring a Caching-Only Server

Although all DNS name servers cache queries that they have resolved, caching-only servers are DNS name servers that only perform queries, cache the answers, and return the results. They are not authoritative for any domains, and the information that they contain is limited to what has been cached while resolving queries. Accordingly, they don't have any zone files, and they don't participate in zone transfers. When a caching-only server is first started, it has no information in its cache; the cache is gradually built over time.

Caching-only servers are easy to configure. After installing the DNS service, simply make sure the root hints are configured properly. One new advantage to Windows Server 2016 is the ability to also support IPv6 root hints.

1. Right-click your DNS server and choose the Properties command.

2. When the Properties dialog box appears, switch to the Root Hints tab (see Figure 2.11).

3. If your server is connected to the Internet, you should see a list of root hints for the root servers maintained by ICANN and the Internet Assigned Numbers Authority (IANA). If not, click the Add button to add root hints as defined in the cache.dns file.

FIGURE 2.11   The Root Hints tab of the DNS server's Properties dialog box

You can obtain current cache.dns files on the Internet by using a search engine. Just search for *cache.dns* and download one. (I always try to get cache·dns files from a university or a company that manages domain names.)

Setting Zone Properties

There are six tabs on the Properties dialog box for a forward or reverse lookup zone. You only use the Security tab to control who can change properties and to make dynamic updates to records on that zone. The other tabs are discussed in the following sections.

 Secondary zones don't have a Security tab, and their SOA tab shows you the contents of the master SOA record, which you can't change.

General Tab

The General tab includes the following:

- The Status indicator and the associated Pause button let you see and control whether this zone can be used to answer queries. When the zone is running, the server can use it to answer client queries; when it's paused, the server won't answer any queries it gets for that particular zone.

- The Type indicator and its Change button allow you to select the zone type. The options are Standard Primary, Standard Secondary, and AD-Integrated. (See "Introducing DNS Database Zones" earlier in this chapter.) As you change the type, the controls you see below the horizontal dividing line change too. For primary zones, you'll see a field that lets you select the zone filename; for secondary zones, you'll get controls that allow you to specify the IP addresses of the primary servers. But the most interesting controls are the ones you see for AD Integrated zones. When you change to the AD Integrated zones, you have the ability to make the dynamic zones Secure Only.

- The Replication indicator and its Change button allow you to change the replication scope if the zone is stored in Active Directory. You can choose to replicate the zone data to any of the following:

    - All DNS servers in the Active Directory forest

    - All DNS servers in a specified domain

    - All domain controllers in the Active Directory domain (required if you use Windows 2000 domain controllers in your domain)

    - All domain controllers specified in the replication scope of the application directory partition

- The Dynamic Updates field gives you a way to specify whether you want to support Dynamic DNS updates from compatible DHCP servers. As you learned earlier in the section "Dynamic DNS and Non-Dynamic DNS," the DHCP server or DHCP client must know about and support Dynamic DNS in order to use it, but the DNS server has to participate too. You can turn dynamic updates on or off, or you can require that updates be secured.

Start Of Authority (SOA) Tab

The following options in the Start Of Authority (SOA) tab, shown in Figure 2.12, control the contents of the SOA record for this zone.

- The Serial Number field indicates which version of the SOA record the server currently holds. Every time you change another field, you should increment the serial number so that other servers will notice the change and get a copy of the updated record.

- The Primary Server and Responsible Person fields indicate the location of the primary name server for this zone and the email address of the administrator responsible for the maintenance of this zone, respectively. The standard username for this is hostmaster.

- The Refresh Interval field controls how often any secondary zones of this zone must contact the primary zone server and get any changes that have been posted since the last update.

- The Retry Interval field controls how long secondary servers will wait after a zone transfer fails before they try again. They'll keep trying at the interval you specify (which should be shorter than the refresh interval) until they eventually succeed in transferring zone data.

- The Expires After field tells the secondary servers when to throw away zone data. The default of 1 day (24 hours) means that a secondary server that hasn't gotten an update in 24 hours will delete its local copy of the zone data.

- The Minimum (Default) TTL field sets the default TTL for all RRs created in the zone. You can assign specific TTLs to individual records if you want.

- The TTL For This Record field controls the TTL for the SOA record itself.

FIGURE 2.12   The Start Of Authority (SOA) tab of the zone Properties dialog box

Name Servers Tab

The *name server (NS) record* for a zone indicates which name servers are authoritative for the zone. That normally means the zone primary server and any secondary servers you've configured for the zone. (Remember, secondary servers are authoritative read-only copies of the zone.) You edit the NS record for a zone using the Name Servers tab (see Figure 2.13). The tab shows you which servers are currently listed, and you use the Add, Edit, and Remove buttons to specify which name servers you want included in the zone's NS record.

FIGURE 2.13   The Name Servers tab of the zone Properties dialog box

WINS Tab

The WINS tab allows you to control whether this zone uses WINS forward lookups or not. These lookups pass on queries that DNS can't resolve to WINS for action. This is a useful setup if you're still using WINS on your network. You must explicitly turn this option on with the Use WINS Forward Lookup check box in the WINS tab for a particular zone.

Zone Transfers Tab

Zone transfers are necessary and useful because they're the mechanism used to propagate zone data between primary and secondary servers. For primary servers (whether AD Integrated or not), you can specify whether your servers will allow zone transfers and, if so, to whom.

You can use the following controls on the Zone Transfers tab to configure these settings per zone:

- The Allow Zone Transfers check box controls whether the server answers zone transfer requests for this zone at all—when it's not checked, no zone data is transferred. The Allow Zone Transfers selections are as follows:

  - To Any Server allows any server anywhere on the Internet to request a copy of your zone data.

  - Only To Servers Listed On The Name Servers Tab (the default) limits transfers to servers you specify. This is a more secure setting than To Any Server because it limits transfers to other servers for the same zone.

  - Only To The Following Servers allows you to specify exactly which servers are allowed to request zone transfers. This list can be larger or smaller than the list specified on the Name Servers tab.

- The Notify button is for setting up automatic notification triggers that are sent to secondary servers for this zone. Those triggers signal the secondary servers that changes have occurred on the primary server so that the secondary servers can request updates sooner than their normally scheduled interval. The options in the Notify dialog box are similar to those in the Zone Transfers tab. You can enable automatic notification and then choose either Servers Listed On The Name Servers Tab or The Following Servers.

Configuring Zones for Dynamic Updates

In Exercise 2.2, you will create and then modify the properties of a forward lookup zone. In addition, you'll configure the zone to allow dynamic updates.

EXERCISE 2.2

Configuring a Zone for Dynamic Updates

1. Open the DNS management snap-in by selecting Server Manager. Once in Server Manager, click DNS on the left side. In the Servers window (center screen), right-click your server name and choose DNS Manager.

2. Click the DNS server to expand it and then click the Forward Lookup Zones folder. Right-click the Forward Lookup Zones folder and choose New Zone.

3. At the New Zone Welcome screen, click Next.

4. At the Zone Type screen, choose the Primary Zone option. If your DNS server is also a domain controller, do not check the box to store the zone in Active Directory. Click Next when you are ready.

5. Enter a new zone name in the Zone Name field and click Next. (I used my last name—Panek.com.)

EXERCISE 2.2 *(continued)*

6. Leave the default zone filename and click Next.

7. Select the Do Not Allow Dynamic Updates radio button and click Next.

8. Click Finish to end the wizard.

9. Right-click the zone you just created and choose the Properties command.

10. Click the down arrow next to Dynamic Updates. Notice that there are only two options (None and Nonsecure And Secure). The Secure Only option is not available because you are not using Active Directory Integrated. Make sure Nonsecure And Secure is chosen.

11. Click OK to close the Properties box.

12. Close the DNS management snap-in.

13. Close the Server Manager snap-in.

Delegating Zones for DNS

DNS provides the ability to divide the namespace into one or more zones, which can then be stored, distributed, and replicated to other DNS servers. When deciding whether to divide your DNS namespace to make additional zones, consider the following reasons to use additional zones:

- A need to delegate management of part of your DNS namespace to another location or department within your organization

- A need to divide one large zone into smaller zones for distributing traffic loads among multiple servers, for improving DNS name-resolution performance, or for creating a more fault-tolerant DNS environment

- A need to extend the namespace by adding numerous subdomains at once, such as to accommodate the opening of a new branch or site

Each newly delegated zone requires a primary DNS server just as a regular DNS zone does. When delegating zones within your namespace, be aware that for each new zone you create, you need to place delegation records in other zones that point to the authoritative DNS servers for the new zone. This is necessary both to transfer authority and to provide correct referral to other DNS servers and clients of the new servers being made authoritative for the new zone.

In Exercise 2.3, you'll create a delegated subdomain of the domain you created in Exercise 2.2. Note that the name of the server to which you want to delegate the subdomain must be stored in an A or CNAME record in the parent domain.

EXERCISE 2.3

Creating a Delegated DNS Zone

1. Open the DNS management snap-in by selecting Server Manager. Once in Server Manager, click DNS on the left side. In the Servers window (center screen), right-click your server name and choose DNS Manager.

2. Expand the DNS server and locate the zone you created in Exercise 2.2.

3. Right-click the zone and choose the New Delegation command.

4. The New Delegation Wizard appears. Click Next to dismiss the initial wizard page.

5. Enter **ns1** (or whatever other name you like) in the Delegated Domain field of the Delegated Domain Name page. This is the name of the domain for which you want to delegate authority to another DNS server. It should be a subdomain of the primary domain (for example, to delegate authority for farmington.example.net, you'd enter **farmington** in the Delegated Domain field). Click Next to complete this step.

6. When the Name Servers page appears, click the Add button to add the names and IP addresses of the servers that will be hosting the newly delegated zone. For the purpose of this exercise, enter the server name you used in Exercise 2.2. Click the Resolve button to resolve this domain name's IP address automatically into the IP address field. Click OK when you are finished. Click Next to continue with the wizard.

7. Click the Finish button. The New Delegation Wizard disappears, and you'll see the new zone you just created appear beneath the zone you selected in step 3. The newly delegated zone's folder icon is drawn in gray to indicate that control of the zone is delegated.

DNS Forwarding

If a DNS server does not have an answer to a DNS request, it may be necessary to send that request to another DNS server. This is called *DNS forwarding*. You need to understand the two main types of forwarding:

External Forwarding   When a DNS server forwards an external DNS request to a DNS server outside of your organization, this is considered *external forwarding*. For example, a resolver requests the host www.microsoft.com. Most likely, your internal DNS server is not going to have Microsoft's web address in its DNS database. So, your DNS server is going to send the request to an external DNS (most likely your ISP).

Conditional Forwarding   *Conditional forwarding* is a lot like external forwarding except that you are going to forward requests to specific DNS servers based on a condition. Usually this is an excellent setup for internal DNS resolution. For example, let's say that you have two companies, Stormwind.com and Stormtest.com. If a request comes in for Stormwind.com, it gets forwarded to the Stormwind DNS server, and any requests for Stormtest.com will get forwarded to the Stormtest DNS server. Requests are forwarded to a specific DNS server depending on the condition that an administrator sets up.

Manually Creating DNS Records

From time to time you may find it necessary to add resource records manually to your Windows Server 2016 DNS servers. Although Dynamic DNS frees you from the need to fiddle with A and PTR records for clients and other such entries, you still have to create other resource types (including MX records, required for the proper flow of SMTP email) manually. You can manually create A, PTR, MX, SRV, and many other record types.

There are only two important things to remember for manually creating DNS records:

- You must right-click the zone and choose either the New Record command or the Other New Records command.

- You must know how to fill in the fields of whatever record type you're using.

  For example, to create an MX record, you need three pieces of information (the domain, the mail server, and the priority). To create an SRV record, however, you need several more pieces of information.

In Exercise 2.4, you will manually create an MX record for a mailtest server in the zone you created in Exercise 2.2.

EXERCISE 2.4

Manually Creating DNS RRs

1. Open the DNS management snap-in by selecting Server Manager. Once in Server Manager, click DNS on the left side. In the Servers window (center screen), right-click your server name and choose DNS Manager.

2. Expand your DNS server, right-click its zone, and choose New Host (A record).

3. Enter **mailtest** in the Name field. Enter a TCP/IP number in the IP Address field. (You can use any number for this exercise, such as, for example, 192.168.1.254.) Click the Add Host button.

4. A dialog box appears stating that the host record was created successfully. Click OK. Click Done.

5. Right-click your zone name and choose New Mail Exchanger (MX).

6. Enter **mailtest** in the Host Or Child Domain field and enter **mailtest.yourDomain.com** (or whatever domain name you used in Exercise 2.2) in the Fully-Qualified Domain Name (FQDN) Of Mail Server field and then click OK. Notice that the new record is already visible.

7. Next create an alias (or CNAME) record to point to the mail server. (It is assumed that you already have an A record for mailtest in your zone.) Right-click your zone and choose New Alias (CNAME).

8. Type **mail** into the Alias Name field.

9. Type **mailtest.yourDomain.com** into the Fully-Qualified Domain Name (FQDN) For Target Host field.

10. Click the OK button.

11. Close the DNS management snap-in.

DNS Aging and Scavenging

When using dynamic updates, computers (or DHCP) will register a resource record with DNS. These records get removed when a computer is shut down properly. A major problem in the industry is that laptops are frequently removed from the network without a proper shutdown. Therefore, their resource records continue to live in the DNS database.

Windows Server 2016 DNS supports two features called *DNS aging* and *DNS scavenging*. These features are used to clean up and remove stale resource records. DNS zone or DNS server aging and scavenging flag old resource records that have not been updated in a certain amount of time (determined by the scavenging interval). These stale records will be scavenged at the next cleanup interval. DNS uses time stamps on the resource records to determine how long they have been listed in the DNS database.

By default, DNS aging and scavenging are disabled by default. Microsoft states that these features should only be enabled if you have users that are not logging off the network properly. If your users are all using desktops or if your users log off the network properly every day, you should keep these features disabled.

The issue that you can run into if this feature is enabled and DNS deletes records that should not be deleted, is that this can stop users from access resources on the network because their DNS records have been deleted improperly.

If you decide that you want to enable DNS aging and scavenging, you must enable these features on both at the DNS server and on the zone.

DNS aging and scavenging is done by using time stamps. Time stamps are a date and time value that is used by the DNS server. The date and time is used to determine removal of the resource record when it performs the aging and scavenging operations.

Monitoring and Troubleshooting DNS

Now that you have set up and configured your DNS name server and created some resource records, you will want to confirm that it is resolving and replying to client DNS requests. A couple of tools allow you to do some basic monitoring and managing. Once you are able to monitor DNS, you'll want to start troubleshooting.

The simplest test is to use the ping command to make sure that the server is alive. A more thorough test would be to use nslookup to verify that you can actually resolve addresses for items on your DNS server.

In the following sections, you'll look at some of these monitoring and management tools and how to troubleshoot DNS.

Monitoring DNS with the DNS Snap-In

You can use the DNS snap-in to do some basic server testing and monitoring. More important, you use the snap-in to monitor and set logging options. On the Event Logging tab of the server's Properties dialog box (see Figure 2.14), you can pick which events you want logged. The more events you select, the more logging information you'll get. This is useful when you're trying to track what's happening with your servers, but it can result in a very large log file if you're not careful.

FIGURE 2.14   The Event Logging tab of the server's Properties dialog box

The Monitoring tab (see Figure 2.15) gives you some testing tools. When the check box labeled A Simple Query Against This DNS Server is checked, a test is performed that asks for a single record from the local DNS server. It's useful for verifying that the service is running and listening to queries, but not much else. When the check box labeled A Recursive Query To Other DNS Servers is checked, the test is more sophisticated—a recursive query checks whether forwarding is working okay. The Test Now button and the Perform Automatic Testing At The Following Interval check box allow you to run these tests now or later as you require.

Another tab in the server's properties that allows you to monitor the activity of the DNS server is the Debug Logging tab. The Debug Logging tab allows you to monitor all outbound and inbound DNS traffic, packet content, packet type, and which transport protocol (TCP or UDP) you want to monitor on the DNS server.

FIGURE 2.15   The Monitoring tab of the server's Properties dialog box

WINSRV2016 Properties   ?   ×

| Interfaces | Forwarders | Advanced | Root Hints |
| Debug Logging | Event Logging | Monitoring | Security |

To verify the configuration of the server, you can perform manual or automatic testing.

Select a test type:

☐ A simple query against this DNS server

☐ A recursive query to other DNS servers

To perform the test immediately, click Test Now.   [Test Now]

☐ Perform automatic testing at the following interval:

Test interval: 1   minutes ▽

Test results:

| Date | Time | Simple Query | Recursive Q... |

[OK]   [Cancel]   [Apply]   [Help]

If the simple query fails, check that the local server contains the zone `1.0.0.127.in-addr.arpa`. If the recursive query fails, check that your root hints are correct and that your root servers are running.

In Exercise 2.5, you will enable logging, use the DNS MMC to test the DNS server, and view the contents of the DNS log.

EXERCISE 2.5

Simple DNS Testing

1. Open the DNS management snap-in by selecting Server Manager. Once in Server Manager, click DNS on the left side. In the Servers window (center screen), right-click your server name and choose DNS Manager.

2. Right-click the DNS server name on the top left and select Properties.

3. Switch to the Debug Logging tab, check all the debug logging options except Filter Packets By IP Address and enter a full path and filename in the File Path And Name field. Click the Apply button.

4. Switch to the Monitoring tab and check both A Simple Query Against This DNS Server and A Recursive Query To Other DNS Servers.

EXERCISE 2.5 *(continued)*

5.   Click the Test Now button several times and then click OK.

6.   Press the Windows key on the keyboard (left side between the Ctrl and Alt keys) and then choose Computer. Navigate to the folder that you specified in step 3 and use WordPad or Notepad to view the contents of the log file.

Troubleshooting DNS

When troubleshooting DNS problems, ask yourself the following basic questions:

▪   What application is failing? What works? What doesn't work?

▪   Is the problem basic IP connectivity, or is it name resolution? If the problem is name resolution, does the failing application use NetBIOS names, DNS names, or hostnames?

▪   How are the things that do and don't work related?

▪   Have the things that don't work ever worked on this computer or network? If so, what has changed since they last worked?

Windows Server 2016 provides several useful tools, discussed in the following sections, which can help you answer these questions:

▪   Nslookup is used to perform DNS queries and to examine the contents of zone files on local and remote servers.

▪   DNSLint is a command-line utility used for troubleshooting many common DNS issues.

▪   Ipconfig allows you to perform the following tasks:

    ▪   View DNS client settings

    ▪   Display and flush the resolver cache

    ▪   Force a dynamic update client to register its DNS records

▪   The DNS log file monitors certain DNS server events and logs them for your edification.

Using *Nslookup*

Nslookup is a standard command-line tool provided in most DNS server implementations, including Windows Server 2016. Windows Server 2016 gives you the ability to launch nslookup from the DNS snap-in.

When nslookup is launched from the DNS snap-in, a command prompt window opens automatically. You enter nslookup commands in this window.

Nslookup offers you the ability to perform query testing of DNS servers and to obtain detailed responses at the command prompt. This information can be useful for diagnosing and solving name resolution problems, for verifying that resource records are added or updated correctly in a zone, and for debugging other server-related problems. You can do a number of useful things with nslookup:

- Use it in noninteractive mode to look up a single piece of data
- Enter interactive mode and use the debug feature
- Perform the following from within interactive mode:
    - Set options for your query
    - Look up a name
    - Look up records in a zone
    - Perform zone transfers
    - Exit nslookup

> **NOTE** When you are entering queries, it is generally a good idea to enter FQDNs so that you can control what name is submitted to the server. However, if you want to know which suffixes are added to unqualified names before they are submitted to the server, you can enter **nslookup** in debug mode and then enter an unqualified name.

Using *Nslookup* on the Command Line

To use nslookup in plain-old command-line mode, enter the following in the command prompt window:

```
nslookup DNS_name_or_IP_address server_IP_address
```

This command will look up a DNS name or address using a server at the IP address you specify.

Using *Nslookup* in Interactive Mode

Nslookup is a lot more useful in interactive mode because you can enter several commands in sequence. Entering **nslookup** by itself (without specifying a query or server) puts it in interactive mode, where it will stay until you type **exit** and press Enter. Before that point, you can look up lots of useful stuff. The following are some of the tasks that you can perform with nslookup in interactive mode:

Setting Options with the set Command   While in interactive mode, you can use the set command to configure how the resolver will carry out queries. Table 2.5 shows a few of the options available with set.

TABLE 2.5   Command-line options available with the set command

Option	Purpose
set all	Shows all the options available.
set d2	Puts nslookup in debug mode so that you can examine the query and response packets between the resolver and the server.
set domain=*domain name*	Tells the resolver what domain name to append for unqualified queries.
set timeout=*timeout*	Tells the resolver how long to keep trying to contact the server. This option is useful for slow links where queries frequently time out and the wait time must be lengthened.
set type=*record type*	Tells the resolver which type of resource records to search for (for example, A, PTR, or SRV). If you want the resolver to query for all types of resource records, type **settype=all**.

Looking Up a Name   While in interactive mode, you can look up a name just by typing it: **stormwind.com**. In this example, stormwind is the owner name for the record for which you are searching, and .com is the server that you want to query.

You can use the wildcard character (*) in your query. For example, if you want to look for all resource records that have *k* as the first letter, just type **k*** as your query.

Looking Up a Record Type   If you want to query a particular type of record (for instance, an MX record), use the set type command. The command set type=mx tells nslookup that you're interested only in seeing MX records that meet your search criteria.

Listing the Contents of a Domain   To get a list of the contents of an entire domain, use the ls command. To find all the hosts in your domain, you'd type **set type=a** and then type **ls -t yourdomain.com**.

Troubleshooting Zone Transfers   You can simulate zone transfers by using the ls command with the -d switch. This can help you determine whether the server you are querying allows zone transfers to your computer. To do this, type the following: **ls -d domain__name**.

Nslookup Responses and Error Messages

A successful nslookup response looks like this:

```
Server: Name_of_DNS_server
Address: IP_address_of_DNS_server
Response_data
```

Nslookup might also return an error message. Some common messages are listed in Table 2.6.

TABLE 2.6 Common nslookup error messages

Error message	Meaning
DNS request timed out. Timeout was x seconds. *** Can't find server name for address IP_Address: Timed out *** Default servers are not available Default Server: Unknown Address: IP_address_of_DNS_server	The resolver did not locate a PTR resource record (containing the hostname) for the server IP address you specified. Nslookup can still query the DNS server, and the DNS server can still answer queries.
*** Request to Server timed-out	A request was not fulfilled in the allotted time. This might happen, for example, if the DNS service was not running on the DNS server that is authoritative for the name.
*** Server can't find Name_or_IP_address_ queried_for: No response from server	The server is not receiving requests on User Datagram Protocol (UDP) port 53.
*** Server can't find Name_or_IP_address_ queried_for: Non-existent domain	The DNS server was unable to find the name or IP address in the authoritative domain. The authoritative domain might be on the remote DNS server or on another DNS server that this DNS server is unable to reach.
*** Server can't find Name_or_IP_address_ queried_for: Server failed	The DNS server is running, but it is not working properly. For example, it might include a corrupted packet, or the zone in which you are querying for a record might be paused. However, this message can also be returned if the client queries for a host in a domain for which the DNS server is not authoritative. You will also receive the error if the DNS server cannot contact its root servers, it is not connected to the Internet, or it has no root hints.

In Exercise 2.6, you'll get some hands-on practice with the `nslookup` tool.

Using the `nslookup` Command

1. Press the Windows key on the keyboard and then choose Computer. Navigate to the `C:\Windows\System32` folder and double-click `CMD.exe`. (When you get to this file, you can right-click the file and choose Send To Desktop. The shortcut will then always be available on the desktop.)

2. Type **nslookup** and press the Enter key. (For the rest of the exercise, use the Enter key to terminate each command.)

3. Try looking up a well-known address: Type www.microsoft.com.

4. Try looking up a nonexistent host: Type **www.example.ccccc**. Notice that your server indicates that it can't find the address and times out. This is normal behavior.

5. Type **Exit** at the prompt. Type **Exit** again to leave the command prompt.

Using *DNSLint*

Microsoft Windows Server 2016 DNS can use the `DNSLint` command-line utility to help diagnose some common DNS name-resolution issues and to help diagnose potential problems of incorrect delegation. You need to download `DNSLint` from the Microsoft Download Center.

DNSLint uses three main functions to verify DNS records and to generate a report in HTML:

dnslint /d   This function helps diagnose the reasons for "lame delegation" and other related DNS problems.

dnslint /ql   This function helps verify a user-defined set of DNS records on multiple DNS servers.

dnslint /ad   This function helps verify DNS records pertaining to Active Directory replication.

Here is the syntax for DNSLint:

```
dnslint /d domain_name | /ad [LDAP_IP_address] | /ql input_file
[/c [smtp,pop,imap]] [/no_open] [/r rcport_name]
[/t] [/test_tcp] [/s DNS_IP_address] [/v] [/y]
```

The following are some sample queries:

```
dnslint /d stormwind.com
dnslint /ad /s 192.168.36.201
dnslint /ql dns_server.txt
dnslint /ql autocreate
dnslint /v /d stormwind.com
dnslint /r newfile /d stormwind.com
dnslint /y /d stormwind.com
dnslint /no_open /d stormwind.com
```

Table 2.7 explains the command options.

TABLE 2.7   DNSLint command options

Command option	Meaning
/d	Domain name that is being tested.
/ad	Resolves DNS records that are used for Active Directory forest replication.
/s	TCP/IP address of host.
/ql	Requests DNS query tests from a list. This switch sends DNS queries specified in an input file.
/v	Turns on verbose mode.
/r *filename*	Allows you to create a report file.
/y	Overwrites an existing report file without being prompted.
/no_open	Prevents a report from opening automatically.

Using *Ipconfig*

You can use the command-line tool ipconfig to view your DNS client settings, to view and reset cached information used locally for resolving DNS name queries, and to register the resource records for a dynamic update client. If you use the ipconfig command with no parameters, it displays DNS information for each adapter, including the domain name and DNS servers used for that adapter. Table 2.8 shows some command-line options available with ipconfig.

TABLE 2.8 Command-line options available for the `ipconfig` command

Command	What It Does
`ipconfig /all`	Displays additional information about DNS, including the FQDN and the DNS suffix search list.
`ipconfig /flushdns`	Flushes and resets the DNS resolver cache. For more information about this option, see the section "Configuring DNS" earlier in this chapter.
`ipconfig /displaydns`	Displays the contents of the DNS resolver cache. For more information about this option, see "Configuring DNS" earlier in this chapter.
`ipconfig /registerdns`	Refreshes all DHCP leases and registers any related DNS names. This option is available only on Windows 2000 and newer computers that run the DHCP client service.

You should know and be comfortable with the `ipconfig` commands related to DNS for the exam.

Using *DNSCmd*

`DNSCmd` allows you to display and change the properties of DNS servers, zones, and resource records through the use of command-line commands. The `DNSCmd` utility allows you to modify, create, and delete resource records and/or zones manually, and it allows you to force replication between two DNS servers.

Table 2.9 lists some of the `DNSCmd` commands and their explanations.

TABLE 2.9 DNSCmd command-line options

Command	Explanation
`dnscmd /clearcache`	Clears the DNS server cache
`dnscmd /config`	Resets DNS server or zone configuration
`dnscmd /createdirectorypartition`	Creates a DNS application directory partition
`dnscmd /deletedirectorypartition`	Deletes a DNS application directory partition
`dnscmd /enumrecords`	Shows the resource records in a zone

Command	Explanation
dnscmd /exportsettings	Creates a text file of all server configuration information
dnscmd /info	Displays server information
dnscmd /recordadd	Adds a resource record to a zone
dnscmd /recorddelete	Deletes a resource record from a zone
dnscmd /zoneadd	Creates a new DNS zone
dnscmd /zonedelete	Deletes a DNS zone
dnscmd /zoneexport	Creates a text file of all resource records in the zone
dnscmd /zoneinfo	Displays zone information
dnscmd /zonerefresh	Forces replication of the master zone to the secondary zone

Using the DNS Log File

You can configure the DNS server to create a log file that records the following information:

- Queries
- Notification messages from other servers
- Dynamic updates
- Content of the question section for DNS query messages
- Content of the answer section for DNS query messages
- Number of queries this server sends
- Number of queries this server has received
- Number of DNS requests received over a UDP port
- Number of DNS requests received over a TCP port
- Number of full packets sent by the server
- Number of packets written through by the server and back to the zone

The DNS log appears in systemroot\System32\dns\Dns.log. Because the log is in RTF format, you must use WordPad or Word to view it.

Once the log file reaches the maximum size, Windows Server 2016 writes over the beginning of the file. You can change the maximum size of the log. If you increase the size value, data persists for a longer time period, but the log file consumes more disk space. If you decrease the value, the log file uses less disk space, but the data persists for a shorter time period.

 WARNING Do not leave DNS logging turned on during normal operation because it sucks up both processing and hard disk resources. Enable it only when diagnosing and solving DNS problems.

Troubleshooting the .(*root*) Zone

The *DNS root zone* is the top-level DNS zone in the DNS hierarchy. Windows Server 2016–based DNS servers will build a .(root) zone when a connection to the Internet can't be found.

Because of this, the .(root) zone may prevent access to the Internet. The DNS forwarding option and DNS root hints will not be configurable. If you want your DNS to work as a DNS forwarder or you want to use root hints, you must remove the .(root) zone.

Issues with Non-Microsoft DNS Servers

Another troubleshooting problem that you may run into is working with both Microsoft DNS servers and non-Microsoft DNS servers. One of the most common non-Microsoft DNS servers is the Unix-based BIND DNS server.

If you need to complete a zone transfer from Microsoft DNS to a BIND DNS server, you need to enable BIND Secondaries on the Microsoft DNS server (see Figure 2.16).

FIGURE 2.16   Enabling BIND Secondaries

If you need to enable Bind Secondaries, complete the following steps:

1. Open DNS management.
2. Right-click the server name and choose Properties.
3. Click the Advanced tab.
4. Check the Enable BIND Secondaries box.
5. Click OK.

Integrating Dynamic DNS and IPv4 DHCP

DHCP integration with Dynamic DNS is a simple concept but powerful in action. By setting up this integration, you can pass addresses to DHCP clients while still maintaining the integrity of your DNS services.

The DNS server can be updated in two ways. One way is for the DHCP client to tell the DNS server its address. Another way is for the DHCP server to tell the DNS server when it registers a new client.

Neither of these updates will take place, however, unless you configure the DNS server to use Dynamic DNS. You can make this change in two ways:

- If you change it at the scope level, it will apply only to the scope.
- If you change it at the server level, it will apply to all scopes and superscopes served by the server.

Which of these options you choose depends on how widely you want to support Dynamic DNS; most of the sites I visit have enabled DNS updates at the server level.

To update the settings at either the server or scope level, you need to open the scope or server properties by right-clicking the appropriate object and choosing Properties. The DNS tab of the Properties dialog box includes the following options:

Enable DNS Dynamic Updates According To The Settings Below   This check box controls whether this DHCP server will attempt to register lease information with a DNS server. It must be checked to enable Dynamic DNS.

> **Dynamically Update DNS A And PTR Records Only If Requested By The DHCP Clients**
> This radio button (which is on by default) tells the DHCP server to register the update only if the DHCP client asks for DNS registration. When this button is active, DHCP clients that aren't hip to DDNS won't have their DNS records updated. However, Windows 2000, XP, Vista, Windows 7, Windows 8 / 8.1, Windows 10, Server 2003, Server 2008/2008 R2, and Server 2012/2016 DHCP clients are smart enough to ask for the updates.

> **Always Dynamically Update DNS A And PTR Records**   This radio button forces the DHCP server to register any client to which it issues a lease. This setting may add DNS registrations for DHCP-enabled devices that don't really need them, such as print servers. However, it allows other clients (such as Mac OS, Windows NT, and Linux machines) to have their DNS information automatically updated.

Discard A And PTR Records When Lease Is Deleted This check box has a long name but a simple function. When a DHCP lease expires, what should happen to the DNS registration? Obviously, it would be nice if the DNS record associated with a lease vanished when the lease expired. When this check box is checked (as it is by default), that's exactly what happens. If you uncheck this box, your DNS will contain entries for expired leases that are no longer valid. When a particular IP address is reissued on a new lease, the DNS will be updated, but in between leases you'll have incorrect data in your DNS—something that's always best to avoid.

Dynamically Update DNS A And PTR Records For DHCP Clients That Do Not Request Updates This check box lets you handle these older clients graciously by making the updates using a separate mechanism.

In Exercise 2.7, you will enable a scope to participate in Dynamic DNS updates.

EXERCISE 2.7

Enabling DHCP-DNS Integration

1. Open the DHCP snap-in by selecting Administrative Tools ➤ DHCP.

2. Right-click the IPv4 item, and select Properties.

3. The Server Properties dialog box appears. Click the DNS tab.

4. Verify that the check box labeled Enable DNS Dynamic Updates According To The Settings Below is checked, and verify that the radio button labeled Dynamically Update DNS A And PTR Records Only If Requested By The DHCP Clients is selected.

5. Verify that the check box labeled Discard A And PTR Records When Lease Is Deleted is checked. If not, then check it.

6. Click the OK button to apply your changes and close the Server Properties dialog box.

DNS PowerShell Commands

When talking about PowerShell commands for DNS, I must let you know that there are dozens of commands that you can use to configure and maintain a DNS server. Before I show you the table of DNS PowerShell commands, let's look at two commands first.

When we install DNS onto a server, we can use PowerShell to do the install. But when we are talking about Nano server, the PowerShell commands are a bit different.

Let's first look at how you install DNS on a regular Windows server using PowerShell. The following command is the command used to install DNS on a Windows Server.

```
Install-WindowsFeature DNS -IncludeManagementTools
```

Now let's take a look at the PowerShell command for installing DNS on a Nano server. The following commands are used to install DNS on a Nano server. The first command downloads DNS to the Nano server and the second command installs it on the server.

```
Install-NanoServerPackage Microsoft-NanoServer-DNS-Package -Culture en-us
Enable-WindowsOptionalFeature -Online -FeatureName DNS-Server-Full-Role
```

Nano servers have no GUI interface and all installations have to be done using remote tools or PowerShell commands. There are dozens of possible PowerShell commands. Nano servers are excellent servers to use as DNS servers. Just be sure that you know what Roles can be installed onto a Nano server and which Roles can't be installed on a Nano server (like DHCP).

In Table 2.10, I will show you just some of the possible PowerShell commands that are available for DNS.

 For a complete list of DNS PowerShell commands, please visit Microsoft's website at `https://technet.microsoft.com/itpro/powershell/windows/dnsserver/dnsserver`.

TABLE 2.10 PowerShell Commands for DNS

PowerShell Command	Description
Add-DnsServerClientSubnet	This command allows an administrator to add a client subnet to a DNS server.
Add-DnsServerConditionalForwarderZone	Administrators can use this command to add a conditional forwarder to a DNS server.
Add-DnsServerForwarder	This command allows an administrator to add forwarders to a DNS server.
Add-DnsServerPrimaryZone	Administrators can use this command to add a primary zone to a DNS server.
Add-DnsServerQueryResolutionPolicy	This command allows an administrator to add a query resolution policy to DNS.
Add-DnsServerResourceRecord	Administrators can use this command to add a resource record to a DNS zone.
Add-DnsServerResourceRecordA	This command allows an administrator to add an A record to a DNS zone.
Add-DnsServerResourceRecordAAAA	This command allows an administrator to add an AAAA record to a DNS zone.

TABLE 2.10 PowerShell Commands for DNS *(continued)*

PowerShell Command	Description
Add-DnsServerResourceRecordCName	This command allows an administrator to add a CNAME record to a DNS zone.
Add-DnsServerResourceRecordDnsKey	Administrators can use this command to add a DNSKEY record to a DNS zone.
Add-DnsServerResourceRecordDS	This command allows an administrator to add a DS record to a DNS zone.
Add-DnsServerResourceRecordMX	This command allows an administrator to add a MX record to a DNS zone.
Add-DnsServerResourceRecordPtr	This command allows an administrator to add a PTR record to a DNS zone.
Add-DnsServerSecondaryZone	Administrators can use this command to add a secondary zone.
Add-DnsServerSigningKey	This command adds a KSK or ZSK to a signed zone.
Add-DnsServerStubZone	This command adds a stub zone to a DNS server.
Add-DnsServerTrustAnchor	Admins can use this command to add a trust anchor to a DNS server.
Add-DnsServerZoneDelegation	This command allows an administrator to add a new delegated DNS zone to an existing zone.
Clear-DnsServerCache	Administrators use this command to clear resource records from a DNS cache.
ConvertTo-DnsServerPrimaryZone	This command converts a zone to a primary zone.
Get-DnsServer	This command retrieves configuration information for a DNS server.
Get-DnsServerDsSetting	This command allows you to gather information about DNS Active Directory settings.
Get-DnsServerRootHint	Administrators use this command to view root hints on a DNS server.

PowerShell Command	Description
Get-DnsServerScavenging	Administrators use this command to view DNS aging and scavenging settings.
Get-DnsServerSetting	This command allows you to view DNS server settings.
Get-DnsServerSigningKey	This command allows you to view zone signing keys.
Import-DnsServerResourceRecordDS	This command allows an administrator to import DNS resource records from a file.
Import-DnsServerRootHint	This command imports root hints from a DNS server.
Remove-DnsServerZone	Administrators use this command to remove a DNS zone from a server.
Resume-DnsServerZone	This command allows you to resume resolution on a suspended zone.
Set-DnsServer	Administrators can use this command to set the DNS server configuration.
Set-DnsServerRootHint	This command allows an administrator to replace a server's root hints.
Set-DnsServerSetting	Administrators can use this command to change DNS server settings.
Test-DnsServer	This command allows an administrator to test a functioning DNS server.

Summary

DNS was designed to be a robust, scalable, and high-performance system for resolving friendly names to TCP/IP host addresses. This chapter presented an overview of the basics of DNS and how DNS names are generated. You then looked at the many new features available in the Microsoft Windows Server 2016 version of DNS, and you learned how to install, configure, and manage the necessary services. Microsoft's DNS is based on a widely accepted set of industry standards. Because of this, Microsoft's DNS can work with both Windows- and non-Windows-based networks.

Exam Essentials

Understand the purpose of DNS.   DNS is a standard set of protocols that defines a mechanism for querying and updating address information in the database, a mechanism for replicating the information in the database among servers, and a schema of the database.

Understand the different parts of the DNS database.   The SOA record defines the general parameters for the DNS zone, including who is the authoritative server. NS records list the name servers for a domain; they allow other name servers to look up names in your domain. A host record (also called an address record or an A record) statically associates a host's name with its IP addresses. Pointer records (PTRs) map an IP address to a hostname, making it possible to do reverse lookups. Alias records allow you to use more than one name to point to a single host. The MX record tells you which servers can accept mail bound for a domain. SRV records tie together the location of a service (like a domain controller) with information about how to contact the service.

Know how DNS resolves names.   With iterative queries, a client asks the DNS server for an answer, and the client, or resolver, returns the best kind of answer it has. In a recursive query, the client sends a query to one name server, asking it to respond either with the requested answer or with an error. The error states either that the server can't come up with the right answer or that the domain name doesn't exist. With inverse queries, instead of supplying a name and then asking for an IP address, the client first provides the IP address and then asks for the name.

Understand the differences among DNS servers, clients, and resolvers.   Any computer providing domain name services is a DNS server. A DNS client is any machine issuing queries to a DNS server. A resolver handles the process of mapping a symbolic name to an actual network address.

Know how to install and configure DNS.   DNS can be installed before, during, or after installing the Active Directory service. When you install the DNS server, the DNS snap-in is installed too. Configuring a DNS server ranges from easy to difficult, depending on what you're trying to make it do. In the simplest configuration, for a caching-only server, you don't have to do anything except to make sure that the server's root hints are set correctly. You can also configure a root server, a normal forward lookup server, and a reverse lookup server.

Know how to create new forward and reverse lookup zones.   You can use the New Zone Wizard to create a new forward or reverse lookup zone. The process is basically the same for both types, but the specific steps and wizard pages differ somewhat. The wizard walks you through the steps, such as specifying a name for the zone (in the case of forward lookup zones) or the network ID portion of the network that the zone covers (in the case of reverse lookup zones).

Know how to configure zones for dynamic updates.   The DNS service allows dynamic updates to be enabled or disabled on a per-zone basis at each server. This is easily done in the DNS snap-in.

Know how to delegate zones for DNS.   DNS provides the ability to divide the namespace into one or more zones; these can then be stored, distributed, and replicated to other DNS servers. When delegating zones within your namespace, be aware that for each new zone you create, you need delegation records in other zones that point to the authoritative DNS servers for the new zone.

Understand the tools that are available for monitoring and troubleshooting DNS.   You can use the DNS snap-in to do some basic server testing and monitoring. More important, you use the snap-in to monitor and set logging options. Windows Server 2016 automatically logs DNS events in the event log under a distinct DNS server heading. Nslookup offers the ability to perform query testing of DNS servers and to obtain detailed responses at the command prompt. You can use the command-line tool ipconfig to view your DNS client settings, to view and reset cached information used locally for resolving DNS name queries, and to register the resource records for a dynamic update client. Finally, you can configure the DNS server to create a log file that records queries, notification messages, dynamic updates, and various other DNS information.

Review Questions

1. You are the network administrator for the ABC Company. Your network consists of two DNS servers named *DNS1* and *DNS2*. The users who are configured to use DNS2 complain because they are unable to connect to Internet websites. The following table shows the configuration of both servers.

   DNS1   DNS2

   `_msdcs.abc.comabc.com`   `.(root)_msdcs.abc.comabc.com`

   The users connected to DNS2 need to be able to access the Internet. What needs to be done?

   A. Build a new Active Directory Integrated zone on DNS2.

   B. Delete the `.(root)` zone from DNS2, and configure conditional forwarding on DNS2.

   C. Delete the current `cache.dns` file.

   D. Update your `cache.dns` file and root hints.

2. You are the network administrator for a large company that has one main site and one branch office. Your company has a single Active Directory forest, `ABC.com`. You have a single domain controller (ServerA) in the main site that has the DNS role installed. ServerA is configured as a primary DNS zone. You have decided to place a domain controller (ServerB) in the remote site and implement the DNS role on that server. You want to configure DNS so that, if the WAN link fails, users in both sites can still update records and resolve any DNS queries. How should you configure the DNS servers?

   A. Configure ServerB as a secondary DNS server. Set replication to occur every 5 minutes.

   B. Configure ServerB as a stub zone.

   C. Configure ServerB as an Active Directory Integrated zone, and convert ServerA to an Active Directory Integrated zone.

   D. Convert ServerA to an Active Directory Integrated zone, and configure ServerB as a secondary zone.

3. You are the network administrator for a mid-size computer company. You have a single Active Directory forest, and your DNS servers are configured as Active Directory Integrated zones. When you look at the DNS records in Active Directory, you notice that there are many records for computers that do not exist on your domain. You want to make sure only domain computers register with your DNS servers. What should you do to resolve this issue?

   A. Set dynamic updates to None.

   B. Set dynamic updates to Nonsecure And Secure.

   C. Set dynamic updates to Domain Users Only.

   D. Set dynamic updates to Secure Only.

4. Your company consists of a single Active Directory forest. You have a Windows Server 2016 domain controller that also has the DNS role installed. You also have a Unix-based DNS server at the same location. You need to configure your Windows DNS server to allow zone transfers to the Unix-based DNS server. What should you do?

   A. Enable BIND secondaries.

   B. Configure the Unix machine as a stub zone.

   C. Convert the DNS server to Active Directory Integrated.

   D. Configure the Microsoft DNS server to forward all requests to the Unix DNS server.

5. You are the network administrator for Stormwind Corporation. Stormwind has two trees in its Active Directory forest, Stormwind.com and abc.com. Company policy does not allow DNS zone transfers between the two trees. You need to make sure that when anyone in abc.com tries to access the Stormwind.com domain, all names are resolved from the Stormwind.com DNS server. What should you do?

   A. Create a new secondary zone in abc.com for Stormwind.com.

   B. Configure conditional forwarding on the abc.com DNS server for Stormwind.com.

   C. Create a new secondary zone in Stormwind.com for abc.com.

   D. Configure conditional forwarding on the Stormwind.com DNS server for abc.com.

6. You are the network administrator for your organization. A new company policy states that all inbound DNS queries need to be recorded. What can you do to verify that the IT department is compliant with this new policy?

   A. Enable Server Auditing - Object Access.

   B. Enable DNS debug logging.

   C. Enable server database query logging.

   D. Enable DNS Auditing - Object Access.

7. You are the network administrator for a small company with two DNS servers: DNS1 and DNS2. Both DNS servers reside on domain controllers. DNS1 is set up as a standard primary zone, and DNS2 is set up as a secondary zone. A new security policy was written stating that all DNS zone transfers must be encrypted. How can you implement the new security policy?

   A. Enable the Secure Only setting on DNS1.

   B. Enable the Secure Only setting on DNS2.

   C. Configure Secure Only on the Zone Transfers tab for both servers.

   D. Delete the secondary zone on DNS2. Convert both DNS servers to use Active Directory Integrated zones.

8. You are responsible for DNS in your organization. You look at the DNS database and see a large number of older records on the server. These records are no longer valid. What should you do?

A. In the zone properties, enable Zone Aging and Scavenging.

B. In the server properties, enable Zone Aging and Scavenging.

C. Manually delete all the old records.

D. Set Dynamic Updates to None.

9. Your IT team has been informed by the compliance team that they need copies of the DNS Active Directory Integrated zones for security reasons. You need to give the Compliance department a copy of the DNS zone. How should you accomplish this goal?

A. Run dnscmd /zonecopy.

B. Run dnscmd /zoneinfo.

C. Run dnscmd /zoneexport.

D. Run dnscmd /zonefile.

10. You are the network administrator for a Windows Server 2016 network. You have multiple remote locations connected to your main office by slow satellite links. You want to install DNS into these offices so that clients can locate authoritative DNS servers in the main location. What type of DNS servers should be installed in the remote locations?

A. Primary DNS zones

B. Secondary DNS zones

C. Active Directory Integrated zones

D. Stub zones

Chapter

3

Configuring DHCP

THE FOLLOWING 70-741 EXAM OBJECTIVES ARE COVERED IN THIS CHAPTER:

✓ **Install and configure DHCP**

▪ This objective may include but is not limited to: Install and configure DHCP servers; authorize a DHCP server; create and configure scopes; create and configure superscopes and multicast scopes; configure a DHCP reservation; configure DHCP options; configure DNS options from within DHCP; configure policies; configure client and server for PXE boot; configure DHCP Relay Agent; implement IPv6 addressing using DHCPv6; perform export and import of a DHCP server; perform DHCP server migration.

✓ **Manage and maintain DHCP**

▪ This objective may include but is not limited to: Configure a lease period; back up and restore the DHCP database; configure high availability using DHCP failover; configure DHCP name protection; troubleshoot DHCP.

In this chapter, I will show you the different methods of setting up an IP address network. If you want systems to be able to share network resources, the computers must all talk the same type of language. This is where DHCP comes into play.

DHCP allows your users to get the required information so that they can properly communicate on the network. I will show you how to install and configure DHCP. I will also show you the advantages of using DHCP and how DHCP can save you hours of configuration time.

Understanding DHCP

When you're setting up a network, the computers need to communicate with each other using the same type of computer language. This is referred to as a protocol. TCP/IP is the priority protocol for Windows Server 2016. For all of your machines to work using TCP/IP, each system must have its own unique IP address. There are two ways to have clients and servers get TCP/IP addresses:

- You can manually assign the addresses.

- The addresses can be assigned automatically.

Manually assigning addresses is a fairly simple process. An administrator goes to each of the machines on the network and assigns TCP/IP addresses. The problem with this method arises when the network becomes midsized or larger. Think of an administrator trying to individually assign 4,000 TCP/IP addresses, subnet masks, default gateways, and all other configuration options needed to run the network.

DHCP's job is to centralize the process of IP address and option assignment. You can configure a DHCP server with a range of addresses (called a *pool*) and other configuration information and let it assign all of the IP parameters—addresses, default gateways, DNS server addresses, and so on.

One of the nice advantages of DHCP is that you can install DHCP onto a Server Core server. DHCP is one of the roles that can be deployed onto a Server Core server. At the time this book was written, DHCP was not supported on a Nano Server. So you can NOT load DHCP on a Windows Server 2016 Nano Server.

DHCP is defined by a series of Request for Comments documents, notably 2131 and 2132.

Introducing the DORA Process

An easy way to remember how DHCP works is to learn the acronym DORA. *DORA* stands for Discover, Offer, Request, and Acknowledge. In brief, here is DHCP's DORA process:

1. **Discover:** When IP networking starts up on a DHCP-enabled client, a special message called a DHCPDISCOVER is broadcast within the local physical subnet.

2. **Offer:** Any DHCP server that hears the request checks its internal database and replies with a message called a DHCPOFFER, which contains an available IP address.

   The contents of this message depend on how the DHCP server is configured—there are numerous options aside from an IP address that you can specify to pass to the client on a Windows Server DHCP server.

3. **Request:** The client receives one or more DHCPOFFERs (depending on how many DHCP servers exist on the local subnet), chooses an address from one of the offers, and sends a DHCPREQUEST message to the server to signal acceptance of the DHCPOFFER.

   This message might also request additional configuration parameters.

   Other DHCP servers that sent offers take the request message as an acknowledgment that the client didn't accept their offer.

4. **Acknowledge:** When the DHCP server receives the DHCPREQUEST, it marks the IP address as being in use (that is, usually, though it's not required). Then it sends a DHCPACK to the client.

   The acknowledgment message might contain requested configuration parameters.

   If the server is unable to accept the DHCPREQUEST for any reason, it sends a DHCPNAK message. If a client receives a DHCPNAK, it begins the configuration process over again.

5. When the client accepts the IP offer, the address is assigned to the client for a specified period of time, called a *lease*. After receiving the DHCPACK message, the client performs a final check on the parameters (sometimes it sends an ARP request for the offered IP address) and makes note of the duration of the lease. The client is now configured. If the client detects that the address is already in use, it sends a DHCPDECLINE.

If the DHCP server has given out all of the IP addresses in its pool, it won't make an offer. If no other servers make an offer, the client's IP network initialization will fail, and the client will use Automatic Private IP Addressing (APIPA).

DHCP Lease Renewal

No matter how long the lease period, the client sends a new lease request message directly to the DHCP server when the lease period is half over (give or take some randomness required by RFC 2131). This period goes by the name *T1* (not to be confused with the T1 type of network connection). If the server hears the request message and there's no reason to reject it, it sends a DHCPACK to the client. This resets the lease period.

If the DHCP server isn't available, the client realizes that the lease can't be renewed. The client continues to use the address, and once 87.5 percent of the lease period has elapsed (again, give or take some randomness), the client sends out another renewal request. This interval is known as *T2*. At that point, any DHCP server that hears the renewal can respond to this *DHCP request message* (which is a request for a lease renewal) with a DHCPACK and renew the lease. If at any time during this process the client gets a negative DHCPNACK message, it must stop using its IP address immediately and start the leasing process over from the beginning by requesting a new lease.

When a client initializes its IP networking, it always attempts to renew its old address. If the client has time left on the lease, it continues to use the lease until its end. If the client is unable to get a new lease by that time, all IP communications with the network will stop until a new, valid address can be obtained.

DHCP Lease Release

Although leases can be renewed repeatedly, at some point they might run out. Furthermore, the lease process is "at will." That is, the client or server can cancel the lease before it ends. In addition, if the client doesn't succeed in renewing the lease before it expires, the client loses its lease and reverts to APIPA. This release process is important for reclaiming extinct IP addresses used by systems that have moved or switched to a non-DHCP address.

Advantages and Disadvantages of DHCP

DHCP was designed from the start to simplify network management. It has some significant advantages, but it also has some drawbacks.

Advantages of DHCP

The following are advantages of DHCP:

- Configuration of large and even midsized networks is much simpler. If a DNS server address or some other change is necessary to the client, the administrator doesn't have to touch each device in the network physically to reconfigure it with the new settings.

- Once you enter the IP configuration information in one place—the server—it's automatically propagated to clients, eliminating the risk that a user will misconfigure some parameters and require you to fix them.

- IP addresses are conserved because DHCP assigns them only when requested.

- IP configuration becomes almost completely automatic. In most cases, you can plug in a new system (or move one) and then watch as it receives a configuration from the server. For example, when you install new network changes, such as a gateway or DNS server, the client configuration is done at only one location—the DHCP server.

- It allows a preboot execution environment (PXE) client to get a TCP/IP address from DHCP. PXE clients (also called Microsoft Windows Deployment Services [WDS] clients) can get an IP address without needing to have an operating system installed. This allows WDS clients to connect to a WDS server through the TCP/IP protocol and download an operating system remotely.

Disadvantages of DHCP

Unfortunately, there are a few drawbacks with DHCP:

- DHCP can become a single point of failure for your network. If you have only one DHCP server and it's not available, clients can't request or renew leases.

- If the DHCP server contains incorrect information, the misinformation will automatically be delivered to all of your DHCP clients.

- If you want to use DHCP on a multisegment network, you must put either a DHCP server or a relay agent on each segment, or you must ensure that your router can forward Bootstrap Protocol (BOOTP) broadcasts.

Ipconfig Lease Options

The ipconfig command-line tool is useful for working with network settings. Its /renew and /release switches make it particularly handy for DHCP clients. These switches allow you to request renewal of, or give up, your machine's existing address lease. You can do the same thing by toggling the Obtain An IP Address Automatically button in the Internet Protocol (TCP/IP) Properties dialog box, but the command-line option is useful especially when you're setting up a new network.

For example, I spend about a third of my time teaching MCSA or MCSE classes, usually in temporary classrooms set up at conferences, hotels, and so on. Laptops are used in these classes, with one brawny one set up as a DNS/DHCP/DC server. Occasionally, a client will lose its DHCP lease (or not get one, perhaps because a cable has come loose). The quickest way to fix it is to pop open a command-line window and type **ipconfig /renew**.

You can configure DHCP to assign options only to certain classes. *Classes*, defined by an administrator, are groups of computers that require identical DHCP options. The /setclassid*classID* switch of ipconfig is the only way to assign a machine to a class.

More specifically, the switches do the following:

ipconfig /renew   Instructs the DHCP client to request a lease renewal. If the client already has a lease, it requests a renewal from the server that issued the current lease. This is equivalent to what happens when the client reaches the half-life of its lease. Alternatively, if the client doesn't currently have a lease, it is equivalent to what happens when you boot a DHCP client for the first time. It initiates the DHCP mating dance, listens for lease offers, and chooses one it likes.

ipconfig /release   Forces the client to give up its lease immediately by sending the server a DHCP release notification. The server updates its status information and marks the client's old IP address as "available," leaving the client with no address bound to its network interface. When you use this command, most of the time it will be immediately followed by ipconfig/renew. The combination releases the existing lease and gets a new one, probably with a different address. (It's also a handy way to force your client to get a new set of settings from the server before the lease expiration time.)

ipconfig /setclassidclassID   Sets a new class ID for the client. You will see how to configure class options later in the section "Setting Scope Options for IPv4." For now, you should know that the only way to add a client machine to a class is to use this command. Note that you need to renew the client lease for the class assignment to take effect.

If you have multiple network adapters in a single machine, you can provide the name of the adapter (or adapters) upon which you want the command to work, including an asterisk (*) as a wildcard. For example, one of my servers has two network cards: an Intel EtherExpress (ELNK1) and a generic 100 Mbps card. If you want to renew DHCP settings for both adapters, you can type **ipconfig/renew ***. If you just want to renew the Intel EtherExpress card, you can type **ipconfig/renew ELNK1**.

Understanding Scope Details

By now you should have a good grasp of what a lease is and how it works. To learn how to configure your servers to hand out those leases, however, you need to have a complete understanding of some additional topics: scopes, superscopes, exclusions, reservations, address pool, and relay agents.

Scope

Let's start with the concept of a *scope*, which is a contiguous range of addresses. There's usually one scope per physical subnet, and a scope can cover a Class A, Class B, or Class C network address or a TCP/IP v6 address. DHCP uses scopes as the basis for managing and assigning IP addressing information.

Each scope has a set of parameters, or scope options, that you can configure. *Scope options* control what data is delivered to DHCP clients when they're completing the DHCP negotiation process with a particular server. For example, the DNS server name, default gateway, and default network time server are all separate options that can be assigned. These settings are called *option types*. You can use any of the types provided with Windows Server 2016, or you can specify your own.

Superscope

A *superscope* enables the DHCP server to provide addresses from more than one scope to clients on the same physical subnet. This is helpful when clients within the same subnet have more than one IP network and thus need IPs from more than one address pool. Microsoft's DHCP snap-in allows you to manage IP address assignment in the superscope, though you must still configure other scope options individually for each child scope.

Exclusions and Reservations

The scope defines what IP addresses could potentially be assigned, but you can influence the assignment process in two additional ways by specifying exclusions and reservations:

Exclusions   These are IP addresses within the range that you never want automatically assigned. These excluded addresses are off-limits to DHCP. You'll typically use exclusions to tag any addresses that you never want the DHCP server to assign at all. You might use exclusions to set aside addresses that you want to assign permanently to servers that play a vital role in your organization.

Reservations   These are IP addresses within the range for which you want a permanent DHCP lease. They essentially reserve a particular IP address for a particular device. The device still goes through the DHCP process (that is, its lease expires and it asks for a new one), but it always obtains the same addressing information from the DHCP server.

Exclusions are useful for addresses that you don't want to participate in DHCP at all. *Reservations* are helpful for situations in which you want a client to get the same settings each time they obtain an address.

An address cannot be simultaneously reserved and excluded. Be aware of this fact for the exam, possibly relating to a troubleshooting question.

 Real World Scenario

Using Reservations and Exclusions

Deciding when to assign a reservation or exclusion can sometimes be confusing. In practice, you'll find that certain computers in the network greatly benefit by having static IP network information. Servers such as DNS servers, the DHCP server itself, SMTP servers, and other low-level infrastructure servers are good candidates for static assignment. There are usually so few of these servers that the administrator is not overburdened if a change in network settings requires going out to reconfigure each individually. Chances are that the administrator would still need to reconfigure these servers manually (by using ipconfig /release and then ipconfig /renew), even if they did not have IP addresses reserved. Even in large installations, I find it preferable to manage these vital servers by hand rather than to rely on DHCP.

Reservations are also appropriate for application servers and other special but nonvital infrastructure servers. With a reservation in DHCP, the client device will still go through the DHCP process but will always obtain the same addressing information from the DHCP server. The premise behind this strategy is that these nonvital servers can withstand a short outage if DHCP settings change or if the DHCP server fails.

Address Pool

The range of IP addresses that the DHCP server can assign is called its *address pool*. For example, let's say you set up a new DHCP scope covering the 192.168.1 subnet. That gives you 255 IP addresses in the pool. After adding an exclusion from 192.168.1.240 to 192.168.1.254, you're left with 241 (255 – 14) IP addresses in the pool. That means (in theory, at least) that you can service 241 unique clients at a time before you run out of IP addresses.

DHCP Relay Agent

By design, DHCP is intended to work with clients and servers on a single IP network. But RFC 1542 sets out how BOOTP (on which DHCP is based) should work in circumstances in which the client and server are on different IP networks. If no DHCP server is available on the client's network, you can use a DHCP relay agent to forward DHCP broadcasts from the client's network to the DHCP server. The relay agent acts like a radio repeater, listening for DHCP client requests and retransmitting them through the router to the server.

Installing and Authorizing DHCP

Installing DHCP is easy using the Windows Server 2016/2012 R2 installation mechanism. Unlike some other services discussed in this book, the installation process installs just the service and its associated snap-in, starting it when the installation is complete. At that point, it's not delivering any DHCP service, but you don't have to reboot.

Installing DHCP

Exercise 3.1 shows you how to install a DHCP Server using Server Manager. This exercise was completed on a Windows Server 2016 Member Server since Active Directory is not installed yet.

EXERCISE 3.1

Installing the DHCP Service

1. Choose Server Manager by clicking the Server Manager icon on the Taskbar.

2. Click Add Roles And Features.

3. Choose role-based or feature-based installation and click Next.

4. Choose your server and click Next.

5. Choose DHCP (as shown in Figure 3.1) and click Next.

FIGURE 3.1   Choosing DHCP

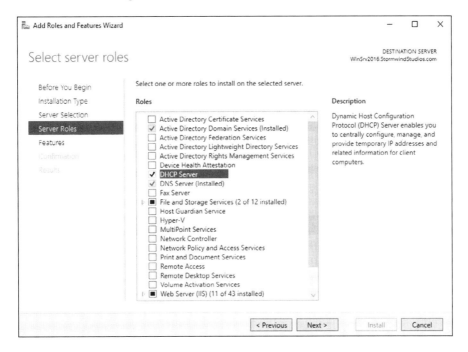

6. At the Features screen, click Next.

7. Click Next at the DHCP screen.

8. At the DHCP confirmation screen, click the Install button.

9. When the installation is complete, click the Close button.

10. On the left side, click the DHCP link.

11. Click the More link next to Configuration Required For DHCP Server.

12. Under Action, click Complete DHCP Configuration.

13. At the DHCP Description page, click Commit.

14. Click Close at the Summary screen.

15. Close Server Manager.

Introducing the DHCP Snap-In

When you install the DHCP server, the DHCP snap-in is also installed. You can open it by selecting Administrative Tools ➤ DHCP. Figure 3.2 shows the snap-in.

FIGURE 3.2   DHCP snap-in

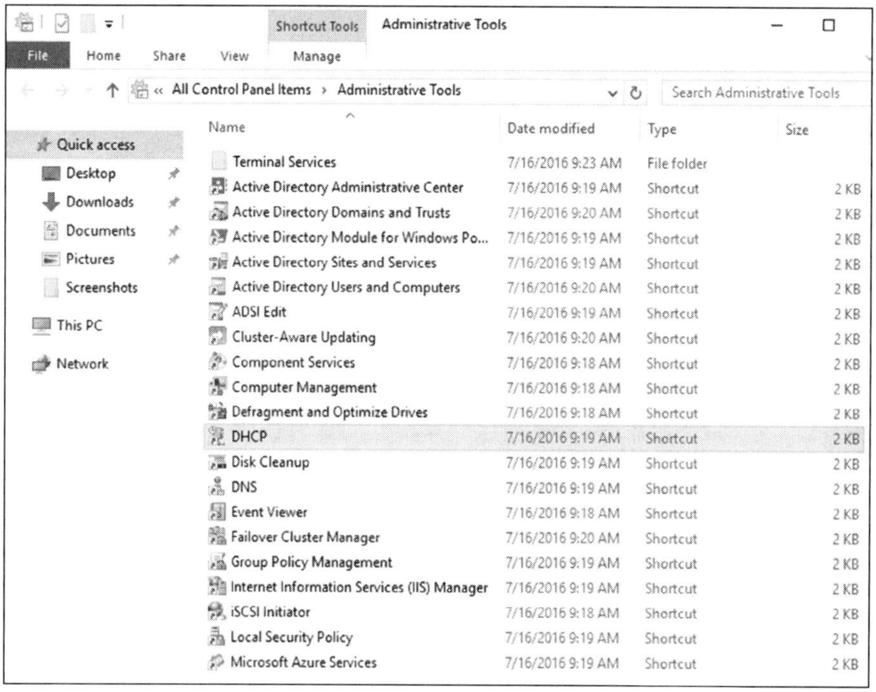

As you can see, the snap-in follows the standard MMC model. The left pane displays IPv4 and IPv6 sections and which servers are available; you can connect to servers other than the one to which you're already connected. A `Server Options` folder contains options that are specific to a particular DHCP server. Each server contains subordinate items grouped into folders. Each scope has a folder named after the scope's IP address range. Within each scope, four subordinate views show you interesting things about the scope, such as the following:

- The Address Pool view shows what the address pool looks like.

- The Address Leases view shows one entry for each current lease. Each lease shows the computer name to which the lease was issued, the corresponding IP address, and the current lease expiration time.

- The Reservations view shows the IP addresses that are reserved and which devices hold them.

- The Scope Options view lists the set of options you've defined for this scope.

Authorizing DHCP for Active Directory

Authorization creates an Active Directory object representing the new server. It helps keep unauthorized servers off your network. Unauthorized servers can cause two kinds of problems. They may hand out bogus leases, or they may fraudulently deny renewal requests from legitimate clients.

When you install a DHCP server using Windows Server 2016 and Active Directory is present on your network, the server won't be allowed to provide DHCP services to clients until it has been authorized. If you install DHCP on a member server in an Active Directory domain or on a stand-alone server, you'll have to authorize the server manually. When you authorize a server, you're adding its IP address to the Active Directory object that contains the IP addresses of all authorized DHCP servers.

 You also have the ability to authorize a DHCP server during the installation of DHCP if you are installing DHCP onto an Active Directory machine.

At start time, each DHCP server queries the directory, looking for its IP address on the "authorized" list. If it can't find the list or if it can't find its IP address on the list, the DHCP service fails to start. Instead, it adds a message to the event log, indicating that it couldn't service client requests because the server wasn't authorized.

Exercise 3.2 and Exercise 3.3 show you how to authorize and unauthorize a DHCP server onto a network with Active Directory. If you installed DHCP onto a network with a domain, you can complete the following two exercises, but if you are still on a member server, you *cannot* do these exercises. These are here to show you how to do it after you have Active Directory on your network.

EXERCISE 3.2

Authorizing a DHCP Server

1. From Administrative Tools, choose DHCP to open the DHCP snap-in.

2. Right-click the server you want to authorize and choose the Authorize command (see Figure 3.3).

FIGURE 3.3 Choosing Authorize

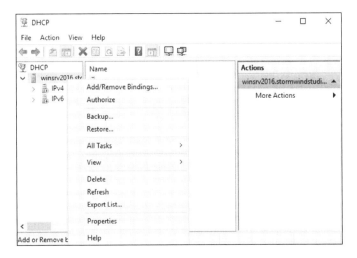

3. Wait a few seconds and then hit F5. This will refresh the server. You should now see that the red down arrows are now green.

EXERCISE 3.3

Unauthorizing a DHCP Server

1. From Administrative Tools, choose DHCP to open the DHCP snap-in.

2. Right-click the server you want to authorize and choose the Unauthorize command (as shown in Figure 3.4).

FIGURE 3.4   Choosing Unauthorize

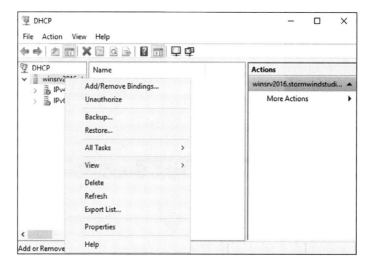

3. Wait a few seconds and then hit F5. This will refresh the server. You should now see that the green arrows are now red.

4. Now let's reauthorize the server. Right-click the server and choose the Authorize command. Wait a few seconds and hit F5.

Creating and Managing DHCP Scopes

You can use any number of DHCP servers on a single physical network if you divide the range of addresses that you want assigned into multiple scopes. Each scope contains a number of useful pieces of data, but before you can understand them, you need to know some additional terminology.

You can perform the following management tasks on DHCP scopes:

▪   Create a scope

▪   Configure scope properties

▪   Configure reservations and exclusions

- Set scope options
- Activate and deactivate scopes
- Create a superscope
- Create a multicast scope
- Integrate Dynamic DNS and DHCP

I will cover each task in the following sections.

Creating a New Scope in IPv4

Like many other things in Windows Server 2016, a wizard drives the process of creating a new scope. You will most likely create a scope while installing DHCP, but you may need to create more than one. The overall process is simple, as long as you know beforehand what the wizard is going to ask. If you think about what defines a scope, you'll be well prepared. You need to know the following:

- The IP address range for the scope you want to create.
- Which IP addresses, if any, you want to exclude from the address pool.
- Which IP addresses, if any, you want to reserve.
- Values for the DHCP options you want to set, if any. This item isn't strictly necessary for creating a scope. However, to create a useful scope, you'll need to have some options to specify for the clients.

To create a scope, under the server name, right-click the IPv4 option in the DHCP snap-in, and use the Action ➤ New Scope command. This starts the New Scope Wizard (see Figure 3.5). You will look at each page of the wizard in the following sections.

FIGURE 3.5   Welcome page of the New Scope Wizard

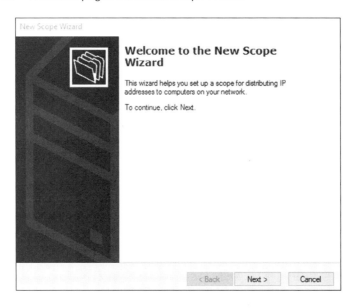

Setting the Screen Name

The Scope Name page allows you to enter a name and description for your scope. These will be displayed by the DHCP snap-in.

> It's a good idea to pick sensible names for your scopes so that other administrators will be able to figure out the purpose of the scope. For example, the name DHCP is likely not very helpful, whereas a name like 1st Floor Subnet is more descriptive and can help in troubleshooting.

Defining the IP Address Range

The IP Address Range page (see Figure 3.6) is where you enter the start and end IP addresses for your range. The wizard does minimal checking on the addresses you enter, and it automatically calculates the appropriate subnet mask for the range. You can modify the subnet mask if you know what you're doing.

FIGURE 3.6   IP Address Range page of the New Scope Wizard

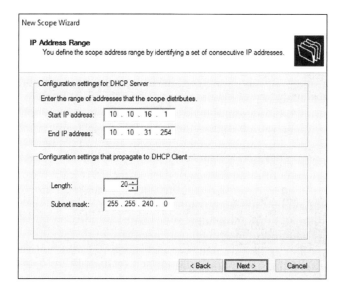

Adding Exclusions and Delay

The Add Exclusions And Delay page (see Figure 3.7) allows you to create exclusion ranges. Exclusions are TCP/IP numbers that are in the pool, but they do not get issued to clients. To exclude one address, put it in the Start IP Address field. To exclude a range, also fill in the

End IP Address field. The delay setting is a time duration by which the server will delay the transmission of a DHCPOFFER message.

FIGURE 3.7 Add Exclusions And Delay page of the New Scope Wizard

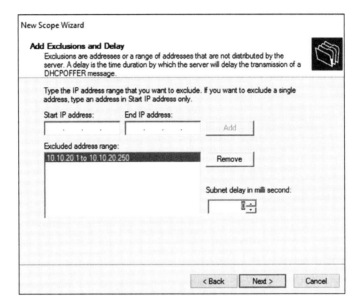

 Although you can always add exclusions later, it's best to include them when you create the scope so that no excluded addresses are ever passed out to clients.

Setting a Lease Duration

The Lease Duration page (see Figure 3.8) allows you to set how long a device gets to use an assigned IP address before it has to renew its lease. The default lease duration is eight days. You may find that a shorter or longer duration makes sense for your network. If your network is highly dynamic, with lots of arrivals, departures, and moving computers, set a shorter lease duration; if it's less active, make it longer.

 Remember that renewal attempts begin when approximately half of the lease period is over (give or take a random interval), so don't set them too short.

FIGURE 3.8   Lease Duration page of the New Scope Wizard

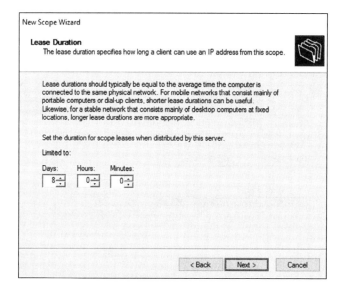

Configuring Basic DHCP Options

The Configure DHCP Options page (see Figure 3.9) allows you to choose whether you want to set up basic DHCP options such as default gateway and DNS settings. The options are described in the following sections. If you choose not to configure options, you can always do so later. However, you should not activate the scope until you've configured the options you want assigned.

FIGURE 3.9   Configure DHCP Options page of the New Scope Wizard

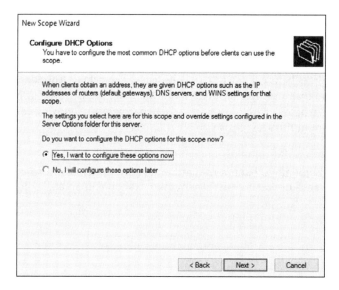

Configuring a Router

The first option configuration page is the Router (Default Gateway) page (see Figure 3.10), in which you enter the IP addresses of one or more routers (more commonly referred to as *default gateways*) that you want to use for outbound traffic. After entering the IP addresses of the routers, use the Up and Down buttons to order the addresses. Clients will use the routers in the order specified when attempting to send outgoing packets.

FIGURE 3.10   Router (Default Gateway) page of the New Scope Wizard

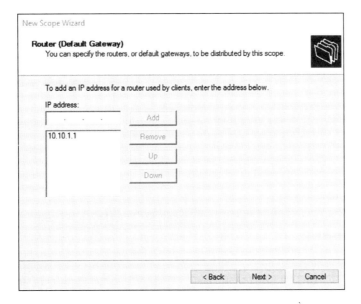

Providing DNS Settings

On the Domain Name And DNS Servers page (see Figure 3.11), you specify the set of DNS servers and the parent domain you want passed down to DHCP clients. Normally, you'll want to specify at least one DNS server by filling in its DNS name or IP address. You can also specify the domain suffix that you want clients to use as the base domain for all connections that aren't fully qualified. For example, if your clients are used to navigating based on server name alone rather than the fully qualified domain name (FQDN) of server.willpanek.com, then you'll want to place your domain here.

Providing WINS Settings

If you're still using Windows Internet Name Service (WINS) on your network, you can configure DHCP so that it passes WINS server addresses to your Windows clients. (If you want the Windows clients to honor it, you'll also need to define the WINS/NBT Node Type option for the scope.) As on the DNS server page, on the WINS Servers page (see Figure 3.12) you can enter the addresses of several servers and move them into the order in which you want clients to try them. You can enter the DNS or NetBIOS name of each server, or you can enter an IP address.

FIGURE 3.11   Domain Name And DNS Servers page of the New Scope Wizard

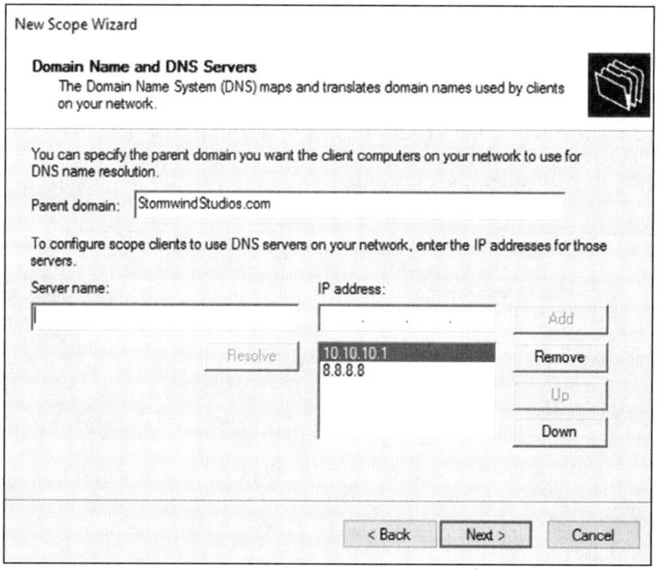

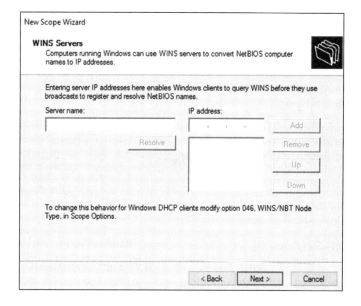

FIGURE 3.12   WINS Servers page of the New Scope Wizard

Here are some of the more common options you can set on a DHCP server:

003 Router   Used to provide a list of available routers or default gateways on the same subnet.

006 DNS Servers   Used to provide a list of DNS servers.

015 DNS Domain Name   Used to provide the DNS suffix.

028 Broadcast Address   Used to configure the broadcast address, if different than the default, based on the subnet mask.

44 WINS/NBNS Servers   Used to configure the IP addresses of WINS servers.

46 WINS/NBT Node Type   Used to configure the preferred NetBIOS name resolution method. There are four settings for node type:

   B node (0x1)   Broadcast for NetBIOS resolution

   P node (0x2)   Peer-to-peer (WINS) server for NetBIOS resolution

   M node (0x4)   Mixed node (does a B node and then a P node)

   H node (0x8)   Hybrid node (does a P node and then a B node)

051 Lease   Used to configure a special lease duration.

Activating the Scope

The Activate Scope page (see Figure 3.13) gives you the option to activate the scope immediately after creating it. By default, the wizard assumes that you want the scope activated unless you select the No, I Will Activate This Scope Later radio button, in which case the scope will remain dormant until you activate it manually.

FIGURE 3.13   Activate Scope page of the New Scope Wizard

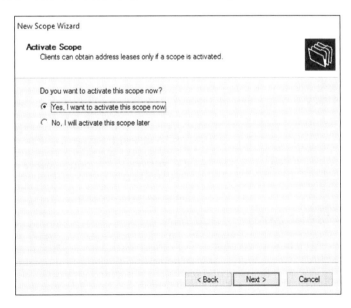

WARNING   Be sure to verify that there are no other DHCP servers assigned to the address range you choose!

In Exercise 3.4, you will create a new scope for the 192.168.0.xprivate Class C network. First you need to complete Exercise 3.1 before beginning this exercise.

EXERCISE 3.4

Creating a New Scope

1. Open the DHCP snap-in by selecting Administrative Tools ➢ DHCP.

2. Right-click the IPv4 folder and choose New Scope. The New Scope Wizard appears.

3. Click the Next button on the welcome page.

4. Enter a name and a description for your new scope and click the Next button.

5. On the IP Address Range page, enter **192.168.0.2** as the start IP address for the scope and **192.168.0.250** as the end IP address. Leave the subnet mask controls alone (though when creating a scope on a production network, you might need to change them). Click the Next button.

6. On the Add Exclusions And Delay page, click Next without adding any excluded addresses or delays.

7. On the Lease Duration page, set the lease duration to 3 days and click the Next button.

8. On the Configure DHCP Options page, click the Next button to indicate you want to configure default options for this scope.

9. On the Router (Default Gateway) page, enter **192.168.0.1** for the router IP address and then click the Add button. Once the address is added, click the Next button.

10. On the Domain Name And DNS Servers page, enter the IP address of a DNS server on your network in the IP Address field (for example, you might enter **192.168.0.251**) and click the Add button. Click the Next button.

11. On the WINS Servers page, click the Next button to leave the WINS options unset.

12. On the Activate Scope page, if your network is currently using the 192.168.0.x range, select Yes, I Want To Activate This Scope Now. Click the Next button.

13. When the wizard's summary page appears, click the Finish button to create the scope.

Creating a New Scope in IPv6

Now that you have seen how to create a new scope in IPv4, I'll go through the steps to create a new scope in IPv6.

To create a scope, right-click the IPv6 option in the DHCP snap-in under the server name and select the Action ➤ New Scope command. This starts the New Scope Wizard. Just as with creating a scope in IPv4, the welcome page of the wizard tells you that you've launched the New Scope Wizard. You will look at each page of the wizard in the following sections.

Setting the Screen Name

The Scope Name page (see Figure 3.14) allows you to enter a name and description for your scope. These will be displayed by the DHCP snap-in.

FIGURE 3.14   IPv6 Scope Name page of the New Scope Wizard

 It's a good idea to pick a sensible name for your scopes so that other administrators will be able to figure out what the scope is used for.

Scope Prefix

The Scope Prefix page (see Figure 3.15) gets you started creating the IPv6 scope. IPv6 has three types of addresses, which can be categorized by type and scope.

FIGURE 3.15   Scope Prefix page of the New Scope Wizard

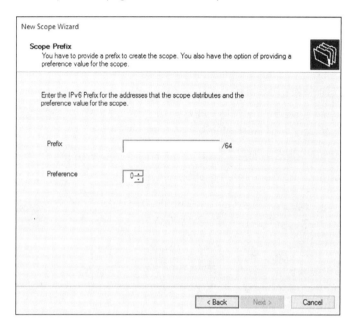

Unicast Addresses   *One-to-one*: A packet from one host is delivered to another host. The following are some examples of IPv6 unicast:

- The unicast prefix for site-local addresses is FEC0::/48.
- The unicast prefix for link-local addresses is FE80::/64.

The 6to4 address allows communication between two hosts running both IPv4 and IPv6. The way to calculate the 6to4 address is by combining the global prefix 2002::/16 with the 32 bits of a public IPv4 address of the host. This gives you a 48-bit prefix. 6to4 is described in RFC 3056.

Multicast addresses   *One-to-many*: A packet from one host is delivered to multiple hosts (but not everyone). The prefix for multicast addresses is FF00::/8.

Anycast addresses   A packet from one host is delivered to the nearest of multiple hosts (in terms of routing distance).

Adding Exclusions

As with the IPv4 New Scope Wizard, the Add Exclusions page allows you to create exclusion ranges. *Exclusions* are TCP/IP numbers that are in the pool but do not get issued to clients. To exclude one address, put it in the Start IPv6 Address field. To exclude a range, also fill in the End IPv6 Address field.

Setting a Lease Duration

The Scope Lease page allows you to set how long a device gets to use an assigned IP address before it has to renew its lease. You can set two different lease durations. The section labeled Non Temporary Address (IANA) is the lease time for your more permanent hosts (such as printers and server towers). The one labeled Temporary Address (IATA) is for hosts that might disconnect at any time, such as laptops.

Activating the Scope

The Completing The New Scope Wizard page gives you the option to activate the scope immediately after creating it. By default, the wizard will assume you want the scope activated. If you want to wait to activate the scope, choose No in the Activate Scope Now box.

Changing Scope Properties (IPv4 and IPv6)

Each scope has a set of properties associated with it. Except for the set of options assigned by the scope, you can find these properties on the General tab of the scope's Properties dialog box (see Figure 3.16). Some of these properties, such as the scope name and description, are self-explanatory. Others require a little more explanation.

- The Start IP Address and End IP Address fields allow you to set the range of the scope.
- For IPv4 scopes, the settings in the section Lease Duration For DHCP Clients control how long leases in this scope are valid.

  The IPv6 scope dialog box includes a Lease tab where you set the lease properties.

FIGURE 3.16 General tab of the scope's Properties dialog box for an IPv4 scope

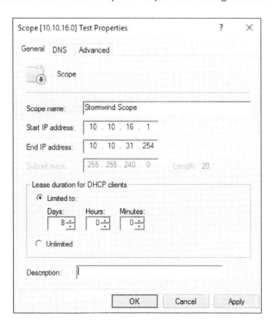

When you make changes to these properties, they have no effect on existing leases. For example, say you create a scope from 172.30.1.1 to 172.30.1.199. You use that scope for a while and then edit its properties to reduce the range from 172.30.1.1 to 172.30.1.150. If a client has been assigned the address 172.30.1.180, which was part of the scope before you changed it, the client will retain that address until the lease expires but will not be able to renew it.

Changing Server Properties

Just as each scope has its own set of properties, so too does the server itself. You access the server properties by right-clicking the IPv4 or IPv6 object within the DHCP management console and selecting Properties.

IPv4 Server Properties

Figure 3.17 shows the IPv4 Properties dialog box.

FIGURE 3.17   General tab of the IPv4 Properties dialog box for the server

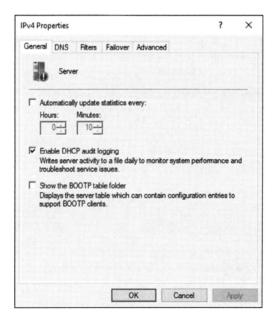

The IPv4 Properties dialog box has five tabs: General, DNS, Network Access Protection, and Advanced.

The Advanced tab, shown in Figure 3.18, contains the following configuration parameters:

- Audit Log File Path is where you enter the location for log files.

- Conflict Detection Attempts specifies how many ICMP echo requests (pings) the server sends for an address it is about to offer. The default is 0. Conflict detection is a way to verify that the DHCP server is not issuing IP addresses that are already being used on the network.

FIGURE 3.18   Advanced tab of the IPv4 Properties dialog box for the server

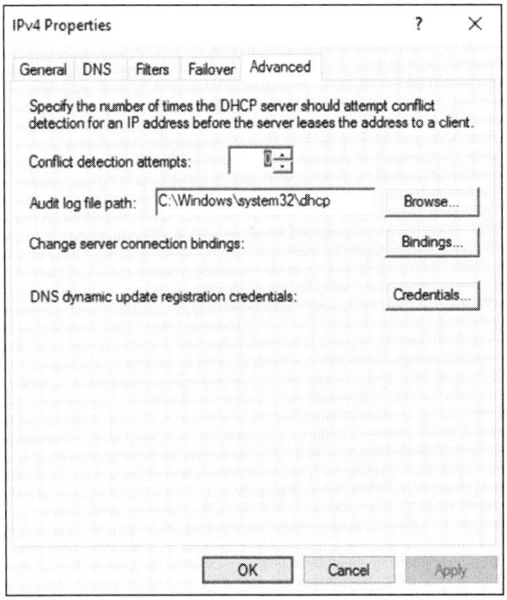

IPv6 Server Properties

The IPv6 Properties dialog box for the server has two tabs: General and Advanced. On the General tab, you can configure the following settings:

- Frequency with which statistics are updated
- DHCP auditing

  The Advanced tab allows you to configure the following settings:

- Database path for the audit log file path.
- Connection bindings.
- Registration credentials for dynamic DNS. The registration credential is the user account that DHCP will use to register clients with Active Directory.

Managing Reservations and Exclusions

After defining the address pool for your scope, the next step is to create reservations and exclusions, which reduce the size of the pool. In the following sections, you will learn how to add and remove exclusions and reservations.

Adding and Removing Exclusions

When you want to exclude an entire range of IP addresses, you need to add that range as an exclusion. Ordinarily, you'll want to do this before you enable a scope because that prevents any of the IP addresses you want excluded from being leased before you have a chance to exclude them. In fact, you can't create an exclusion that includes a leased address—you have to get rid of the lease first.

Adding an Exclusion Range

Here's how to add an exclusion range:

1. Open the DHCP snap-in and find the scope to which you want to add an exclusion (either IPv4 or IPv6).

2. Expand the scope so that you can see its Address Pool item for IPv4 or the Exclusion section for IPv6.

3. Right-click the Address Pool or Exclusion section and choose the New Exclusion Range command.

4. When the Add Exclusion dialog box appears, enter the IP addresses you want to exclude. To exclude a single address, type it in the Start IP Address field. To exclude a range of addresses, also fill in the End IP Address field.

5. Click the Add button to add the exclusion.

When you add exclusions, they appear in the Address Pool node, which is under the Scope section for IPv4 and under the Exclusion section of IPv6.

Removing an Exclusion Range

To remove an exclusion, just right-click it and choose the Delete command. After confirming your command, the snap-in removes the excluded range and the addresses become immediately available for issuance.

Adding and Removing Reservations

Adding a reservation is simple as long as you have the MAC address of the device for which you want to create a reservation. Because reservations belong to a single scope, you create and remove them within the Reservations node beneath each scope.

Adding a Reservation

To add a reservation, perform the following tasks:

1. Right-click the scope and select New Reservation.

   This displays the New Reservation dialog box, shown in Figure 3.19.

2. Enter the IP address and MAC address or ID for the reservation.

> To find the MAC address of the local computer, use the `ipconfig` command. To find the MAC address of a remote machine, use the `nbtstat -acomputername` command.

3. If you want, you can also enter a name and description.

4. For IPv4, in the Supported Types section, choose whether the reservation will be made by DHCP only, BOOTP only (useful for remote-access devices), or both.

FIGURE 3.19   New Reservation dialog box for IPv4 and IPv6

New Reservation   ?   ×

Provide information for a reserved client.

Reservation name: [   ]

IP address: [10 . 10 . 16 .   ]

MAC address: [   ]

Description: [   ]

Supported types
  ⦿ Both
  ○ DHCP
  ○ BOOTP

                        [Add]   [Close]

Removing a Reservation

To remove a reservation, right-click it and select Delete. This removes the reservation but does nothing to the client device.

There's no way to change a reservation once it has been created. If you want to change any of the associated settings, you'll have to delete and re-create the reservation.

Setting Scope Options for IPv4

Once you've installed a server, authorized it in Active Directory, and fixed up the address pool, the next step is to set scope options that you want sent out to clients, such as router (that is, default gateway) and DNS server addresses. You must configure the options you want sent out before you activate a scope. If you don't, clients may register in the scope without getting any options, rendering them virtually useless. Thus, configure the scope options, along with the IP address and subnet mask that you configured earlier in this chapter.

In the following sections, you will learn how to configure and assign scope options on the DHCP server.

Understanding Option Assignment

You can control which DHCP options are doled out to clients in five (slightly overlapping) ways:

Predefined Options   *Predefined options* are templates that are available in the Server, Scope, or Client Options dialog box.

Server Options   *Server options* are assigned to all scopes and clients of a particular server. That means if there's some setting you want all clients of a DHCP server to have, no matter what scope they're in, this is where you assign it. Specific options (those that are set at the class, scope, or client level) will override server-level options. That gives you an escape valve; it's a better idea, though, to be careful about which options you assign if your server manages multiple scopes.

Scope Options   If you want a particular option value assigned only to those clients in a certain subnet, you should assign it as a *scope option*. For example, it's common to specify different routers for different physical subnets; if you have two scopes corresponding to different subnets, each scope would probably have a separate value for the router option.

Class Options   You can assign different options to clients of different types, that is, *class options*. For example, Windows 2000, XP, Vista, Windows 7, Windows 8/8.1, Windows 10, Server 2003, Server 2003 R2, Server 2008, Server 2008 R2, and Server 2016/2012 R2 machines recognize a number of DHCP options that Windows 98, Windows NT, and Mac OS machines ignore, and vice versa. By defining a Windows 2000 or newer class (using the `ipconfig /setclassid` command you saw earlier), you could assign those options only to machines that report themselves as being in that class.

Client Options   If a client is using DHCP reservations, you can assign certain options to that specific client. You attach *client options* to a particular reservation. Client options override scope, server, and class options. The only way to override a client option is to configure the client manually. The DHCP server manages client options.

> Client options override class options, class options override scope options, and scope options override server options.

Assigning Options

You can use the DHCP snap-in to assign options at the scope, server, reserved address, or class level. The mechanism you use to assign these options is the same for each; the only difference is where you set the options.

When you create an option assignment, remember that it applies to all of the clients in the server or the scope from that point forward. Option assignments aren't retroactive, and they don't migrate from one scope to another.

Creating and Assigning a New Option

To create a new option and have it assigned, follow these steps:

1. Select the scope or server where you want the option assigned.

2. Select the corresponding Options node and choose Action ➤ Configure Options.

    To set options for a reserved client, right-click its entry in the Reservations node and select Configure Options.

    Then you'll see the Scope Options dialog box, which lists all of the options that you might want to configure.

3. To select an individual option, check the box next to it and then use the controls in the Data Entry control group to enter the value you want associated with the option.

4. Continue to add options until you've specified all of the ones you want attached to the server or scope. Then click OK.

Configuring the DHCP Server for Classes

Now it is time for you to learn how to configure the DHCP server to recognize your customized classes and configure options for them. In Exercise 3.5, you will create a new user class and configure options for the new class. Before you begin, make sure that the computers you want to use in the class have been configured with the `ipconfig /setclassid` command.

EXERCISE 3.5

Configuring User Class Options

1. Open the DHCP snap-in by selecting Administrative Tools ➤ DHCP.

2. Right-click the IPv4 item and select Define User Classes.

3. Click the Add button in the DHCP User Classes dialog box.

4. In the New Class dialog box, enter a descriptive name for the class in the Display Name field. Enter a class ID in the ID field. (Typically, you will enter the class ID in the ASCII portion of the ID field.) When you have finished, click OK.

5. The new class appears in the DHCP User Classes dialog box. Click the Close button to return to the DHCP snap-in.

6. Right-click the Scope Options node and select Configure Options.

7. Click the Advanced tab. Select the class you defined in step 4 from the User Class pop-up menu.

8. Configure the options you want to set for the class. Click OK when you have finished. Notice that the options you configured (and the class with which they are associated) appear in the right pane of the DHCP window.

About the Default Routing and Remote Access Predefined User Class

Windows Server 2016 includes a predefined user class called the *Default Routing and Remote Access class*. This class includes options important to clients connecting to Routing and Remote Access, notably the 051 Lease option.

 Be sure to know that the 051 Lease option is included within this class and that it can be used to assign a shorter lease duration for clients connecting to Routing and Remote Access.

Activating and Deactivating Scopes

When you've completed the steps in Exercise 3.4 and you're ready to unleash your new scope so that it can be used to make client assignments, the final required step is activating the scope. When you activate a scope, you're just telling the server that it's OK to start handing out addresses from that scope's address pool. As soon as you activate a scope, addresses from its pool may be assigned to clients. Of course, this is a necessary precondition to getting any use out of your scope.

If you later want to stop using a scope, you can, but be aware that it's a permanent change. When you deactivate a scope, DHCP tells all clients registered with the scope that they need to release their leases immediately and renew them someplace else—the equivalent of a landlord who evicts tenants when the building is condemned!

Don't deactivate a scope unless you want clients to stop using it immediately.

Creating a Superscope for IPv4

A *superscope* allows the DHCP server to provide multiple logical subnet addresses to DHCP clients on a single physical network. You create superscopes with the New Superscope command, which triggers the New Superscope Wizard.

You can have only one superscope per server.

The steps in Exercise 3.6 take you through the process of creating a superscope.

EXERCISE 3.6

Creating a Superscope

1. Open the DHCP snap-in by selecting Administrative Tools ≻ DHCP.

2. Follow the instructions in Exercise 3.4 to create two scopes: one for 192.168.0.2 through 192.168.0.127 and one for 192.168.1.12 through 192.168.1.127.

3. Right-click IPv4 and choose the New Superscope command. The New Superscope Wizard appears. Click the Next button.

4. On the Superscope Name page, name your superscope and click the Next button.

5. The Select Scopes page appears, listing all scopes on the current server. Select the two scopes you created in step 2 and then click the Next button.

6. The wizard's summary page appears. Click the Finish button to create your scope.

7. Verify that your new superscope appears in the DHCP snap-in.

Deleting a Superscope

You can delete a superscope by right-clicking it and choosing the Delete command. A superscope is just an administrative convenience, so you can safely delete one at any time—it doesn't affect the "real" scopes that make up the superscope.

Adding a Scope to a Superscope

To add a scope to an existing superscope, find the scope you want to add, right-click it, and choose Action ➤ Add To Superscope. A dialog box appears, listing all of the superscopes known to this server. Pick the one to which you want the current scope appended and click the OK button.

Removing a Scope from a Superscope

To remove a scope from a superscope, open the superscope and right-click the target scope. The pop-up menu provides a Remove From Superscope command that will do the deed.

Activating and Deactivating Superscopes

Just as with regular scopes, you can activate and deactivate superscopes. The same restrictions and guidelines apply. You must activate a superscope before it can be used, and you must not deactivate it until you want all of your clients to lose their existing leases and be forced to request new ones.

To activate or deactivate a superscope, right-click the superscope name and select Activate or Deactivate, respectively, from the pop-up menu.

Creating IPv4 Multicast Scopes

Multicasting occurs when one machine communicates to a network of subscribed computers rather than specifically addressing each computer on the destination network. It's much more efficient to multicast a video or audio stream to multiple destinations than it is to unicast it to the same number of clients, and the increased demand for multicast-friendly network hardware has resulted in some head scratching about how to automate the multicast configuration.

In the following sections, you will learn about MADCAP, the protocol that controls multicasting, and about how to build and configure a multicast scope.

Understanding the Multicast Address Dynamic Client Allocation Protocol

DHCP is usually used to assign IP configuration information for *unicast* (or one-to-one) network communications. With multicast, there's a separate type of address space assigned from 224.0.0.0 through 239.255.255.255. Addresses in this space are known as *Class D addresses*, or simply *multicast addresses*. Clients can participate in a multicast just by knowing (and using) the multicast address for the content they want to receive. However, multicast clients also need to have an ordinary IP address.

How do clients know what address to use? Ordinary DHCP won't help because it's designed to assign IP addresses and option information to one client at a time. Realizing this, the Internet Engineering Task Force (IETF) defined a new protocol: *Multicast Address Dynamic Client Allocation Protocol (MADCAP)*. MADCAP provides an analog to DHCP but for multicast use. A MADCAP server issues leases for multicast addresses only. MADCAP clients can request a multicast lease when they want to participate in a multicast.

DHCP and MADCAP have some important differences. First you have to realize that the two are totally separate. A single server can be a DHCP server, a MADCAP server, or both; no implied or actual relation exists between the two. Likewise, clients can use DHCP and/or MADCAP at the same time—the only requirement is that every MADCAP client has to get a unicast IP address from somewhere.

> Remember that DHCP can assign options as part of the lease process but MADCAP cannot. The only thing MADCAP does is dynamically assign multicast addresses.

Building Multicast Scopes

Most of the steps you go through when creating a multicast scope are identical to those required for an ordinary unicast scope. Exercise 3.7 highlights the differences.

EXERCISE 3.7

Creating a New Multicast Scope

1. Open the DHCP snap-in by selecting Administrative Tools ➤ DHCP.

2. Right-click IPv4 and choose New Multicast Scope. The New Multicast Scope Wizard appears. Click the Next button on the welcome page.

3. In the Multicast Scope Name page, name your multicast scope (and add a description if you'd like). Click the Next button.

4. The IP Address Range page appears. Enter a start IP address of **224.0.0.0** and an end IP address of **224.255.0.0**. Adjust the TTL to 1 to make sure that no multicast packets escape your local network segment. Click the Next button when you're finished.

5. The Add Exclusions page appears; click its Next button.

6. The Lease Duration page appears. Since multicast addresses are used for video and audio, you'd ordinarily leave multicast scope assignments in place somewhat longer than you would with a regular unicast scope, so the default lease length is 30 days (instead of 8 days for a unicast scope). Click the Next button.

7. The wizard asks you if you want to activate the scope now. Click the No radio button and then the Next button.

8. The wizard's summary page appears; click the Finish button to create your scope.

9. Verify that your new multicast scope appears in the DHCP snap-in.

Setting Multicast Scope Properties

Once you create a multicast scope, you can adjust its properties by right-clicking the scope name and selecting Properties.

The Multicast Scope Properties dialog box has two tabs. The General tab allows you to change the scope's name, its start and end addresses, its Time To Live (TTL) value, its lease duration, and its description—in essence, all of the settings you provided when you created it in the first place.

The Lifetime tab allows you to limit how long your multicast scope will be active. By default, a newly created multicast scope will live forever, but if you're creating a scope to provide MADCAP assignments for a single event (or a set of events of limited duration), you can specify an expiration time for the scope. When that time is reached, the scope disappears from the server but not before making all of its clients give up their multicast address leases. This is a nice way to make sure that the lease cleans up after itself when you're finished with it.

Integrating Dynamic DNS and IPv4 DHCP

DHCP integration with Dynamic DNS is a simple concept but powerful in action. By setting up this integration, you can pass addresses to DHCP clients while still maintaining the integrity of your DNS services.

The DNS server can be updated in two ways. One way is for the DHCP client to tell the DNS server its address. Another way is for the DHCP server to tell the DNS server when it registers a new client.

Neither of these updates will take place, however, unless you configure the DNS server to use Dynamic DNS. You can make this change in two ways:

- If you change it at the scope level, it will apply only to the scope.

- If you change it at the server level, it will apply to all scopes and superscopes served by the server.

Which of these options you choose depends on how widely you want to support Dynamic DNS; most of the sites I visit have enabled DNS updates at the server level.

To update the settings at either the server or scope level, you need to open the scope or server properties by right-clicking the appropriate object and choosing Properties. The DNS tab of the Properties dialog box (see Figure 3.20) includes the following options:

Enable DNS Dynamic Updates According To The Settings Below   This check box controls whether this DHCP server will attempt to register lease information with a DNS server. It must be checked to enable Dynamic DNS.

> **Dynamically Update DNS A And PTR Records Only If Requested By The DHCP Clients**
> This radio button (which is on by default) tells the DHCP server to register the update only if the DHCP client asks for DNS registration. When this button is active, DHCP clients that aren't hip to DDNS won't have their DNS records updated. However, Windows 2000, XP, Vista, Windows 7, Windows 8/8.1, Windows 10, Server 2003/2003 R2, Server 2008/2008 R2, and Server 2016/2012 R2 DHCP clients are smart enough to ask for the updates.

FIGURE 3.20 DNS tab of the scope's IPv4 Properties dialog box

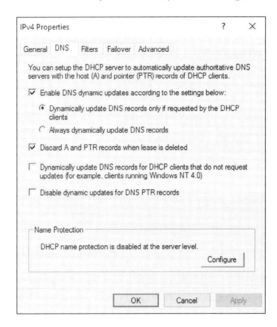

Always Dynamically Update DNS A And PTR Records   This radio button forces the DHCP server to register any client to which it issues a lease. This setting may add DNS registrations for DHCP-enabled devices that don't really need them, such as print servers. However, it allows other clients (such as Mac OS, Windows NT, and Linux machines) to have their DNS information automatically updated.

Discard A And PTR Records When Lease Is Deleted   This check box has a long name but a simple function. When a DHCP lease expires, what should happen to the DNS registration? Obviously, it would be nice if the DNS record associated with a lease vanished when the lease expired. When this check box is checked (as it is by default), that's exactly what happens. If you uncheck this box, your DNS will contain entries for expired leases that are no longer valid. When a particular IP address is reissued on a new lease, the DNS will be updated, but in between leases you'll have incorrect data in your DNS—something that's always best to avoid.

Dynamically Update DNS A And PTR Records For DHCP Clients That Do Not Request Updates   This check box lets you handle these older clients graciously by making the updates using a separate mechanism.

In Exercise 3.8, you will enable a scope to participate in Dynamic DNS updates.

EXERCISE 3.8

Enabling DHCP-DNS Integration

1. Open the DHCP snap-in by selecting Administrative Tools ➢ DHCP.

2. Right-click the IPv4 item and select Properties.

3. The Server Properties dialog box appears. Click the DNS tab.

4. Verify that the check box labeled Enable DNS Dynamic Updates According To The Settings Below is checked and verify that the radio button labeled Dynamically Update DNS A And PTR Records Only If Requested By The DHCP Clients is selected.

5. Verify that the check box labeled Discard A And PTR Records When Lease Is Deleted is checked. If not, then check it.

6. Click the OK button to apply your changes and close the Server Properties dialog box.

Using DHCP Failover Architecture

DHCP can become a single point of failure within a network if there is only one DHCP server. If that server becomes unavailable, clients will not be able to obtain new leases or renew existing leases. For this reason, it is recommended that you have more than one DHCP server in the network. However, more than one DHCP server can create problems if they both are configured to use the same scope or set of addresses. Microsoft recommends the 80/20 rule for redundancy of DHCP services in a network.

Implementing the 80/20 rule calls for one DHCP server to make approximately 80 percent of the addresses for a given subnet available through DHCP while another server makes the remaining 20 percent of the addresses available. For example, with a /24 network of 254 addresses, say 192.168.1.1 to 192.168.1.254, you might have Server 1 offer 192.168.1.10 to 192.168.1.210 while Server 2 offers 192.168.1.211 to 192.168.254.

DHCP Load Sharing

Load sharing is the normal default way that you use multiple DHCP servers (as explained earlier). Both servers cover the same subnets (remember that a DHCP server can handle multiple subnets at the same time) simultaneously, and both servers assign IP addresses and options to clients on the assigned subnets. The client requests are load balanced and shared between the two servers.

This is a good option for a company that has multiple DHCP servers in the same physical location. The DHCP servers are set up in a failover relationship at the same site, and both servers respond to all DHCP client requests from the subnets to which they are associated. The DHCP server administrator can set the load distribution ratio between the multiple DHCP servers.

DHCP Hot Standby

When thinking of a DHCP hot standby setup, think of the old server failover cluster. You have two servers where one server does all of the work and the other server is a standby server in the event that the first server crashes or goes down.

In a DHCP hot standby situation, the two DHCP servers operate in a failover relationship where one server acts as an active server and is responsible for leasing IP addresses to all clients in a scope or subnet. The secondary DHCP server assumes the standby role, and it is ready to go in the event that the primary DHCP server becomes unavailable. If the primary server becomes unavailable, the secondary DHCP server is given the role of the primary DHCP server and takes over all the responsibilities of the primary DHCP server.

This failover situation is best suited to DHCP deployments where a company has DHCP servers in multiple locations.

 To learn more about DHCP failover situations, please visit Microsoft at http://technet.microsoft.com/en-us/library/hh831385.aspx. Microsoft has been known for taking questions right off its websites, and this website is the perfect solution for doing this.

Working with the DHCP Database Files

DHCP uses a set of database files to maintain its knowledge of scopes, superscopes, and client leases. These files, which live in the *systemroot*\System32\DHCP folder, are always open when the DHCP service is running. DHCP servers use Joint Engine Technology (JET) databases to maintain their records.

 You shouldn't modify or alter the DHCP database files when the service is running.

The primary database file is dhcp.mdb—it has all of the scope data in it.

The following files are also part of the DHCP database:

Dhcp.tmp   This is a backup copy of the database file created during reindexing of the database. You normally won't see this file, but if the service fails during reindexing, it may not remove the file when it should.

J50.log   This file (plus a number of files named J50*xxxxx*.log, where *xxxxx* stands for 00001, 00002, 00003, and so on) is a log file that stores changes before they're written to the database. The DHCP database engine can recover some changes from these files when it restarts.

J50.chk   This is a checkpoint file that tells the DHCP engine which log files it still needs to recover.

In the following sections, you will see how to manipulate the DHCP database files.

Removing the Database Files

If you're convinced that your database is corrupt because the lease information that you see doesn't match what's on the network, the easiest repair mechanism is to remove the database files and start over with an empty database.

 If you think the database is corrupt because the DHCP service fails at startup, you should check the event log.

To start over, follow these steps:

1. Stop the DHCP service by typing **net stop dhcpserver** at the command prompt.

2. Remove all of the files from the *systemroot*\system32\DHCP folder.

3. Restart the service (at command prompt, type **net start dhcpserver**).

4. Reconcile the scope.

Changing the Database Backup Interval

By default, the DHCP service backs up its databases every 60 minutes. You can adjust this setting by editing the Backup Interval value under HKEY_LOCAL_MACHINE\SYSTEM\ CurrentControlSet\Services\DHCPServer\Parameters. This allows you to make backups either more frequently (if your database changes a lot or if you seem to have ongoing corruption problems) or less often (if everything seems to be on an even keel).

Moving the DHCP Database Files

You may find that you need to dismantle or change the role of your DHCP server and offload the DHCP functions to another computer. Rather than spend the time re-creating the DHCP database on the new machine by hand, you can copy the database files and use them directly. This is especially helpful if you have a complicated DHCP database with lots of reservations and option assignments.

By copying the files, you also minimize the amount of human error that could be introduced by reentering the information by hand.

Compacting the DHCP Database Files

There may be a time when you need to compact the DHCP database. Microsoft has a utility called jetpack.exe that allows you to compact the JET database. Microsoft JET databases are used for WINS and DHCP databases. If you wanted to use the jetpack command, the proper syntax is:

```
JETPACK.EXE <database name><temp database name>
```

After you compact the database, you rename the temp database to dhcp.mdb.

Working with Advanced DHCP Configuration Options

DHCP makes the life of an administrator easy when it comes to managing the IP addresses of devices within an organization. Could you imagine having to keep track of each device and that device's IP manually? With Windows Server 2016's DHCP high availability and load balancing options available, life gets even easier. The next few sections will cover how to implement advanced DHCP solutions in detail.

Implement DHCPv6

In Windows Server 2016, administrators can create and manage both IPv4 and IPv6 DHCP scopes for their organization. Even though they are managed separately, they have the same capabilities of being able to configure reservations, exclusions, and other DHCP options. Unlike an IPv4 client, a DHCPv6 client uses a device unique identifier (DUID) instead of a MAC address to get an IP address from the DHCP server.

DHCPv6 supports both stateful address configuration and stateless address configuration. An easy way to think of the difference between a stateful configuration and a stateless configuration is that, with a stateful configuration, the DHCPv6 client receives its IPv6 address and its additional DHCP options from the DHCPv6 server. With a stateless configuration, the IPv6 client can automatically assign itself an IPv6 address without ever having to communicate with the DHCPv6 server. The stateless configuration process is also known as *DHCPv6 autoconfiguration*. Exercise 3.9 will walk you through the process of creating and activating a new DHCPv6 scope.

EXERCISE 3.9

Creating and Activating a New DHCPv6 Scope

1. Open the DHCP Management Console.

2. Right-click IPv6 and choose the New Scope command. The New Scope Wizard appears. Click the Next button.

3. On the Welcome To The New Scope Wizard page, click the Next button.

4. On the Scope Name page, provide a name and description for your new DHCPv6 scope. Click the Next button.

5. On the Scope Prefix page, input the corresponding prefix for your organization's IPv6 network settings. In the event that you have more than one DHCPv6 server, you can set a preference value that will indicate your server priority. The lower the preference value, the higher the server priority. Click Next.

6. On the Add Exclusions page of the wizard, you can configure either a single IP exclusion or a range of IPs to exclude from obtaining an address automatically. Exclusions should include any device or range of devices that have been manually set with a static IP on that particular scope. Click Next.

7. Keep the default selections on the Scope Lease page. Click Next.

8. Make sure the Activate Scope Now radio button is toggled to Yes. Click Finish to complete the creation and activation of your new DHCPv6 scope.

9. Verify that your new scope appears in the DHCP Management Console to complete this exercise.

Configure High Availability for DHCP, Including DHCP Failover and Split Scopes

DHCP failover provides load balancing and redundancy for DHCP services, enabling administrators to deploy a highly resilient DHCP service for their organization. The idea is to share your DHCP IPV4 scopes between two Windows Server 2016 servers so that if one of the failover partners goes down, then the other failover partner will continue providing DHCP services throughout the environment. DHCP failover supports large-scale DHCP deployments without the challenges of a split-scope DHCP environment.

Here are a few of the benefits that DHCP failover provides:

Multisite   DHCP failover supports a deployment architecture that includes multiple sites. DHCP failover partner servers do not need to be located at the same physical site.

Flexibility   DHCP failover can be configured to provide redundancy in hot standby mode; or, with load balancing mode, client requests can be distributed between two DHCP servers.

Seamless   DHCP servers share lease information, allowing one server to assume the responsibility for servicing clients if the other server is unavailable. DHCP clients can keep the same IP address when a lease is renewed, even if a different DHCP server issues the lease.

Simplicity   A wizard is provided to create DHCP failover relationships between DHCP servers. The wizard automatically replicates scopes and settings from the primary server to the failover partner.

Configuring DHCP Failover

One of the nice things about DHCP failover is that the configured scope is replicated between both clustered DHCP nodes whether or not you are running the cluster in hot standby or load balancing mode. If one server fails, the other can manage the entire pool of IP addresses on behalf of the environment. Exercise 3.10 provides step-by-step DHCP failover configuration in Windows Server 2016.

EXERCISE 3.10

Configuring DHCP Failover

1. Open the DHCP Management Console.

2. Right-click IPv4 and choose the Configure Failover command to launch the Configure Failover Wizard. Click Next on the Introduction page.

3. On the Specify The Partner Server To Use For Failover page, select your partner DHCP server from the drop-down menu or by browsing the Add Server directory. Click Next.

4. On the Create A New Failover Relationship page, provide a relationship name, select the Load Balance mode from the drop-down, and provide a shared secret password that will be used to authenticate the DHCP failover relationship between the two servers in the failover cluster. Click Next.

EXERCISE 3.10 *(continued)*

5. Review your configuration settings and click the Finish button to configure your new DHCP failover configuration. Click Close upon successful completion.

6. After the wizard successfully completes on the primary DHCP server, verify that the new failover scope has been created and activated on the secondary DHCP server in the DHCP Management Console to complete this exercise.

You can always go back in and change the properties of the failover scope if you want. Test both hot standby and load balancing modes to decide which deployment configuration option best suits your organization's needs. Expect to see exam scenarios discussing both DHCP failover configuration modes and the differences between them.

DHCP Split Scopes

Even though you have the capabilities of DHCP failover in Windows Server 2016, for exam purposes you will need to understand how DHCP split scopes work. Split scopes are configurable only on IPv4 IP addresses and cannot be configured on IPv6 scopes. The idea of DHCP split scopes is to have two stand-alone DHCP servers that are individually responsible for only a percentage of the IP addresses on a particular subnet.

For example, DHCP Server 1 would be responsible for 70 percent of the IP addresses, and DHCP Server 2 would be responsible for the other 30 percent of IP addresses. The two DHCP servers in a split-scope configuration do not share any lease information between one another, and they do not take over for one another in the event that one of the two DHCP servers fails. As you can see, a split-scope configuration is less fault tolerant than a full DHCP failover configuration. However, a split-scope configuration does split the load of DHCP leases and renewals between two servers, providing a basic level of native load balancing in a Windows Server 2016 environment.

DHCP Allow and Deny Filtering

One of the nice things about DHCP is that administrators can use allow or deny filtering to control which devices get an IP address and which devices do not on your network. DHCP filtering is controlled by recording a client's MAC address in a list and then enabling either the Allow or Deny filter. One thing to keep in mind about DHCP filtering is that by enabling the allow list, you automatically deny DHCP addresses to any client computer not on the list. In Exercise 3.11, you will configure DHCP filtering by adding a client machine to the Deny filter by MAC address.

EXERCISE 3.11

Configuring DHCP Filtering

1. Open the DHCP Management Console.

2. Expand IPv4 until you reach the Deny filter object in your DHCP hierarchy.

3. Right-click the Deny filter object and select New Filter.

4. Enter the MAC address of the device you want to exclude from your network, provide a description such as Unwanted Device, click Add, and then click Close.

5. Right-click the Deny filter and select Enable to complete this exercise.

One of the good things about these filters is that you can move devices from one filter to the other quite easily at any time by right-clicking the device in the list and selecting either Move To Allow or Move To Deny. Test both Allow and Deny filters thoroughly while preparing for the exam. You will most likely see multiple scenarios surrounding DHCP filtering.

Configure DHCP Name Protection

DHCP name protection is an additional configuration option that administrators should consider when working DHCP within their environment. Name protection protects a DHCP leased machine's name from being overwritten by another machine with the same name during DNS dynamic updates so that you can configure a Windows 2016 DHCP server to verify and update the DNS records of a client machine during the lease renewal process. If the DHCP server detects that a machine's DNS A and PTR records already exist in the environment when a DHCP update occurs, then that DHCP update will fail on that client machine, making sure not to overwrite the existing server name. There are just a few simple steps needed in order to configure DHCP name protection. Exercise 3.12 will walk you through these steps.

EXERCISE 3.12

Enabling DHCP Name Protection

1. Open the DHCP Management Console.

2. Right-click IPv4 and select Properties.

3. The Server Properties dialog box appears. Click the DNS tab.

4. Verify that Enable DNS Dynamic Updates According To The Settings Below is checked, and verify that the radio button labeled Dynamically Update DNS A And PTR Records Only If Requested By The DHCP Clients is selected.

5. Verify that Discard A And PTR Records When Lease Is Deleted is checked. If not, then check it.

6. Click Configure under Name Protection, and select Enable Name Protection.

7. Click OK twice to complete this exercise.

PowerShell Commands

When talking about PowerShell commands for DHCP, I must let you know that there are dozens of commands that you can use to configure and maintain a DHCP server.

In Table 3.1, I will show you just some of the possible PowerShell commands that are available for DHCP.

 The following list are just some of the PowerShell commands available for DHCP. To see the complete list, visit Microsoft's website at https://technet.microsoft.com/en-us/itpro/powershell/windows/dhcpserver/dhcpserver.

TABLE 3.1 DHCP PowerShell commands

Command	Description
Add-DhcpServerInDC	This command allows an administrator to authorize the DHCP server services in Active Directory.
Add-DhcpServerv4Class	This command allows an administrator to add an IPv4 vendor or user class.
Add-DhcpServerv4ExclusionRange	Administrators can use this command to add an exclusion range to an IPv4 scope.
Add-DhcpServerv4Failover	Administrators can use this command to add an IPv4 failover.
Add-DhcpServerv4Lease	This command allows an administrator to add a new IPv4 address lease.
Add-DhcpServerv4MulticastScope	Administrators use this command to add a multicast scope server.
Add-DhcpServerv4OptionDefinition	This command allows an administrator to add a DHCPv4 option definition.
Add-DhcpServerv4Policy	Admins can use this command to add a new policy to either the server or scope level.
Add-DhcpServerv4Reservation	This command allows an admin to reserve a client IPv4 address in the scope.
Add-DhcpServerv4Scope	This command adds an IPv4 scope.

Command	Description
Add-DhcpServerv6Class	This command allows an administrator to add an IPv6 vendor or user class.
Add-DhcpServerv6ExclusionRange	Administrators can use this command to add an exclusion range to an IPv6 scope.
Add-DhcpServerv6Lease	This command allows an administrator to add a new IPv6 address lease.
Add-DhcpServerv6OptionDefinition	This command allows an administrator to add a DHCPv6 option definition.
Add-DhcpServerv6Reservation	This command allows an admin to reserve a client IPv6 address in the scope.
Add-DhcpServerv6Scope	This command adds an IPv6 scope.
Backup-DhcpServer	Administrators can use this command to back up the DHCP database.
Export-DhcpServer	This command allows an administrator to export the DHCP server configuration and lease data.
Get-DhcpServerAuditLog	This command shows you the audit log for the DHCP configuration.
Get-DhcpServerDatabase	Administrators can use this command to view the configuration parameters of the DHCP database.
Get-DhcpServerSetting	This command allows an admin to view the configuration parameters of the DHCP database.
Get-DhcpServerv4Class	Administrators use this command to view the IPv4 vendor or user class settings.
Set-DhcpServerDatabase	This command allows an administrator to modify configuration settings of the DHCP database.
Set-DhcpServerDnsCredential	Administrators can set the credentials of the DHCP Server service, which help register or deregister client records.
Set-DhcpServerSetting	This command allows an administrator to configure the server-level settings.

TABLE 3.1   DHCP PowerShell commands *(continued)*

Command	Description
Set-DhcpServerv4Class	This command allows an administrator to configure the IPv4 vendor class or user class settings.
Set-DhcpServerv4Failover	This command allows an admin to configure the settings for an existing failover relationship.
Set-DhcpServerv4Policy	Administrators can use this command to configure the settings of a DHCP policy.
Set-DhcpServerv4Reservation	This command allows an administrator to configure an IPv4 reservation.
Set-DhcpServerv4Scope	Admins can use this command to configure the settings of an existing IPv4 scope.
Set-DhcpServerv6Reservation	This command allows an administrator to configure an IPv4 reservation.
Set-DhcpServerv6Scope	Admins can use this command to configure the settings of an existing IPv6 scope.

Summary

In this chapter, I explained how DHCP can help your company by issuing all of the TCP/IP settings to your corporate clients. There are two ways to set up a TCP/IP network: manually or automatic. Manually means that an administrator needs to set up the TCP/IP for each client. Automatic means that your corporate clients get their TCP/IP settings from DHCP.

This chapter covered the DHCP lease process as it relates to TCP/IP configuration information for clients. The following stages were covered: IP discovery, IP lease offer, IP lease selection, and IP lease acknowledgment. I showed you how to install and configure the DHCP server on Windows Server 2016 and how to create and manage DHCP scopes and scope options.

I also discussed the authorization of DHCP servers within Active Directory and scopes for IPv4 and IPv6, and then I showed you how to create them. I also covered superscopes as well as managing client leases with their options.

Exam Essentials

Know how to install and authorize a DHCP server.   You install the DHCP Server service using the Add/Remove Windows Components Wizard. You authorize the DHCP server using the DHCP snap-in. When you authorize a server, you're actually adding its IP address to the Active Directory object that contains a list of the IP addresses of all authorized DHCP servers.

Know how to create a DHCP scope.   You use the New Scope Wizard to create a new scope for both IPv4 and IPv6. Before you start, you'll need to know the IP address range for the scope you want to create; which IP addresses, if any, you want to exclude from the address pool; which IP addresses, if any, you want to reserve; and the values for the DHCP options you want to set, if any.

Understand how relay agents help with multiple physical network segments.   A question about relay agents on the exam may appear to be a DHCP-related question. Relay agents assist DHCP message propagation across network or router boundaries where such messages ordinarily wouldn't pass.

Understand the difference between exclusions and reservations.   When you want to exclude an entire range of IP addresses, you need to add that range as an exclusion. Any IP addresses within the range for which you want a permanent DHCP lease are known as reservations. Remember that exclusions are TCP/IP numbers in a pool that do not get issued and reservations are numbers in a TCP/IP pool that get issued only to the same client each time.

Understand DHCP Failover.   DHCP failover (and load sharing) is one of the hottest new features in Windows Server 2016. It is easy to deploy, and it provides an added level of redundancy when compared to using a DHCP split-scope configuration.

Know How to Configure DHCP Name Protection.   DHCP name protection protects DNS Host A records from being overwritten by other clients' Host A records during DNS dynamic updates. DHCP name protection is configured using the DHCP Management Console.

Review Questions

1. You are the network administrator for a midsize computer company. You have a single Active Directory forest, and you have a requirement to implement DHCP for the organization. You need to ensure that your DHCP deployment configuration is both fault tolerant and redundant. Out of the options provided, which is the most reliable DHCP configuration that you could implement?

   A. DHCP split scope

   B. DHCP multicast scope

   C. DHCP failover

   D. DHCP super scope

2. You are the network administrator for your organization. You need to configure the settings of an existing IPv4 scope. What PowerShell cmdlet would you use?

   A. `Set-DhcpServerScope`

   B. `Set-Serverv4Scope`

   C. `Set-DhcpServerv4Scope`

   D. `Set-DhcpScope`

3. You have decided to split the DHCP scope between two DHCP servers. What is the recommended split that Microsoft states that you should use?

   A. 50/50

   B. 60/40

   C. 70/30

   D. 80/20

4. You are the network administrator for an organization with two servers. The servers are named Server1 and Server2. Server2 is a DHCP server. You want Server1 to help lease addresses for Server2. You add the DHCP role to Server1. What should you do next?

   A. In the DHCP console, run the Configure Failover Wizard.

   B. In the DHCP console, run the Configure Zone Wizard.

   C. On Server2, set the DHCP role to Enabled.

   D. On Server1, start the Share Zone Information Wizard.

5. True or False? You can load DHCP on a Nano Server.

   A. True

   B. False

6. You are the network administrator for a large training company. You have been asked to set up the default gateway setting using DHCP. Which option would you configure?

   A. 003 Router

   B. 006 DNS

    C. 015 DNS Domain Name

    D. 028 Broadcast Address

7. You are the network administrator for your organization. Your DHCP server (Server1) has a scope of 10.10.16.0 to 10.10.16.254 with a subnet mask of /20. You need to ensure that all of the client computers obtain an IP address from Server1. What PowerShell cmdlet would you use?

    A. `Reconcile-DHCPServerv4IPRecord`

    B. `Get-Serverv4Scope`

    C. `Get- DHCPServerv4IPRecord`

    D. `Set-DhcpServerv4Scope`

8. You are the network administrator for a large training company. You have been asked to set up the DNS setting of all your clients using DHCP. Which option would you configure?

    A. 003 Router

    B. 006 DNS

    C. 015 DNS Domain Name

    D. 028 Broadcast Address

9. Your network contains two servers named ServerA and ServerB that run Windows Server 2016. ServerA is a DHCP server that is configured to have a scope named Scope1. ServerB is configured to obtain an IP address automatically. In the scope on ServerA, you create a reservation named ServerB_Reservation for ServerB. A technician replaces the network adapter on ServerB. You need to make sure that ServerB can obtain the same IP address as it did before the network card got replaced. What should you modify on Server1?

    A. The Advanced settings of ServerB_Reservation

    B. The MAC address of ServerB_Reservation

    C. The Network Access Protection settings of Scope1

    D. The Name Protection settings of Scope1

10. You are the network administrator for a large training company. You have one DHCP server called DHCP1. DHCP1 has an IPv4 scope named Scope1. Users report that when they boot up their systems, it takes a long time to access the network. After auditing your network, you notice that it takes a long time for computers to receive their IP addresses from DHCP because the DHCP server sends out five (5) pings before issuing the IP address to the client machine. How do you reduce the amount of time it takes for computers to receive their IP addresses?

    A. Run the DHCP Configuration Wizard.

    B. Create a new IPv4 filter.

    C. Modify the Conflict Detection Attempts setting.

    D. Modify the Ethernet properties of DHCP1.

Chapter

4

Implement IP Address Management

THE FOLLOWING 70-741 EXAM OBJECTIVES ARE COVERED IN THIS CHAPTER:

✓ **Install and configure IP Address Management (IPAM)**

  ▪ This objective may include but is not limited to: Provision IPAM manually or by using Group Policy; configure server discovery; create and manage IP blocks and ranges; monitor utilization of IP address space; migrate existing workloads to IPAM; configure IPAM database storage using SQL Server; determine scenarios for using IPAM with System Center Virtual Machine Manager for physical and virtual IP address space managementDeploy and manage IPAM.

✓ **Manage DNS and DHCP using IPAM**

  ▪ This objective may include but is not limited to: Manage DHCP server properties using IPAM; configure DHCP scopes and options; configure DHCP policies and failover; manage DNS server properties using IPAM; manage DNS zones and records; manage DNS and DHCP servers in multiple Active Directory forests; delegate administration for DNS and DHCP using role-based access control (RBAC); Create and manage IP blocks and ranges.

✓ **Audit IPAM Migrate to IPAM**

  ▪ This objective may include but is not limited to: Audit the changes performed on the DNS and DHCP servers; audit the IPAM address usage trail; audit DHCP lease events and user logon events.

In this book, I have shown you how to work with and configure protocols and services like TCP/IP, DNS, and DHCP. In this chapter, I will show you a tool that allows you to manage and manipulate these services and protocols from one application.

I will show you how you can use the IP Address Management application to manage and configure all of your TCP/IP services. I will show you how you can use this application to do your entire TCP/IP configuration from one location.

Understanding IPAM

One of the great features of Windows Server 2016 is the *IP Address Management (IPAM)* utility. IPAM is a built-in utility that allows an administrator to discover, monitor, audit, and manage the TCP/IP schema used on your network. IPAM provides an administrator with the ability to observe and administer the servers that are running the Dynamic Host Configuration Protocol (DHCP) and the Domain Name System (DNS). IPAM includes some of the following advantages:

Automatic IP Address Infrastructure Discovery IPAM has the ability to discover automatically the domain's DHCP servers, DNS servers, and domain controllers. IPAM can do the discovery for any of the domains you specify. Administrators also have the ability to enable or disable management of these servers using the IPAM utility.

Management of DHCP and DNS Services IPAM gives administrators the capability to monitor and manage Microsoft DHCP and DNS servers across an entire network using the IPAM console. IPAM allows you to configure things as easy as adding a resource record to DNS or as complex as configuring DHCP policies and failover servers.

Custom IP Address Management Administrators now have the ability to customize the display of IP addresses and tracking and utilization data. IPAM allows the IP address space to be organized into IP address blocks, IP address ranges, and individual IP addresses. To help you organize the IP address space further, built-in or user-defined fields are also assigned to the IP addresses.

Multiple Active Directory Forest Support Administrators can manage multiple Active Directory forests using IPAM as long as there is a two-way trust between the two forests.

There may be times when an organization needs to have multiple forests in their structure or when a company purchases another company. Once both forests are connected by a trust, administrators can manage both companies IP services through one application.

Purge Utilization Data   Administrators now have the ability to reduce the size of the IPAM database. This is done by purging the IP address utilization data older than the date that the administrator specifies.

Auditing and Tracking of IP Address   IPAM allows administrators to track and audit IP addresses through the use of the IPAM console. IPAM allows IP addresses to be tracked using DHCP lease events and user logon events. These events are collected from the Network Policy Server (NPS) servers, domain controllers, and DHCP servers. Administrators can track IP data by following the IP address, client ID, hostname, or username.

PowerShell Support   Windows Server 2016 now allows an administrator to manage access scopes on IPAM objects using PowerShell commands.

As an administrator, you should understand a few things before installing the IPAM feature. There are three main methods to deploy an IPAM server:

Distributed   This method allows an IPAM server deployment at every site in an enterprise network.

Centralized   This method allows only one IPAM server in an enterprise network.

Hybrid   This method uses a central IPAM server deployment along with dedicated IPAM servers at each site in the enterprise network.

Installing IPAM

Now that I have started explaining what IPAM can do for your organization, the next step is to install IPAM. When you are thinking of installing IPAM, there are a few considerations that you must think about. So let's start with looking at the hardware and software requirements needed for IPAM.

IPAM Hardware and Software Requirements

So let's start with the main requirement. IPAM must be loaded onto a Windows Server. Since this is a Windows Server 2016 book, I would recommend that you use Windows Server 2016. However, you can load IPAM onto a Windows Server 2008, 2008 R2, 2012, or 2012 R2 system.

You can also load an IPAM client (this allows you to remotely operate IPAM) onto any Windows 7 or higher system. Before the IPAM client can be used, you must first install the Remote Server Administration Tools (RSAT). You need to make sure that you install the proper version of RSAT based on the version of Windows you have installed.

Your network needs to be a domain. Workgroup networks are not supported by IPAM. So the server on which you decide to install IPAM needs to be part of a domain but it can't be a domain controller. Domain controllers are servers that are part of a domain and have a copy of the Active Directory database. When you install IPAM, you HAVE to load it on a Member Server.

IPAM will work on both an IPv4 and IPv6 network. The member server that you install IPAM onto must be able to see and connect to the other servers on your network. If the IPAM server is not able to access the other servers (like DNS and DHCP), the IPAM server will not be able to help monitor and maintain these servers.

One of the advantages of IPAM is that the IPAM server will automatically discover other servers on your network. Server discovery requires the IPAM server to be able to access at least one domain controller and an authoritative DNS server.

Microsoft's best practices are to place the IPAM server onto its own server. You should *NOT* put the IPAM server on a server with other network services like DNS or DHCP. For example, DHCP server discovery will be automatically disabled if you install IPAM and DHCP onto the same server.

This makes IPAM a good candidate for virtual machines or containers. By using a virtual machine or container for the IPAM installation, you don't give up all of the hardware resources of a powerful server for just one feature. Some other IPAM specifications and features are as follows:

- Server discovery for IPAM is limited to a single Active Directory forest.

- IPAM can manage DNS and DHCP servers belonging to a different AD forest as long as a two-way trust relationship is set up between your forest and the other forest. The servers in the other forest will need to be manually entered into IPAM.

- IPAM only works with Microsoft servers (domain controllers, DHCP, DNS, and NPS) using Windows Server 2008 and above.

- IPAM only supports Microsoft-based systems. IPAM does not support non-Microsoft network devices.

- IPAM only supports Windows Internal Database (WID) or SQL Server. Other database engines are not supported.

- Windows Server 2016 IPAM now supports /31, /32, and /128 subnets.

- Windows Server 2016 IPAM now supports DNS resource records, conditional forwarders, and DNS zone management for both primary zones and primary zones with Active Directory integration.

- You can now purge IP address utilization data, thus reducing the size of the IPAM database.

So let's go ahead and install the IPAM feature. Exercise 4.1 will show you how to install the IPAM feature. You will install and configure the IPAM feature using Server Manager. Remember, this exercise has to be done on a member server.

EXERCISE 4.1

Installing the IPAM Feature

1. Open Server Manager.

2. Click the number 2 link, Add Roles And Features. If the Before You Begin screen appears, just click Next.

3. Choose a role-based or feature-based installation and click Next.

4. Choose your server and click Next.

5. On the Roles screen, just click Next.

6. On the Features screen, click the box for the IP Address Management (IPAM) server (see Figure 4.1). Click the Add Features button when the box appears. Click Next.

FIGURE 4.1   Choosing the IPAM feature

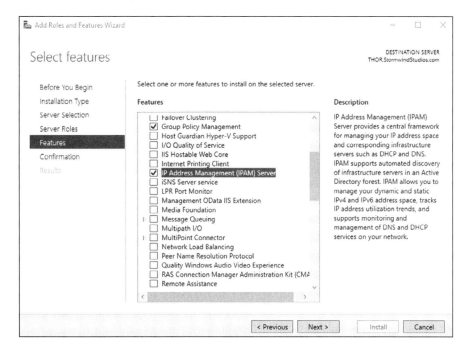

7. At the Confirmation screen, make sure the check box Restart The Destination Server Automatically If Required is selected (see Figure 4.2) and then click the Install button.

EXERCISE 4.1 *(continued)*

FIGURE 4.2 Confirmation Screen

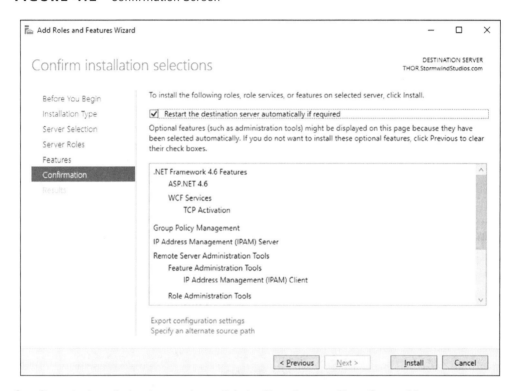

8. Once the installation is complete, click the Close button. Close Server Manager.

9. In the Add Servers box, click the DNS tab. In the search box, type the name of your DNS server and click the magnifying glass.

10. Under Name, double-click the server name. The server will be added to the right-side box. Click OK. Close Server Manager.

Provision IPAM Manually or by Using Group Policy

When setting up an IPAM server, you must determine how the IPAM server will communicate with your other servers. This is called IPAM provisioning. IPAM provisioning can be set up two ways, manually or by using GPOs.

IPAM will try to locate your DNS servers, DHCP servers, and domain controllers as long as those servers are within the searching scope that you have configured. An administrator can configure whether the servers (DNS, DHCP, and domain controllers) are managed by IPAM or unmanaged. Please note that this will work only with Microsoft products; it won't find Infoblox or Unix-based DNS/DHCP.

If you want your servers to be managed by IPAM, you must make sure you set up the network and the servers properly. For example, you will need to configure the security settings and firewall ports properly on the servers (DNS, DHCP, and domain controllers) in order to allow IPAM to access these servers and perform its configuration and monitoring.

Once you have decided to use the Group Policy provisioning method, you will be required to create a GPO name prefix in the provisioning wizard (I use IPAM1 in Exercise 4.2). Once you have set up the GPO name prefix, the provisioning wizard will show you the names of the GPOs that you will need to create. You will be required to either manually create or automatically create (using PowerShell) the GPOs for the different servers.

If you decide to manually create the GPOs, then you will need to open the Group Policy Management Console and then create a GPO for each of the different server types that IPAM will manage. This is a more difficult way to create the GPOs. It is easier to create the provisioned GPOs automatically.

To create these provisioned GPOs automatically, you will need to use the `Invoke-IpamGpoProvisioning` cmdlet at an elevated Windows PowerShell prompt.

The following is an example of the `Invoke-IpamGpoProvisioning` command. In this example, the IPAM server is named IPAMServer. The name of our domain is StormWindStudios.com and the GPO Prefix name will be IPAM1. As you will see in the command, I added a `-Force` switch to the end of the command. This switch forces the PowerShell command to run without asking the user for confirmation.

```
Invoke-IpamGPOProvioning -Domain StormWindStudios.com -GpoPrefixName IPAM1
-IpamServerFqdn IPAMServer.StormWindStudios.com -Force
```

After you run the `Invoke-IpamGpoProvisioning` command, new GPOs will be created based on your network setup. For example, I am running a domain controller and NPS together. So the GPOs may look like the following:

- \<GPO-prefix>_DHCP

- \<GPO-prefix>_DNS

- \<GPO-prefix>_DC_NPS

The created GPOs will all have the GPO prefix name that you used in the `Invoke-IpamGpoProvisioning` command. For example, I used IPAM1 in the above `Invoke-IpamGPOProvisioning` command. So my actual GPOs look like the following:

- IPAM1_DHCP

- IPAM1_DNS

- IPAM1_DC_NPS

In order for IPAM to automatically manage these servers, you must create these GPOs. After the GPOs are created, IPAM will be able to manage these servers through the IPAM console. When an IPAM server no longer manages these servers (servers will be shown as unmanaged), the GPOs can be removed.

The IPAM server needs to be able to manipulate the GPOs directly. To ensure that IPAM can manage the GPOs directly, you must make sure that the GPO security filtering includes the IPAM servers. If the IPAM servers are not added to the security filtering for the GPOs, the IPAM server will not be able to manage these other servers (DNS, DHCP, and NPS).

In Exercise 4.2, I will walk you through the process of provisioning your IPAM server. I will also show you how to create the GPOs needed for the IPAM provisioning and then I will show you how to add the IPAM servers to the GPOs security filter. To complete this exercise properly, you will need to log into the IPAM server with a domain admin account or higher.

EXERCISE 4.2

Provisioning an IPAM Server

1. Open Server Manager.

2. Click the IPAM link on the left side. This opens the IPAM Overview page.

3. Click number 2, Provision the IPAM Server (see Figure 4.3).

FIGURE 4.3   IPAM Overview screen

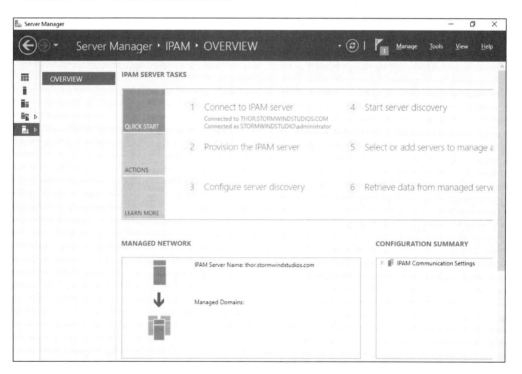

4. Click Next at the Before You Begin screen.

5. At this screen, you will need to setup a database for IPAM. You can either use the Windows Internal Database (WID) or a Microsoft SQL Server. If you choose to use a WID (I am using a WID in this exercise), you will need to put in a location for the database storage. Make your database selection on the Configure Database screen and click Next.

6. At the Select Provisioning Method screen, choose GPO and put in a GPO suffix name. I used IPAM1 for the GPO suffix name (see Figure 4.4).

FIGURE 4.4   Select Provisioning

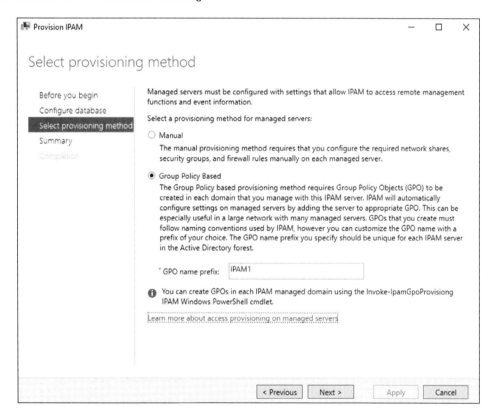

7. At the Summary screen, write down the names of the GPOs that you need to create (see Figure 4.5). Click the Apply button.

FIGURE 4.5 GPOs Needed

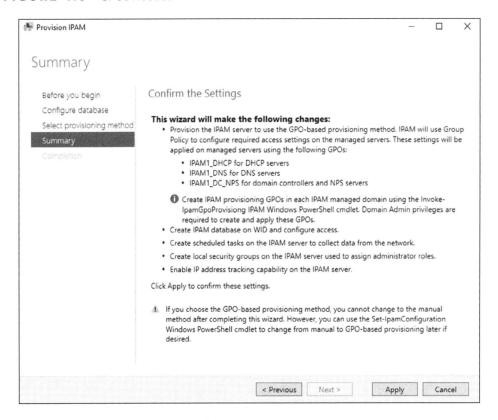

8. Once the process is completed, click the Close button.

9. Close Server Manager.

10. Open PowerShell

11. Type in the following command and hit Enter. Make sure to change the domain name, GPO suffix name, and the IPAM server name to match your settings. I used StormWindStudios.com as my domain, IPAM1 as my GPO Prefix name, and Mercury as my IPAM server name.

    ```
    Invoke-IpamGPOProvisioning -Domain StormwindStudios.com
    -GPOPrefixName IPAM1 -IpamServerFqdn Mercury.StormwindStudios.com -Force
    ```

12. You will be asked to confirm the installation of the GPOs. This is normally asked three times. When asked to confirm, click Y and hit Enter for all three.

13. After the command has finished, close PowerShell.

14. On your domain controller, open the Group Policy Management Console.

15. Under the Forest, expand Domains and then expand the name of your domain. You should now see the three new GPOs (see Figure 4.6).

FIGURE 4.6   New GPOs

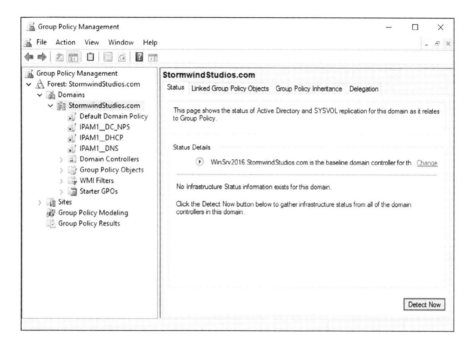

16. Click on the GPO that you want to configure. For example, if you are adding a managed DHCP server, click the GPO name ending in _DHCP.

17. On the Scope tab, under the Security Filtering section, click the Add button.

18. In the Select User, Computer, or Group window, click the Object Types button.

19. Select the Computers check box, and then click OK.

20. Under the section called Enter The Object Name To Select, type the name of the IPAM server and click the Check Names button. If the name is proper, the server name will become underlined. Click OK.

21. Repeat steps 16 through 20 for the other IPAM GPOs. Only do these steps for every server that you currently have. For example, if you only have a DHCP and DNS server, do these steps for just these two servers.

22. When you've completed the GPOs, close the Group Policy Management Console.

Configure Server Discovery

Once you have successfully installed and provisioned the IPAM feature on your Windows Server 2016 machine, you can begin server discovery. One of the great things about IPAM is that you can define multiple domains within the same forest to be managed by a single IPAM server.

Once initiated, server discovery will automatically search for all of the machines running on the specified domain. Administrator privileges are required for the domain against which you are running server discovery. Exercise 4.3 will walk you through the server discovery process.

EXERCISE 4.3

Configuring IPAM Server Discovery

1. Open Server Manager and select IPAM.

2. On the IPAM Overview page, select option 3, Configure Server Discovery.

3. On the Configure Server Discovery page, select and add the forest and domains you want to discover and click OK. When you add the domain, it should appear under the Select The Server Roles To Discover section and Domain Controller, DNS, and DHCP should be checked (see Figure 4.7).

FIGURE 4.7   Configuring server discovery

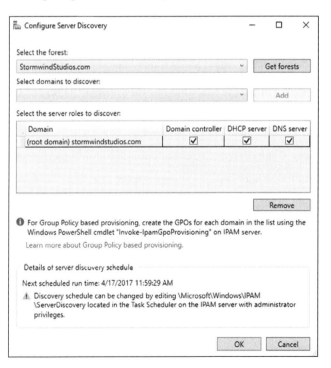

4. On the IPAM Overview page, select option 4, Start Server Discovery. The task will run in the background. You will receive notification once server discovery has completed.

5. On the IPAM home page, select Server Inventory to review the now-completed server discovery of the requested domain (see Figure 4.8). This may take a few minutes and you may need to refresh Server Manager.

FIGURE 4.8   Server Inventory screen

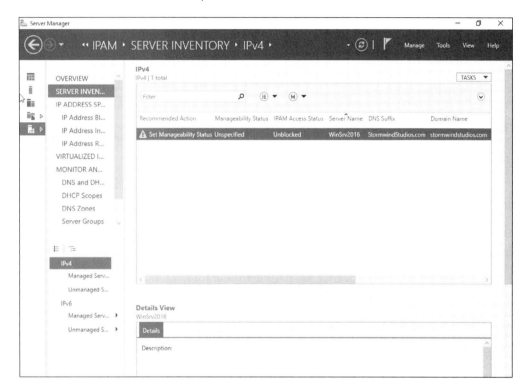

6. Close Server Manager.

Create and Manage IP Blocks and Ranges

In IPAM, IP address space is divided into addresses, ranges, and blocks. Blocks are groups of ranges, and ranges are groups of IP Addresses. Here you will find a breakdown of each IP Management space found within IPAM:

IP Addresses   Individual IP addresses map to a single IP address range. When you map an IP address to a range, it enables actions to be taken on a range that affect all IP addresses in the range, such as adding, updating, or deleting IP address fields.

IP Address Ranges   IP address ranges are smaller chunks of IP addresses that typically correspond to a DHCP scope. IP address ranges are contained within, or "mapped to," IP address blocks. IP address ranges cannot map to multiple IP address blocks, and ranges that map to the same block cannot overlap.

IP Address Blocks   IP address blocks are large chunks of IP addresses that are used to organize address space at a high level. For example, you might use one IP address block for all private IP addresses in your organization and another block for public IP addresses. You can think of IP address blocks as containers that hold IP address ranges. IP address blocks are not deployed and managed on the network like IP address ranges or individual IP addresses.

When you have an IPAM-managed DHCP server, the IP address ranges found within the scopes of that DHCP server are automatically entered into the IPAM database during the discovery process. Individual IP addresses and IP blocks are not automatically added to the IPAM database.

Exercise 4.4 will demonstrate how to add an IP address manually and also on how to add an IP address block. I will be adding the IP address of my DNS/DHCP server.

EXERCISE 4.4

Manually Add IPAM IP Address and Blocks

1.   Open Server Manager and select IPAM.

2.   Select IP Address Blocks.

3.   Right-click IPv4 and select Add IP Address.

4.   Enter the IP address of the device that is to be managed by IPAM. Keep all other defaults.

5.   Click Apply.

6.   On the Summary page, verify that the task completed successfully. Click OK.

7.   Your new IP address is now managed by IPAM. You can now both create and delete DHCP reservations and DNS records for this IP address space from inside the IPAM management console.

8.   Right-click IPv4 and select Add IP Address Block.

9.   Fill in the following fields and click OK:

     Network ID: 10.10.16.0

     Leave all other fields as defaults.

10. Close Server Manager.

Managing Services

One of the nicest advantages of using IPAM is the ability to manage and maintain your DNS and DHCP servers from one location. Normally in a corporate environment, the IT department will use the DNS console and the DHCP console to configure these services. With IPAM, you can open one application and configure many of the IP services from one location.

So let's start by learning how to configure and manage your DNS servers from IPAM.

Managing DNS

Domain Name System (DNS) is the default name resolution service used by Windows Server 2016. Let's talk about TCP/IP for a moment. TCP/IP is just like a telephone number. Every computer gets its own telephone number (TCP/IP address). Now just like the telephone system, when you don't know a number, you call information and ask for the number. This is exactly what DNS does. DNS turns a host name into a TCP/IP number.

There are many different ways to configure and manage a DNS server. IPAM is just another tool for doing DNS management but the nice advantage of using IPAM is the ability to also manage other IP services.

In Windows Server 2016, IPAM allows an administrator to configure DNS resource record, conditional forwarder, server properties, and DNS zone management. IPAM allows an administrator to manage DNS for both Active Directory integration and file based DNS servers (see Figure 4.9). Finally, IPAM can manage and maintain DNS servers in multiple Active Directory forests.

FIGURE 4.9   IPAM DNS Management

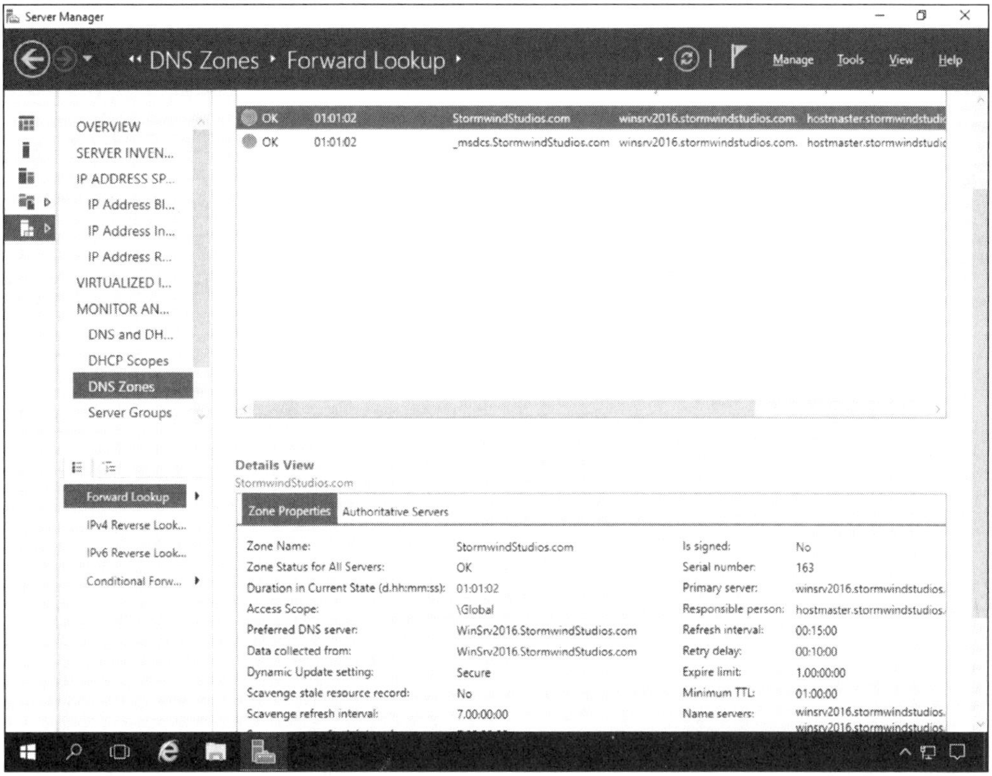

When using the IPAM console to configure DNS, it's easy to manage and maintain the DNS settings. Let's start with some of the basics like adding DNS resource records.

Resource records are the database records used by DNS. There are many types of records including Host records (A or AAAA), Reverse Lookup records (PTR), Mail Exchange records (MX), and Name Server records (NS) to just name a few.

In Exercise 4.5, I will show you how to add a few resource records to the DNS zone using IPAM.

EXERCISE 4.5

Adding Resource Records

1. Open Server Manager.

2. Click on the IPAM section and choose DNS Zones (under Monitor and Manage).

3. Right click the name of your zone and choose Add DNS Resource record (see Figure 4.10).

FIGURE 4.10 Adding DNS records

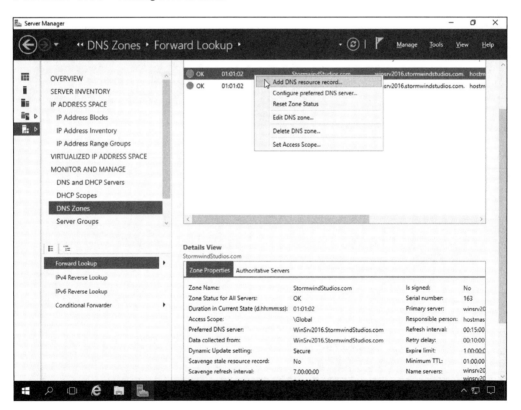

4. When the Add Resource Record wizard starts, make sure the DNS zone is chosen along with the DNS server. Click the New button.

5. Fill in the following properties and click Create Resource record (see Figure 4.11);

Resource record type: A

Name: TestBox

FQDN: Testbox.YourDNSDomain.xxx

IP Address: Enter an IP address of an Unused IP.

Make sure the Checkbox is checked for Create assoiciated pointer (PTR) record.

FIGURE 4.11   Adding A Record

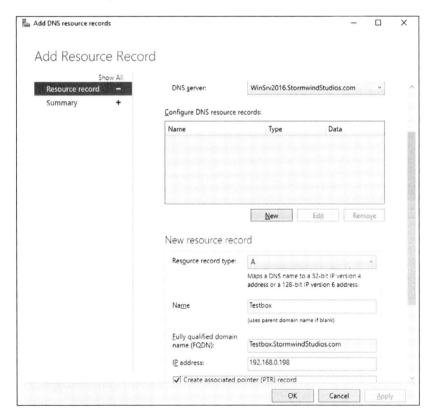

6. Once the record is added to the list, click the OK button for the wizard.

7. Open your DNS server and verify that the record is created as shown in Figure 4.12.

EXERCISE 4.5 *(continued)*

FIGURE 4.12 Verifying the DNS record

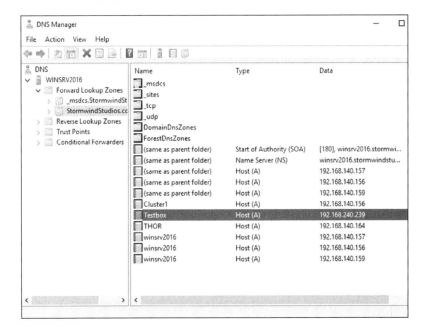

In Exercise 4.5, I showed you how to add a Resource Record to DNS using IPAM. Now let's take a look at configuring the DNS zone using IPAM. In Exercise 4.6, I will show you how to manage the DNS zone using IPAM.

EXERCISE 4.6

Managing the DNS zone

1. Open Server Manager.

2. Click on IPAM on left side.

3. Click on DNS Zones under Monitor and Manage.

4. Right click on the zone name and choose Edit DNS Zone (see Figure 4.13).

5. The Edit DNS Zone wizard appears. Make sure all zone information is correct. Click on Advanced.

6. In the Advanced settings, set the No-refresh interval and Refresh interval for 5 days (see Figure 4.14). Make sure all the other settings are correct. Once everything is verified, click on the SOA link.

FIGURE 4.13   Managing the DNS Zone

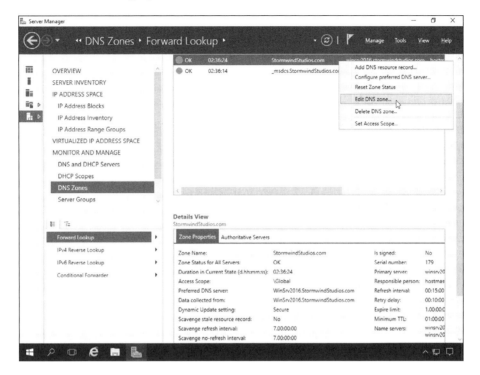

FIGURE 4.14   DNS Zone Advanced Properties

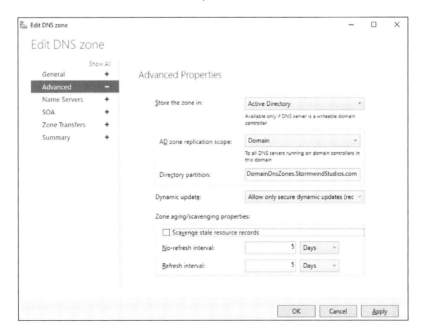

EXERCISE 4.6 *(continued)*

7. Check all of the values under the SOA page and make sure that everything is setup correctly. If you would like to force replication between DNS servers, increase the Serial Number by 1. Then click on Zone Transfers.

8. Make sure that the zone transfers are setup to only DNS servers that you trust. Click on the Summary link.

9. At this point, you will need to click on the Apply button to save your changes.

10. Close Server Manager.

As you have seen from exercises 4.5 and 4.6, you can manage and manipulate DNS from IPAM. Besides adding Resource Records or changing the zone properties, administrators can also configure the DNS preferred server, reset zone status, delete the DNS zone, and set access scopes. IPAM allows you to configure both IPv4 and IPv6 networks.

Now that we have looked at configuring DNS using IPAM, now it's time to look at how to configure DHCP using IPAM.

Managing DHCP

In the section called "Managing DNS," I used an example of TCP/IP working just like the telephone system. DHCP in this example would be the telephone company that issues you a telephone number. DHCP issues TCP/IP addresses to all of your users.

Administrators can use IPAM to configure many of the DHCP options. For example, you can use IPAM to configure the following DHCP options (as seen in Figure 4.15):

- DHCP Server Properties
- DHCP Server Options
- Create DHCP Scope
- Configure Predefined DHCP Options
- Configure DHCP User Classes
- Configure DHCP Vendor Classes
- Configure DHCP Policy
- Import DHCP Policy
- Add DHCP MAC Address Filtering
- Launch the DHCP Console
- Activate or Deactivate Policies

- Setup DHCP Failover Servers
- Replicate DHCP Servers
- Set Access Scope
- Retrieve Server Data

FIGURE 4.15   Configuring DHCP using IPAM

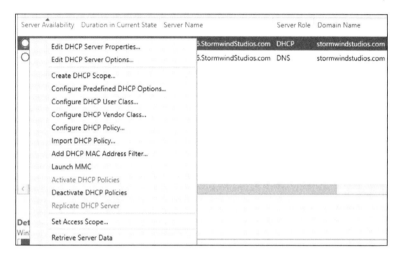

In Exercise 4.7, I will show you how to start configuring DHCP using IPAM. I will start by showing you how to use IPAM to create a new DHCP Scope.

EXERCISE 4.7

Creating a DHCP Scope

1. Open Server Manager.

2. Click on IPAM.

3. Click on DNS and DHCP Servers link under Monitor and Manage.

4. Right click on the DHCP server in the right hand window. Choose Create DHCP Scope (see Figure 4.16).

5. When the Create Scope wizard appears, fill in the following information (as seen in Figure 4.17).

    Scope Name: Scope1

    Description: Scope for Sybex Book

Start IP: 10.10.16.1

Ending IP: 10.10.31.254

Subnet Mask: 255.255.240.0

DHCP Lease: 8 Days

Activate Scope on Creation: NO

All DNS Settings leave blank.

　　Under Scope Options, add the following information:

　　　　003 Router: 10.10.10.1

　　　　006 DNS: 10.10.10.2

FIGURE 4.16　Create DHCP Scope

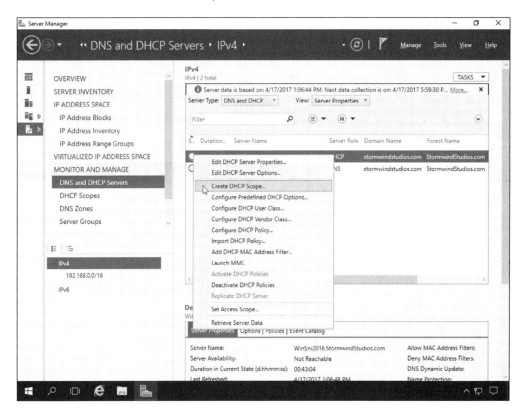

FIGURE 4.17   DHCP Scope settings

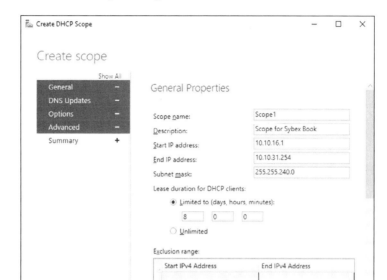

6.   Once all the settings are completed, click OK.

7.   Once the wizard completes, close Server Manager.

Now that you have setup your DHCP Scope using IPAM, now I will show you how to setup DHCP Policies. In Exercise 4.8, I will show you how to setup DHCP Policies for MAC addresses and lease times. What this will do for us is give us a shorter lease for any system with the same beginning MAC address.

EXERCISE 4.8

Setting up DHCP Policies

1.   Open Server Manager.

2.   Click on IPAM.

3.   Click on DNS and DHCP Servers link under Monitor and Manage.

4.   Right click on the DHCP server in the right hand window. Choose Configure DHCP Policy (see Figure 4.18).

FIGURE 4.18   Configuring DHCP Policy

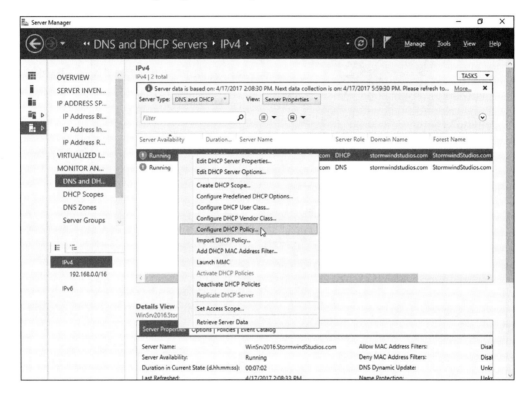

5.   Fill in the following properties (see Figure 4.19):

Name: Test Policy

Description: DHCP Policy for Sybex Book

Set lease duration for Policy Checked and set for 1 day

Under Policy Conditions - Click the New button

Criteria: MAC Address

Operation: Equals

Value: 462F68

Use Wildcard (*): Checked

Click the Add button next to Value. Then click the Add Condition button. Then hit the OK button.

FIGURE 4.19   DHCP Policy settings

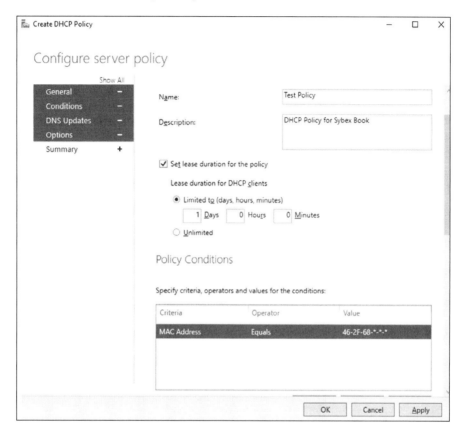

6.   Close Server Manager.

Now that I have shown you how to use IPAM to configure DNS and DHCP, I will now show you how to setup IPAM auditing.

IPAM Access and Auditing

It is essential for network administrators to be able to monitor and manage their IP address infrastructure well. This grows increasingly difficult as your network gets bigger and becomes more complex. Unfortunately, quite a few administrators still rely on spreadsheets and basic database applications for IP tracking and usage. The problem is that manual tracking is time-consuming and prone to error.

IPAM tracks the service status of the DNS and DHCP servers on the network. By aggregating multiple DHCP servers, the Multiserver Management (MSM) module enables an administrator to perform editing and configuration of important properties on multiple DHCP servers and scopes. It also facilitates surveillance and tracking of DHCP service status and utilization of DHCP scopes. IPAM allows for monitoring the condition of a DNS zone on multiple DNS servers by exposing the collected status of a zone across all authoritative DNS servers.

IPAM also comes with its own event catalog that allows administrators to track both DHCP and DNS correlated events. Administrators can use the event catalog to audit the changes performed on the DNS and DHCP servers, audit the IPAM address usage trail, monitor utilization of IP address space, and audit DHCP lease events and user logon events.

The nice thing about this event log is that you can easily search by client hostname, client ID, username, or IP address for a full list of both DNS and DHCP related events on that client. You can also export these event logs to an Excel workbook. The event catalog (see Figure 4.20) is found toward the bottom of the IPAM hierarchical navigation window.

FIGURE 4.20   IPAM event catalog

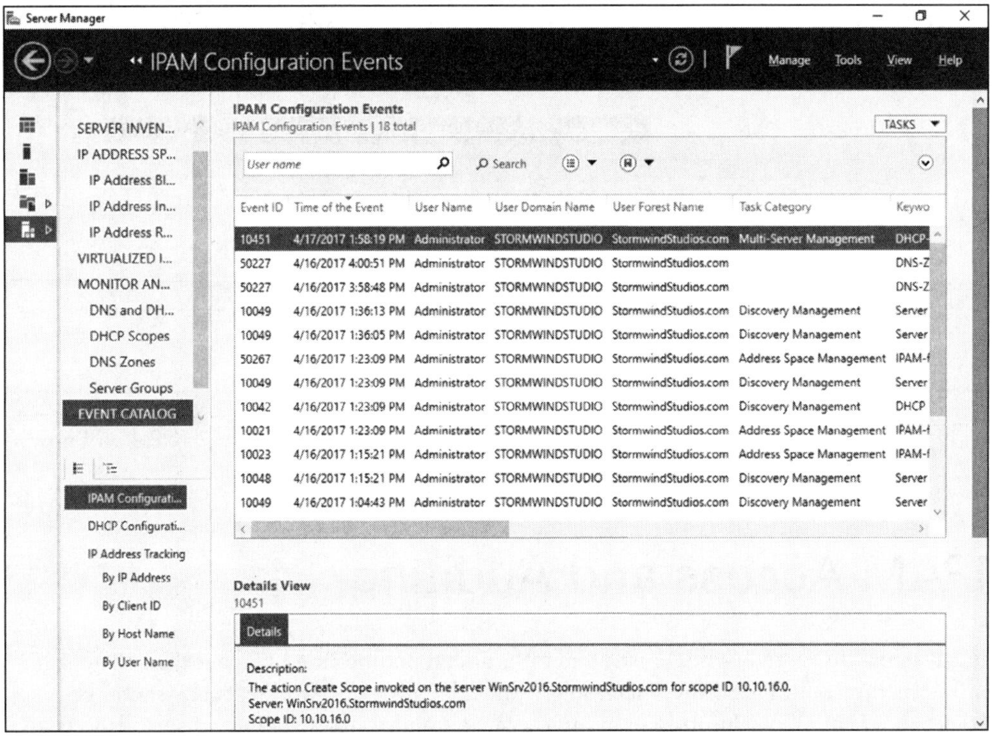

If you want to use the event catalog to check errors or issues with DNS and DHCP, click on the event message. You want to look at the event ID and the task category. You can enter these into TechNet or your favorite search engine and see what the event issue is and how to fix it.

When I first starting using TechNet in Windows NT 4.0, I learned how valuable it could be to help me locate and fix issues with my server. Microsoft still uses TechNet on the Internet, and you can search the event IDs and find out how to solve many of your issues.

 If you would like to use Microsoft TechNet, go to the following Microsoft website and enter your search in the search bar: `https://technet .microsoft.com/en-us/`.

Migrate to IPAM

There are two possible IPAM database storage solutions. An administrator can use either a Windows Internal Database (WID) or a dedicated Microsoft SQL Server instance for their IPAM configuration. For smaller networks, a WID backend will work just fine for the initial IPAM deployment. If in the future the need arises to expand past a WID to a SQL database, then you already know that IPAM comes with migration functionality just for that situation. The database configuration options are chosen during the provisioning steps of an IPAM deployment.

Fully deploy and test the capabilities of the IPAM feature set to help track and forecast IP address utilization within your organization. IPAM is a great way to discover, monitor, and manage all of the TCP/IP devices on your network.

The situation may arise in which you must migrate your IPAM database infrastructure either from a Windows Internal Database (WID) to a Microsoft SQL database or from one SQL server to another. Windows Server 2016 IPAM comes with the functionality to migrate an IPAM database via PowerShell. The `Move-IpamDatabase` cmdlet is used to complete this operation. When this cmdlet is run, a new IPAM schema is created, and then all of the IP address information is copied over. You can also use the `Get-IpamDatabase` cmdlet to review and compare pre- and post-database configuration settings during an IPAM database migration.

Delegate IPAM Administration

The delegation of IPAM administration is similar to the delegation of DNS. When IPAM is installed and provisioned, new security groups become available to administrators to configure role-based access control (RBAC) within your IPAM infrastructure. The five security groups for IPAM administration are as follows:

IPAM Administrators   Members of this group have full permissions to manage and administer an IPAM infrastructure.

IPAM IP Audit Administrators   Members of this group can perform common IPAM management tasks and can carry out IPAM audits.

IPAM ASM Administrators   Members of this group can perform tasks related to IP address space management (ASM) functionality.

IPAM MSM Administrator   Members of this group can perform tasks across multiple IPAM servers through the IPAM multiserver management (MSM) functionality.

IPAM Users   Members of this group can only view information about server discovery, ASM, and MSM in IPAM. They can also view operational events, but they have no access to tracking or auditing information.

One new feature to Windows Server 2016 IPAM is the ability to configure Role Based Access Control using Windows PowerShell. IPAM also comes with an Access Control feature, which allows administrators to get even more granular with IPAM permissions by using up to eight different preconfigured roles.

You can also create your own custom IPAM administration roles for full IPAM permissions flexibility within your environment. Figure 4.21 illustrates the new Access Control panel for IPAM delegation of administration. Take the time to add and remove users from each of these groups and roles to get used to IPAM permission sets.

FIGURE 4.21   IPAM Access Control

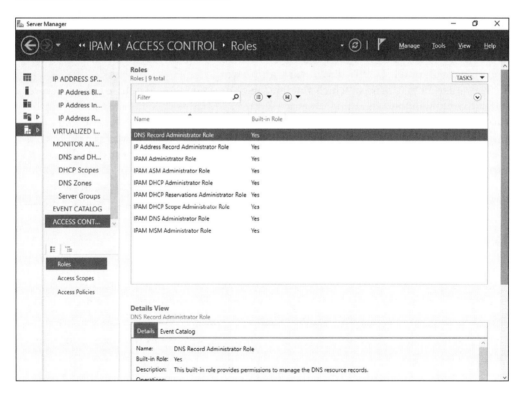

In Exercise 4.9, I will show you how to configure RBAC for IPAM using Server Manager.

EXERCISE 4.9

Configuring Role-Based Access Control

1. Open Server Manager.

2. Click on IPAM.

3. Click Access Control in the navigation window. Click Roles in the lower navigation window.

4. Right-click Roles and choose Add User Role (see Figure 4.22).

FIGURE 4.22   Add User Role

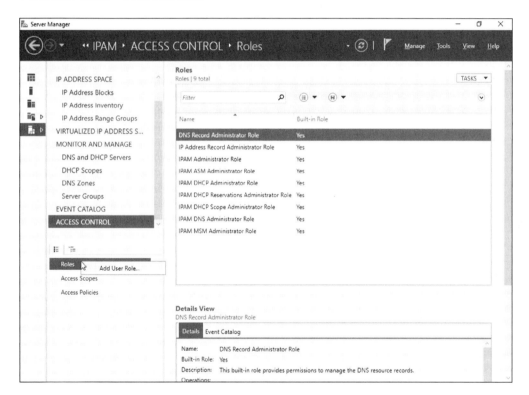

5. Fill in the following fields and check boxes (see Figure 4.23). Then click OK. In the Operations section, you can expand any of the operations and choose more fine-grained options. I am choosing a few random operations. You can choose whichever operations you want this account to have access to.

Name: IPAM_TeamMember

Description: IPAM Role for IT Team

EXERCISE 4.9 *(continued)*

Operations:

DHCP Server Operations

DHCP Scope Operations

DHCP Reservation Operations

DNS Zone Operations

IP Address Subnet Operations

IP Address Operations

DNS Server Operations

FIGURE 4.23 User Operations

6. You should be able to see your new role under the Roles section. Close Server Manager.

Manage IPAM Collections

In IPAM, server groups are logical groups used to organize managed DHCP and DNS servers. Servers are members of a server group based on values of custom fields that are assigned to the server. Having servers of the same type sorted into their own IPAM collections makes it easier to manage your server lists within the IPAM Management Console. Drop-down menus will allow you to filter server and task lists by IPAM service categories such as DNS or DHCP servers.

Virtual Machine Manager and IPAM

IPAM gives you the ability to work with virtual machines and set up and monitor both physical and virtual IP address spaces. Inside the IPAM console, there is a link called Virtualized IP Address Space. Once you have clicked on this link, you can then add or view both customer and provider IP address spaces. For example, administrators have the ability to view logical networks under the Provider IP Address Space.

Administrators can also create a logical network within IPAM. To do this, an administrator would click Virtualized IP Address Space in the IPAM console and then right-click Provider IP Address Space in the lower navigation window. They would then choose Add IP Address Space and then need to fill in all of the fields.

 If you would like to see all the steps needed for creating a virtual and logical network, visit Microsoft's website at

https://technet.microsoft.com/en-us/library/
dn783485(v=ws.11).aspx

There may be times when you want to have your virtual machines and your IPAM server to work even more closely together. You can do this by integrating System Center Virtual Machine Manager (SCVMM) and IPAM. To do this, you need to first configure a user account (you must be part of the Administrators group or higher) that can be used on both the IPAM server and the System Center Virtual Machine Manager server. Then you need to configure the IPAM network service plug-in in VMM.

You must then give permission for the VMM server to be able to view and configure the IP address space in the IPAM server. The VMM server must also be able to perform management of the IPAM server remotely. To set this up, the VMM server uses the "Run As" account to achieve the permissions needed to configure the IPAM network service plug-in.

The following are the steps needed to create the VMM user account.

1. Open an elevated command prompt on the IPAM server. At the command prompt, type **lusrmgr.msc** and press Enter. This will open the Local Users and Groups MMC.

2. You need to create a new group. To do this, right-click Groups and choose New Group.

3. When the New Group dialog box appears, type **VMM Users** in the Group Name spot.

4. In the Enter The Object Names To Select section, click Add. Then type in the username of the user account that you will use for the VMM server and click OK.

5. Click Create to create the group and then click Close.

6. Close the Local Users and Groups MMC.

After the group is created, you need to next assign the necessary permissions to the VMM user account that you chose in the previous steps:

1. On the IPAM server, open Server Manager and choose the IPAM server console.

2. Choose Access Control in the upper navigation pane.

3. In the lower navigation windows, Right-click on Access Policies and then click Add Access Policy.

4. Click the Add button and then add the name of the VMM Users group that you created previously. Then click the OK button.

5. Next you need to click on Access Settings. Then click New and then from the drop-down list under Select Role, choose the IPAM ASM Administrator Role. Make sure the Global Access Scope is selected and then click the OK button.

6. Right-click Remote Management Users in the Local Users and Groups console, and then click Add to Group.

7. Next you will need to click the Add button and then type in the VMM user account under Enter the object names to select. Click the OK button.

8. Close the Remote Management Users Properties by clicking the OK button.

Finally, you need to configure the VMM server. To configure the server, you would need to complete the following steps:

1. Expand the Networking node in the Fabric workspace and then click Network Service.

2. Right-click Network Service and then click Add Network Service. This will start the Add Network Service Wizard.

3. On the Name page, type **IPAM** next to Name. You can add something to the Description field or leave it blank. Click Next.

4. The Manufacturer And Model screen is next. Choose Microsoft next to Manufacturer and choose Microsoft Windows Server IP Address Management next to the Model field. Click Next.

5. When the Credentials page appears, click the Browse button next to Run As Account. Click the Create Run As Account button.

6. When the Create Run As Account page appears, type a name for the account. I used VMM User1. Enter the username and password created earlier on the IPAM server. Click OK once you're finished.

7. At the Select A Run As Account dialog box, click the OK button to close. Click Next.

8. At the Connection String screen, enter the fully qualified domain name (FQDN) of the IPAM server. Then click Next.

9. The Provider screen will be next. Make sure the Microsoft IPAM Provider is chosen (at the Configuration provider field) and then click Test.

10. Make sure that there is a Passed message next to the Test open connection, Test capability discovery, and Test system info sections. Click Next.

11. On the Host Group screen, select the check box All Hosts. This enables IPAM integration with SCVMM. Click Next.

12. Click the Finish button at the Summary screen.

13. Make sure that the Completed status is next to the Add network service device and Create new RunAs Account fields. Close all applications.

Auditing IPAM

One of the nicest advantages to IPAM is the ability to audit the different services that you are monitoring. In today's complex IT world, we all have many different servers and applications that we are running to get our job done. We use Microsoft products and non-Microsoft products to accomplish the tasks that help our end users do their jobs more efficiently.

One of the issues that we have because of using all of these different servers and applications is knowing how they all operate and making sure we are keeping these products operating at max performance.

As an IT member today, you have to be a jack-of-all-trades when it comes to networking technologies. This is where auditing really comes into play. Being able to audit a server, services, or applications allows us to make sure that we are running these products the way they should be run.

Once you decide that you are going to be using IPAM for all of your IP based services, you now also get a single application to monitor all of these services.

IPAM allows you to audit the changes performed on the DNS and DHCP servers, audit the IPAM address usage trail, audit DHCP lease events, and audit user logon events (to just name a few).

This is very easy to do since we are using the same IPAM console that we have used for everything else IPAM related. That's the nice advantage. Normally if you want to audit these services, you have to open a different application. With IPAM, the auditing is located in the same console as the rest of the IPAM services.

IPAM allows you to audit all of the IPAM events using the Event Catalog (see Figure 4.24) or you can audit events just for the individual services like DHCP (see Figure 4.25).

In Exercise 4.10 I will show you how to configure auditing for IPAM using Server Manager. I will show you how to audit the changes performed on the DNS and DHCP servers, audit the IPAM address usage trail, audit DHCP lease events, and audit user logon events.

FIGURE 4.24   Event Catalog

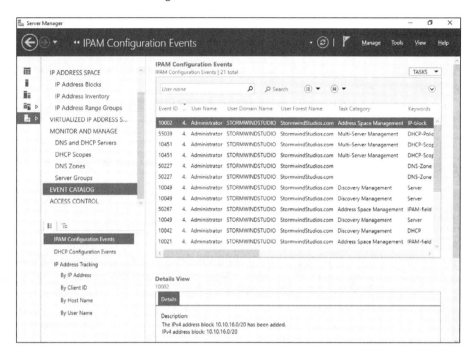

FIGURE 4.25   DHCP Event Catalog

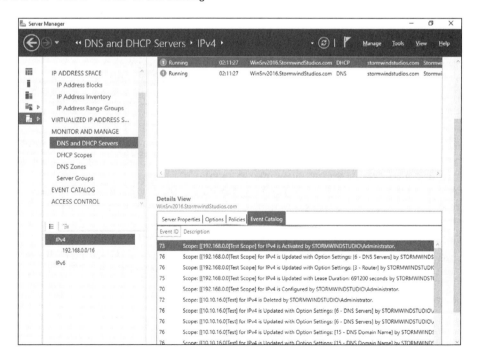

Configuring Auditing

1. Open Server Manager.

2. Click on IPAM.

3. Click Event Catalog in the navigation window. In the right hand side under IPAM Configuration Event, you will see all of the IPAM configuration events that have been logged.

4. In the lower window, click on DHCP configuration events. This will show you any configuration changes made to the DHCP servers.

5. Now click on IP address tracking. This allows you to audit the IP address usage. You can search this By IP Address, By Client ID, By Host Name or By User Name. Click on any of the categories to view the DHCP events.

6. Under the Monitor and Manage section, click on DNS and DHCP servers. In the right hand windows, click either of the two servers and then choose Event Catalog under the Details View (see Figure 4.26). This allows you to monitor DNS and DHCP events independently. You can look at DHCP lease events or look at DNS zone events. It just depends on which server you are monitoring.

FIGURE 4.26   DNS Event Catalog

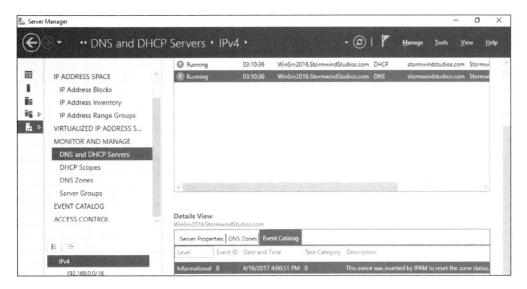

7. Under the Monitor and Manage section, you can choose any server that you want to monitor, including your domain controllers. Just click on the server and then choose Event Catalog under the Details View. You can search DCs for user logon information or you can choose NPS and see policy changes that were performed.

8. Once you are finished looking at all of the different servers you have in IPAM, close Server Manager.

PowerShell Commands for IPAM

As I have shown you in most chapters, PowerShell is a big part of the Microsoft management process. In Table 4.1, I will show you some of the possible PowerShell commands for IPAM.

 For a complete list of IPAM PowerShell commands, please visit Microsoft's website at `https://technet.microsoft.com/en-us/itpro/powershell/windows/ipamserver/ipamserver`.

TABLE 4.1 PowerShell commands for IPAM

Command	Description
Add-IpamAddress	This command allows an administrator to add an IP address to IPAM.
Add-IpamAddressSpace	This command allows an administrator to add an address space to IPAM.
Add-IpamBlock	Administrators can use this command to add an IP address block to IPAM.
Add-IpamCustomField	This command is used to add a custom field to IPAM.
Add-IpamCustomValue	Administrators can use this command to add an IPAM value to a custom field.
Add-IpamDiscoveryDomain	This command allows an administrator to add a new domain in which IPAM discovers infrastructure servers.
Add-IpamRange	Administrators can use this command to add an IP address range to an IPAM server.
Disable-IpamCapability	This command allows an administrator to disable an IPAM optional capability.
Enable-IpamCapability	This command allows an administrator to enable an IPAM optional capability.
Export-IpamAddress	Administrators can use this command to export IP addresses from an IPAM server.

Command	Description
Export-IpamRange	Administrators can use this command to export all of the IP address ranges.
Export-IpamSubnet	This command allows an administrator to export the subnets of an IP address.
Find-IpamFreeAddress	This command will show you the available subnets for allocation, given an IP block, prefix length, and number of requested subnets.
Get-IpamAddress	This command shows an administrator a requested IP addresses from IPAM.
Get-IpamAddressSpace	This command shows an administrator an address spaces in IPAM.
Get-IpamBlock	This command shows an administrator a set of address blocks from IPAM.
Get-IpamDatabase	Administrators can use this command to view the IPAM database configuration settings.
Get-IpamDhcpScope	Administrators can use this command to view DHCP scopes on an IPAM server.
Get-IpamDhcpServer	This command allows an administrator to view DHCP server information from an IPAM database.
Get-IpamDnsResourceRecord	Administrators can use this command to view DNS resource records in an IPAM database.
Get-IpamDnsServer	This command allows an administrator to view DNS server information from an IPAM database.
Get-IpamDnsZone	This command allows an administrator to view DNS zone information from an IPAM database.
Get-IpamIpAddressAuditEvent	Administrators can use this command to view IP address audit events in IPAM.
Import-IpamAddress	This command allows an admin to import an IP address into the IPAM server.
Import-IpamRange	This command allows an admin to import an IP address range into the IPAM server.

TABLE 4.1 PowerShell commands for IPAM *(continued)*

Command	Description
Import-IpamSubnet	This command allows an admin to import an IP address subnet into the IPAM server.
Invoke-IpamGpoProvisioning	Administrators can create and link IPAM group policies (GPOs) for provisioning.
Move-IpamDatabase	This command allows an admin to move an IPAM database to a SQL Server database.
Remove-IpamAddress	Administrators use this command on an IPAM server to remove a set of IP addresses.
Remove-IpamAddressSpace	Administrators use this command on an IPAM server to remove a set of IP address spaces.
Set-IpamAccessScope	This command allows an administrator to set up an IPAM access scope.
Set-IpamAddress	Administrators can use this command to configure an IP address in IPAM.
Set-IpamAddressSpace	Administrators can use this command to configure an IP address space in IPAM.
Set-IpamBlock	Administrators can use this command to configure an IP address block in IPAM.
Set-IpamConfiguration	Administrators can adjust the configuration of a computer that hosts the IPAM server.
Set-IpamDatabase	This command allows an administrator to change the settings on how IPAM connects to the IPAM database.
Set-IpamDiscoveryDomain	Administrators use this command to change the IPAM discovery configuration.
Set-IpamRange	This command is used to modify an existing IP address range.
Set-IpamSubnet	This command is used to modify an existing IP subnet.
Update-IpamServer	Administrators can use this command to update the IPAM server after an operating system upgrade.

Summary

This chapter talked about the advanced configuration options of IPAM. You learned step-by-step how to configure core network services and features using the IPAM console. IPAM allows an administrator to manage TCP/IP network services easily in a large or complex environment.

I showed you how to install and configure IPAM. I explained how you need to setup the required GPOs using PowerShell and the different types of role-based administration IPAM allows.

Understanding how DHCP, DNS, and IPAM all work together is essential for ensuring success when taking the exam. Focus your attention on completing the labs found within the chapter and learning the ins and outs of managing TCP/IP services using IPAM administration.

Exam Essentials

Understand IP Address Management.   IPAM allows administrators to track and audit IP addresses through the use of the IPAM console. IPAM allows IP addresses to be tracked using DHCP lease events and user logon events.

Know how to provision IPAM and configure server discovery.   IPAM is managed and monitored in Server Manager. Know that there are two separate provisioning models—manual and GPO—and know how to configure each. Know how to configure IPAM server discovery.

Know how to delegate IPAM administration.   Active Directory has specific security groups for IPAM. IPAM has its own internal delegation of administration. A user does not need to be a member of the Domain Admins group in order to manage IPAM.

Video Resources

There are videos available for the following exercises:

Exercise 4.1

Exercise 4.2

Exercise 4.3

You can access the videos at http://sybextestbanks.wiley.com on the Other Study Tools tab.

Review Questions

1. You are the network administrator for your company. You need to use a PowerShell command to configure an IP address block in IPAM. What command do you use?

   A. `Set-IpamIP`

   B. `Set-IpamBlock`

   C. `Set-IPBlock`

   D. `Set-IPAddressBlock`

2. You are the network administrator for your company. You need to use a PowerShell command to add an IP address range to an IPAM server. What command do you use?

   A. `Get-IpRange`

   B. `Set-IpRange`

   C. `Add-IpamRange`

   D. `Set-IPBlock`

3. You are the administrator for StormWind Studios online training company. You need to change the IPAM discovery configuration. What PowerShell command do you use?

   A. `Get-IpamDiscovery`

   B. `Get-IpamDiscoveryDomain`

   C. `Set-IpamDiscovery`

   D. `Set-IpamDiscoveryDomain`

4. You are the network administrator for a large training company. You need to view the DNS zone information from the IPAM database. What PowerShell command do you use?

   A. `Get-IpamDnsZone`

   B. `Add-IpamDnsZone`

   C. `Set-IpamDnsZone`

   D. `View-IpamDnsZone`

5. You are the administrator for StormWind Studios. You are installing and configuring IPAM. You have already installed IPAM and now you need to set up the GPOs for IPAM Provisioning. What PowerShell command creates the Provisioned GPOs needed for IPAM to function properly?

   A. `Get-IpamGpoProvisioning`

   B. `Add-IpamGpoProvisioning`

   C. `Invoke-IpamGpoProvisioning`

   D. `Set-IpamGpoProvisioning`

6. You are the infrastructure team lead for a high-tech hardware development company. You need to delegate some of the team's IPAM administration responsibilities between team members. You decide that Noelle will be managing IPAM address spaces, but she will not

be managing IP address tracking and auditing. Which IPAM security group would best fit Noelle's new responsibilities?

A. IPAM Administrators

B. IPAM Users

C. IPAM ASM Administrators

D. IPAM MSM Administrators

7. You are the network administrator for a large communications company. You have recently decided to implement IPAM within your organization with the release of Windows Server 2016. You want to set up your IPAM infrastructure so that one primary server can manage your entire enterprise. Which IPAM deployment method would fulfill this requirement?

A. Isolated

B. Centralized

C. Hybrid

D. Distributed

8. You are the administrator of a company who is using IPAM. You need to change the IPAM GPO prefix. What command would you use?

A. `Set-IPAMConfiguration`

B. `Set-IPAM`

C. `Get-IPAMConfiguration`

D. `Get-IPAM`

9. You are the lead network administrator for a web hosting company. You have recently made the decision to implement IPAM within your organization. You have already installed and provisioned the IPAM feature on your dedicated Windows Server 2016 server. What is the next logical step in your IPAM deployment?

A. Create a new IP block.

B. Delegate IPAM administration.

C. Configure server discovery.

D. Create a new IP range.

10. You are a system administrator for the Stellacon Corporation. Because of the unusual growth of TCP/IP devices on your corporate network over the last year, you need to scale out your IPAM database capabilities. You are currently using a Windows Internal Database (WID) for your IPAM infrastructure, and you want to migrate your IPAM database to a Microsoft SQL Server. Which PowerShell cmdlet would you use to verify current IPAM database configuration settings?

A. `Move-IpamDatabase`

B. `Show-IpamDatabaseConfig`

C. `Show-IpamStatistics`

D. `Get-IpamMigrationSettings`

Chapter

5

Configuring Network Access

THE FOLLOWING 70-741 EXAM OBJECTIVES ARE COVERED IN THIS CHAPTER:

✓ **Implement network connectivity solutions**

 ▪ This objective may include but is not limited to: Implement Network Address Translation (NAT); configure routing.

✓ **Implement virtual private network (VPN) and DirectAccess solutions**

 ▪ This objective may include but is not limited to: Implement remote access and site-to-site (S2S) VPN solutions using remote access gateway; configure different VPN protocol options; configure authentication options; configure VPN reconnect; create and configure connection profiles; determine when to use remote access VPN and site-to-site VPN and configure appropriate protocols; install and configure DirectAccess; implement server requirements; implement client configuration; troubleshoot DirectAccess; Configure Network Access Protection (NAP).

✓ **Implement Network Policy Server (NPS)**

 ▪ This objective may include but is not limited to: Configure a RADIUS server including RADIUS proxy; configure RADIUS clients; configure NPS templates; configure RADIUS accounting; configure certificates; configure Connection Request Policies; configure network policies for VPN and wireless and wired clients; import and export NPS policies.

So in the first few chapters, I talked about using TCP/IP and the services that help support TCP/IP. Now I will show you how to access your network both locally and remotely.

Routing and Remote Access Services (RRAS) includes some security features necessary to provide remote access effectively. For example, you'll probably want the ability to restrict user dial-up access by group membership, time of day, or other factors. You'll also need a way to specify the various callback, authentication, and encryption options that the protocols support.

In this chapter, you'll learn about *virtual private networks (VPNs)*, which provide remote access to private networks across public connections. That is, using the Internet, clients can dial in to an Internet service provider (ISP) and connect to your private network.

The main benefit of VPNs is reduced cost because it means that long-distance calls are unnecessary. VPNs are becoming more popular because of the increased popularity of high-speed Internet connections, such as cable and digital subscriber line (DSL) connections.

I will also talk to you about a VPN replacement called DirectAccess. DirectAccess allows a user to remotely access your network without the need for the user to initiate the remote connection.

I will also talk about how to protect your network by using the Network Policy Server. Network Policy Server allows you to put rules on the way your users access your network.

Before I can get into the details of what these features do and how to configure them to provide remote access for your network, you need to understand some of the basic terms and concepts specific to RRAS. That's where you'll begin in this chapter, and then you'll move on to learning about the features and configuration settings that you need to understand to meet the exam objectives.

Overview of Dial-Up Networking

LANs provide relatively high-speed connectivity to attached machines, but where does that leave those of us who work from home, who travel, or who need to access data on a remote computer? Until wireless access is available worldwide, we have the option of using dial-up networking in which the client computer uses a modem to dial in and connect to a remote server. Once the connection is established, a variety of protocols and services make it possible for us to view web pages, transfer files and email, and do pretty much anything we could do with a hardwired LAN connection, albeit at a reduced speed.

In the following sections, you will learn more about what dial-up networking does and how it works by examining the specific technologies and protocols associated with remote access.

What DUN Does

At this point in the book, you should understand that Windows Server 2016 network protocols are actually implemented as drivers. These drivers normally work with hardware network interfaces to get data from point A to point B. How do dial-up connections fit in? Many people may read this and say, "Who still uses dial-up?" Well, as a person who lives in New Hampshire, I can tell you that we still have many areas that can't get broadband or even satellite access.

Think back to the OSI model. Each layer has a function, and each layer serves as an intermediary between the layer above it and the one below it. By substituting one driver for another at some level in the stack, you can dramatically change how things work. That's exactly what the Windows Server 2016's *Dial-Up Networking (DUN)* subsystem does. It makes the dial-up connection appear to be just another network adapter.

The DUN driver takes care of the task of making a slow asynchronous modem appear to work just like a fast LAN interface. Applications and services that use TCP/IP on your DUN connection never know the difference. In fact, you can configure Windows Server 2016 to use your primary connection first and then to pass traffic over a secondary connection (such as a dial-up link) if the primary connection is down. This does not affect the applications with which you're working (except that they might run more slowly).

Depending on how you configure the DUN server, users who dial in can see the whole network or only specific resources on the server. You also get to control who can log on, when they can log on, and what they can do once they've logged on. As far as Windows Server 2016 is concerned, a user connected via DUN is no different from one using resources over your LAN, so all the access controls and permissions you apply remain in force for DUN users.

How DUN Works

A lot of pieces are required to complete a dial-up call successfully from your computer to a server at another physical location. Understanding what these pieces are, how they work, and what they do for you is important. The following sections will cover the DUN infrastructure, how the *Point-to-Point Protocol (PPP)* helps with this connection, the relationship between PPP and the network protocols, and how multilink can be used to increase the speed and efficiency of your remote connections.

The DUN Infrastructure

This section covers the physical layer that underlies voice and data calls. Most of the following material will be familiar to anyone who has ever used a modem, but you should still understand the details you may not have considered before.

Plain Old Telephone Service

Plain Old Telephone Service (POTS) connections offer a theoretical maximum speed of 56 Kbps; in practice, many users routinely get connections at 51 Kbps or 52 Kbps.

The word *modem* is actually short for *modulator-demodulator*. The original Bell System modems took digital data and modulated it into screechy analog audio tones suitable for use on regular phone lines. Because phone lines are purposely designed to pass only the low end of the audible frequency range that most can hear, the amount of data was limited. However, in the early 1990s, an engineer discovered that you could communicate much faster when the path between the sender and receiver was all digital.

An all-digital path doesn't have any analog components that induce signal loss, so it preserves the original signal quality faithfully. This in turn makes it possible to put more information into the original signal. As it happens, phone companies nationwide were in the process of making major upgrades to replace their analog equipment with newer and better digital equivalents. These upgrades made it possible for people in most areas to get almost 56 Kbps speeds without changing any of the wiring in their homes or offices. The connection between the house and the phone office was still analog, but the connections between phone offices were digital, ensuring high-quality connections.

Integrated Services Digital Network

In the mid-1970s, *Integrated Services Digital Network (ISDN)* was designed. At the time, no one had any idea that you'd be able to get 56 Kbps speeds out of an ordinary phone line. ISDN speeds of up to 128 Kbps over a single pair of copper wires seemed pretty revolutionary. In addition, ISDN had features such as call forwarding, caller ID, and multiple directory numbers (so you could have more than one number, perhaps with different ringing patterns, associated with a single line).

Unfortunately, ISDN requires an all-digital signal path. It also requires special equipment on both ends of the connection. The phone companies were slow to promote ISDN as a faster alternative to regular dial-up service, so customers avoided it.

ISDN still has some advantages, though. Because it's all digital, call setup times are much shorter than they are for analog modems—it takes only about half a second to establish a new ISDN call. Modern ISDN adapters and ISDN-capable routers can seamlessly stitch together multiple ISDN channels to deliver bandwidth in 64 Kbps increments. Because you can use ISDN lines for regular analog voice, data, and fax traffic, you can make a single ISDN act like two voice lines, a single 128 Kbps data line, or a 64 Kbps data line plus a voice line.

 ISDN is quickly being replaced by faster broadband services such as DSL and cable modems. In fact, you should resort to ISDN only if these other solutions are not available in your area. Note that DSL (a misnomer because they are all digital) and cable modems do not use PPP (discussed later), so they are technically not considered dial-up connections.

Other Connection Methods

Any other on-demand connection that's established using the Point-to-Point Protocol can be thought of as a dial-up connection, and Windows Server 2016 doesn't make any distinction between POTS, ISDN, and other dial-ups—they're all treated identically.

Connecting with PPP

The Point-to-Point Protocol enables any two devices to establish a TCP/IP connection over a serial link. That usually means a dial-up modem connection, but it could just as easily be a direct serial cable connection, an infrared connection, or any other type of serial connection. When one machine dials another, the machine that initiates the connection is referred to as a *client*, and the machine that receives the call is referred to as a *server*—even though PPP itself makes no such distinction.

PPP negotiation involves three phases that are required to establish a remote access connection. Actually, at least six distinct protocols run on top of PPP. Understanding what they do helps to make the actual PPP negotiation process clearer. These protocols are as follows:

The Link Control Protocol   The *Link Control Protocol (LCP)* handles the details of establishing and configuring the lowest-level PPP link. In that regard, you can think of LCP as if it were almost part of the Physical layer. When one PPP device calls another, the devices use LCP to agree that they want to establish a PPP connection.

The Challenge Handshake Authentication Protocol   *The Challenge Handshake Authentication Protocol (CHAP)*—as well as MS-CHAPv2 and PAP—allow the client to authenticate itself to the server. This authentication functions much like a regular network logon; once the client presents its logon credentials, the server can figure out what access to grant.

The Callback Control Protocol   The *Callback Control Protocol (CBCP)* is used to negotiate whether a callback is required, whether it's permitted, and when it happens. Once the client has authenticated itself, the server can decide whether it should hang up and call the client back. The client can also request a callback at a number it provides. Although this isn't as secure as having the server place a call to a predetermined number, it provides some additional flexibility. If a callback occurs, the connection is reestablished and reauthenticated, but the CBCP stage is skipped.

The Compression Control Protocol   The *Compression Control Protocol (CCP)* allows the two sides of the connection to determine what kind of compression, if any, they want to use on the network data. Because PPP traffic actually consists of wrapped-up IP datagrams and because IP datagram headers tend to be fairly compressible, negotiating effective compression can significantly improve overall PPP throughput.

The IP Control Protocol   At this point in the call, the two sides have agreed to authentication, compression, and a callback. They haven't yet agreed on what IP parameters to use for the connection. These parameters, which include the maximum packet size to be sent over the link (the *maximum transmission unit*, or *MTU*), have a great impact on the overall link performance, so the client and server use the *IP Control Protocol (IPCP)* to negotiate them based on the traffic they expect to be passed.

The Internet Protocol   Once the IPCP negotiation has been completed, each end has complete knowledge of how to communicate with its peer. That knowledge allows the two sides to begin exchanging Internet Protocol (IP) datagrams over the link, just as they would over a standard LAN connection.

The Relationship Between PPP and Network Protocols

Usually, when you hear about network communication, you hear about using TCP/IP on a hardwired LAN. How does this protocol fit in with PPP? In the case of TCP/IP, that's an easy question to answer: The client routes all (or some) of its outgoing TCP/IP traffic to its PPP peer, which can then inspect the IP datagrams it gets back from the PPP stack to analyze and route them properly.

Windows Server 2016 supports only TCP/IP, so consider what has to happen when a client using AppleTalk needs to connect via dial-up. Because the server will not use those other protocols, it will drop the call or cause the client to warn its user (that's what Windows Server 2016 does). After the other PPP setup steps are finished, the client and server can wrap other types of network traffic inside an IP datagram. This process, called *encapsulation*, allows the client to take a packet with some kind of private content, wrap it inside an IP datagram, and send it to the server. The server, in turn, processes the IP datagram, routing real datagrams normally and handling any encapsulated packets with the appropriate protocol. At that point, the client can communicate with the server without knowing that its non-TCP/IP packets are being encapsulated in any way—that detail is hidden deep in the layers of the OSI model.

Understanding the Benefits of Multilink

Many parts of the world don't have high-speed broadband access yet. In fact, many places don't have ISDN or even phone lines that support 56 Kbps modems. The *multilink extensions* to the Point-to-Point Protocol provide a way to take several independent PPP connections and make them look like one line so that they act as a single connection.

For example, if you use two phone lines and modems to place a two-line multilink call to your ISP, instead of getting the usual 48 Kbps connection, you would end up with an apparent bandwidth of 96 Kbps. The multilink PPP software on your Windows Server 2016 machine and on the ISP's router takes care of stringing all of the packets together to make this process seamless. Windows Server 2012's RRAS supports multilink PPP for inbound and outbound calls.

The primary drawback to multilink calls is that they take up more than one phone line apiece.

Overview of Virtual Private Networks

Private networks offer superior security. You own the wires, so you have control over what they're used for, who can use them, and what kind of data passes over them. However, they're not very flexible because they require you to configure and manage costly leased lines between remote locations. To make things worse, most private networks face a dilemma: Implementing enough capacity to handle peak loads almost guarantees that much of that capacity will remain idle much of the time, even though it still has to be paid for.

One way to work around this problem is to maintain private dial-up services. Such services allow, for example, a field rep in Chicago to dial into the home office in Boston. But dial-ups are expensive, and they have the same excess capacity problem as truly private networks. As an added detriment, someone has to pay long-distance or toll-free number charges.

Virtual private networks (VPNs) offer a solution. You get the security of a true private network with the flexibility, ubiquity, and low cost of the Internet. In the following sections, I will cover VPNs, including what they are used for and how they work (in general and with Windows Server 2016).

What VPNs Do

At any time, two parties can create a connection over the Internet. The idea behind a VPN is that you can use these connections to let two parties establish an *encrypted tunnel* between them using the Internet as a transportation medium. The VPN software on each end takes care of encrypting the VPN packets as they go; when the packets leave one end of the tunnel, their payloads are encrypted and encapsulated inside regular IP packets that cause them to be delivered to the remote machine. Figure 5.1 shows one way to conceptualize this process.

FIGURE 5.1   Drilling a tunnel through the Internet

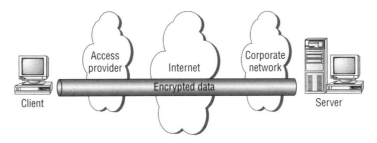

As an example, let's say you're in the field at a client site. As long as you're somewhere that your ISP serves, you can dial into the client's local point of presence and get connected to the Internet. At that point, you can open a VPN connection back to the servers at your office and do whatever you could do when sitting in front of a regular desktop machine.

VPNs and Windows Server 2016

Windows Server 2016 includes support for Microsoft's proprietary *Point-to-Point Tunneling Protocol* and Layer 2 Tunneling Protocol. *Layer 2 Tunneling Protocol (L2TP)* provides a more generic tunneling mechanism than PPTP, and when combined with IPsec, L2TP also allows you to establish VPNs using a wide range of Microsoft or non-Microsoft hardware and software products, including routers and access devices from companies such as Cisco, Red Creek, and Nortel.

Windows Server 2016's VPN support includes the following worthwhile features:

- You can set up account lockout policies for dial-up and VPN users. This capacity has existed for network and console users for some time.

- The *Extensible Authentication Protocol (EAP)* allows Microsoft or third parties to write modules that implement new authentication methods and retrofit them to servers. One example is the EAP-TLS module, which implements access control based on smart cards and certificates for VPN and dial-up users.

How you enable VPN support on your Windows Server 2016 machine depends on whether you're using a server or a client (Windows XP, Windows Vista, Windows 7, Windows 8, and so on).

Client configuration is easy. Just install the Dial-Up Networking service and then use the Make New Connection Wizard to create a new VPN connection. On the server side, you'll need to install and configure RRAS and then enable it to accept incoming VPN connections.

How VPNs Work

The VPN client assumes that the VPN server is already connected to the Internet in some way. Here's how the VPN connection process works:

1. The client establishes a connection to the Internet. Dial-up networking or any other connection method can be used for this connection. The client must be able to send packets to the Internet.

2. The client sends a VPN connection request to the server. The exact format of the request varies, depending on whether the VPN is using PPTP, L2TP, or SSTP.

3. The client authenticates itself to the server. Again, the exact process varies according to the VPN protocol in use. If the client can't provide valid credentials, the connection is terminated.

4. The client and server negotiate parameters for the VPN session. This negotiation allows the two ends to agree on an encryption algorithm and strength.

5. The client and server go through the PPP negotiation process because both L2TP and PPTP depend on the lower-level PPP.

Because the contents of data passed around in step 2 and step 3 vary according to the tunneling protocol in use, I'll explain the differences. First, though, you should understand encapsulation and how VPNs use it to wrap one kind of data inside another.

An Encapsulation Primer

Most of yesterday's networks could carry only one kind of data. Each network vendor had its own protocol, and most of the time there was no way to intermingle data using different protocols on the same line. Over time, vendors began to find ways to allow a single network to carry many different types of traffic, resulting in the current assortment of traffic types found on most large networks. However, the Internet works only with IP, which is why it's called *Internet Protocol*. If you need to send other types of traffic, such as AppleTalk, across the Internet, you can encapsulate it within IP.

How does encapsulation work? Software at each level of the OSI model has to see header information to figure out where a packet is coming from and where it's going. However, the payload contents aren't important to most of those components, and the payload is what's encapsulated. By fabricating the right kind of header and prepending it for whatever you want in the payload, you can route foreign traffic types through IP networks with no trouble.

VPNs depend on encapsulation because their security method depends on being able to keep the payload information encrypted. The following steps demonstrate what happens to a typical packet as it goes from being a regular IP datagram to a PPTP packet (see Figure 5.2).

FIGURE 5.2   The encapsulation process

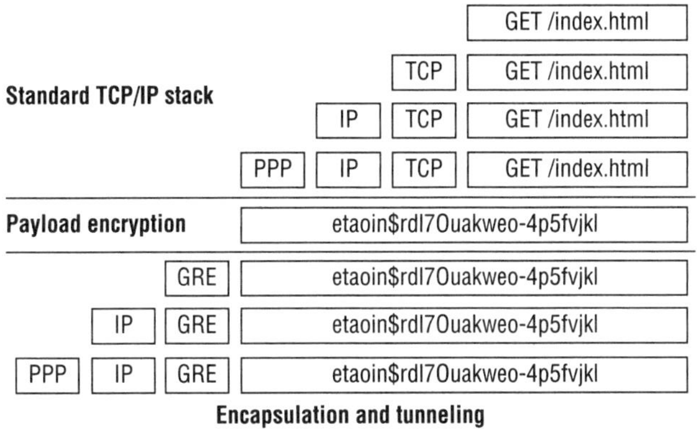

1. An application creates a block of data bound for a remote host. In this case, it's a web browser.

2. The client-side IP stack takes the application's data and turns it into an IP packet, first by adding a TCP header and then by adding an IP header. This is called the *IP datagram* because it contains all of the necessary addressing information to be delivered by IP.

3. The client is connected via PPP, so it adds a PPP header to the IP datagram. This PPP+IP combination is called a *PPP frame*.

4. If you are using PPP instead of a VPN protocol, the packet goes across the PPP link without further modification. When you are using a VPN (as in this example), the next step is for the VPN to encrypt the PPP frame, turning it into unreadable information to be transported over the Internet.

5. A *Generic Routing Encapsulation (GRE) header* is combined with the encrypted payload. GRE really is generic; in this case, the protocol ID field in the GRE header says that this is an encapsulated PPTP packet.

6. Now that there is a tag to tell you what's in the payload, the PPTP stack can add an IP header (specifying the destination address of the VPN server) and a PPP header.

7. Now the packet can be sent out over your PPP connection. The IP header specifies that it should be routed to the VPN server.

8. When the packet arrives at the VPN server, the server reverses steps 1 through 6 to extract the payload.

Encapsulation allows the use of VPN data inside ordinary-looking IP datagrams, which is part of what makes VPNs so powerful—you don't have to change any of your applications, routers, or network components (unless they have to be configured to recognize and pass GRE packets).

PPTP Tunneling

PPTP is a pretty straightforward protocol. It works by encapsulating packets using the mechanism described in the previous section, "An Encapsulation Primer," and performs encryption (step 4) using the *Microsoft Point-to-Point Encryption (MPPE) algorithm*. The encryption keys used to encrypt the packets are generated dynamically for each connection; in fact, the keys can be changed periodically during the connection.

When the client and server have successfully established a PPTP tunnel, the authorization process begins. This process is an exchange of credentials that allows the server to decide whether the client is permitted to connect:

1. The server sends a challenge message to the client.

2. The client answers with an encrypted response.

3. The server checks the response to see whether the answer is right. The challenge-response process allows the server to determine which account is trying to make a connection.

4. The server determines whether the user account is authorized to make a connection.

5. If the account is authorized, the server accepts the inbound connection; any access controls or remote access restrictions still apply.

L2TP/IPsec Tunneling

L2TP is much more flexible than PPTP, but it's also more complicated. It was designed to be a general-purpose tunneling protocol not limited to VPN use.

L2TP itself doesn't offer any kind of security. When you use L2TP, you're setting up an unencrypted, unauthenticated tunnel. Using L2TP by itself over the Internet, therefore, would be dangerous because anyone who wanted to could read your traffic.

The overall flow of an L2TP/IPsec tunnel session looks a little different from that of a PPTP session because IPsec security is different. Here's how the L2TP/IPsec combination works:

1. The client and server establish an IPsec security association using the ISAKMP and Oakley protocols. At this point, the two machines have an encrypted channel between them.

2. The client builds a new L2TP tunnel to the server. Because this happens after the channel has been encrypted, there's no security risk.

3. The server sends an authentication challenge to the client.

4. The client encrypts its answer to the challenge and returns it to the server.

5. The server checks the challenge response to see whether it's valid; if so, the server can determine which account is connecting. At this point, the server can accept the inbound connection, subject to whatever access policies you've put in place.

Note that steps 3 through 5 mirror the steps described for PPTP tunneling. This is because the authorization process is a function of the remote access server, not the VPN stack. All the VPN does is to provide a secure communications channel, and something else has to decide who gets to use it.

SSTP Tunneling

The *Secure Sockets Tunneling Protocol (SSTP)* is a secure way to make a VPN connection using the Secure Sockets Layer v.3 (SSL) port 443. The following steps show how SSTP operates and functions:

1. The client connects to the server through the Internet using port 443.

2. During the TCP session, SSL negotiation takes place.

3. During the SSL authentication phase, the client machine receives the server certificate.

4. The client machine will send HTTPS requests on top of the encrypted SSL session.

5. The client machine will then also send SSTP control packets on top of the HTTPS session.

6. PPP negotiation now takes place on both ends of the connection.

7. After PPP is finished, both ends are ready to send IP packets to each other.

Configuring Your Remote Access Server

Most of the configuration necessary for a remote access server happens at the server level. You use the server's Properties dialog box to control whether the server allows remote connections, what protocols and options it supports, and so forth. Because all of the protocols are carried via PPP, you can set some generic PPP options as well. I will cover these options in the following sections. You also have to configure settings for your users, which you'll read about in the next section, and you will install and configure the Remote Access role for the server in the first exercise.

Configuring PPP Options

You can use the PPP tab of the RRAS server's Properties dialog box (see Figure 5.3) to control the PPP layer options available to clients that call in. The settings you specify here control whether the related PPP options are available to clients; you can use remote access policies to control whether individual connections can use them.

FIGURE 5.3   The PPP tab of the RRAS server's Properties dialog box

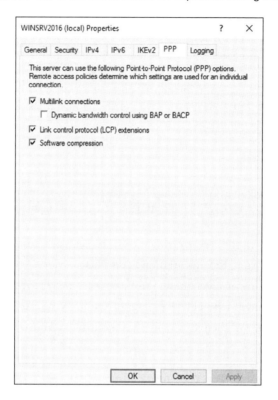

This tab has four check boxes:

- The Multilink Connections check box, which is selected by default, controls whether the server will allow clients to establish multilink connections when they call in.

- The Dynamic Bandwidth Control Using BAP Or BACP check box determines whether clients and servers are allowed to add or remove links dynamically during a multilink session. If you enable this feature, you can throttle the amount of available bandwidth up or down on demand. It's available only when the Multilink Connections check box is selected. (BAP stands for Bandwidth Allocation Protocol, and BACP stands for Bandwidth Allocation Control Protocol.)

- The Link Control Protocol (LCP) is used to establish a PPP link and negotiate its settings. A variety of LCP extensions are defined in various RFCs; these extensions allow a client and server to agree dynamically about which protocols are being passed back and forth, among other things. The Link Control Protocol (LCP) Extensions check box controls whether these extensions are available. Windows 9x, NT, 2000, Vista, XP, Windows 7, Windows 8/8.1, and Windows 10 clients depend on the LCP extensions, so you should leave this check box selected.

- The Software Compression check box controls whether RRAS will allow a remote client to use the Compression Control Protocol (CCP) to compress PPP traffic. In some cases, hardware compression at the modem level is more efficient, but not everyone has a compression-capable modem. You should leave this check box selected as well.

Configuring IP-Based Connections

TCP/IP is far and away the most commonly used remote access protocol; coincidentally, it's also the most configurable of the protocols that Windows Server 2016 supports. Both of these facts are reflected in the IPv4 and IPv6 tabs of the server's Properties dialog box. Figure 5.4 shows the IPv4 tab.

FIGURE 5.4   The IPv4 tab of the RRAS server's Properties dialog box

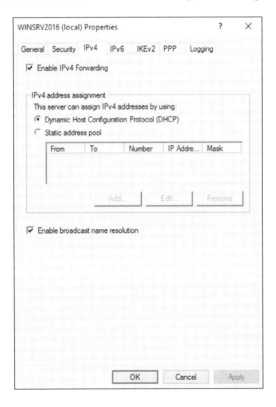

The controls on the IPv4 tab do the following:

- The Enable IPv4 Forwarding check box controls whether RRAS will route IPv4 packets between the remote client and other interfaces on your RRAS server. When this box is checked, as it is by default, remote clients' packets can go to the RRAS server or to any other host to which the RRAS server has a route. To allow clients to access resources on the RRAS server only, uncheck this box.

- The IP Address Assignment control group lets you specify how you want remote clients to get their IP addresses. The default settings here depend on what you told the RRAS Setup Wizard during setup:

  - If you want to use a DHCP server on your network as the source of IP addresses for remote clients, select the Dynamic Host Configuration Protocol (DHCP) radio button and make sure that you have the DHCP relay agent installed and running.

  - If you'd rather use static address allocation, select the Static Address Pool radio button. Then, in the list below, specify which IP address ranges you want issued to clients.

  - The Enable Broadcast Name Resolution option allows remote clients to resolve TCP/IP names without the use of a WINS or DNS server. This feature is enabled by default, and it was new in Windows Server 2012.

Figure 5.5 shows the IPv6 tab of the RRAS server's Properties dialog box.

FIGURE 5.5   The IPv6 tab of the RRAS Server's Properties dialog box

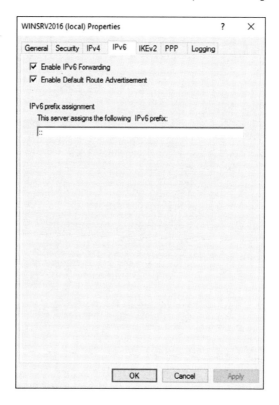

The controls on the IPv6 tab do the following:

- The Enable IPv6 Forwarding check box controls whether RRAS will route IPv6 packets between the remote client and other interfaces on your RRAS server. When this box is checked, as it is by default, remote clients' packets can go to the RRAS server or to any other host to which the RRAS server has a route. To allow clients to access resources on the RRAS server only, uncheck this box.

- The Enable Default Route Advertisement check box (enabled by default) makes the *Border Gateway Protocol (BGP)* routing protocol available. BGP can exchange routing information between Windows Server 2016 routers. When this box is checked, your Windows Server 2016 router can announce its route to other routers.

- On the IPv6 tab, you can also set up your IPv6 prefix assignment.

In Exercise 5.1, I will show you how to install and configure the Remote Access role onto your server. Just as with many of our installations, you will use Server Manager to install the Remote Access role. This role also installs the DirectAccess role onto your server.

EXERCISE 5.1

Installing the Remote Access Role

1. Open Server Manager.

2. On the Server Manager dashboard, click the Add Roles And Features link (number 2).

3. If a Before You Begin screen appears, click Next.

4. On the Selection type page, choose a role-based or feature-based installation and click Next.

5. Click the top radio button, Select A Server From The Server Pool, and choose the server in the Server Pool section. Click Next.

6. On the Select Server Roles screen, click the Remote Access check box (see Figure 5.6). If a pop-up window appears telling you that you need to add features, click the Add Features button. Click Next.

7. On the Add Features page, click Next.

8. On the Remote Access page, click Next.

9. On the Select Role Services page, choose the first two check boxes: DirectAccess And VPN (RAS) and Routing (see Figure 5.7). If a pop-up window appears telling you that you need to add additional features, click the Add Features button. Click Next.

10. At the Confirmation screen, click the Install button.

11. After the Installation screen finishes, click the Close button.

12. In Server Manager, click the Remote Access link on the left window pane.

FIGURE 5.6 Remote Access check box

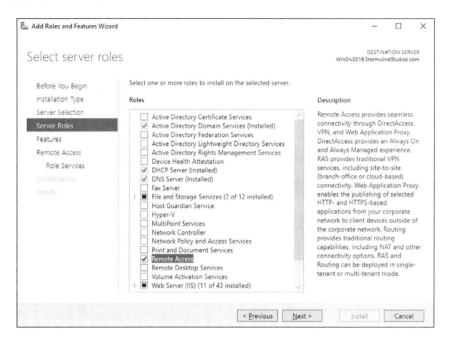

FIGURE 5.7 Remote Access

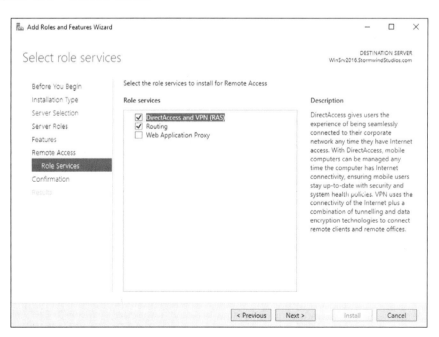

13. Click the more link (see Figure 5.8).

FIGURE 5.8 Remote Access configuration needed

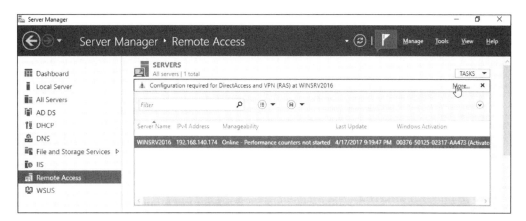

14. At the Post-deployment Configuration task, click the link for Open The Getting Started Wizard (see Figure 5.9).

FIGURE 5.9 Opening the Getting Started Wizard

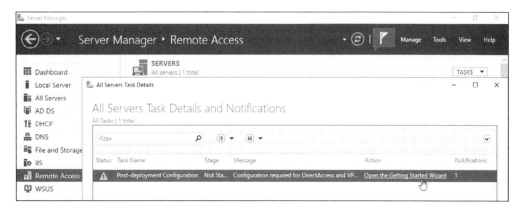

15. At the Configure Remote Access screen, choose the Deploy VPN Only link.

16. At this point we can configure the Remote Access VPN role. We will configure this role in a later exercise. Close Server Manager.

Understanding a VPN

Conventional dial-up access works well, but as you saw earlier, it can be expensive to implement, painful to manage, and extremely slow by today's standards. VPNs offer a way around these problems by providing low initial and ongoing costs, easy management, and excellent speeds (depending on your connection). Windows Server 2012's RRAS component includes two complete VPN implementations: one using Microsoft's PPTP and one using a combination of the Internet-standard IPsec protocol and L2TP or SSTP.

The basic process of setting up a VPN is simple, but you need to think some things through before plunging ahead. Getting the VPN installation right may require small hardware or networking changes plus proper configuration of the VPN service. You will look at this process in the following sections.

How a VPN Works

A VPN sits between your internal network and the Internet, accepting connections from clients in the outside world. In Figure 5.10, clients 1 and 2 are using different ISPs (probably because they're at different physical locations). For example, a packet from client 1 goes from its computer to its ISP and then through some route, unknown to you, that eventually delivers it to the VPN server, which transforms it into a packet suitable for use on the internal network.

FIGURE 5.10   VPNs provide private connections between clients and servers across the Internet.

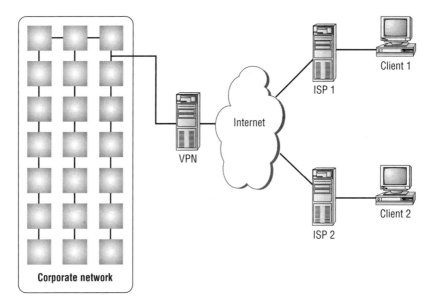

Imagine a line around the internal network, and think of it as a security boundary. In general, you'll want your VPN server to be outside any firewalls or network security measures that you have in place. The most common configuration is to use two NICs: One connects to the Internet, and the other connects either to the private network or to an intermediate network that itself connects to the private network. Of course, you can use any type of Internet connection you want for the VPN server, such as cable modem, DSL, T1, satellite, or whatever.

The point behind giving the VPN its own network adapter is that your VPN clients need a public IP address to which they can connect, and you probably don't want them calling directly into your internal network. That also means that things will be easiest for your VPN users if the IP address for your VPN server's external interface is statically assigned so that it won't be changing on them when they least expect it.

Enabling RRAS as a VPN

If you're already using RRAS for IP routing or remote access, you can enable it as a VPN server without reinstalling.

The General tab of the server's Properties dialog box allows you to specify whether your RRAS server is a router, a remote access server, or both. The first step in converting your existing RRAS server to handle VPN traffic is to make sure that the IPv4 Remote Access Server or IPv6 Remote Access Server check box is selected on this tab.

Making this change requires you to stop and restart the RRAS service, but that's OK because the snap-in will do it for you. Then you must configure VPN ports, as shown in the following sections.

Configuring a VPN

VPN configuration is extremely simple, at least for PPTP. Either a server can accept VPN calls or it can't. If it can, it will have a certain number of VPN ports, all of which are configured identically. You don't have to change or tweak much to get a VPN server set up, but you can adjust a few things as you like.

Configuring VPN Ports

The biggest opportunity to configure your VPN server is to adjust the number and kind of VPN ports available for clients to use. You can enable or disable either PPTP or L2TP, depending on what you want your remote users to be able to access. You accomplish this through the Ports Properties dialog box.

For conventional remote access servers, this dialog box shows you a list of hardware ports, but for servers that support VPN connections, there are two WAN Miniport device selections: one for PPTP and one for L2TP. (These aren't really devices; they're actually virtual ports maintained by RRAS for accepting VPN connections.) You configure these ports by selecting one and clicking the Configure button, which displays the Configure Device – WAN Miniport (PPTP) dialog box.

Three controls are pertinent to a VPN configuration:

- The Remote Access Connections (Inbound Only) check box must be activated in order to accept VPN connections with this port type. To disable a VPN type (for instance, if you want to turn off L2TP), uncheck this box.

- The Demand-Dial Routing Connections (Inbound And Outbound) check box controls whether this VPN type can be used for demand-dial connections. By default, this box is checked; you'll need to uncheck it if you don't want to use VPN connections to link your network with other networks.

- The Maximum Ports control lets you set the number of inbound connections that this port type will support. By default, you get 5 PPTP and 5 L2TP ports when you install RRAS; you can use from 0 to 250 ports of each type by adjusting the number here.

You can also use the Phone Number For This Device field to enter the IP address of the public interface to which VPN clients connect. You might want to do this if your remote access policies accept or reject connections based on the number called by the client. Because you can assign multiple IP addresses to a single adapter, you can control VPN traffic by throttling which clients can connect to which addresses through a policy.

Troubleshooting VPNs

The two primary problems you might encounter with VPN are as follows:

- Inability to establish a connection at all
- Inability to reach some needed resource once connected

There's a lot of common ground between the process of troubleshooting a VPN connection and the process of troubleshooting an ordinary remote access connection.

The following are some extremely simple—but sometimes overlooked—things to check when your VPN clients can't connect. First, make sure your clients can make the underlying connection to their ISP; then, check the following:

- Is RRAS installed and configured on the server?
  - Is the server configured to allow remote access? Check the General tab of the server's Properties dialog box.
  - Is the server configured to allow VPN traffic? Check the Ports Properties dialog box to make sure that the appropriate VPN protocol is enabled and that the number of ports for that protocol is greater than 0.
  - Are there any available VPN ports? If you have 10 L2TP ports allocated, the 11th caller will not be able to connect.

- Do the client and server match?

  - Is the VPN protocol used by the client enabled on the server? Windows 2000 and newer clients will try L2TP first and switch to PPTP as a second choice. However, clients on other OSs (including Windows NT) can normally expect L2TP, PPTP, or SSTP (2008 or higher).

- Are the client and server authenticated correctly?

  - Are the username and password correct?

  - Does the user account in question have remote access permissions, either directly on the account or through a policy?

  - Do the authentication settings in the server's policies (if any) match the supported set of authentication protocols?

If you check all of the simple stuff and find nothing wrong, it's time to move on to checking more complex issues. These tend to affect more than one user, as opposed to the simple (and generally user-specific) issues just outlined. The problems include the following:

Policy Problems   If you're using a native-mode Windows Server 2016 domain and you're using policies, those policies may cause some subtle problems that show up under some circumstances:

- Are there any policies whose Allow or Deny settings conflict with each other? Remember that all conditions of all policies must match to gain user access; if any condition of any policy fails or if there are any policies that deny access, the connection will be denied.

- Does the user match all of the necessary conditions that are in place, such as time and date?

Network Problems   If you're using dynamic IP addressing, are there any addresses left in the pool? If the VPN server can't assign an address, it won't accept the connection.

Domain Problems   Windows Server 2016 RRAS servers can coexist with Windows NT RRAS servers, and both of them can interoperate with RADIUS servers from Microsoft and other vendors. Sometimes, though, this interoperation doesn't work exactly as you'd expect. Here are some questions to ask:

- Is the RRAS server's domain membership correct? Your RRAS servers don't have to be domain members unless you want to use native-mode features such as remote access policies.

- If you're in a domain, are the server's group memberships correct? The server account must be a member of the RAS group and Internet Authentication Servers security group.

So now that you understand what a VPN does, let's go ahead and configure your VPN server. In Exercise 5.2, I will show you how to configure your VPN server.

EXERCISE 5.2

Setting Up a VPN Server

1. Open Routing and Remote Access by clicking the Start button and choosing Administrative tools and then choose Routing and Remote Access.

2. Right-click on the server name and choose Configure and Enable Routing and Remote Access.

3. The Routing and Remote Access wizard starts. Click Next at the Welcome screen.

4. At the Configuration screen, choose the first option Remote access (dial-up or VPN) as shown in Figure 5.11.

FIGURE 5.11 Remote access choice

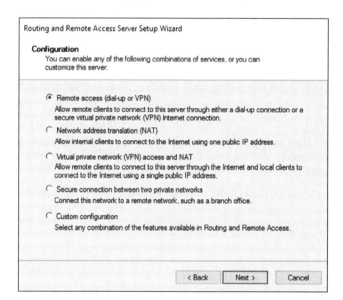

5. At the Remote Access screen, choose the VPN check box. Click Next.

6. Click the Ethernet adapter that will be connected to the internet. Make sure the check box for Enable security on the selected interface is selected. Click Next.

7. At the IP Address Assignment screen, choose Automatically and choose Next.

8. At the Managing Multiple Remote Access Servers screen, click the No button and click Next.

9. At the Summary screen, click the Finish button.

10. If you get a message about setting up a DHCP Relay Agent, click OK.

Managing Your Remote Access Server

RRAS server management is generally pretty easy because, in most cases, there's not much to manage. You set up the server, and it answers calls. You'll probably find it necessary to monitor the server's ongoing activity, however, and you may find it necessary to log activity for accounting or security purposes.

You can monitor your server's activity in a number of ways, including having the server keep local copies of its logs or having it send logging data to a remote RADIUS server. In addition, you can monitor the current status of any of the ports on your system.

Microsoft's documentation distinguishes between event logging, which records significant things that happen such as the RRAS service starting up and shutting down, and authentication and accounting logging, which tracks things like when a user logged on and logged off. The settings for both types of logging are intermingled in the RRAS snap-in.

Managing Remote Users with a RADIUS Server

Remote Authentication Dial-In User Service (RADIUS) allows for maintaining and managing your remote users. A RADIUS server allows Remote Access Service (RAS) clients and dial-up routers to be authenticated.

Network Policy Server (NPS) is Microsoft's implementation of a RADIUS server in Windows Server 2016. NPS replaced Windows Server 2003 Internet Authentication Service (IAS) in Windows Server 2008. NPS, working as a RADIUS server, allows for authentication, authorization, and accounting for wireless and VPN networks.

NPS allows a server to perform the duties of a RADIUS proxy. A RADIUS proxy allows the routing of RADIUS messages between RADIUS clients (RAS) and RADIUS servers. NPS also gives you the ability to record information about forwarded messages in an accounting log.

Monitoring Overall Activity

The Server Status node in the RRAS snap-in shows you a summary of all the RRAS servers known to the system. When you select the Server Status item, the right pane of the MMC will list each known RRAS server. Each entry in the list tells you whether the server is up, what kind of server it is, how many ports it has, how many ports are currently in use, and how long the server has been up. You can right-click any Windows Server 2016 RRAS server in this view to start, stop, restart, pause, or resume its RRAS service; disable RRAS on the server; or remove the server's advertisement from Active Directory (provided, of course, that you're using Active Directory).

Controlling Remote Access Logging

A standard RRAS installation will always log some data locally, but that's pretty useless unless you know what gets logged and where it goes. Each RRAS server on your network has its own set of logs, which you manage through the `Remote Access Logging` folder. Within that folder, you'll usually see a single item labeled *Local File*, which is the log file stored on that particular server.

If you don't have Windows accounting or Windows authentication turned on, you won't have a local log file. Depending on whether you're using RADIUS accounting and logging, you may see additional entries.

Setting Server Logging Properties

You can control server logging at the server level. You use the Logging tab to control what level of detail you want in the server's event log.

These controls regulate all logging by RRAS, not just remote access log entries.

You have four choices for the level of logged detail:

- The Log Errors Only radio button instructs the server to log errors and nothing else. This gives you an adequate indication of problems after they happen, but it doesn't point out potential problems noted by warning messages.

- The Log Errors And Warnings radio button is the default choice. This forces the server to log error and warning messages to the event log, giving you a nice balance between information content and log volume.

- The Log All Events radio button causes the RRAS service to log mass quantities of messages, literally covering everything the server does. Although this voluminous output is useful for troubleshooting (or even for getting a better understanding of how remote access works), it's overkill for everyday use.

- The Do Not Log Any Events radio button turns off all event logging for RRAS.

Don't use the Do Not Log Any Events option. The service's logs are important in case of a problem.

The Log Additional Routing And Remote Access Information check box allows you to turn on the logging of all PPP negotiations and connections. This can provide valuable information when you're trying to figure out what's wrong, but it adds a lot of unnecessary bulk to your log files. Don't turn it on unless you're trying to pin down a problem.

Setting Log File Properties

By selecting an individual log file in the snap-in, you can change what events will be logged in that file. The Local Log File Properties dialog box has two tabs:

- The Settings tab controls what gets logged in the file:

  - Accounting Requests governs whether events related to the service will be logged (as well as accounting data). You should always leave this checked.

- Authentication Requests adjusts whether successful and failed logon requests are logged. You should always leave this checked.

- Periodic Status controls whether interim accounting packets are permanently stored on disk. You should usually leave this checked.

- Periodic Authentication Requests adjusts whether successful and failed logon requests are periodically logged. You should always leave this checked.

- The Log File tab (see Figure 5.12) controls the format of the file, specifically, how the log file is written to disk. You use this tab to designate three things:

  - The Directory field shows where the log file is stored. By default, each server logs its data in *systemroot*\system32\LogFiles. You can change this location to wherever you want.

  - The Format controls determine the format of the log file. By default, Windows Server 2016 uses the database-compatible file format ODBC (legacy) as shown in Figure 5.12. This format makes it easy for you to take log data and store it in a database, enabling more sophisticated post-processing for things such as billing and chargebacks.

  - The Create A New Log File section determines how often new log files are created. For example, some administrators prefer to start a new log file each week or each month, whereas others are content to let the log file grow without end. You can choose to have RRAS start new log files every day, week, month, never, or when the log file reaches a certain size.

FIGURE 5.12   The Log File tab

Having correct accounting and authorization data is critical to maintaining a good level of security. Exercise 5.3 walks you through configuring remote access logging.

EXERCISE 5.3

Changing Remote Access Logging Settings

1. Open the RRAS MMC snap-in by pressing the Windows key and selecting Adminis-
    trative Tools ➤ Routing And Remote Access.

2. Navigate to the Remote Access Logging and Policies folder. Right-click the folder
    and select Launch NPS.

3. On the left pane, click Accounting. On the right side, click Change Log File Properties
    (see Figure 5.13).

FIGURE 5.13   Change Log File Properties

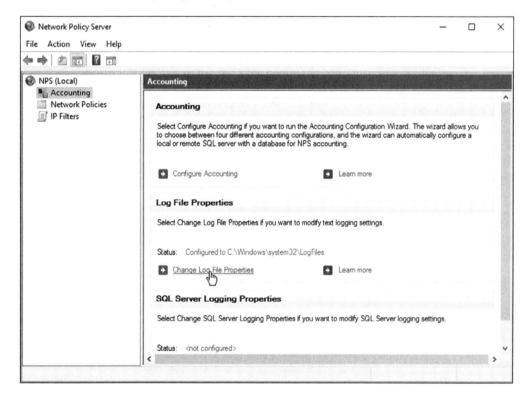

4. The Local File Logging dialog box appears. On the Settings tab, make sure that all
    check boxes are marked.

5. Switch to the Log File tab, and in the Create A New Log File section, select the When Log
    File Reaches This Size option. Enter **50** to set the maximum size of the log file to 50 MB.

6. Click the OK button. Close the Network Policy Server window.

Reviewing the Remote Access Event Log

You use the Log File tab to specify the format, size, and location of the log file. Once you have a log file, however, what do you do with the log information? Windows Server 2016 online help has an exhaustive list of all of the fields logged for each connection attempt and accounting record. Because of the availability of online help, you don't need to have all of those fields memorized, and you don't have to remember exactly how to make sense of the log entries.

Why bother reviewing the logs? One nice feature is that each entry in the authentication log indicates which remote access policy was applied (either to accept or to reject the connection). This is a good way to identify problems with policies because sometimes multiple policies can combine to have an effect that you didn't expect.

Furthermore, if it's desirable in your environment, you can use the logged data to generate accounting reports to tell you things such as the average utilization of your dial-in ports, the top 10 users of dial-in connect time, or how much online time accounts or certain Windows groups use.

Monitoring Ports and Port Activity

You can monitor port status and activity from the RRAS snap-in. The Ports folder under the server contains one entry for each defined port. When you select the Ports folder, you'll see a list of the ports and their current status. The list indicates whether each port is a dial-in or VPN port and whether it's active, so you can get a quick summary of your server's workload at any time.

Double-clicking an individual port displays the Port Status dialog box (see Figure 5.14). This dialog box shows information such as a port's line speed (Line BPS), the amount of transmitted and received data (Bytes In and Bytes Out), and the network address for each protocol being carried on the port. This is a useful tool for verifying whether a port is in active use, and it gives you a count of the number of transmission and reception errors on the port.

FIGURE 5.14   The Port Status dialog box

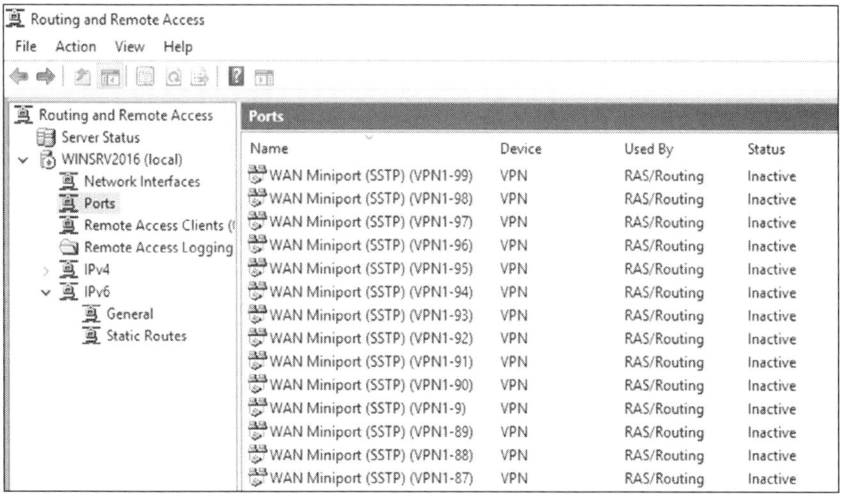

Network Address Translation

Network Address Translation (NAT) provides an advantage with routing and tunneling. NAT (also referred to as network masquerading) allows a router to translate one IP address to another across the tunnel. This allows you to use private IP addressing internally but use pubic addresses between the tunnels.

The huge advantage of NAT is the ability for you to share a single public IP address and single Internet connection between multiple locations using private IP addressing schemes. The nodes on the private network use nonroutable private addresses. NAT maps the private addresses to the public address.

Implementing NAT

Implementing NAT is an easy process. I am going to show you the steps needed to implement NAT, but I am not going to do it as an exercise. To set up NAT in an exercise without a tunnel or without multiple networks is not always an easy thing to do. So, I will just show you how to implement NAT in case you need to do it at work. To run these steps, you must be a member of at least the local Administrators group or higher. The following steps show you how to implement NAT:

1. Start the Routing and Remote Access MMC snap-in (under Administrative Tools). Right-click your server name and choose Configure And Enable Routing And Remote Access.

2. At the Welcome Screen, click Next.

3. Choose the Custom Configuration radio button. Click Next.

4. Click NAT and click Next.

5. Start Service.

6. Expand your server name.

7. Expand IPv4.

At this point, you can configure NAT. If you need to install NAT, you must have a system with multiple NIC devices or a demand-dial setup.

NAT is also commonly used for Internet connections, but this is done through your firewall or router. For example, let's say you have an Internet service provider that issues you only four valid Internet TCP/IP addresses for you to use on your network. You can set up NAT and program it to use those four valid addresses. Then, when a user from the network wants to access the Internet, NAT swaps the user's internal IP address for one of the valid IP addresses.

Configuring Routes

If you are familiar with routers, then you understand that most routers need to have their routing tables built. Well, using a Microsoft Server as a router is no different. When you decide to use a multihomed server as a router, you have to decide how you want to set up the routing table. The routers can be programmed by using the Routing and Remote Access MMC or by using a command prompt.

Any subnet that is connected directly to the router does not need programming. Since the router can see the subnet, it knows what computers can be on that subnet. But you need to program any subnets that are not directly connected to the router.

If I have three subnets, subnet A, subnet B, and subnet C and router1 is connected to subnet A and subnet B, then I have to program router1 to know how to get to subnet C. I don't need to program router1 for subnets A or B. If I have a router (router2) connected to subnet B and subnet C, then router2 needs a route for subnet A.

To program the route in the Microsoft router, you would need to use the Route command. To add a route, you would type in **Route add** and the parameters of the route path. Let's take a look at Figure 5.15.

FIGURE 5.15   Network Layout

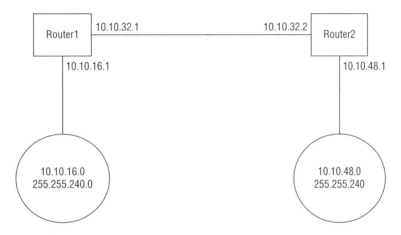

Router1 can NOT see the 10.10.48.0 subnet and Router2 can NOT see 10.10.16.0. So you would need to use the Route command to set these routes up. To use the Route command, you state what you are doing (Route add, Route delete, etc.). Then you put in the subnet you are trying to get to, the mask, and the gateway that you use to get to that subnet. So for Router1 you would use the following command:

Route add 10.10.48.0 mask 255.255.240.0 10.10.32.2 -p

As you can see in this command, you are trying to program for the 10.10.48.0 subnet. The mask is 255.255.240.0 and the gateway you would use from Router1 is the next router (10.10.32.2). The -p stands for persistent and it puts the route into the registry. This is important because when you type Route commands, they are put into Cache. So if the machine reboots, you lose your routes. By using the -p, these routes are entered into the registry and the routes will be reloaded if the server reboots. If you were on Router2, the command would be as follows:

Route add 10.10.16.0 mask 255.255.240.0 10.10.32.1 -p

Now you do have a second option to programming the router. Not do it. You can add a router protocol that will automatically build the routing tables. Microsoft uses the Routing Information Protocol (RIP) to automatically program routes. RIP is a broadcast-based protocol and it can be added to any Microsoft router. The downside to using RIP is the extra broadcast traffic. So if you only have a few routers, it's best to just configure the routes manually. On a large network with many subnets, you may want to consider using RIP.

RAS Gateway

In Windows Server 2016, RAS Gateways are a software router and gateway that routes network traffic between your physical and virtual networks. No matter where the resources are located. So let's say you have a physical and virtual network located at the same physical location. You can implement a Hyper-V server that is also configured with a RAS Gateway virtual machine to act as a forwarding gateway and route traffic between the virtual and physical networks.

When setting up a RAS Gateway, you can use the RAS Gateway in either single tenant mode or multitenant mode.

Single Tenant Mode   In the single tenant mode, administrators can deploy RAS Gateways as an edge VPN server, an edge DirectAccess server, or both simultaneously. Using RAS Gateways this way provides remote users with connectivity to your network by using either VPN or DirectAccess connections. Also, single tenant mode allows administrators to connect offices at different physical locations through the Internet.

Multitenant Mode   When an administrator chooses Multitenant mode, Cloud Service Providers (CSPs) and Enterprise networks can use RAS Gateways to allow datacenter and cloud network traffic routing between both the virtual and physical networks. For multitenant mode, it is recommended that you deploy RAS Gateways on virtual machines that are running Windows Server 2016.

Configuring a VPN Client

Dial-up RAS clients and VPN clients are similar. Almost all of the options that are available when you set up a RAS client are also available when you set up a VPN client. The main differences are as follows:

- VPN clients specify the server's IP address, whereas RAS clients specify the server's phone number.
- VPN clients require an underlying connection to the Internet.

Client configuration is not a focus of the exam, so in this chapter you will learn how to configure a VPN client but not a RAS client. Just remember that the RAS client configuration is extremely similar and that RAS clients are slowly fading away. Thus, here I will focus on VPN settings only.

VPN connections are almost always created on client workstations, so this section describes the settings in Windows 7 / 8 / 8.1 / 10.

When you establish a virtual private network connection, you're actually building an encrypted tunnel between you and some other machine. The tunneled data is carried over an insecure network, such as the Internet.

Once you've created a connection, you can change its properties at any time by opening its Properties dialog box. The Dial-Up Connection Properties dialog box has a total of five tabs that you can use to adjust all of the pertinent settings for each connection.

 Don't confuse these settings with the ones in the Local Area Connection Properties dialog box; they serve entirely different purposes.

The General Tab

The General tab of the Connection Properties dialog box (the box is called Dial-Up Connections or VPN Connections, depending on whether you're configuring dial-up RAS or VPN) is where you specify either the IP address of the VPN server or the modem and phone number to use with this particular connection. Some fields have been filled in already from when you used the Network Connection Wizard. Figure 5.16 shows the VPN settings.

FIGURE 5.16   General tab of the VPN Connection Properties dialog box

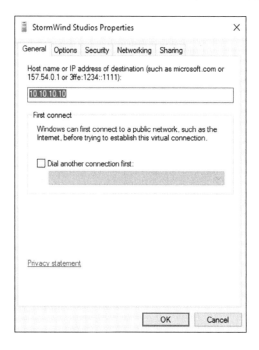

The General tab has a field where you enter the VPN server address or hostname. The First Connect group lets you specify which dial-up connection, if any, you want brought up before the VPN connection is established.

With the General tab, you can also do the following:

- Set VPN options:

  - Enter the VPN server address or hostname.

  - Specify whether to dial another connection automatically first and then specify the connection to dial.

- Set RAS options:

  - Change the modem this connection uses, or the settings for the modem you already have, with the Configure button.

 When configuring dial-up, you can also use the Phone And Modem Options control panel to adjust a broader range of modem settings.

The Options Tab

The Options tab holds settings that control how DUN dials and redials the connection. The controls in this dialog box are segregated into two groups. The Dialing Options group holds controls that govern DUN's interface behavior while dialing, and the Redialing Options group controls whether and how DUN will redial if it doesn't immediately connect (see Figure 5.17).

FIGURE 5.17 Options tab of the VPN Connection Properties dialog box

Dialing Options

Four dialing options are available in the Dialing Options group:

- The Display Progress While Connecting check box (selected by default) instructs DUN to keep you updated on its progress as it attempts to raise the connection.

- The Prompt For Name And Password, Certificate, Etc. check box is also selected by default. When it's on, Windows will prompt you for any credentials it needs to authenticate your connection to the remote server. This may be a username, a password, a public key certificate, or some combination of the three, depending on what the remote end requires.

- The Include Windows Logon Domain check box is unchecked by default. It forces DUN to include the domain name of the domain to which you're logged on as part of the authentication credential. Leave this unchecked unless you're dialing into a Windows NT/2000 network that has a trust relationship with your logon domain.

- For RAS connections, a Prompt For Phone Number check box tells DUN to display the phone number in the connection dialog box. This box is checked by default. This gives you a chance to edit the phone number before dialing; you may want to uncheck it if you (or your users) are prone to making accidental changes.

Redialing Options

The settings in the Redialing Options group control how DUN will attempt to redial the specified number if the remote end is busy or doesn't answer with a recognizable carrier tone. These settings are as follows:

- The Redial Attempts field controls how many attempts DUN will make to raise the other end before giving up. The default value is 3, but you can set any value from 0 (meaning that DUN won't attempt to redial) to 999,999,999.

- The Time Between Redial Attempts drop-down menu controls how long DUN will wait after each failed call before it tries again. Values in the drop-down menu range from 1 second all the way up to 10 minutes, with various increments in between.

- The Idle Time Before Hanging Up drop-down menu lets you specify an inactivity timer. If your connection is idle for longer than the specified period, your client will terminate the call. Note that the remote end may drop the call sooner than your client, depending on how it's configured. By default, this drop-down menu is set to Never, meaning that your client will never drop a call. If you want an inactivity timer, you can pick values ranging from 1 minute to 24 hours.

- The Redial If Line Is Dropped check box automatically redials the number if you are disconnected.

The Security Tab

How useful you find the Security tab will depend on whom you're calling. The default settings it provides will work fine with most Internet service providers and corporate dial-up facilities, but Windows 7 / 8 / 8.1 / 10 have a broad range of security settings that you can change if you require. The Security Options group contains controls that directly affect the security of your connection. The Advanced (Custom Settings) radio button controls settings such as encryption and authentication protocols.

Security Options

The controls in the Security Options group are pretty straightforward. The security settings in effect for this connection are governed by your choice between the Typical (Recommended Settings) and Advanced (Custom Settings) radio buttons (see Figure 5.18).

FIGURE 5.18   Security tab of the VPN Connection Properties dialog box

Typical (Recommended Settings)

Usually, it's best to stick with the Typical (Recommended Settings) option and use its subordinate controls to pick a canned setting that matches your needs. These subordinate controls are as follows:

- The Validate My Identity As Follows drop-down menu lets you choose among the following authentication methods:
  - Unsecured passwords (the default, and the only type of authentication that most networks support)
  - Secured passwords
  - Smart card authentication (useful only when calling another Windows network)

- If you choose to require a secured password, the Automatically Use My Windows Logon Name And Password (And Domain If Any) check box instructs DUN to offer to the remote end the logon credentials you used to log on to the computer or domain. This is useful only if you're dialing into a network that has access to your domain authentication information.

- If you require a secured password or smart card authentication, the Require Encryption (Disconnect If None) check box allows you to have either an encrypted connection or none at all. If you check this box, your client and the remote server will attempt to negotiate a common encryption method. If they can't (perhaps because the remote end doesn't offer encryption), your client will hang up.

Advanced (Custom Settings)

If you select the Advanced (Custom Settings) radio button and then click the Settings button, you'll see the Advanced Security Settings dialog box. Its controls are more complex than the ones on the Security tab.

The first field is the Data Encryption drop-down menu. Windows 10 offers you the opportunity to encrypt both sides of network connections using IPsec. This capability extends to dial-up connections too. The drop-down menu gives you the following four choices:

- No Encryption Allowed means that the server will drop your call if it requires encryption because you can't provide it.

- Optional Encryption tells the client to request encryption but to continue the call if it's not available.

- Require Encryption tells the client to request encryption and to refuse to communicate with servers that don't support it.

- Maximum Strength Encryption tells the client to communicate only with servers that offer the same strength encryption it does. For example, with this setting in force, a North American Windows Server 2016 machine running 3DES won't communicate with a French Windows XP machine because the French machine uses the weaker exportable encryption routines.

The Authentication section controls which authentication protocols this client can use. The default setting, Use Extensible Authentication Protocol (EAP), is for standard Windows authentication (using the MD5-Challenge method) or certificate-based authentication (using the Smart Card Or Other Certificate choice in the drop-down menu).

The Allow These Protocols radio button is followed by a long list of authentication protocols. Although the specifics of how they work are different, the basic idea behind all of these protocols is the same. Each provides a secure way for a client to prove its identity to a server. By selecting the appropriate check boxes, you can make your client use the same protocols as the remote end.

The Networking Tab

You use the Networking tab (see Figure 5.19) to control which protocols your client will attempt to use when communicating with other servers.

FIGURE 5.19   Networking tab of the VPN Connection Properties dialog box

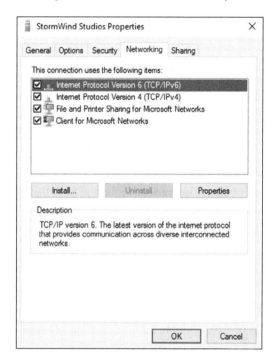

The list box in the middle of the tab shows the network protocols installed on the client. Protocols marked with a check are available for use with this connection. Usually, when configuring RAS, you'll see TCP/IP and Client For Microsoft Networks marked, which indicates that those two protocols can be used over the connection.

The Install, Uninstall, and Properties buttons work just as they do in the Local Area Connection Properties dialog box. By using them, you can control which protocols are on your machine and their settings.

It's worth mentioning that selecting Internet Protocol (TCP/IP) in the protocols list and opening its Properties dialog box gives you access to a set of properties that are completely distinct from any TCP/IP settings that may apply to your LAN interfaces. Usually, the dial-up TCP/IP settings are configured to obtain an IP address and DNS information from the remote server, although if you need to, you can override these settings.

The Sharing Tab

Internet Connection Sharing allows other users to connect to the Internet through this machine. The machine on which you enable this feature works like a gateway to the Internet (see Figure 5.20).

FIGURE 5.20   Sharing tab of the VPN Connection Properties dialog box

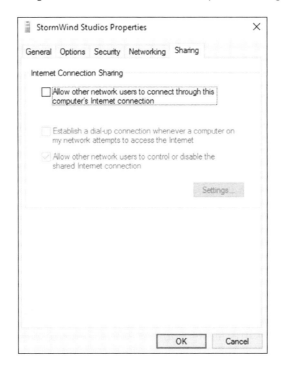

Configuring a Web Application Proxy

One of the new advantages of using the Remote Access role service in Windows Server 2016 is the Web Application Proxy. Normally, your users access applications on the Internet from your corporate network. The *Web Application Proxy* reverses this feature, and it allows your corporate users to access applications from any device outside the network.

Administrators can choose which applications to provide reverse proxy features, and this allows administrators the ability to give access selectively to corporate users for the desired application that you want to set up for the Web Application Proxy service.

The Web Application Proxy feature allows applications running on servers inside the corporate network to be accessed by any device outside the corporate network. The process of allowing an application to be available to users outside of the corporate network is known as *publishing*.

Publishing Applications

One disadvantage to corporate networks are that the machines that access the network are normally devices issued by the organization. That's where Web Application Proxy publishing can help.

Web Application Proxy allows an administrator to publish an organization's applications, thus allowing corporate end users the ability to access the applications from their own devices. This is becoming a big trend in the computer industry, called *bring your own device (BYOD)*.

In today's technology world, users are buying and using many of their own devices, even for business work. Because of this, the users are comfortable with their own devices. Web Application Proxy allows an organization to set up applications and enable their corporate users to use these applications with the devices the users already own, including computers, tablets, and smartphones.

The client side is easy to use as long as the end user has a standard browser or Office client. End users can also use apps from the Microsoft Windows Store that allow the client system to connect to the Web Application Proxy.

Configuring Pass-Through Authentication

Now when setting up the Web Application Proxy so that your users can access applications, you must have some kind of security or everyone with a device would be able to access and use your applications.

Because of this, Active Directory Federation Services (AD FS) must always be deployed with Web Application Proxy. AD FS gives you features such as single sign-on (SSO). *Single sign-on* allows you to log in one time with a set of credentials and use that set of credentials to access the applications over and over.

Pass-through authentication is truly a great benefit for your end users. Think of having a network where a user has to log in every time that user wants to access an application. The more times you make your end users log into an application, the more chances there are that the end user will encounter possible issues. Pass-through authentication works in the following way:

1. The client enters a URL address on their device, and the client system attempts to access the published web application.

2. The Web Application Proxy sends the request to the proxy server.

3. If the backend server needs the user to authenticate, the end user needs to enter their credentials only once.

4. After the server authenticates the credentials, the client has access to the published web application.

When an administrator sets up applications to use pass-through preauthentication, additional features of AD FS will not function. For example, you will not be able to use AD FS Workplace Join, multifactor authentication (MFA), and multifactor access control.

Understanding DirectAccess

DirectAccess was a new technology that was introduced in the Windows Server 2008 R2 and Windows 7 operating systems. DirectAccess has been improved upon, and it is also available for Windows 10 and Windows Server 2016.

DirectAccess allows a remote user to work on their corporate network when they are away from the office without the need for a VPN. As long as the remote user is connected to the Internet, DirectAccess will automatically connect the remote user to the corporate network without the need for any user intervention.

When a user's DirectAccess-enabled laptop is connected to the Internet, a bidirectional connection is automatically established with the user's corporate network. Because the connection is bidirectional, the IT administrator can also remotely manage the Windows 10 machine while the machine is away from the network.

DirectAccess vs. VPNs

There really is no debate between VPN or DirectAccess—DirectAccess is the better way to go. The downside to DirectAccess is that it requires a great deal of time, resources, and knowledge to set it up properly.

There are a few problems with using VPNs to connect to a network. One issue is that when a user gets disconnected from their VPN connection, they must reestablish the VPN connection.

Another issue with VPNs is that many organizations filter VPN connection traffic. It may not be possible for an organization to open a firewall to allow VPN traffic. Also, if your intranet and your Internet connections are the same as your VPN connections, this can cause your Internet to be slower.

DirectAccess does not face the same limitations of a VPN. DirectAccess allows a laptop or desktop that is configured properly to connect automatically using a bidirectional connection between the client and the server.

To establish this connection, DirectAccess uses Internet Protocol Security (IPsec) and IPv6. IPsec provides a high level of security between the client and the server, and IPv6 is the protocol that the machines use.

Understanding the DirectAccess Process

Before you can set up the features and benefits of DirectAccess, there are some prerequisites that I must first go over. DirectAccess is a great way to get your users to access the network from the road, but it is not the easiest thing to set up, and it must be done correctly.

DirectAccess Prerequisites

As with any software package, role, or feature, when you install any one of these, there are always prerequisites that you must deal with. DirectAccess is no different. The following is a list of DirectAccess Server with Advanced Settings prerequisites:

- A public key infrastructure must be deployed.

- ISATAP in the corporate network is not supported. If you are using ISATAP, you should remove it and use native IPv6.

- Computers that are running the following operating systems are supported as DirectAccess clients:

  - Windows Server 2016

  - Windows Server 2012 R2

  - Windows Server 2012

  - Windows Server 2008 R2

  - Windows 10 Enterprise

  - Windows 8.1 Enterprise

  - Windows 8 Enterprise

  - Windows 7 Ultimate

  - Windows 7 Enterprise

- Force tunnel configuration is not supported with KerbProxy authentication.

- Changing policies by using a feature other than the DirectAccess management console or Windows PowerShell cmdlets is not supported.

- Separating NAT64/DNS64 and IPHTTPS server roles on another server is not supported.

  The following is the list of prerequisites if you want to manage DirectAccess clients remotely:

- Windows Firewall must be enabled on all profiles.

- ISATAP in the corporate network is not supported. If you are using ISATAP, you should remove it and use native IPv6.

- Computers that are running the following operating systems are supported as DirectAccess clients:

  - Windows Server 2016

  - Windows Server 2012 R2

  - Windows Server 2012

  - Windows Server 2008 R2

  - Windows 10 Enterprise

  - Windows 8.1 Enterprise

- ▪ Windows 8 Enterprise
- ▪ Windows 7 Ultimate
- ▪ Windows 7 Enterprise
- Changing policies by using a feature other than the DirectAccess management console or Windows PowerShell cmdlets is not supported.

Understanding DirectAccess

To understand DirectAccess better, it helps to understand the process involved with how DirectAccess operates. The following steps, taken from the Microsoft white papers, show how DirectAccess operates.

1. The Windows 8 DirectAccess client determines whether the machine is connected to a network or the Internet.

2. The Windows 8 DirectAccess computer tries to connect to the web server specified during the DirectAccess setup configuration.

3. The Windows 8 DirectAccess client computer connects to the Windows Server 2016 DirectAccess server using IPv6 and IPsec. Because most users connect to the Internet using IPv4, the client establishes an IPv6-over-IPv4 tunnel using 6to4 or Teredo.

4. If an organization has a firewall that prevents the DirectAccess client computer using 6to4 or Teredo from connecting to the DirectAccess server, the Windows 8 client automatically attempts to connect using the IP-HTTPS protocol.

5. As part of establishing the IPsec session, the Windows 8 DirectAccess client and server authenticate each other using computer certificates for authentication.

6. The DirectAccess server uses Active Directory membership, and the DirectAccess server verifies that the computer and user are authorized to connect using DirectAccess.

7. The DirectAccess server begins forwarding traffic from the DirectAccess client to the intranet resources to which the user has been granted access.

Now that you understand how DirectAccess works, let's look at the requirements for setting up DirectAccess on your network.

Knowing the DirectAccess Infrastructure Requirements

To set up DirectAccess, you must make sure that your network infrastructure meets some minimum requirements. The following are the requirements for setting up DirectAccess:

- Windows Server 2016 configured to use DirectAccess. The Windows Server 2016 machine will be set up as a multihomed system. This means your server will need two network adapters so that one adapter is connected directly to the Internet and a second adapter is connected to the intranet. Each network adapter will be configured with its own TCP/IP address.

- Windows 7 / 8 / 8.1 / 10 client machines configured to use DirectAccess.

- Minimum of one domain controller and one Domain Name System (DNS) server running Windows Server 2008 SP2, Windows Server 2008 R2, Windows Server 2012, Windows Server 2012 R2, or Windows Server 2016.

- Certificate authority (CA) server that will issue computer certificates, smart card certificates, or health certificates.

- IPsec policies to specify protection for traffic.

- IPv6 on the DirectAccess server that uses ISATAP, Teredo, or 6to4.

Overview of Wireless Access

In today's computer world, it seems like everyone has a laptop. We all do a lot of traveling, and at any airport it seems like everyone is working on a laptop while waiting for a plane.

Because laptops have grown in popularity, IT professionals must account for them on their networks. Laptops offer IT administrators a unique set of challenges that must be dealt with on a day-to-day basis.

One major concern for IT administrators is security. Years ago, we never had to worry about users copying documents to a desktop computer and then walking out with the computer. However, today users can copy company documents to laptop computers and then walk out the door with the computer and the documents. So, I will discuss wireless networks, protocols, and security.

Windows 7 / 8 / 8.1 / 10, Windows 2008 / 2008 R2, Windows Server 2012 / 2012 R2, and Windows Server 2016 have enhanced the IEEE 802.11 wireless support to include some of the following changes:

- Single sign-on

- 802.11 wireless diagnostics

- WPA2 support

- Native Wi-Fi architecture

- User interface improvements for wireless connections

- Wireless Group Policy enhancements

- Changes in wireless auto-configuration

- Integration with Network Access Protection when using 802.1X authentication

- EAP host infrastructure

- Command-line support for configuring wireless settings

- Network location awareness and network profiles

- Next-generation TCP/IP stack enhancements for wireless environments

Configuring Wireless Access

Windows 7 / 8 / 8.1 / 10, Windows 2008 / 2008 R2, Windows Server 2012 / 2012 R2, and Windows Server 2016 provide built-in support for 802.11 wireless LAN networking. Inside the Network Connections folder, an installed 802.11 wireless LAN network adapter appears as a wireless network connection. The following are some of the items you can configure:

Operating Modes   There are two types of operating modes:

Infrastructure Mode   This mode uses at least one wireless access point (WAP) and/or a device that bridges the wireless computers to each other.

Ad Hoc Mode   Using this mode, wireless network computers connect directly to each other without the use of an access point (AP) or bridge.

Wired Equivalent Privacy   All of us (on a laptop) have tried to find a wireless network at one time or another. *Wired Equivalent Privacy (WEP)* is a wireless encryption that was originally defined in 802.11. WEP helps to prevent unauthorized wireless users from accessing your wireless network by the use of a shared secret key:

- If your wireless network is using the infrastructure mode, the WEP key must be configured on the wireless AP and all of the wireless clients.

- If your wireless network is using the ad hoc mode, the WEP key must be configured on all of the wireless clients.

The WEP key can be either 40-bit or 104-bit, depending on what your hardware can accommodate.

Wi-Fi Protected Access   An organization of wireless equipment vendors called the Wi-Fi Alliance created an interim standard called *Wi-Fi Protected Access (WPA)* while the IEEE 802.11i wireless LAN security standard was still being completed. WPA uses a strong encryption method called the *Temporal Key Integrity Protocol (TKIP)* to replace the weaker WEP standard. You have the ability to use the *Advanced Encryption Standard (AES)* for encryption that is provided by WPA.

WPA can be used in two different mode types:

WPA-Personal   This is used for a home office or small company. In the WPA-Personal model, you would use a preshared or passphrase code to gain authorization onto the network.

WPA-Enterprise   This was designed for a midsize to large organization. WPA-Enterprise has all of the same features as WPA-Personal, but it also includes the ability to use a 802.1X RADIUS server.

Wi-Fi Protected Access 2   Wi-Fi Protected Access 2 (WPA2) was officially designed to replace the WEP standard. WPA2 certifies that equipment used in a wireless network is compatible with the IEEE 802.11i standard. This certification is used to help standardize the use of the additional security features of the IEEE 802.11i standard that are not already included in WPA.

WPA2 can be used in two different mode types:

WPA2-Personal   This is used for a home office or small company. In the WPA-Personal model, you would use a preshared or passphrase code to gain authorization onto the network.

WPA2-Enterprise   This was designed for a midsize to large organization. WPA-Enterprise has all of the same features as WPA-Personal, but it also includes the ability to use a 802.1X RADIUS server.

Service Set Identifier   To specify a wireless network by name, you specify the *service set identifier (SSID)*, also known as the *wireless network name*:

Infrastructure Mode   The SSID is configured on the wireless access point.

Ad Hoc Mode   The SSID is configured on the initial wireless client.

To help wireless clients discover and join the wireless network, the wireless AP or the initial wireless client periodically advertises the SSID. (This can be disabled for security.)

Group Policies for Wireless   You have the ability to use Group Policy settings for Vista, Windows 7, Windows 8, Windows 10, Windows 2008/2008 R2, Windows Server 2012/2012 R2, and Windows Server 2016 for WPA2. Group Policy settings allow you to configure WPA2 options at the server for all wireless clients.

Remote Access Security

In the past, remote access was seldom part of most companies' networks. It was too hard to implement, too hard to manage, and too hard to secure. It's reasonably easy to secure your networks from unauthorized physical access, but it was perceived to be much harder to do so for remote access. Recently, a number of security policies, protocols, and technologies have been developed to ease this problem. First I'll discuss the user authentication protocols.

User Authentication

One of the first steps in establishing a secure remote access connection involves allowing the user to present some credentials to the server. You can use any or all of the following authentication protocols that Windows Server 2016 supports:

Password Authentication Protocol   The *Password Authentication Protocol (PAP)* is the simplest authentication protocol. It transmits all authentication information in cleartext with no encryption, which makes it vulnerable to snooping if attackers can put themselves between the modem bank and the remote access server. However, this type of attack is unlikely in most networks. The security risk with PAP is largely overemphasized considering the difficulty of setting up a sniffer in between the modems and the remote access server. If an attacker has the ability to install a sniffer this deep in the network, you have larger problems to address. PAP is the most widely supported authentication protocol, and therefore you may find that you need to leave it enabled.

Microsoft CHAPv2   Microsoft created *Microsoft CHAPv2 (MS-CHAPv2)* as an extension of the CHAP protocol to allow the use of Windows authentication information. Version 2 is more secure than version 1, and version 1 is not supported by Windows Server 2008 and newer. Some other operating systems (besides Microsoft) support MS-CHAP version 1.

Extensible Authentication Protocol   The *Extensible Authentication Protocol (EAP)* doesn't provide any authentication itself. Instead, it relies on external third-party authentication methods that you can retrofit to your existing servers. Instead of hardwiring any one authentication protocol, a client-server pair that understands EAP can negotiate an authentication method. The computer that asks for authentication (the *authenticator*) is free to ask for several pieces of information, making a separate query for each one. This allows the use of almost any authentication method, including smart cards, secure access tokens such as SecurID, one-time password systems such as S/Key, or ordinary username/password systems.

Each authentication scheme supported in EAP is called an *EAP type*. Each EAP type is implemented as a plug-in module. Windows Server 2016 can support any number of EAP types at once; the Routing and Remote Access Services (RRAS) server can use any EAP type to authenticate if you've allowed that module to be used and the client has the module in question.

Windows Server 2016 comes with *EAP-Transport Level Security (EAP-TLS)*. This EAP type allows you to use public key certificates as an authenticator. TLS is similar to the familiar Secure Sockets Layer (SSL) protocol used for web browsers. When EAP-TLS is turned on, the client and server send TLS-encrypted messages back and forth. EAP-TLS is the strongest authentication method you can use; as a bonus, it supports smart cards. However, EAP-TLS requires your RRAS server to be part of a Windows 2000, Windows Server 2003, Windows Server 2008/2008 R2, Windows Server 2012/2012 R2, or Windows Server 2016 domain.

EAP-RADIUS is another authentication method included with Windows Server 2016. EAP-RADIUS is a fake EAP type that passes any incoming message to a Remote Authentication Dial-In User Service (RADIUS) server for authentication.

PEAP-MS-CHAP v2   This protocol is founded on the authenticated wireless access design, and it's based on Protected Extensible Authentication Protocol Microsoft Challenge Handshake Authentication Protocol version 2 (PEAP-MS-CHAP v2). This authentication protocol utilizes the user account credentials (username and password) stored in Active Directory Domain Services to authenticate wireless access clients instead of using smart cards or user and computer certificates for client authentication.

PEAP-MS-CHAP v2 is an EAP-type protocol that is easier to deploy than Extensible Authentication Protocol with Transport Level Security (EAP-TLS). It is easier because user authentication is accomplished by using password-based credentials (username and password) instead of digital certificates or smart cards. Only servers running Network Policy Server or PEAP-MS-CHAP v2 are required to have a certificate. The server certificate used by NPS can be issued by your organization's private trusted root CA deployed on your network or by a public CA that is already trusted by the client computer.

Just in case you missed the very important line above, I will say it again: Servers that are running Network Policy Server or PEAP-MS-CHAP v2 are *required* to have a certificate.

TLS/SSL (Schannel) *TLS/SSL (Schannel)* implements both the Secure Sockets Layer and Transport Layer Security Internet standard authentication protocols. Administrators can use TLS/SSL to authenticate servers and client computers. Administrators also have the ability to use the protocol to encrypt messages between the authenticated parties (client and server).

The Transport Layer Security protocol, Secure Sockets Layer protocol, Datagram Transport Layer Security (DTLS), and Private Communications Transport (PCT) protocol are all based on the public key cryptography. The Security Channel authentication protocol suite provides these protocols, and this protocol is based on the client-server model.

NTLMv2 *NTLMv2* (Windows NT LAN Manager) helps the authentication process for Windows NT 4 systems or earlier, and it allows for transactions between any two computers running these older systems. Networks that use NTLMv2 are referred to as *mixed mode*.

Kerberos The *Kerberos authentication protocol* is used to perform Active Directory domain authentication. By default, all computers joined to a Windows Server 2016 domain use the Kerberos authentication protocol. Kerberos allows for a single sign-on to network resources on a domain or on a trusted domain. Administrators have the ability to control certain parameters through the Kerberos security settings of the account policies.

802.1X The IEEE has a standard for wireless authentication called 802.1X. 802.1X allows wireless networks to authenticate onto wired Ethernet networks or wireless 802.11 networks. The IEEE 802.1X standard uses EAP for exchanging messages during the authentication process.

Connection Security

You can use some additional features to provide connection-level security for your remote access clients:

- The *Callback Control Protocol (CBCP)* allows your RRAS servers or clients to negotiate a callback with the other end. When CBCP is enabled, either the client or the server can ask the server at the other end to call the client back at a number supplied by the client or a prearranged number stored on the server.

- You can program the RRAS server to accept or reject calls based on the caller ID or automatic number identification (ANI) information transmitted by the phone company. For example, you can instruct your primary RRAS server to accept calls from only your home analog line. This means you can't call the server when you're on the road, and it also keeps the server from talking to strangers.

- You can specify various types and levels of encryption to protect your connection from interception or tampering.

> ### 🌐 Real World Scenario
>
> #### The Limits of Caller ID
>
> It's risky to rely on ANI information for any type of authentication or caller verification. First, caller ID information can be forged. Therefore, if an attacker knows the telephone numbers from which your network accepted calls, they could make their ANI report as one of those numbers and be authenticated onto the network.
>
> Another problem with relying on ANI for authentication is that not all telephone companies pass ANI information with the call. Therefore, if your users are in remote locations (which is why they'd be dialing in anyway), they might not be able to authenticate. Even when ANI information is sent, some telephone companies pass different pieces of the information, which can also result in authentication failures.
>
> Finally, not all incoming line types support ANI. If your site uses a network access server or modem bank that doesn't receive this information based on the type of T1 connection used for incoming calls, the ANI information might not be there at all.

Access Control

Apart from the connection-level measures that you can use to prohibit outside callers from talking to your servers, you can restrict which users can make remote connections in a number of ways:

- You can allow or disallow remote access from individual user accounts. This is the same limited control you have in Windows NT, but it's just the start for Windows Server 2016.

- You can use network access policies to control whether users can get access.

  Like group policies, network access policies give you an easy way to apply a consistent set of policies to groups of users. However, the policy mechanism is a little different: You create rules that include or exclude the users whom you want in the policy.

  Unlike group policies, network access policies are available only in Windows 2003 or higher domain functional level.

  In the next sections, you will learn how to configure user access control.

Configuring User Access

Now it's time to determine who can actually use the remote access services. You do this in two ways:

- By setting up remote access profiles on individual accounts
- By creating and managing network access policies that apply to groups of users

This distinction is subtle but important because you manage and apply profiles and policies in different places.

Setting Up User Profiles

Windows Server 2016 stores a lot of information for each user account. Collectively, this information is known as the account's *profile*, and it's normally stored in Active Directory. Some settings in the user's profile are available through one of the two user-management snap-ins:

- If your RRAS server is part of an Active Directory domain, the user profile settings are in the Active Directory Users and Computers snap-in.

- If your RRAS server is *not* part of an Active Directory domain, the user profile settings are in the Local Users and Groups snap-in.

In either case, the interesting part of the profile is the Dial-In tab of the user's Properties dialog box (see Figure 5.21). This tab has a number of controls that regulate how the user account can be used for dial-in access.

FIGURE 5.21   The Dial-In tab of the user's Properties dialog box

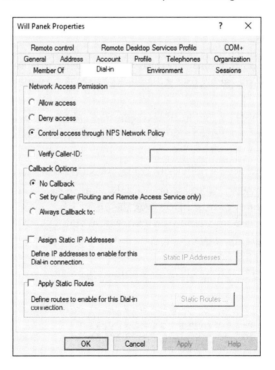

These controls include the following:

Network Access Permission Control Group   The first, and probably most familiar, controls on this tab are in the Network Access Permission control group. These options control whether the user has dial-in permission. Windows Server 2016 has a feature that, in addition to explicitly allowing or denying access, lets you control access through Network Access Protection.

Verify Caller-ID Check Box   RRAS can verify a user's caller ID information and use the results to allow or deny access. When you check the Verify Caller-ID check box and enter a phone number in the field, you're telling RRAS to reject a call from anyone who provides that username and password but whose caller ID information doesn't match what you enter. This means the user can call in only from a single phone number.

Callback Options Control Group   The Callback Options control group gives you three choices for regulating callback:

No Callback   This is the default setting. It means that the server will never honor callback requests from this account.

Set By Caller   This setting allows the calling system to specify a number at which it wants to be called back. The RRAS server will call the client back at that number.

Always Callback To   This setting allows you to enter a number that the server will call back no matter from where the client is actually calling. This option is less flexible but more secure than the Set By Caller option.

Assign Static IP Addresses Check Box   If you want this user always to get the same static IP address, you can arrange to do so by selecting the Assign Static IP Addresses check box and then entering the desired IP address. This allows you to set up nondynamic DNS records for individual users, guaranteeing that their machines will always have a valid DNS entry. On the other hand, this can be more prone to typographical errors on setup than the dynamic DNS-DHCP combination you could use instead.

Apply Static Routes Check Box   In an ordinary LAN, you don't have to do anything special to clients to enable them to route packets—just configure them with a default gateway, and the gateway handles the rest. For dial-up connections, though, you may want to define a list of static routes that will enable the remote client to reach hosts on your network, or elsewhere, without requiring that packets be sent to a gateway in between. Depending on the remote access server, though, the client may be able to use Address Resolution Protocol (ARP) for local devices too. If you want to define a set of static routes on the client, you'll have to do it manually. If you want to assign static routes on the server, select the Apply Static Routes check box and then use the Static Routes button to add and remove routes as necessary.

Remember that these settings apply to individual users, so you can assign different routes, caller ID, or callback settings to each user.

Using Network Access Policies

Windows Server 2016 includes support for additional configuration systems:

- Network access policies (which used to be called *remote access policy*).
- Remote access profiles.
- Network Policy Server (NPS) is the Microsoft implementation of a Remote Authentication Dial-in User Service (RADIUS) server and proxy in Windows Server 2012. NPS is the replacement for Internet Authentication Service (IAS) in Windows Server 2003.

Policies determine who can and cannot connect; you define rules with conditions that the system evaluates to see whether a particular user can connect.

You can have any number of policies in a native Windows Server 2016 domain; each policy must have exactly one profile associated with it.

> Settings in an individual user's profile override settings in a network access policy.

You manage network access policies through the Remote Access Logging & Policies folder in the RRAS snap-in. Policies contain conditions that you pick from a list. When a caller connects, the policy's conditions are evaluated, one by one, to see whether the caller gets in. All of the conditions in the policy must match for the user to gain access. If there are multiple policies, they're evaluated according to an order you specify.

In the following sections, you will see how to create and configure network access policies.

Network Policy Attributes

To create a policy, right-click the Remote Access Logging & Policies folder and select Launch NPS. Then right-click Network Policies and choose New. This command starts the New Network Policy Wizard, which uses a series of steps to help you define the policy.

The Select Condition dialog box is part of the New Network Policy Wizard. It lists the attributes you can evaluate in a policy. Table 5.1 describes the attributes that you can set. These attributes are drawn from the RADIUS standards, so you can (and in some cases, should) intermix your Windows Server 2016 RRAS servers with RADIUS servers.

> When setting up any policies, you must base your policy on company rules and standards. Remember, policies can allow or restrict users from remotely accessing your network. The needs of the organization determine the policy and when to use it.

Once you choose an attribute and click the Add button, its corresponding editor appears. You use the editor to set the value of the attribute. For example, if you select the Day And Time Restrictions attribute, you'll see the Time Of Day Constraints dialog box, which offers a calendar grid that lets you select which days and times are available for logging on.

TABLE 5.1   Network access policy attributes

Attribute Name	What It Specifies
Authentication Type	Specifies the authentication methods required to match this policy.
Allowed EAP Types	Specifies the EAP types required for the client computer authentication method configuration to match this policy.
Called Station ID	Specifies the phone number of the remote access port called by the caller.
Calling Station ID	Specifies the caller's phone number.
Client Friendly Name	Specifies the name of the RADIUS server that's attempting to validate the connection.
Client IP Address (IPv4 and IPv6)	Specifies the IP address of the RADIUS server that's attempting to validate the connection.
Client Vendor	Specifies the vendor of the remote access server that originally accepted the connection. This is used to set different policies for different hardware.
Day And Time Restrictions	Specifies the weekdays and times when connection attempts are accepted or rejected.
Framed Protocol	Specifies the protocol to be used for framing incoming packets (for example, PPP, SLIP, and so on).
HCAP (Host Credential Authorization Protocol) User Groups	Used for communications between NPS and some third-party network access servers (NASs).
Location Groups	Specifies the HCAP location groups required to match this policy. This is used for communications between HCAP and some third-party network access servers (NASs).
MS RAS Vendor	Specifies the vendor identification number of the network access server (NAS) that is requesting authentication.
NAS Identifier	Specifies the friendly name of the remote access server that originally accepted the connection.
NAS IP Address (IPv4 and IPv6)	Specifies the IP address of the remote access server that originally accepted the connection.

TABLE 5.1 Network access policy attributes *(continued)*

Attribute Name	What It Specifies
NAS Port Type	Specifies the physical connection (for example, ISDN, POTS) used by the caller.
Service Type	Specifies Framed or Async (for PPP) or login (Telnet).
Tunnel Type	Specifies which tunneling protocol should be used (L2TP or PPTP).
Windows Groups	Specifies which Windows groups are allowed access.

After you select an attribute and give it a value, you can add more attributes or move to the next page by clicking the Next button on the Select Condition page.

Once you're finished setting attributes, you arrive at the Specify Access Permission page of the wizard. This page has only two radio buttons: Grant Remote Access Permissions and Deny Remote Access Permissions. These buttons specify whether the policy you create *allows* users to connect or *prevents* users from connecting. The page also includes an Access Is Determined By User Dial-In Properties check box. If this box is checked and there is a conflict between the network policy and user dial-in properties, the user dial-in properties take precedence.

Creating a Network Access Policy

In Exercise 5.4, you'll create an adjunct policy that adds time and day restrictions to the default policy. (An *adjunct policy* is one used in conjunction with another policy.) This exercise requires that you have completed the previous exercises in this chapter.

EXERCISE 5.4

Creating a Network Access Policy

1. Open the RRAS MMC snap-in by pressing the Windows key and selecting Administrative Tools ➤ Routing And Remote Access.

2. Expand the server you want to configure in the left pane of the MMC.

3. Right-click the Remote Access Logging And Policies folder.

4. Right-click and then select Launch NPS.

5. Once the Network Policy Server page appears, right-click Network Policies and then choose New.

6. The New Network Policy Wizard starts. In the Policy Name box, enter **Test Policy** and then click Next (leave the other settings as they are).

7. On the Specify Conditions page, click the Add button.

8. In the Select Condition dialog box, scroll down and click Day And Time Restrictions. Click Add.

9. The Time Of Day Constraints dialog box appears. Use the calendar controls to allow remote access Monday through Saturday from 7 a.m. to 7 p.m. and then click the OK button.

10. The Select Conditions dialog box reappears, this time with the new condition listed. Click the Next button.

11. The Specify Access Permission page appears. Select the Access Granted radio button and click Next to continue.

12. The Configure Authentication Methods page appears next. This page is where you choose which authentication methods will be used for this connection. Make sure that MS-CHAP and MS-CHAPv2 are both checked, along with the check boxes associated with them. Click Next.

13. The Configure Constraints page appears. Under Constraints, click Session Timeout. On the right side, click the Disconnect After The Following Maximum Session Time box, and type **60** in the field (the value represents minutes). Click Next.

14. The Configure Settings page appears. This page allows you to configure any additional settings for this network policy. Click Next.

15. On the Completing New Network Policy page, click Finish.

NPS as a RADIUS Proxy Server

When a user tries to log into a domain through the use of a RADIUS server, the RADIUS server processes the connection request and helps the user log into the network.

RADIUS proxy servers work in a different way. When a connection request comes into a RADIUS proxy server, the RADIUS proxy server forwards the request to another RADIUS server for authentication onto the network. Servers that are running Network Policy Server can act both as a RADIUS server and as a RADIUS proxy.

When an administrator sets up NPS as a RADIUS server, NPS provides some of the following actions to help the RADIUS server work properly:

- RADIUS clients send an access request to the central authentication and authorization service. NPS uses Active Directory to authenticate the user's credentials. NPS accesses the Active Directory user's dial-in properties and policies to authorize the connection.

- When using NPS, the RADIUS server also records all accounting information on how much the RADIUS server is used. This is helpful when you have to bill other departments for the RADIUS use. Many organizations require that each department pay for its RADIUS use for its users, and using NPS allows an administrator to do this.

When you set up NPS as a RADIUS proxy, NPS provides all of the routing between all of the RADIUS servers and RADIUS clients. NPS is the main switching and routing service when you use RADIUS as a proxy server.

NPS Configuration

Now that you know that NPS can be set up as a RADIUS server, let's take a look at some of those details of how to do it. When an administrator sets up NPS as a RADIUS proxy, network access servers are then configured as the RADIUS clients. The RADIUS proxy server receives requests from the RADIUS clients, and then the RADIUS server forwards those requests to the appropriate servers. Using NPS to set up a RADIUS proxy should be done when the following conditions are needed:

- If you are the administrator of an organization that offers VPN or wireless network access to multiple clients, the RADIUS server can authenticate and authorize the user through their authentication server.

- If you are an administrator of a domain and you want users who are not members of your domain to authenticate into your domain, you can use an NPS server with a RADIUS proxy. To make this situation work, you must set up a two-way trust (two one-way trusts in opposite directions).

- Another great example of when to set up a RADIUS proxy server is when you are using a non-Microsoft-based database. RADIUS servers have the ability to communicate with different types of databases, allowing users still to be authenticated even when it's not a Microsoft authentication database; an example is a Novell Directory Services (NDS) database.

Another configuration that you may need to set when configuring NPS and RADIUS is the priority. The higher the RADIUS priority number, the less that the RADIUS server gets used. For example, if I have two RADIUS servers named Server1 and Server2 and I want Server2 used only when Server1 is unavailable, I would set the RADIUS priority from 1 to 10. This way it will get used only when Server1 is having issues or is unresponsive.

RADIUS Clients

Network access servers that are RADIUS RFC compliant (2865 and 2866) are considered RADIUS clients when used with NPS and a RADIUS server or proxy.

NPS allows an administrator to enable the use of wireless, switches, remote access, or VPN equipment as long as they are heterogeneous or homogenous sets. Network administrators can allow authentication and authorization through the use of NPS network connection requests as long as administrators deploy the following types of network access servers and technologies:

- Wired access with 802.1X-secured and RADIUS-compliant authenticating switches
- Wireless access with 802.1X-secured and RADIUS-compliant wireless access points

NPS Templates

Templates can be a valuable tool when used properly. Templates allow you to create something once and then use that template to create the same thing over and over again.

You can use templates when creating Active Directory users, when setting up GPOs, and now even when setting up NPS. NPS templates allow an administrator to save time and thus also save the cost required to manage and configure NPS on multiple servers. Multiple NPS templates are available in the Templates Management MMC for an administrator to configure:

- Shared Secrets
- RADIUS Clients
- Remote RADIUS Servers
- IP Filters
- Health Policies
- Remediation Server Groups

One advantage of creating a template is that once the template is created, there is no interference with the actual NPS server's performance. Creating templates does not affect an operational NPS server in any way. Once you load the template to the appropriate location, the template becomes active.

Creating Templates

To create a template in the Template Management MMC, right-click the template type you want to create (such as Health Policies) and click New. The New Template dialog box appears, and you just fill in all of your configuration information.

Importing and Exporting NPS Policies

Importing/exporting NPS is a pretty easy thing. It just happens to depend on which version of Windows you are exporting from. In the following examples, I will explain how to export from Windows Server 2012 R2 using the Windows MMC and how to import into Windows Server 2016.

Exporting from Windows Server 2012 R2

To export NPS from Windows Server 2012 R2, follow these steps:

1. On the source server, open Server Manager.
2. In the Server Manager console tree, open Roles\Network Policy and Access Services\NPS.
3. Right-click NPS and then click Export Configuration.
4. In the dialog box that appears, select the check box I Am Aware That I Am Exporting All Shared Secrets and then click OK.

5. For File Name, type **file.xml,** navigate to the migration store file location, and then click Save.

6. In the console tree, right-click Templates Management and then click Export Templates To A File.

7. For File Name, type **iastemplates.xml,** navigate to the migration store file location, and then click Save.

8. If you have configured SQL logging, you must manually record detailed SQL configuration settings.

    To record these settings, follow these steps:

    a. In the NPS console tree, click Accounting and then click Change SQL Server Logging Properties.

    b. Record the configuration settings on the Settings tab and then click Configure.

    c. Manually record all configuration settings from the Connection and Advanced tabs by copying them into the `sql.txt` file. Alternatively, you can click the All tab and enter Name and Value settings displayed on each line into the `sql.txt` file.

9. Copy the `file.xml`, `iastemplates.xml`, and `sql.txt` files to the migration store file location. This information will be required to configure the destination server.

Importing to Windows Server 2016

To import NPS from Windows Server 2016, follow these steps:

1. Copy the configuration files `file.xml`, `iastemplates.xml`, and `sql.txt` that were exported to the migration store file location to the destination NPS server. Alternatively, you can import configuration settings directly from the migration store file location by supplying the appropriate path to the file in the import command. If you have custom settings that were recorded using the NPS Server Migration: Appendix A—Data Collection Worksheet, they must be configured manually on the destination server.

2. On the destination server, open Server Manager.

3. In the Server Manager console tree, click All Servers; then, from the list of servers in the right pane, right-click the relevant server and select Network Policy Server.

4. To import template configuration settings, complete the remaining steps in this list. If you do not have template settings, skip to step 7.

5. In the console tree, right-click Templates Management and then click Import Templates from a file.

6. Select the template configuration file `iastemplates.xml` that you copied from the source server and then click Open.

7. In the console tree, right-click NPS and then click Import Configuration.

8. Select the configuration file `file.xml` or `ias.txt` that you copied from the source server and then click Open.

9. Verify that a message appears indicating the import was successful.

10. Configure SQL accounting if required using the `sql.txt` file and the data collection worksheet. To configure SQL accounting, complete the remaining steps in this list.

11. In the NPS console tree, click Accounting and then click Change SQL Server Logging Properties in the details pane.

12. Modify the properties on the Settings tab if required and then click Configure to enter detailed settings.

13. Using information recorded in the `sql.txt` file, enter the required settings on the Connection and Advanced tabs and then click OK.

Using Remote Access Profiles

Remote access profiles are an integral part of network access policies. Profiles determine what happens during call setup and completion. Each policy has a profile associated with it; the profile determines what settings will be applied to connections that meet the conditions stated in the policy.

For security reasons, it's usually a good idea to limit access to the administrative accounts on your network. In particular, as a consultant, I usually tell clients to restrict remote access for the administrator account; that way, the potential exposure from a dial-up compromise is reduced. In Exercise 5.5, you will learn how to configure the administrator account's user profile to restrict dial-up access.

EXERCISE 5.5

Restricting a User Profile for Dial-In Access

1. Log on to your computer using an account that has administrative privileges.

2. If you're using an RRAS server that's part of an Active Directory domain, open the Active Directory Users and Computers snap-in by pressing the Windows key and selecting Administrative Tools ➢ Active Directory Users And Computers. If not, open the Local Users and Groups snap-in by pressing the Windows key and selecting Administrative Tools ➢ Computer Management ➢ Local Users And Groups.

3. Expand the tree to the Users folder. Right-click the Administrator account in the right pane and choose Properties. The Administrator Properties dialog box appears.

4. Switch to the Dial-In tab. On machines that participate in Active Directory, make sure the Control Access Through NPS Network Policy option (in the Permissions group) is selected.

5. Click the Deny Access radio button to prevent the use of this account over a dial-in connection.

6. Click the OK button.

You can create one profile for each policy. The profile contains settings that fit into specific areas. Each area has its own link in the profile's Properties dialog box.

The Constraints Tab

The Constraints tab has most of the settings that you think of when you consider dial-in access controls. The controls here allow you to adjust how long the connection can be idle before it gets dropped, how long it can be up, the dates and times for establishing the connection, and what dial-in port and medium can be used to connect.

Authentication Link

In the Authentication Methods pane, you can specify which authentication methods are allowed on this specific policy. Note that these settings, like the other policy settings, will be useful only if the server's settings match. For example, if you turn EAP authentication off in the server's Properties dialog box, turning it on in the Authentication Methods pane of the profile's Properties dialog box will have no effect.

You'll notice that each authentication method has a check box. Check the appropriate boxes to control the protocols that you want this profile to use. If you enable EAP, you can also choose which specific EAP type you want the profile to support. You can also choose to allow totally unauthenticated access (which is unchecked by default).

Settings Tab

The Settings tab of the policy's Properties dialog box has several useful sections, which are described in the following list:

IP Settings Pane   The IP Settings pane gives you control over the IP-related settings associated with an incoming call. If you think back to the server-specific settings covered earlier, you'll remember that the server preferences include settings for protocols other than IP; this is not so in the network access profile. In this pane, you can specify where the client gets its IP address.

Multilink And Bandwidth Allocation Protocol (BAP) Pane   The profile mechanism gives you a degree of control over how the server handles multilink calls. You exert this control through the Multilink And Bandwidth Allocation Protocol (BAP) pane of the profile Properties dialog box. Your first choice is to decide whether to allow multilink calls at all and, if so, how many ports you want to let a single client use at once. Normally, this setting is configured so that the server-specific settings take precedence, but you can override them.

Bandwidth Allocation Protocol Group   The Bandwidth Allocation Protocol control group gives you a way to control what happens during a multilink call when the bandwidth usage drops below a certain threshold. For example, why tie up three analog lines to provide 168 Kbps of bandwidth when the connection is using only 56 Kbps? You can tweak the capacity and time thresholds. By default, a multilink call will drop one line every time the bandwidth usage falls to less than 50 percent of the available bandwidth and stays there for two minutes. The Require BAP For Dynamic Multilink Requests check box allows you to refuse calls from clients that don't support BAP. This is an easy way to make sure that no client can hog your multilink bandwidth.

Encryption Pane   The Encryption pane of the Settings tab controls which type of encryption you want your remote users to be able to access.

The following radio buttons are on the Encryption pane:

- Basic Encryption (MPPE 40-Bit) means single Data Encryption Standard (DES) for IPsec or 40-bit Microsoft Point-to-Point Encryption (MPPE) for Point-to-Point Tunneling Protocol (PPTP).

- Strong Encryption (MPPE 56-Bit) means 56-bit encryption (single DES for IPsec; 56-bit MPPE for PPTP).

- Strongest Encryption (MPPE 128-Bit) means triple DES for IPsec or 128-bit MPPE for PPTP connections.

- No Encryption allows users to connect using no encryption at all. Unless this button is selected, a remote connection must be encrypted or it'll be rejected.

In Exercise 5.6, you'll force all connections to your server to use encryption. Any client that can't use encryption will be dropped. You must complete Exercise 5.4 before you do this exercise.

 Don't do this exercise on your production RRAS server unless you're sure that all of your clients are encryption-capable.

EXERCISE 5.6

Configuring Encryption

1. Open the RRAS MMC snap-in by pressing the Windows key and selecting Administrative Tools ➢ Routing And Remote Access.

2. Expand the server you want to configure in the left pane of the MMC.

3. Right-click the `Remote Access Logging & Policies` folder.

4. Select Launch NPS.

5. Once the Network Policy Server page appears, click the hours policy you created in Exercise 5.4. (I named mine Test Policy.)

6. Select Action ➢ Properties. The policy's Properties dialog box appears.

7. Click the Settings tab. Select Encryption in the left pane.

8. In the right pane, uncheck the No Encryption check box. Make sure that the Basic, Strong, and Strongest check boxes are all selected.

9. Click the OK button. When the policy Properties dialog box reappears, click the OK button.

Setting Up a VPN Network Access Policy

Earlier in this chapter, you learned how to use the Network Access Policy mechanism on a Windows Server 2016 domain. Now it's time to apply what you've learned to a virtual private network (VPN). Recall that you have two ways to control which specific users can access a remote access server:

- You can grant and deny dial-up permission to individual users in each user's Properties dialog box.

- You can create a network access policy that embodies whatever restrictions you want to impose.

It turns out that you can do the same thing for VPN connections, but there are a few additional things to consider.

Granting and Denying Per-User Access

To grant or deny VPN access to individual users, all you have to do is make the appropriate change on the Dial-In tab of each user's Properties dialog box. Although this is the easiest method to understand, it gets tedious quickly if you need to change VPN permissions for more than a few users. Furthermore, this method offers you no way to distinguish between dial-in and VPN permissions.

Creating a Network Access Policy for VPNs

You may find it helpful to create network access policies that enforce the permissions that you want end users to have. You can accomplish this result in a number of ways; which one you use will depend on your overall use of network access policies.

The simplest way is to create a policy that allows all of your users to use a VPN. Earlier in this chapter, you learned how to create network access policies and specify settings for them; one thing you may have noticed was that there's a NAS-Port-Type attribute that you can use in the policy's conditions. That attribute is the cornerstone of building a policy that allows or denies remote access via VPN because you use it to accept or reject connections arriving over a particular type of VPN connection. For best results, you'll use the Tunnel-Type attribute in conjunction with the NAS-Port-Type attribute, as described in Exercise 5.7.

EXERCISE 5.7

Creating a VPN Network Access Policy

1. Open the RRAS MMC snap-in by pressing the Windows key and selecting Administrative Tools ➢ Routing And Remote Access.

2. Expand the server you want to configure in the left pane of the MMC.

3. Right-click the `Remote Access Logging & Policies` folder.

4. Select Launch NPS.

5. Once the Network Policy Server page appears, right-click Network Policies and choose New.

6. The New Network Policy Wizard starts. In the Policy Name box, enter VPN Network Policy and click Next (leave the other settings as they are).

7. On the Specify Conditions page, click the Add button.

8. On the Select Condition page, scroll down, click NAS-Port-Type Attribute, and click Add. When the NAS Port Type page appears, click Virtual VPN in the Common Dial-Up And VPN Tunnel Types box. Click OK and then click the Next button.

9. The Specify Conditions page reappears, this time with the new condition listed. Click the Next button.

10. The Specify Access Permission page appears. Select the Access Granted radio button and click Next to continue.

11. Next the Configure Authentication Methods page will appear. This page is where you choose which authentication methods will be used for this connection. Make sure that MS-CHAP and MS-CHAPv2 are both checked along with their associated check boxes. Click Next.

12. The Configure Constraints page appears. Under Constraints, click Session Timeout. On the right side, click the Disconnect After The Following Maximum Session Time box and type 60 in the box (the value specifies minutes). Click Next.

13. The Configure Settings page appears. This page allows you to configure any additional settings for this network policy. Click Next.

14. At the Completing New Network Policy page, click Finish.

If you don't want to grant VPN access to everyone, you can make some changes to the process in Exercise 5.7 to fine-tune it. First you'll probably want to move the VPN policy to the top of the list. (When you first add the policy described in the exercise, it is placed at the end of the policy list. Unless you move it, the default policies will take effect before the VPN-specific policy does.)

Next you can create an Active Directory group and put your VPN users in it. You can then create a policy using the two conditions outlined in Exercise 5.7 plus a condition that uses the Windows-Groups attribute to specify the new group. You can also use this process to allow everyone dial-up access and reserve VPN capability for a smaller group.

Connection Manager

To help administrators create and manage remote access connections, Microsoft includes a suite of components called Connection Manager within Windows Server 2016. Connection Manager is not installed by default. You can install the Connection Manager using Server Manager ➢ Add Roles ➢ Network Access Services.

Connection Manager allows an administrator to create remote access connections called *service profiles*. These profiles then appear on client machines as network connections. You can use these network connections to connect client machines to VPNs or remote networks.

Configuring Security

When configuring remote access security, you must consider several aspects, the most fundamental of which involves configuring the types of authentication and encryption that the server will use when accepting client requests. You will look at each of these in the following sections.

Controlling Server Security

The Security tab of the server's Properties dialog box (see Figure 5.22) allows you to specify which authentication and accounting methods RRAS uses. You can choose one of two authentication providers by using the Authentication Provider drop-down list.

FIGURE 5.22 The Security tab of the RRAS server's Properties dialog box

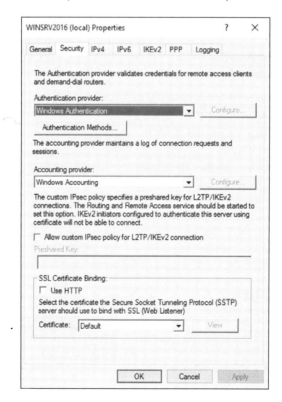

Your choices include the following:

Windows Authentication   This is a built-in authentication suite included with Windows Server 2016.

RADIUS Authentication   This authentication allows you to send all authentication requests heard by your server to a RADIUS server for approval or denial.

You can also use the Accounting Provider drop-down list on the Security tab to choose between the following:

Windows Accounting   With this type of accounting, connection requests are maintained in the event log.

RADIUS Accounting   In this type of accounting, all accounting events, such as call start and call stop, are sent to a RADIUS server for action.

RADIUS Authentication Settings

When you select the RADIUS Authentication option from the Authentication Provider drop-down menu, you are enabling a RADIUS client that passes authentication duties to a RADIUS server. This communication is sent via UDP on port 1645 or 1812, depending on the version of RADIUS being used.

Click the Configure button to open the RADIUS Authentication dialog box. From here, you can set the following options:

- Click the Add button to add the name or address of a RADIUS server to which the RAS server will pass authentication duties.

- You must also enter the correct secret, which is initially set by the RADIUS server.

- The Time-Out option determines how long the RRAS server will attempt to authenticate the remote user before giving up.

- The Initial Score option is similar to the cost value used by routers. The RAS server will attempt to authenticate users on the RADIUS server with the highest score first. If that attempt fails, the RAS server will use the RADIUS server with the next highest score, and so on.

- Although the Port option can be changed, the default setting is part of RFC 2866, "RADIUS Accounting," and it should not be altered unless extraordinary circumstances call for it.

    The Internet Assigned Numbers Authority (IANA) is the official source for port number assignment. You can view current port number assignments and other valuable information at www.iana.org/assignments/port-numbers.

Windows Authentication Settings

Select the Windows Authentication option from the Authentication Provider drop-down menu if you want the local machine to authenticate your remote access users. To configure the server by telling it which authentication methods you want it to use, click the Authentication Methods button, which displays the Authentication Methods dialog box. If you look at the list of authentication protocols earlier in the chapter, you'll find that each one has a corresponding check box here: EAP, MS-CHAPv2, CHAP, and PAP. You can also turn on unauthenticated access by checking the Allow Remote Systems To Connect Without Authentication box, but that is not recommended because it allows anyone to connect to, and use, your server (and thus by extension your network).

There's actually a special set of requirements for using CHAP because it requires access to each user's encrypted password. Windows Server 2016 normally doesn't store user passwords in a format that CHAP can use, so you have to take some additional steps if you want to use CHAP:

1. Enable CHAP at the server and policy levels.

2. Edit the default domain GPO's Password Policy object to turn on the Store Password Using Reversible Encryption policy setting.

3. Change or reset each user's password, which forces Windows Server 2016 to store the password using reversible encryption.

After these steps are completed for an account, that account can be used with CHAP.

 These steps aren't required for MS-CHAPv2; for that protocol, you just enable MS-CHAPv2 at the server and policy levels.

Configuring Network Access Protection

Another way that you can have security is to allow users to access resources based on the identity of the client computer. This security solution is called *Network Access Protection (NAP)*. Determined by the client needs, network administrators now have the ability to define granular levels of network access using NAP. NAP also allows administrators to determine client access based on compliancy with corporate governance policies. The following are some of the NAP features:

Network Layer Protection *Network layer protection* is the ability to secure communications at the Network layer of the OSI model.

All communications travel through the seven layers of the OSI model. Starting at the top (layer 7), the seven layers are the Application, Presentation, Session, Transport, Network, Data-Link, and Physical layers.

VPN Enforcement VPN enforcement verifies the compliancy of the system before the VPN connection is given full access to the network.

IPsec Enforcement *IPsec enforcement* will allow a computer to communicate with other computers as long as the computers are IPsec compliant. You have the ability to configure the requirements for secure communications between the two compliant computer systems. You can configure the IPsec communications based on IP address or TCP/UDP port numbers.

802.1X Enforcement   For a computer system to have 802.1X unlimited access to network connections (Ethernet 802.11 or wireless access point), the computer system must be 802.1X compliant. *802.1X enforcement* verifies that the connecting system is 802.1X connection compliant. Noncompliant computers will obtain only limited access to network connections.

Flexible Host Isolation   *Flexible host isolation* allows a server and domain to isolate computers to help make it possible to design a layer of security between computers or networks. Even if a hacker gains access to your network using an authorized username and password, the server and domain isolation can stop the attack because the computer is not an authorized domain computer.

Multiconfiguration System Health Validator   This feature allows you to specify multiple configurations of a *system health validator (SHV)*. When an administrator configures a network policy for health evaluation, the administrator will select a specific health policy. Using this feature allows you to specify different network policies for different sets of health requirements based on a specific configuration of the SHV. For example, an administrator can create a network policy that specifies that all internal computers must have antivirus software enabled and a different network policy that specifies that VPN-connected computers must have their antivirus software enabled and signature files up-to-date.

NAP Monitoring

There may be many times when you will need to monitor how NAP is running and what NAP policies are being enforced. There are multiple ways that you can monitor NAP. You can use the Network Access Protection MMC snap-in to look at how things are running.

But there is another tool that you can use called Logman. Logman creates and manages Event Trace Session and Performance logs and allows an administrator to monitor many different applications through the use of the command line. Table 5.2 shows some of the different Logman switches you can use.

TABLE 5.2   Logman switches

Switch	Description
Logman create	Creates a counter, trace, configuration data collector, or API
Logman query	Queries data collector properties
Logman start | stop	Starts or stops data collection
Logman delete	Deletes an existing data collector
Logman update	Updates the properties of an existing data collector
Logman import | export	Imports a data collector set from an XML file or exports a data collector set to an XML file

PowerShell for Remote Access

There may be times when you need to use PowerShell to configure Remote Access. Table 5.3 is just some of the PowerShell commands that you can use to configure and manage remote access.

To see the entire list of Remote Access PowerShell commands, visit Microsoft's website at `https://technet.microsoft.com/en-us/itpro/powershell/windows/remoteaccess/remoteaccess`.

TABLE 5.3   PowerShell commands for RAS

Command	Description
Add-DAAppServer	This command allows an administrator to add a new application server security group to the DirectAccess.
Add-DAClient	Administrators use this command to add client computer security groups (SGs) to the DirectAccess (DA).
Add-DAEntryPoint	This command allows you to add an entry point to a multisite deployment.
Add-RemoteAccessIpFilter	Administrators use this command to add filters for network traffic that passes through a particular interface.
Add-RemoteAccessRadius	This command allows an administrator to add a new external RADIUS server for VPN or DirectAccess connectivity.
Disconnect-VpnUser	Administrators can use this command to disconnect a VPN user.
Enable-DAMultiSite	This command allows an admin to enable and configure a multisite deployment while also adding the first entry point.
Get-BgpPeer	Administrators can use this command to show the configuration information for BGP peers.
Get-BgpRouter	This command allows you to see the configuration information for BGP routers.
Get-DAClient	Administrators use this command to see the list of client security groups that are part of the DirectAccess deployment and the client properties.

Command	Description
Get-DAEntryPoint	This command shows the settings for an entry point.
Get-DAServer	Admins can use this command to see the properties of the DirectAccess server.
Get-RemoteAccess	This command shows the configuration of a DirectAccess and VPN server.
Remove-BgpPeer	Administrators can use this command to remove a BGP peer from a router.
Set-DAServer	This command allows an administrator to set the properties specific to the DirectAccess server.
Set-VpnAuthType	Administrators use this command to set the authentication type to be used for a VPN connection.
Set-VpnServerConfiguration	This command allows you to update the S2S server parameters.
Set-VpnSstpProxyRule	Administrators use this command for updating the tenant ID to gateway mapping for SSTP Proxy.
Update-DAMgmtServer	This command is used to update the list of management servers of the DirectAccess deployment.

Summary

In this chapter, you learned how to install and configure Routing and Remote Access Services to handle dial-in connections, how to configure appropriate encryption and security settings so that communication between the client and server is encrypted and authenticated, how to install RRAS to provide VPN service using the PPTP and L2TP protocols, how to configure VPN services on the server and client, and, finally, how to troubleshoot common problems with VPNs. I explained the benefits of DirectAccess and how DirectAccess works.

I talked about the different ways that you can secure your remote access connections. You learned how to configure appropriate security settings so that communication between the client and server is secure because of NAP and NPS settings.

I talked about how to verify that client machines meet the minimum requirements in order to gain either full or limited access to your network.

I also discussed wireless networking and what types of security encryption you can use to help support your wireless network. You learned about the different components of wireless access and using group policies to configure wireless clients.

Exam Essentials

Know how to install and configure RAS at the server level.   The RAS installation process is driven by the Routing and Remote Access Server Setup Wizard, which you use to set up a dial-up server. You can specify whether the server acts as a remote access server, specify what authentication providers and settings you want the server to use, control the settings applied to each protocol you have installed, specify which PPP protocols (including multilink) the clients on this server are allowed to use, and control what level of log detail is kept for incoming connections.

Know how to install and configure a VPN server.   If you don't have RRAS installed, you'll need to install it, activate it, and configure it as a VPN server. If you're already using RRAS for IP routing or remote access, you can enable it as a VPN server without reinstalling. VPN configuration is extremely simple, at least for PPTP. Either a server can accept VPN calls or it can't. If it can, it will have a certain number of VPN ports, all of which are configured identically.

Know how to configure an RRAS client.   Most client connections are made on Windows 8, Windows 7, Windows Vista, or Windows XP Professional workstations. Dial-in and VPN connections are configured similarly, but when creating a VPN connection, you must substitute an IP address for a phone number.

Understand what NAP can do for your network.   Understand that NAP allows administrators to determine client access based on compliancy with corporate governance policies. Some of the settings are Network Layer Protection, VPN Enforcement, IPsec Enforcement, 802.1X Enforcement, Flexible Host Isolation, and Multi-configuration System Health Validator.

Understand what NPS can do for your network.   Understand how to use NPS to manage network access centrally through a variety of network access servers, including RADIUS-compliant 802.1X-capable wireless access points, VPN servers, dial-up servers, and 802.1X-capable Ethernet switches.

Video Resources

There are videos available for the following exercises:

Exercise 5.1

Exercise 5.2

You can access the videos at http://sybextestbanks.wiley.com on the Other Study Tools tab.

Review Questions

1. You are the network administrator for StormWind Studios. You deploy a RAS Gateway server as an edge VPN server and as an edge DirectAccess server. Your users can now access the corporate network by using either VPN or DirectAccess connections. Which RAS Gateway mode is being described?

    A. Multitenant mode

    B. Single tenant mode

2. What PowerShell command would you use to see the configuration information for your BGP routers?

    A. `Get-BgpRouter`

    B. `Get-Router`

    C. `Set-RouterClient`

    D. `Add-BgpClient`

3. You are the administrator of StormWind. You need to see a list of client security groups that are a part of the DirectAccess deployment. What PowerShell command would you use?

    A. `Get-Client`

    B. `Get-DAClient`

    C. `Get-VPNClient`

    D. `Get-RASClient`

4. Your network contains an Active Directory domain named StormWind.com. Network Access Protection (NAP) is deployed to the domain. You need to create NAP event trace log files on a client computer. What should you run?

    A. Register-ObjectEvent

    B. Register-EngineEvent

    C. tracert

    D. logman

5. Your network contains four Network Policy Server (NPS) servers named ServerA, ServerB, ServerC, and ServerD. Server1 is configured as a RADIUS proxy that forwards connection requests to a remote RADIUS server group named Group1. You need to ensure that ServerB and ServerC receive connection requests. ServerD should receive connection requests only if both ServerB and ServerC are unavailable. How should you configure Group1?

    A. Change the weight of ServerB and ServerC to 10.

    B. Change the weight of ServerD to 10.

    C. Change the priority of ServerB and ServerC to 10.

    D. Change the priority of ServerD to 10.

6. You have a Windows Server 2016 server named ServerA. ServerA is located on the perimeter network and only uses inbound TCP port 443 is allowed to connect ServerA from the Internet. You install the Remote Access server role on ServerA. You need to configure ServerA to accept VPN connections over port 443. Which VPN protocol should you use?

    A. PPTP

    B. SSTP

    C. L2TP

    D. IKEv2

7. What PowerShell command would you use to view the configuration of a DirectAccess or VPN server?

    A. `Get-Server`

    B. `View-Server`

    C. `Get-RemoteAccess`

    D. `Get-RASAccess`

8. You are the administrator of a large company. You need to set the setting of your DirectAccess server. What PowerShell command would you use?

    A. `Set-DirectAccessServer`

    B. `Set-DAServer`

    C. `Set-DirectServer`

    D. `Set-RASServer`

9. You have decided to implement a VPN server. You want to set the authentication type for the VPN connect. What PowerShell command would you use?

    A. `Set-VPNType`

    B. `Set-AuthType`

    C. `Set-VPNAuthType`

    D. `Set-VPNAuth`

10. You are the network administrator for a mid-size company. You need to add a new external RADIUS server for VPN connectivity. What PowerShell command would you use?

    A. `Add-RemoteAccessServer`

    B. `Add-RemoteAccess`

    C. `Add-RASServer`

    D. `Add-RemoteAccessRadius`

Chapter

6

Understanding File Services

THE FOLLOWING 70-741 EXAM OBJECTIVES ARE COVERED IN THIS CHAPTER:

✓ **Implement Distributed File System (DFS) and Branch Office solutions**

- This objective may include but is not limited to: Install and configure DFS namespaces; configure DFS replication targets; configure replication scheduling; configure Remote Differential Compression (RDC) settings; configure staging; configure fault tolerance; clone a Distributed File System Replication (DFSR) database; recover DFSR databases; optimize DFS Replication; install and configure BranchCache; implement distributed and hosted cache modes; implement BranchCache for web, file, and application servers; troubleshoot BranchCache.

In this chapter, I will talk about the services that we can use with file servers. File servers are servers that are set up to host files for your organization. Once you have set up a basic server and decided that the server will host files, it's now time to add some other features to that server.

I will start the chapter talking about using the File Server Resource Manager. This is a utility that allows an administrator to manage and configure file servers. This includes setting up how much space your users will get on the file servers. I will also show you how to set up and manage encrypted files using the Encrypting File System (EFS).

I will then introduce you to the Distributed File System (DFS) setup. I will show you how to install and set up a DFS namespace. I will then show you how to add shared folders to the DFS structure.

Configuring File Server Resource Manager

As an administrator, when you need to control and manage the amount and type of data stored on your servers, Microsoft delivers the tools to help you do just that. The *File Server Resource Manager (FSRM)* is a suite of tools that allows an administrator to place quotas on folders or volumes, filter file types, and create detailed storage reports. These tools allow an administrator to properly plan and implement policies on data as needed.

FSRM Features

Many of the advantages of using FSRM come from all of the included features, which allow administrators to manage the data that is stored on their file servers. Some of the advantages included with FSRM are as follows:

Configure File Management Tasks　FSRM allows an administrator to apply a policy or action to data files. Some of the actions that can be performed include the ability to encrypt files or run a custom command.

Configure Quotas　Quotas give an administrator the ability to limit how much disk space a user can use on a file server. Administrators have the ability to limit space to an entire volume or to specific folders.

File Classification Infrastructure   Administrators can set file classifications and then manage the data more effectively by using these classifications. Classifying files, and then setting policies to those classifications, allows an administrator to set policies on those classifications. These policies include restricting file access, file encryption, and file expirations.

Configure File Screens   Administrators can set file screening on a server and limit the types of files that are being stored on that server. For example, an administrator can set a file screen on a server so that any file ending in .bmp gets rejected.

Configure Reports   Administrators can create reports that show them how data is classified and accessed. They also have the ability to see which users are trying to save unauthorized file extensions.

Installing the FSRM Role Service

Installing FSRM is easy when using either Server Manager or PowerShell. To install using Server Manager, you go into Add Roles And Features and choose File And Storage Services ➢ File Services ➢ File Server Resource Manager. To install FSRM using PowerShell, you use the following command:

```
Install-WindowsFeature -Name FS-Resource-Manager -IncludeManagementTools
```

Configuring FSRM using the Windows GUI version is straightforward, but setting up FSRM using PowerShell is a bit more challenging. Table 6.1 describes some of the PowerShell commands for FSRM.

TABLE 6.1   PowerShell commands for FSRM

PowerShell Cmdlet	Description
Get-FsrmAutoQuota	Gets auto-apply quotas on a server
Get-FsrmClassification	Gets the status of the running file classification
Get-FsrmClassificationRule	Gets classification rules
Get-FsrmFileGroup	Gets file groups
Get-FsrmFileScreen	Gets file screens
Get-FsrmFileScreenException	Gets file screen exceptions
Get-FsrmQuota	Gets quotas on the server
Get-FsrmSetting	Gets the current FSRM settings

TABLE 6.1 PowerShell commands for FSRM *(continued)*

PowerShell Cmdlet	Description
Get-FsrmStorageReport	Gets storage reports
New-FsrmAutoQuota	Creates an auto-apply quota
New-FsrmFileGroup	Creates a file group
New-FsrmFileScreen	Creates a file screen
New-FsrmQuota	Creates an FSRM quota
New-FsrmQuotaTemplate	Creates a quota template
Remove-FsrmClassificationRule	Removes classification rules
Remove-FsrmFileScreen	Removes a file screen
Remove-FsrmQuota	Removes an FSRM quota from the server
Set-FsrmFileScreen	Changes the configuration settings of a file screen
Set-FsrmQuota	Changes the configuration settings for an FSRM quota

Configure File and Disk Encryption

Hardware and software encryption are some of the most important actions you can take as an administrator. You must make sure that if anyone steals hardware from your company or from your server rooms that the data they are stealing is secured and cannot be used. This is where BitLocker can help.

Using BitLocker Drive Encryption

To prevent individuals from stealing your computer and viewing personal and sensitive data found on your hard disk, some editions of Windows come with a new feature called BitLocker *Drive Encryption*. BitLocker encrypts the entire system drive. New files added to this drive are encrypted automatically, and files moved from this drive to another drive or computers are decrypted automatically.

Only Windows 7 Enterprise, Windows 7 Ultimate, Windows 8 Pro, Windows 8 Enterprise, Windows 10 Enterprise, Windows 10 Pro, Windows Server 2008, Windows Server 2008 R2,

Windows Server 2012, Windows Server 2012 R2, and Windows Server 2016 include BitLocker Drive Encryption, and only the operating system drive (usually C:) or internal hard drives can be encrypted with BitLocker. Files on other types of drives must be encrypted using BitLocker To Go. BitLocker To Go allows you to put BitLocker on removable media such as external hard disks or USB drives.

BitLocker Recovery Password

The BitLocker recovery password is important. Do not lose it, or you may not be able to unlock the drive. Even if you do not have a TPM, be sure to keep your recovery password in case your USB drive becomes lost or corrupted.

BitLocker uses a *Trusted Platform Module (TPM)* version 1.2 or newer to store the security key. A TPM is a chip that is found in newer computers. If you do not have a computer with a TPM, you can store the key on a removable USB drive. The USB drive will be required each time you start the computer so that the system drive can be decrypted.

If the TPM discovers a potential security risk, such as a disk error or changes made to the BIOS, hardware, system files, or startup components, the system drive will not be unlocked until you enter the 48-digit BitLocker recovery password or use a USB drive with a recovery key as a recovery agent.

BitLocker must be set up either within the Local Group Policy editor or through the BitLocker icon in the Control Panel. One advantage of using BitLocker is that you can prevent any unencrypted data from being copied onto a removable disk, thus protecting the computer.

BitLocker requires that you have a hard disk with at least two partitions, both formatted with NTFS. One partition will be the system partition that will be encrypted. The other partition will be the active partition that is used to start the computer. This partition will remain unencrypted.

Features of BitLocker

As with any version of Windows, Microsoft continues to improve on the technologies used in Windows Server 2016 and Windows 10. The following sections cover some of the features of BitLocker.

BitLocker Provisioning

In previous versions of BitLocker (Windows Vista and Windows 7), BitLocker provisioning (system and data volumes) was completed during the post installation of the BitLocker utility. BitLocker provisioning was done through either the command-line interface (CLI) or the Control Panel. In the Windows 8/Windows Server 2016 version of BitLocker, an administrator can choose to provision BitLocker before the operating system is even installed.

Administrators have the ability to enable BitLocker prior to the operating system deployment from the Windows Preinstallation Environment (WinPE). BitLocker is applied to the formatted volume, and BitLocker encrypts the volume prior to running the Windows setup process.

If an administrator wants to check the status of BitLocker on a particular volume, the administrator can view the status of the drive either in the BitLocker Control Panel applet or in File Explorer.

Used Disk Space–Only Encryption

Windows 7 BitLocker requires that all data and free space on the drive must be encrypted. Because of this requirement, the encryption process can take a long time on larger volumes. In Windows 10 BitLocker, administrators have the ability to encrypt either the entire volume or just the space being used. When you choose the Used Disk Space Only option, only the section of the drive that contains data will be encrypted. Because of this, encryption is completed much faster.

Standard User PIN and Password Change

One issue that BitLocker has had in the past is that you need to be an administrator to configure BitLocker on operating system drives. This could become an issue in a large organization because deploying TPM + PIN to a large number of computers can be challenging.

Even with the new operating system changes, administrative privileges are still needed to configure BitLocker, but now your users have the ability to change the BitLocker PIN for the operating system or change the password on the data volumes.

When a user gets to choose their own PIN and password, they normally choose something that has meaning to them and something that is easy to remember. That is a good and bad thing at the same time. It's a good thing because when your users choose their own PIN and password, they normally don't need to write it down—they just know it. It's a bad thing because if anyone knows the user well, they can have an easier time figuring out the person's PIN and password. Even when you allow your users to choose their own PIN and password, make sure you set a GPO to require password complexity.

Network Unlock

One of the features of BitLocker is called Network Unlock. *Network Unlock* allows administrators to easily manage desktop and servers that are configured to use BitLocker. Network Unlock allows an administrator to configure BitLocker to automatically unlock an encrypted hard drive during a system reboot when that hard drive is connected to their trusted corporate environment. For this to function properly on a machine, there has to be a DHCP driver implementation in the system's firmware.

If your operating system volume is also protected by the TPM + PIN protection, the administrator has to be sure to enter the PIN at the time of the reboot. This protection can actually make using Network Unlock more difficult to use, but they can be used in combination.

Support for Encrypted Hard Drives for Windows

One of the new advantages of using BitLocker is *Full Volume Encryption (FVE)*. BitLocker provides built-in encryption for Windows data files and Windows operating system files. The advantage of this type of encryption is that encrypted hard drives that use *Full Disk Encryption (FDE)* get each block of the physical disk space encrypted. Because each physical block gets encrypted, it offers much better encryption. The only downside to this is that because each physical block is encrypted, it degrades the hard drive speed somewhat. So, as an administrator, you have to decide whether you want better speed or better security on your hard disk.

Windows 7 and 2008 R2 vs. Windows 10 and 2016

The real question is what's the difference between Windows 7/Windows 2008 R2 and Windows 10/Windows Server 2016? Table 6.2 shows you many of the common features and how they work then and now.

TABLE 6.2 BitLocker then and now

Feature	Windows 7/Server 2008 R2	Windows 10/Server 2016
Resetting the BitLocker PIN or password	The user's privileges must be set to an administrator if you want to reset the BitLocker PIN on an operating system drive and the password on a fixed or removable data drive.	Standard users now have the ability to reset the BitLocker PIN and password on operating system drives, fixed data drives, and removable data drives.
Disk encryption	When BitLocker is enabled, the entire disk is encrypted.	When BitLocker is enabled, users have the ability to choose whether to encrypt the entire disk or only the used space on the disk.
Hardware-encrypted drive support	Not supported.	If the Windows logo hard drive comes preencrypted from the manufacturer, BitLocker is supported.
Unlocking using a network-based key to provide dual-factor authentication	Not available.	If a computer is rebooted on a trusted corporate wired-network key protector, then this feature allows a key to unlock and skip the PIN entry.

TABLE 6.2 BitLocker then and now *(continued)*

Feature	Windows 7/Server 2008 R2	Windows 10/Server 2016
Protection for clusters	Not available.	Windows Server 2016 BitLocker includes the ability to support cluster-shared volumes and failover clusters as long as they are running in a domain that was established by a Windows Server 2016 domain controller with the Kerberos Key Distribution Center Service enabled.
Linking a BitLocker key protector to an Active Directory account	Not available.	BitLocker allows a user, group, or computer account in Active Directory to be tied to a key protector. This key protector allows protected data volumes to be unlocked.

In Exercise 6.1, you will enable BitLocker on the Windows Server 2016 system.

EXERCISE 6.1

Enabling BitLocker in Windows Server 2016

1. Open Server Manager by selecting the Server Manager icon or running `servermanager.exe`.

2. Select Add Roles And Features from the dashboard.

3. Select Next at the Before You Begin pane (if shown).

4. Select role-based or feature-based installation and select Next to continue.

5. Select the Select A Server From The Server Pool option and click Next.

6. At the Select Server Roles screen, click Next.

7. At the Select Features screen, click the BitLocker Drive Encryption check box. When the Add Roles and Features dialog box appears, click the Add Features button. Then click Next.

8. Select the Install button on the Confirmation pane of the Add Roles and Features Wizard to begin BitLocker feature installation. The BitLocker feature requires a restart

to complete. Selecting the Restart The Destination Server Automatically If Required option in the Confirmation pane will force a restart of the computer after installation is complete.

9. If the Restart The Destination Server Automatically If Required check box is not selected, the Results pane of the Add Roles And Features Wizard will display the success or failure of the BitLocker feature installation. If required, a notification of additional action necessary to complete the feature installation, such as the restart of the computer, will be displayed in the results text.

You also can install BitLocker by using the Windows PowerShell utility. To install BitLocker, use the following PowerShell commands:

```
Install-WindowsFeature BitLocker -IncludeAllSubFeature -IncludeManagementTools
-Restart
```

Using EFS Drive Encryption

If you have been in the computer industry long enough, you may remember the days when only servers used NTFS. Years ago, most client systems used FAT or FAT32, but NTFS had some key benefits over FAT/FAT32. The main advantages were NTFS security, quotas, compression, and encryption. Encryption is available on a system because you are using a file structure (for example, NTFS) that allows encryption. Windows Server 2016 NTFS allows administrators to use these four advantages including encryption.

Encrypting File System (EFS) allows a user or administrator to secure files or folders by using encryption. Encryption employs the user's security identification (SID) number to secure the file or folder. Encryption is the strongest protection that Windows provides to help you keep your information secure. Some key features of EFS are as follows:

- Encrypting is simple; just select a check box in the file or folder's properties to turn it on.

- You have control over who can read the files.

- Files are encrypted when you close them but are automatically ready to use when you open them.

- If you change your mind about encrypting a file, clear the check box in the file's properties.

To implement encryption, open the Advanced Attributes dialog box for a folder and check the Encrypt Contents To Secure Data box.

If files are encrypted using EFS and an administrator has to unencrypt the files, there are two ways to do this. You can log in using the user's account (the account that encrypted the files) and unencrypt the files using the Cipher command. Alternatively, you can become a recovery agent and manually unencrypt the files.

If you use EFS, it's best not to delete users immediately when they leave a company. Administrators have the ability to recover encrypted files, but it is much easier to gain access to the user's encrypted files by logging in as the user who left the company and unchecking the encryption box.

Using the Cipher Command

The Cipher command is useful when it comes to EFS. Cipher is a command-line utility that allows you to change and/or configure EFS. When it comes to using the Cipher command, you should be aware of a few things:

- Administrators can decrypt files by running `Cipher.exe` in the Command Prompt window (advanced users).
- Administrators can use Cipher to modify an EFS-encrypted file.
- Administrators can use Cipher to import EFS certificates and keys.
- Administrators can also use Cipher to back up EFS certificates and keys.

Let's take a look at some of the different switches that you can use with Cipher. Table 6.3 describes many of the different Cipher switches you can use. This table comes from Microsoft's TechNet site. Microsoft continues to add and improve switches, so make sure you check Microsoft's website to see whether there are any changes.

TABLE 6.3 Using the cipher switches

Cipher switch	Description
/e	This switch allows an administrator to encrypt specified folders. With this folder encrypted, any files added to this folder will automatically be encrypted.
/d	This switch allows an administrator to decrypt specified folders.
/s: dir	By using this switch, the operation you are running will be performed in the specified folder and all subfolders.
/i	By default, when an error occurs, Cipher automatically halts. By using this switch, Cipher will continue to operate even after errors occur.
/f	The force switch (/f) will encrypt or decrypt all of the specified objects, even if the files have been modified by using encryption previously. Cipher, by default, does not touch files that have been encrypted or decrypted previously.

Cipher switch	Description
/q	This switch shows you a report about the most critical information of the EFS object.
/h	Normally, system or hidden files are not touched by encryption. By using this switch, you can display files with hidden or system attributes.
/k	This switch will create a new file encryption key based on the user currently running the Cipher command.
/?	This shows the Cipher help command.

Configuring Distributed File System

One problem that network administrators have is deciding how to share folders and communicating to end users how to find the shares. For example, if you share a folder called StormWind Documents on server A, how do you make sure your users will find the folder and the files within it? The users have to know the server name and the share name. This can be a huge problem if you have hundreds of shares on multiple servers. If you want to have multiple copies of the folder called StormWind Documents for fault tolerance and load balancing, the problem becomes even more complicated.

Distributed File System (DFS) in Windows Server 2016 offers a simplified way for users to access geographically dispersed files. DFS allows you to set up a tree structure of virtual directories that allows users to connect to shared folders throughout the entire network.

Administrators have the ability to take shared folders that are located on different servers and transparently connect them to one or more DFS namespaces—virtual trees of shared folders throughout an organization. The advantage of using DFS is that if one of the folders becomes unavailable, DFS has failover capability that will allow your users to connect to the data on a different server.

Administrators can use the DFS tools to choose which shared folders will appear in the namespace and also to decide how the names of these shared folders will show up in the virtual tree listing.

Advantages of DFS

One of the advantages of DFS is that when a user views this virtual tree, the shared folders appear to be located on a single machine. These are some of the other advantages of DFS:

Simplified Data Migration   DFS gives you the ability to move data from one location to another without the user needing to know the physical location of the data. Because the users do not need to know the physical location of the shared data, administrators can simply move data from one location to another.

Security Integration   Administrators do not need to configure additional security for the DFS shared folders. The shared folders use the NTFS and shared folder permissions that an administrator has already assigned when the share was set up.

Access-Based Enumeration (ABE)   This DFS feature (disabled by default) displays only the files and folders that a user has permissions to access. If a user does not have access to a folder, Windows hides the folder from the user's DFS view. This feature is not active if the user is viewing the files and folders locally.

Types of DFS

The following are types of DFS:

DFS Replication (DFSR)   Administrators have the ability to manage replication scheduling and bandwidth throttling using the DFS management console. Replication is the process of sharing data between multiple machines. As explained earlier in the section, replicated shared folders allow you to balance the load and have fault tolerance. DFS also has read-only replication folders.

DFS Namespace   The DFS Namespace service is the virtual tree listing in the DFS server. An administrator can set up multiple namespaces on the DFS, allowing for multiple virtual trees within DFS. The DFS Namespace service was once known as *Distributed File System* in Windows 2000 Server and Windows Server 2003 (in case you still use Server 2003).

In Exercise 6.2, you will install the DFS Namespace service on the file server. You need to start the installation using the Server Manager MMC.

EXERCISE 6.2

Installing the DFS Namespace Service

1. Open Server Manager by selecting the Server Manager icon or running `servermanager.exe`.

2. Select Add Roles And Features from the dashboard.

3. Select Next at the Before You Begin pane (if shown).

4. Select Role-Based or Feature-Based installation and select Next to continue.

5. Select the Select A Server From The Server Pool option and click Next.

6. At the Select Server Roles screen, expand File And Storage Services and check the DFS Namespace and DFS Replication check boxes (See Figure 6.1). Then click Next. If a dialog box appears, click the Add Features button.

FIGURE 6.1   Select Server Roles

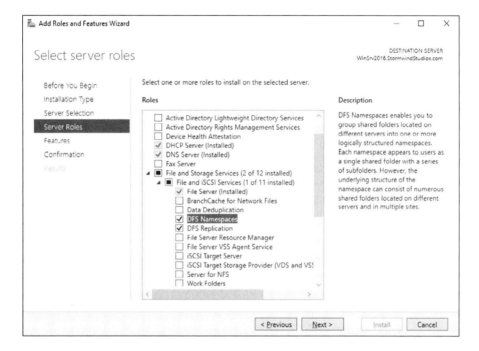

7. At the Select Features screen, click Next.

8. At the Confirmation screen, click the Install button.

9. After the installation is complete, click the Close button.

10. Close Server Manager.

Once you have installed DFS, it's time to learn how to manage DFS with the DFS Management MMC. The DFS Management console (see Figure 6.2) gives you one place to do all of your DFS configurations. The DFS Management console allows you to set up DFS Replication and DFS Namespace. Another task you can do in the DFS Management console is to add a folder target—a folder that you add to the DFS namespace (the virtual tree) for all your users to share.

FIGURE 6.2 DFS Management console

What's New in Windows Server 2016

As with any new version of an operating system, Microsoft is trying to make each version of Windows Server better than the previous ones. This is also true with DFS. Microsoft has added many new features to DFS, and the following are just some of the major changes of Windows Server 2016 DFS.

Windows PowerShell Module for DFS Replication

Windows PowerShell cmdlets for DFS replication modules can help administrators perform the majority of their DFS replication tasks. Administrators can use Windows PowerShell cmdlets to perform common administrative tasks such as creating, modifying, and removing DFS replication settings by using Window PowerShell scripts.

One of the nice new advantages of using Windows PowerShell for DFS is the ability to clone DFS replication databases and also to have the ability to restore those DFS databases in the event of an issue or crash.

Administrators have the ability to manage DFS management and replication through the use of the DNS Management and DFS Replication command-line utilities. Administrators who use the command-line tools are not doing anything incorrectly, but it is an inefficient way to do these tasks as well as being extremely time-consuming.

Administrators can use Windows PowerShell instead of command-line utilities and run hundreds of scripted commands, thus making their jobs easier and more efficient.

For an administrator who wants to use the Windows PowerShell cmdlets, the computer system installed with the DFS Management tools must be running Windows Server 2012

R2 or Windows 8.1 or newer. The DFS Management tools are part of the Remote Server Administration tools.

DFS Replication Windows Management Infrastructure Provider

In this book, I have spoken many times about using Windows Remote Management (WinRM) and how WinRM can help you administer a server remotely.

Windows Management Infrastructure (referred to as WMI v2) allows an administrator, using a properly configured firewall, to provide functionality and which provides programmatic access to manage DFS Replication (DFSR).

Database Cloning

For the first time ever in DFS, Windows Server 2016 includes a new DFS database cloning function. This new feature allows administrators to accelerate replication when creating folders, servers, or recovery systems.

Administrators will now have the ability to extract the DFS database from a single DFS server and then clone that database to multiple DFS servers.

Administrators can use PowerShell and the `Export-DfsrClone` cmdlet to export the volume that contains the DFS database and configuration `.xml` file settings. When executing this PowerShell cmdlet, a trigger is engaged that exports the DFS service, and the system will not proceed until the service is completed. Administrators would then use the PowerShell cmdlet `Import-DfsrClone` to import the data to a specific volume. The service will then validate that the replication was transferred completely.

Recovering a DFS Database

Windows Server 2016 DFS database recovery is a feature that allows DFS to detect a corrupted database, thus allowing DFS to rebuild the database automatically and continue with normal operations of DFS replication. One advantage to this is that when DFS detects and fixes a corrupt database, it does so with no file conflicts.

Prior to this new feature, if a DFS database were determined to be corrupt, DFS Replication would delete the database and start again with an initial nonauthoritative sync process. This would cause newer file versions to be overwritten by older data causing real data loss.

DFS in Windows Server 2016 uses local files and an update sequence number (USN) to fix a corrupt database, allowing for no loss of data.

Optimizing DFS

Windows Server 2016 DFS allows an administrator to configure variable file staging sizes on individual DFS servers. This allows an administrator to set a minimum file size for a file to stage. This increases the staging size of files, and that in turn increases the performance of the replication.

Prior to Windows Server 2016, DFS Replication used a hard-coded 256KB file size to determine staging requirements. If a file size were larger than 256KB, that file would be staged before it replicated. The more file staging that you have, the longer replication takes on a DFS system.

Remote Differential Compression

One issue that can arise occurs when files are changed. There has to be some mechanism that helps files stay accurate. That's where the *Remote Differential Compression (RDC)* feature comes into play. RDC is a group of application programming interfaces (APIs) that programs can use to determine whether files have changed. Once RDC determines that there has been a change, RDC then helps to detect which portions of the files contain the changes. RDC has the ability to detect insertions, removals, and rearrangements of data in files. This feature becomes helpful with limited-bandwidth networks when they replicate changes.

To install the RDC feature, use Server Manager and then run the Add Features Wizard, or type the following command at an elevated command prompt:

```
Servermanagercmd -Install Rdc
```

Now that I have shown you how to install DFS and how DFS works, let's go ahead and setup DFS. In exercise 6.3, I will show you how to configure a DFS Namespace and how to add a shared folder to DFS.

EXERCISE 6.3

Setting Up a DFS Namespace

1. Open DFS Management (Start ➤ Administrative Tools ➤ DFS Management).

2. Right-click Namespaces (see Figure 6.3) and choose New Namespace.

FIGURE 6.3   Adding a Namespace

3. In the Server box, enter the name of the server that will host this namespace (I am using the DFS server). Click Next.

4. At the Namespace screen, enter the namespace you want (see Figure 6.4) to use and hit the Next button.

FIGURE 6.4   Adding a Namespace

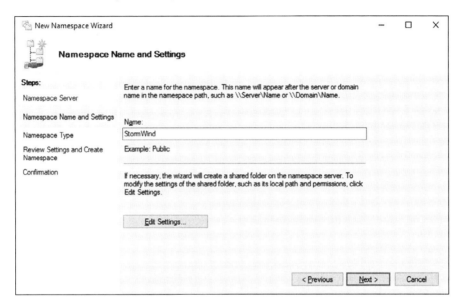

5. Under Namespace Type screen, choose Stand-Alone or Domain Based and click Next. In my lab, I am using a Stand-Alone DFS.

6. At the Review Screen, click Create.

7. Click the Close button. Leave DFS open.

8. Go to Windows Explorer by hitting the Windows Key + E.

9. Create a new folder called Home and share the folder.

10. In DFS under the Actions section (right hand side), choose New Folder (see Figure 6.5).

11. When the New Folder screen appears, Type in the Name for this folder and then hit Add.

12. Add the shared Home Folder and hit OK.

EXERCISE 6.3 *(continued)*

FIGURE 6.5   New Folder

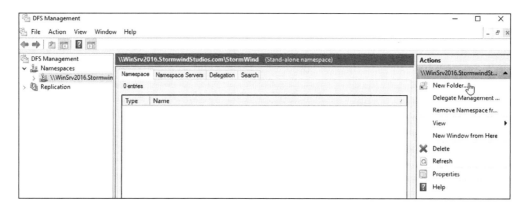

13. After you have entered a name and put in the Home folder (see Figure 6.6), click OK.

FIGURE 6.6   Home Folder

14. The namespace has been created and you have added a shared folder to the namespace. Add any of your other shared folders and then close DFS.

Configure Advanced File Services

Windows Server has come a long way in terms of its file and storage capabilities. I have talked quite a bit about the new features and functionality provided in Windows Server 2016. In this section, you will take a closer look at some of the advanced configuration options available in the Network File System (NFS), BranchCache, and the File Server Resource Manager (FSRM).

Configure the NFS Data Store

The NFS role service and feature set gives IT administrators the ability to integrate a Windows Server–based environment with Unix-based operating systems. Most corporate environments today consist of a mixed operating system infrastructure to some extent. Using a Windows NFS file server, you can configure file shares for use by multiple operating systems throughout the environment.

Windows Server 2016 takes those capabilities even further by enabling you to integrate with platforms such as ESXi. ESXi is VMware's exclusive operating system–independent hypervisor. ESXi is referred to as a *bare-metal* operating system because once it is installed on server virtualization hardware, guest virtual machines can be installed without requiring the use of any other underlying operating system. With Windows Server 2016, you can use an NFS share efficiently as an ESXi data store to house all of your guest virtual machines. Let's take a look at configuring an NFS data store in Exercise 6.4.

For this exercise, you will need the following:

- A Windows Server 2016 server
- A VMware ESXi 5 server

EXERCISE 6.4

Configure the NFS Data Store

1. Open Server Manager on your Windows Server 2016 machine.

2. Launch the Add Roles And Features Wizard from the dashboard.

3. Install the Server for NFS role on the server. A reboot is not required.

4. Create a new folder on your server named NFS_Datastore, right-click and select Properties, and then navigate to the NFS Sharing tab.

5. Click the Manage NFS Sharing button to open the NFS Advanced Sharing page and then check the Share This Folder box. Notice how enabling the share also enables the share's default settings. The share settings let you configure share authentication and user access further if the need arises. The default settings will work just fine for this exercise.

6. Click the Permissions tab to open the NFS Share Permissions page. This is where you will configure the type of access that will be allowed by machines accessing this NFS data store. By default, the NFS share permissions are set to Read-Only and do not include root access. For this exercise, you will need to change the type of access to Read-Write and check the box to allow root access.

7. Click OK to close the NFS Share Permissions page and then click Apply and OK on the NFS Advanced Sharing page. Your new NFS share is now built, ready to be presented as an NFS data store to a VMware ESXi host. Be sure to record the network path displayed on the NFS Sharing tab of the share's Properties page. You will need that information to perform a proper mount on the ESXi host.

8. Switch to your ESXi host and launch the Add Storage Wizard from the Configuration tab.

9. On the Select Storage Type page of the wizard, select the Network File System storage type; click Next to continue to the Locate Network File System page.

10. On this page of the wizard, you will fill in the server and folder information for the NFS share that you will be using as a vSphere data store. Using the information recorded from step 7, properly fill out the server and folder fields and then name your new data store.

11. Click Next to continue to the Ready To Complete page of the wizard. Review the information and click Finish. Once the Create NAS data store task completes on the ESXi host, you are ready to use your Windows Server 2016 shared folder as a vSphere ESXi data store.

The previous exercise shows how versatile Windows Server 2016 shares can be. The same principals can be applied to making Windows Server shares available to other Unix-based operating systems such as ESXi. Now that you have configured a NFS data store, let's take a look at what BranchCache has to offer.

Configure BranchCache

BranchCache is a technology that was introduced with Windows Server 2008 R2 and Windows 7. BranchCache allows an organization with slower links between offices to cache data so that downloads between offices do not have to occur each time a file is accessed.

For example, John comes into work and logs into the network. John accesses the corporate website and downloads a media file that takes four minutes to download. With BranchCache enabled, when Judy comes into work, connects to the corporate website, and tries to download the same media file, the file will be cached from the previous download and Judy will have immediate access to the file.

You can set up two types of BranchCache configurations:

Distributed Cache Mode   In the distributed cache mode configuration, all Windows 7, Windows 8/8.1, and Windows 10 client machines cache the files locally on the client machines. Thus, in the previous example, after John downloaded the media file, Judy would receive the cached media file from John's Windows 7, Windows 8/8.1, or Windows 10 machine.

Hosted Mode   In the hosted mode configuration, the cache files are cached on a local (within the site) Windows Server 2016 machine. So, in the previous example, after John downloads the media file, the cached file would be placed on a Windows Server 2016 machine by default, and all other users (Judy) would download the media file from the Windows Server 2016 machine.

Distributed Cache Mode Requirements

If you decide to install BranchCache in the distributed cache mode configuration, a hosted cache server running Windows Server 2016 is not required at the branch office. To set up distributed cache mode, the client machines must be running Windows 7 Enterprise, Windows 7 Ultimate, Windows 8/8.1 Pro, Windows 8/8.1 Enterprise, Windows 10 Pro or Windows 10 Enterprise.

The Windows client machines would download the data files from the content computer at the main branch office, and then these machines become the local cache servers. To set up distributed cache mode, you must install a content computer (the computer that will hold the original content) at the main office first. After the content server is installed, physical connections (WAN or VPN connections) between the sites and branch offices must be established.

Client computers running Windows 7 Enterprise or higher (from versions listed above) have BranchCache installed by default. However, you must enable and configure BranchCache and configure firewall exceptions. Complete Exercise 6.5 to configure BranchCache firewall rule exceptions.

EXERCISE 6.5

Configuring BranchCache Firewall Exceptions

1.   On a domain controller, open the Group Policy Management Console.

2.   In the Group Policy Management Console, expand the following path: Forest ➤ Domains ➤ Group Policy Objects. Make sure the domain you choose contains the BranchCache Windows 7/Windows 8/Windows 10 client computer accounts that you want to configure.

EXERCISE 6.5 *(continued)*

3. In the Group Policy Management Console, right-click Group Policy Objects and select New. Name the policy **BranchCache Client** and click OK. Right-click BranchCache Client and click Edit. The Group Policy Management Editor console opens.

4. In the Group Policy Management Editor console, expand the following path: Computer Configuration ➢ Policies ➢ Windows Settings ➢ Security Settings ➢ Windows Firewall With Advanced Security ➢ Windows Firewall With Advanced Security – LDAP ➢ Inbound Rules.

5. Right-click Inbound Rules and then click New Rule. The New Inbound Rule Wizard opens.

6. On the Rule Type screen, click Predefined, expand the list of choices, and then click BranchCache – Content Retrieval (Uses HTTP). Click Next.

7. On the Predefined Rules screen, click Next.

8. On the Action screen, ensure that Allow The Connection is selected and then click Finish. You must select Allow The Connection for the BranchCache client to be able to receive traffic on this port.

9. To create the WS-Discovery firewall exception, right-click Inbound Rules and click New Rule. The New Inbound Rule Wizard opens.

10. On the Rule Type screen, click Predefined, expand the list of choices, and then click BranchCache – Peer Discovery (Uses WSD). Click Next.

11. On the Predefined Rules screen, click Next.

12. On the Action screen, ensure that Allow The Connection is selected and then click Finish.

13. In the Group Policy Management Editor console, right-click Outbound Rules and then click New Rule. The New Outbound Rule Wizard opens.

14. On the Rule Type screen, click Predefined, expand the list of choices, and then click BranchCache – Content Retrieval (Uses HTTP). Click Next.

15. On the Predefined Rules screen, click Next.

16. On the Action screen, make sure that Allow The Connection is selected and then click Finish.

17. Create the WS-Discovery firewall exception by right-clicking Outbound Rules and then clicking New Rule. The New Outbound Rule Wizard opens.

18. On the Rule Type screen, click Predefined, expand the list of choices, and then click BranchCache – Peer Discovery (Uses WSD). Click Next.

19. On the Predefined Rules screen, click Next.

20. On the Action screen, make sure that Allow The Connection is selected and then click Finish. Close the Group Policy Management console.

Now that you have looked at the distributed cache mode configuration, let's take a look at the hosted mode configuration.

Hosted Mode Requirements

To set up a hosted mode BranchCache configuration, you must first set up a Windows Server 2016 hosted cache server at the main and branch offices. You also need to be running Windows 7 Enterprise, Windows 7 Ultimate, Windows 8/8.1 Pro, Windows 8/8.1 Enterprise, Windows 10 Pro, or Windows 10 Enterprise computers at the branch offices.

The Windows client machines download the data from the main cache server, and then the hosted cache servers at the branch offices obtain a copy of the downloaded data for other users to access.

Your network infrastructure must also allow for physical connections between the main office and the branch offices. These connections can be VPNs or some type of WAN links. After these requirements are met, your cache server must obtain a server certificate so that the client computers in the branch offices can positively identify the cache servers.

Exercise 6.6 walks you through the process of installing the BranchCache feature on a Windows Server 2016 machine. To begin this exercise, you must be logged into the Windows Server 2016 machine as an administrator.

EXERCISE 6.6

Installing BranchCache on Windows Server 2016

1. Open Server Manager by selecting the Server Manager icon or by running `servermanager.exe`.

2. Select Add Roles And Features.

3. Select Next at the Before You Begin pane (if shown).

4. Select Role-Based Or Feature-Based Installation and select Next to continue.

5. Select the Select A Server From The Server Pool option and click Next.

6. At the Select Server Roles screen, click Next.

7. At the Select Features screen, click the check box for BranchCache (see Figure 6.7). Then click Next.

FIGURE 6.7 BranchCache Option

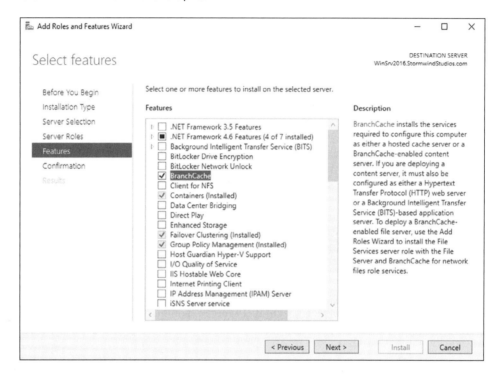

8. Check the Restart The Destination Server If Required box and then click the Install button. If a dialog box appears about restarting, click the Yes button. The system should restart.

9. After the system restarts, log in as the administrator.

Make sure to repeat this exercise on all branch office cache servers. One of the requirements for BranchCache is a physical connection between the main office and the branch offices.

BranchCache and PowerShell

As stated throughout this book, PowerShell is a command-line shell and scripting tool. BranchCache has many different PowerShell cmdlets that allow you to configure and maintain the BranchCache feature. Table 6.4 shows just some of the different PowerShell cmdlets for BranchCache.

TABLE 6.4 PowerShell cmdlets for BranchCache

Cmdlet	Description
Add-BCDataCacheExtension	Increases the amount of cache storage space that is available on a hosted cache server by adding a new cache file
Clear-BCCache	Deletes all data in all data and hash files
Disable-BC	Disables the BranchCache service
Disable-BCDowngrading	Disables downgrading so that client computers that are running Windows 10 do not request Windows 7/8 specific versions of content information from content servers
Enable-BCDistributed	Enables BranchCache and configures a computer to operate in distributed cache mode
Enable-BCHostedClient	Configures BranchCache to operate in hosted cache client mode
Enable-BCHostedServer	Configures BranchCache to operate in hosted cache server mode
Enable-BCLocal	Enables the BranchCache service in local caching mode
Export-BCCachePackage	Exports a cache package
Export-BCSecretKey	Exports a secret key to a file
Get-BCClientConfiguration	Gets the current BranchCache client computer settings
Get-BCContentServerConfiguration	Gets the current BranchCache content server settings
Get-BCDataCache	Gets the BranchCache data cache
Get-BCStatus	Gets a set of objects that provide BranchCache status and configuration information
Import-BCCachePackage	Imports a cache package into BranchCache
Import-BCSecretKey	Imports the cryptographic key that BranchCache uses for generating segment secrets

TABLE 6.4   PowerShell cmdlets for BranchCache *(continued)*

Cmdlet	Description
Set-BCAuthentication	Specifies the BranchCache computer authentication mode
Set-BCCache	Modifies the cache file configuration
Set-BCSecretKey	Sets the cryptographic key used in the generation of segment secrets

Enhanced Features in Windows Server 2016 BranchCache

Microsoft continues to improve on many of the features of Windows Server, and BranchCache is no different. Microsoft has improved BranchCache in Windows Server 2016 and Windows 8/10. The following list includes some of the enhanced features:

Office sizes and the number of branch offices are not limited.   Windows Server 2016 BranchCache allows any number of offices along with any number of users once an administrator deploys hosted cache mode with multiple hosted cache servers.

There are no requirements for a Group Policy object (GPO) for each office location, streamlining deployment.   All that is required to deploy BranchCache is a single GPO that contains a small number of settings.

Client computer configuration is easy.   Administrators have the ability to configure their clients through the use of a Group Policy object. If this is done, client configuration will automatically be configured through the GPO, and if a client can't find a hosted cache server, the client will automatically self-configure as a hosted cache mode client.

BranchCache is deeply integrated with the Windows file server.   BranchCache is automatically integrated with Windows file server technology. Because of this, the process of finding duplicate pieces in independent files is greatly improved.

Duplicate content is stored and downloaded only once.   BranchCache stores only one instance of the content on a hosted cache server or content server, and because of this, you get greater disk storage savings. Since client computers at the remote offices download only one instance of any content, your network saves on additional WAN bandwidth.

Small changes to large files produce bandwidth savings.   One advantage of BranchCache is the file server chunking system that helps divide files and web pages into smaller parts. Now when a file is changed, only the part of that file that has been changed gets replicated. This allows BranchCache to use lower bandwidth requirements.

Offline content creation improves performance.   When BranchCache is deployed as content or file servers, the data is calculated offline before a client even has the chance to request it. Because of this, the systems get faster performance and bandwidth.

Cache encryption is enabled automatically.   BranchCache stores its cached data as encrypted data. This guarantees data security without the need to encrypt the entire drive.

You can deploy multiple hosted cache servers.   In Windows 7 and Windows Server 2008 R2, BranchCache was able to deploy only one hosted cache server per office location. Windows Server 2016 allows you to deploy as many hosted cache servers as are needed at a location.

Implementing an Audit Policy

One of the most important aspects of controlling security in networked environments is ensuring that only authorized users are able to access specific resources. Although system administrators often spend much time managing security permissions, it is almost always possible for a security problem to occur.

Sometimes the best way to find possible security breaches is actually to record the actions that specific users take. Then, in the case of a security breach (the unauthorized shutdown of a server, for example), system administrators can examine the log to find the cause of the problem.

The Windows Server 2016 operating system and Active Directory offer you the ability to audit a wide range of actions. In the following sections, you'll see how to implement auditing for Active Directory.

Overview of Auditing

The act of *auditing* relates to recording specific actions. From a security standpoint, auditing is used to detect any possible misuse of network resources. Although auditing does not necessarily prevent resources from being misused, it does help determine when security violations have occurred (or were attempted). Furthermore, just the fact that others know that you have implemented auditing may prevent them from attempting to circumvent security.

You need to complete several steps in order to implement auditing using Windows Server 2016:

1. Configure the size and storage settings for the audit logs.

2. Enable categories of events to audit.

3. Specify which objects and actions should be recorded in the audit log.

Note that there are trade-offs to implementing auditing. First, recording auditing information can consume system resources. This can decrease overall system performance and use up valuable disk space. Second, auditing many events can make the audit log impractical to view. If too much detail is provided, system administrators are unlikely to scrutinize all of the recorded events. For these reasons, you should always be sure to find a balance between the level of auditing detail provided and the performance-management implications of these settings.

Implementing Auditing

Auditing is not an all-or-none type of process. As is the case with security in general, system administrators must choose specifically which objects and actions they want to audit.

The main categories for auditing include the following:

- Audit account logon events
- Audit account management
- Audit directory service access
- Audit logon events
- Audit object access
- Audit policy change
- Audit privilege use
- Audit process tracking
- Audit system events

In this list of categories, many of the categories are related to Active Directory. Let's discuss these auditing categories in more detail.

Audit Account Logon Events You enable this auditing event if you want to audit when a user authenticates with a domain controller and logs onto the domain. This event is logged in the security log on the domain controller.

Audit Account Management This auditing event is used when you want to watch what changes are being made to Active Directory accounts. For example, when another administrator creates or deletes a user account, it would be an audited event.

Audit Directory Service Access This auditing event occurs whenever a user or administrator accesses Active Directory objects. Let's say an administrator opens Active Directory and clicks a user account; even if nothing is changed on that account, an event is logged.

Audit Logon Events Account logon events are created for domain account activity. For example, you have a user who logs on to a server so that they can access files; the act of logging onto the server creates this audit event.

Audit Object Access Audit object access allows you to audit objects within your network such as folders, files, and printers. If you suspect someone is trying to hack into an object (for example, the finance folder), this is the type of auditing that you would use. You still would need to enable auditing on the actual object (for example, the finance folder).

Audit Policy Change Audit policy change allows you to audit changes to user rights' assignment policies, audit policies, or trust policies. This auditing allows you to see whether anyone changes any of the other audit policies.

Audit Privilege Use Setting the audit privilege use allows an administrator to audit each instance of a user exercising a user right. For example, if a user changes the system time on a machine, this is a user right. Log on locally is another common user right.

To audit access to objects stored within Active Directory, you must enable the Audit Directory Service Access option. Then you must specify which objects and actions should be tracked.

Exercise 6.7 walks through the steps you must take to implement auditing of Active Directory objects on domain controllers.

EXERCISE 6.7

Enabling Auditing of Active Directory Objects

1. Open the Local Security Policy tool (located in the Administrative Tools program group).

2. Expand Local Policies ➢ Audit Policy.

3. Double-click the setting for Audit Directory Service Access.

4. In the Audit Directory Service Access Properties dialog box, place check marks next to Success and Failure. Click OK to save the settings.

5. Close the Local Security Policy tool.

Viewing Auditing Information

One of the most important aspects of auditing is regularly monitoring the audit logs. If this step is ignored, as it often is in poorly managed environments, the act of auditing is useless. Fortunately, Windows Server 2016 includes the *Event Viewer* tool, which allows system administrators to view audited events quickly and easily. Using the filtering capabilities of Event Viewer, they can find specific events of interest.

Exercise 6.8 walks you through the steps that you must take to generate some auditing events and to examine the data collected for these actions. In this exercise, you will perform some actions that will be audited, and then you will view the information recorded within the audit logs.

EXERCISE 6.8

Generating and Viewing Audit Logs

1. Open the Active Directory Users and Computers tool.

2. Within the Engineering OU, right-click any user account and select Properties.

3. On the user's Properties dialog box, add the middle initial *A* for this user account and specify **Software Developer** in the Description box. Click OK to save the changes.

4. Within the Engineering OU, right-click the Robert Admin user account and select Properties.

5. In the Robert Properties dialog box, add the description **Engineering IT Admin** and click OK.

6. Close the Active Directory Users and Computers tool.

7. Open the Event Viewer tool from the Administrative Tools program group. Select the Security item under Windows Logs. You will see a list of audited events categorized under Directory Service Access. Note that you can obtain more details about a specific item by double-clicking it.

8. When you have finished viewing the security log, close the Event Viewer tool.

Using the *Auditpol.exe* Command

There may be a time when you need to look at your actual auditing policies set on a user or a system. This is where an administrator can use the Auditpol.exe command. *Auditpol* gives administrators the ability not only to view an audit policy but also allows an administrator to set, configure, modify, restore, and even remove an audit policy. Auditpol is a command-line utility, and there are multiple switches that can be used with Auditpol. The following is the syntax used with Auditpol.

```
Auditpol command [<sub-command><options>]
```

Here's an example of using the command:

```
Auditpol /get /user:wpanek /category:"Detailed Tracking" /r
```

Table 6.5 describes some of the switches.

TABLE 6.5 Auditpol commands

Command	Description
/backup	Allows an administrator to save the audit policy to a file
/clear	Allows an administrator to clear an audit policy
/get	Gives administrators the ability to view the current audit policy
/list	Allows you to view selectable policy elements
/remove	Removes all per-user audit policy settings and disables all system audit policy settings

Command	Description
/restore	Allows an administrator to restore an audit policy from a file that was previously created using auditpol /backup
/set	Gives an administrator the ability to set an audit policy
/?	Displays help

Windows Server 2016 Auditing Features

Auditing in Windows Server 2016 and Windows 10 has been enhanced in many ways. Microsoft has increased the level of detail in the security auditing logs. Microsoft has also simplified the deployment and management of auditing policies. The following list includes some of the major enhancements:

Global Object Access Auditing Administrators using Windows Server 2016 and Windows 10 have the ability to define computer-wide system access control lists (SACLs). Administrators can define SACLs for either the file system or the registry. After the specified SACL is defined, the SACL is then applied automatically to every single object of that type. This can be helpful to administrators in verifying that all critical files, folders, and registry settings on a computer are protected. This is also helpful for identifying when an issue occurs with a system resource.

"Reason for Access" Reporting When an administrator is performing auditing in Windows Server 2016 and Windows 10, they can see the reason why an operation was successful or unsuccessful. Previously, they lacked the ability to see the reason why an operation succeeded or failed.

Advanced Audit Policy Settings In Windows Server 2016, there are hundreds of Advanced Audit Policy settings that can be used in place of the nine basic auditing settings. These advanced audit settings also help eliminate the unnecessary auditing activities that can make audit logs difficult to manage and decipher.

Expression-Based Audit Policies Administrators have the ability, because of Dynamic Access Control, to create targeted audit policies by using expressions based on user, computer, and resource claims. For example, an administrator has the ability to create an audit policy that tracks all Read and Write operations for files that are considered high-business impact. Expression-based audit policies can be directly created on a file or folder or created through the use of a Group Policy.

Removable Storage Device Auditing Administrators have the ability to monitor attempts to use a removable storage device on your network. If an administrator decides to implement this policy, an audit event is created every time one of your users attempts to copy, move, or save a network resource onto a removable storage device.

Configure and Optimize Storage

Disk storage is a requirement for just about every computer and application used in any corporate environment. Administrators have some familiarity with storage, whether it is internal storage, a locally attached set of disks, or network attached storage (NAS). In this section, you will examine the various aspects of Windows Server 2016 file and storage solutions. Though I'll discuss the various types of file and storage technologies, this section will primarily focus on iSCSI because of the native features in Windows Server 2016. You will also look at some of the advanced configuration options of implementing thin provisioning and trim, managing server free space, and configuring tiered storage.

Configure iSCSI Target and Initiator

Internet Small Computer System Interface (iSCSI) is an Internet protocol used to establish and manage a connection between a computer (initiator) and a storage device (target). It does this by using a connection through TCP port 3260, which allows it to be used over a LAN, a WAN, or the Internet. Each initiator is identified by its iSCSI Qualified Name (iqn), and it is used to establish its connection to an iSCSI target.

iSCSI was developed to allow block-level access to a storage device over a network. This is different from using a NAS device that connects through the use of Common Internet File System (CIFS) or NFS.

Block-level access is important to many applications that require direct access to storage. Microsoft Exchange and Microsoft SQL are examples of applications that require direct access to storage.

By being able to leverage the existing network infrastructure, iSCSI was also developed as an alternative to Fibre Channel storage by alleviating the additional hardware costs associated with a Fibre Channel storage solution.

iSCSI also has another advantage over Fibre Channel in that it can provide security for the storage devices. iSCSI can use Microsoft Challenge Handshake Authentication Protocol (CHAP or MS-CHAP) for authentication and Internet Protocol Security (IPsec) for encryption. Windows Server 2016 is able to connect an iSCSI storage device out of the box with no additional software needing to be installed. This is because the Microsoft iSCSI initiator is built into the operating system.

Windows Server 2016 supports two different ways to initiate an iSCSI session:

▪ Through the native Microsoft iSCSI software initiator that resides on Windows Server 2016

▪ Using a hardware iSCSI host bus adapter (HBA) that is installed in the computer

Both the Microsoft iSCSI software initiator and iSCSI HBA present an iSCSI qualified name that identifies the host initiator. When the Microsoft iSCSI software initiator is used, the CPU utilization may be as much as 30 percent higher than on a computer with a hardware iSCSI HBA. This is because all of the iSCSI process requests are handled within the operating system. Using a hardware iSCSI HBA, process requests can be offloaded to the adapter, thus freeing the CPU overhead associated with the Microsoft iSCSI software initiator. However, iSCSI HBAs can be expensive, whereas the Microsoft iSCSI software initiator is free.

It is worthwhile installing the Microsoft iSCSI software initiator and performing load testing to see how much overhead the computer will have prior to purchasing an iSCSI HBA or HBAs, depending on the redundancy level. Exercise 6.9 explains how to install and configure an iSCSI connection.

EXERCISE 6.9

Configuring iSCSI Storage Connection

1. Press the Windows key or the Start button in the lower-left corner and select Administrative Tools ➢ iSCSI Initiator.

2. If a dialog box appears, click Yes to start the service.

3. Click the Discovery tab.

4. In the Target Portals portion of the page, click Discover Portal.

5. Enter the IP address of the target portal and click OK.

6. The IP address of the target portal appears in the Target Portals box.

7. Click OK.

   To use the storage that has now been presented to the server, you must create a volume on it and format the space.

Configure Internet Storage Name Server

Internet Storage Name Service (iSNS) allows for the central registration of an iSCSI environment because it automatically discovers available targets on the network. The purpose of iSNS is to help find available targets on a large iSCSI network.

The Microsoft iSCSI initiator includes an iSNS client that is used to register with the iSNS. The iSNS feature maintains a database of clients that it has registered either through DCHP discovery or through manual registration. iSNS DHCP is available after the installation of the service, and it is used to allow iSNS clients to discover the location of the iSNS. However, if iSNS DHCP is not configured, iSNS clients must be registered manually with the iscsicli command.

To execute the command, launch a command prompt on a computer hosting the Microsoft iSCSI and type **`iscsicli addisnsserver server_name`**, where server_name is the name of the computer hosting iSNS. Exercise 6.10 walks you through the steps required to install the iSNS feature on Windows Server 2016, and then it explains the different tabs in iSNS.

EXERCISE 6.10

Installing the iSNS Feature on Windows Server 2016

1. Open Server Manager.

2. Launch the Add Roles And Features Wizard.

3. Choose role-based or featured-based installation and click Next.

4. Choose your server and click Next.

5. Click Next at the Roles screen.

6. At the Select Features screen, choose the iSNS Server Service check box. Click Next.

7. At the Confirmation screen, click the Install button.

8. Click the Close button. Close Server Manager and reboot.

9. Log in and open the iSNS server under Administrative Tools.

10. Click the General tab. This tab displays the list of registered initiators and targets. In addition to their iSCSI qualified names, it lists storage node type (Target or Initiator), alias string, and entity identifier (the fully qualified domain name [FQDN] of the machine hosting the iSNS client).

11. Click the Discovery Domains tab. The purpose of discovery domains is to provide a way to separate and group nodes. This is similar to zoning in Fibre Channel.

    The following options are available on the Discovery Domains tab:

    Create creates a new discovery domain.

    Refresh repopulates the Discovery Domain drop-down list.

    Delete deletes the currently selected discovery domain.

    Add adds nodes that are already registered in iSNS to the currently selected discovery domain.

    Add New adds nodes by entering the iSCSI qualified name of the node. These nodes do not have to be currently registered.

    Remove Used removes selected nodes from the discovery domain.

12. Click the Discovery Domain Sets tab. The purpose of discovery domain sets is to separate further discovery domains. Discovery domains can be enabled or disabled, giving administrators the ability to restrict further the visibility of all initiators and targets.

    The options on the Discovery Domain Sets tab are as follows:

    The *Enable* check box indicates the status of the discovery domain sets and turns them off and on.

Create creates new discovery domain sets.

Refresh repopulates the Discovery Domain Sets drop-down list.

Delete deletes the currently selected discovery domain set.

Add adds discovery domains to the currently selected discovery domain set.

Remove removes selected nodes from the discovery domain sets.

13. Close the iSNS server.

Implement Thin Provisioning and Trim

Thin provisioning and trim can be useful features that allow organizations to get the most out of their storage arrays. These solutions apply directly to a virtualized environment using virtual disks that are thin provisioned.

Thin provisioning is a way of providing what is known as just-in-time allocations. Blocks of data are written to disk only as they are used instead of zeroing out all of the blocks of data that have been allocated to the virtual disk configuration. Thin provisioning is tricky to manage properly because you could easily find yourself in a position where you have an over-provisioned environment because of over-allocation.

For example, you have 100 VMs that are all provisioned with 40 GB thin-provisioned virtual disks. Each VM is currently utilizing only 20 GB of the total 40 GB that has been allocated. The problem is that you have only 2 TB worth of storage. Without realizing it, you've over-provisioned your environment by 200 percent because of thin provisioning.

This is where trim comes in to help us manage thin provisioning. *Trim* automatically reclaims free space that is not being used. In addition to trim, Windows Server 2016 provides standardized notifications that will alert administrators when certain storage thresholds are crossed.

Manage Server Free Space Using Features on Demand

Features on Demand was first introduced in Windows Server 2012. This feature lets you conserve disk space within the environment by installing only basic operating system components with every new installation of a Windows Server 2016 or Windows 10 machine. Instead of loading unnecessary payload files, those files are stored in a central repository and used as needed to install roles and features. When I talk about *payload files*, I am talking about the binaries for all permissions, settings, and components of a feature. Features on Demand gives you the ability not only to disable Windows Server features but also to remove all of the payloads. This lets administrators keep a tighter security footprint at the operating system level, which is similar to a Server Core installation but without the limitation of not being able to control which source files are loaded during operating system installation.

Configure Tiered Storage

Tiered storage is an excellent new feature in Windows Server 2016 that gives administrators the ability to use solid-state drives (SSDs) and conventional hard-disk drives (HDDs) within the same storage pool. You can configure virtual disks that span SSD and HDD tiers, which are presented as a single LUN. One of the really nice things about this feature is that with Windows Server 2016, data is automatically saved to either an SSD or an HDD based on actual usage within the environment. Most frequently accessed data is stored on an SSD, and the less frequently accessed data is stored on an HDD.

Quite a few organizations these days use some sort of charge-back or show-back application to track and even charge for hosted solutions and services. Having the capability to tier storage gives users more options in selecting a plan that works for them. It also makes it possible for administrators to keep high I/O servers and applications on faster and better-performing drives without having to move data manually across multiple tiers of storage.

Summary

This chapter took you through the use of many server tools and utilities such as DFS, Encryption, and auditing. Distributed File System allows an administrator to set up a tree structure of virtual directories that allow users to connect to a shared folder anywhere throughout the entire network.

You also learned about EFS and how to use Cipher to modify or configure EFS in a command window. Cipher is the best way to change encrypted directories and files.

This chapter also covered auditing. You looked at what needs to be audited if you are watching Active Directory and its objects. You looked at Auditpol and many of the switches that you would use when configuring Auditpol.

I discussed how configuring file and storage solutions can be highly effective within your organization. You now have a better understanding of how Windows Server 2016 can provide you with extended functionality for effectively controlling corporate data. Quite a few of these solutions are essential to managing a Windows Server environment to the best of your ability. Take the time to complete each exercise thoroughly until you are comfortable with performing the majority of these tasks without documentation.

Exam Essentials

Know how to configure DFS.   Distributed File System in Windows Server 2016 offers a simplified way for users to access geographically dispersed files. The DFS Namespace service allows you to set up a tree structure of virtual directories that lets users connect to shared folders throughout the entire network.

Understand EFS and Cipher.   Users can encrypt their directories and files by using EFS. Understand how Cipher can help an administrator configure or modify an EFS object while in the command prompt.

Understand the purpose and function of auditing.   Auditing helps determine the cause of security violations and helps troubleshoot permissions-related problems. Configure and test the effects of auditing within a file share hierarchy in a lab environment.

Know storage technologies.   Understand how to use the Fibre Channel, iSCSI, and NAS storage technologies. Know how to configure an iSCSI initiator and how to establish a connection to a target. Practice configuring tiered storage and using thin provisioning and trim.

Understand the features and functionality of BranchCache.   BranchCache helps eliminate the problems of slow access and bandwidth issues when sharing data across multiple, geographically disparate locations. By syncing and caching data between sites, users can use company-wide shared resources more efficiently when slower site links exist between site locations.

Review Questions

1. The company for which you work has a multilevel administrative team that is segmented by departments and locations. There are four major locations, and you are in the North-east group. You have been assigned to the administrative group that is responsible for cre-ating and maintaining network shares for files and printers in your region. The last place you worked was a large Windows Server 2012 network, where you had a much wider range of responsibilities. You are excited about the chance to learn more about Windows Server 2016.

    For your first task, you have been given a list of file and printer shares that need to be created for the users in your region. You ask how to create them in Windows Server 2016, and you are told that the process of creating a share is the same as with Windows Server 2012. You create the shares and use NETUSE to test them. Everything appears to work fine, so you send a message that the shares are available. The next day, you start receiving calls from users who say they cannot see any of resources you created. What is the most likely reason for the calls from the users?

    A. You forgot to enable NetBIOS for the shares.

    B. You need to force replication for the shares to appear in the directory.

    C. You need to publish the shares in the directory.

    D. The shares will appear within the normal replication period.

2. You want to publish a printer to Active Directory. Where would you click in order to accomplish this task?

    A. The Sharing tab

    B. The Advanced tab

    C. The Device Settings tab

    D. The Printing Preferences button

3. You are the network administrator for a large organization. You have implemented FSRM on your network. You need to view the quotas on FSRM. Which PowerShell command would you use?

    A. Get-Quota

    B. Get-FsrmQuota

    C. View-Quota

    D. View-FsrmQuota

4. You are the administrator for a company that uses FSRM. You need to create a file group. What PowerShell command would you use?

    A. New-FsrmGroup

    B. New-FsrmFile

    C. New-FsrmFileGroup

    D. New-FileGroup

5. You are the administrator for a company who is using FSRM. You want to create a quota template to use in the future. What PowerShell command would you use to create a FSRM quota template?

   A. `New-FsrmQuotaTemplate`

   B. `New-FsrmTemplate`

   C. `New-QuotaTemplate`

   D. `New-FsrmQuota`

6. You are an administrator for an organization that uses FSRM. Your boss has asked you to remove a FSRM classification rule. Which PowerShell command allows you to do this?

   A. `Delete-FsrmClassificationRule`

   B. `Delete-FsrmClassRule`

   C. `Remove-FsrmClassificationRule`

   D. `Kill-FsrmClassRule`

7. You are the administrator of a company with four Windows 2016 servers, and all of the clients are running Windows 10. All of your sales people use laptops to do their work away from the office. What should you configure to help them work when away from the office?

   A. Online file access

   B. Offline file access

   C. Share permissions

   D. NTFS permissions

8. Your company has decided to implement an external hard drive. The company IT manager before you always used FAT32 as the system partition. Your company wants to know whether it should move to NTFS. Which of the following are some advantages of NTFS? (Choose all that apply.)

   A. Security

   B. Quotas

   C. Compression

   D. Encryption

9. You are the administrator of your network, which consists of two Windows Server 2016 systems. One of the servers is a domain controller, and the other server is a file server for data storage. The hard drive of the file server is starting to fill up. You do not have the ability to install another hard drive, so you decide to limit the amount of space everyone gets on the hard drive. What do you need to implement to solve your problem?

   A. Disk spacing

   B. Disk quotas

   C. Disk hardening

   D. Disk limitations

10. You are the administrator for a large communications company. Your company uses Windows Server 2016, and your users' files are encrypted using EFS. What command-line command would you use to change or modify the EFS files?

    A. Convert

    B. Cipher

    C. Gopher

    D. Encrypt

Chapter

7

Configuring High Availability

THE FOLLOWING 70-741 EXAM OBJECTIVES ARE COVERED IN THIS CHAPTER:

✓ **Implement high performance network solutions**

- This objective may include but is not limited to: Implement NIC Teaming or the Switch Embedded Teaming (SET) solution and identify when to use each; enable and configure Receive Side Scaling (RSS); enable and configure network Quality of Service (QoS) with Data Center Bridging (DCB); enable and configure SMB Direct on Remote Direct Memory Access (RDMA) enabled network adapters; enable and configure SMB Multichannel; enable and configure virtual Receive Side Scaling (vRSS) on a Virtual Machine Queue (VMQ) capable network adapter; enable and configure Virtual Machine Multi-Queue (VMMQ); enable and configure Single Root I/O Virtualization (SR-IOV) on a supported network adapter.

In this chapter, I will show you some of the techniques and components of high availability. I will explain how to set up high availability and I will talk about some of the reasons why you would choose to use high availability. I will also show you how to use PowerShell for high availability.

I will continue the chapter by explaining how to keep your Hyper-V servers up and running by implementing high availability and disaster recovery options in Hyper-V. Finally I will show you the PowerShell commands for Hyper-V high availability.

Components of High Availability

High availability is a buzzword that many application and hardware vendors like to throw around to get you to purchase their products. Many different options are available to achieve high availability, and there also seems to be a number of definitions and variations that help vendors sell their products as high-availability solutions.

When it comes right down to it, however, high availability simply means providing services with maximum uptime by avoiding unplanned downtime. Often, *disaster recovery (DR)* is also closely lumped into discussions of high availability, but DR encompasses the business and technical processes that are used to recover once a disaster has happened.

Defining a high availability plan usually starts with a *service level agreement (SLA)*. At its most basic, an SLA defines the services and metrics that must be met for the availability and performance of an application or service. Often, an SLA is created for an IT department or service provider to deliver a specific level of service. An example of this might be an SLA for a Microsoft Exchange Server. The SLA for an Exchange Server might have uptime metrics on how much time during the month the mailboxes need to be available to end users, or it might define performance metrics for the amount of time it takes for email messages to be delivered.

When determining what goes into an SLA, two other factors need to be considered. However, you will often see them discussed only in the context of disaster recovery, even though they are important for designing a highly available solution. These factors are the *recovery point objective (RPO)* and the *recovery time objective (RTO)*.

An RTO is the length of time an application can be unavailable before service must be restored to meet the SLA. For example, a single component failure would have an RTO of less than five minutes, and a full-site failure might have an RTO of three hours. An RPO is essentially the amount of data that must be restored in the event of a failure. For example, in a single server or component failure, the RPO would be 0, but in a site failure, the RPO might allow for up to 20 minutes of lost data.

SLAs, on the other hand, are usually expressed in percentages of the time the application is available. These percentages are also often referred to by the number of nines the percentage includes. So if someone told you that you need to make sure that the router has a rating of Five 9s, that would mean that the router could only be down for 5.26 minutes a year. Table 7.1 shows you some of the different nines ratings and what each rating allows for downtime.

TABLE 7.1   Availability percentages

Availability Rating	Allowed Unplanned Downtime/Year
99 (two nines) percent	3.65 days
99.9 (three nines) percent	8.76 hours
99.99 (four nines) percent	52.56 minutes
99.999 (five nines) percent	5.26 minutes
99.9999 (six nines) percent	31.5 seconds
99.99999 (seven nines) percent	3.15 seconds

Two important factors that affect an SLA are the *mean time between failure (MTBF)* and the *mean time to recovery (MTTR)*. To be able to reduce the amount of unplanned downtime, the time between failures must be increased, and the time it takes to recover must be reduced. Modifying these two factors will be addressed in the next several sections of this chapter.

Achieving High Availability

Windows Server 2016 is the most secure and reliable Windows version to date. It also is the most stable, mature, and capable of any version of Windows. Although similar claims have been made for previous versions of Windows Server, you can rest assured that Windows Server 2016 is much better than previous versions for a variety of reasons.

An honest look at the feature set and real-world use should prove that this latest version of Windows provides the most suitable foundation for creating a highly available solution. However, more than just good software is needed to be able to offer high availability for applications.

High Availability Foundation

Just as a house needs a good foundation, a highly available Windows server needs a stable and reliable hardware platform on which to run. Although Windows Server 2016 will technically run on desktop-class hardware, high availability is more easily achieved with server-class hardware. What differentiates desktop-class from server-class hardware? *Server-class hardware* has more management and monitoring features built into it so that the health of the hardware is capable of being monitored and maintained.

Another large difference is that server-class hardware has redundancy options. Server-class hardware often has options to protect from drive failures, such as RAID controllers, and to protect against power supply failures, such as multiple power supplies. Enterprise-class servers have even more protection.

More needs to be done than just installing Windows Server 2016 to ensure that the applications remain running with the best availability possible. Just as a house needs maintenance and upkeep to keep the structure in proper repair, so too does a server. In the case of a highly available server, this means *patch management*.

Installing Patches

Microsoft releases monthly updates to fix security problems with its software, both for operating system fixes and for applications. To ensure that your highly available applications are immune to known vulnerabilities, these patches need to be applied in a timely manner during a scheduled maintenance window. Also, to address stability and performance issues, updates and service packs are released regularly for many applications, such as Microsoft SQL Server, Exchange Server, and SharePoint Portal Server. Many companies have a set schedule—daily, weekly, or monthly—to apply these patches and updates after they are tested and approved.

Desired Configuration Manager (DCM), an option in Microsoft System Center Configuration Manager, is a great tool for helping to validate that your cluster nodes are patched. It can leverage the SCCM client to collect installed patches and help reporting within the enterprise on compliancy with desired system states based on the software installed.

To continue with the house analogy, if you were planning to have the master bath remodeled, would you rather hire a college student on spring break looking to make some extra money to do the job or a seasoned artisan? Of course, you would want someone with experience and a proven record of accomplishment to remodel your master bath.

Likewise, with any work that needs to be done on your highly available applications, it's best to hire only decidedly qualified individuals. This is why obtaining a Microsoft certification is definitely an excellent start to becoming qualified to configure a highly available server properly. There is no substitute for real-life and hands-on experience. Working with highly available configurations in a lab and in production will help you know not only what configurations are available but also how the changes should be made.

For example, it may be possible to use Failover Clustering for a DNS server, but in practice DNS replication may be easier to support and require less expensive hardware in order to provide high availability. This is something you would know only if you had enough experience to make this decision.

As with your house, once you have a firm and stable foundation built by skilled artisans and a maintenance plan has been put into place, you need to ascertain what more is needed. If you can't achieve enough uptime with proper server configuration and mature operational processes, a cluster may be needed.

Windows Server 2016 provides two types of high availability: *Failover Clustering* and *Network Load Balancing (NLB)*. Failover clustering is used for applications and services such as SQL Server and Exchange Server. Network Load Balancing is used for network-based services such as web and FTP servers. The remaining sections of this chapter will cover NLB and Hyper-V high availability in depth.

Understanding Network Load Balancing

So the first thing we have to discuss is why an administrator would choose to use NLB. NLB allows an administrator to configure two or more servers as a single virtual cluster. NLB is designed for high availability and scalability of Internet server applications. So this means that Windows Server 2016 NLB is designed to work with web servers, FTP servers, firewalls, proxy servers, and virtual private networks (VPNs).

Network Load Balancing is a form of clustering where the nodes are highly available for a network-based service. This is typically a port listener configuration where a farm of, say, Microsoft Internet Information Services servers all listen on ports 80 and 443 for incoming web traffic from client endpoints. These nodes, while not fully clustered in a technical sense, are load balanced, where each node handles some of the distributed network traffic.

The NLB feature uses the TCP/IP networking protocol to distribute traffic. For web servers and other necessary servers, NLB can provide performance and consistency when two or more computers are combined into a single virtual cluster.

Hosts are servers that make up an NLB cluster. Each host runs their own individual copy of the server applications. The incoming client requests are distributed by NLB to each of the hosts in the cluster. The administrator can configure the load so that it is handled by each host. Hosts can be added to the cluster to increase the load. If NLB has all traffic directed to a specific single host, then it is called a default host.

With the use of NLB, all the computers in a cluster can use the same set of IP addresses while each host maintains its own exclusive IP address. When a host fails for load-balanced applications, the computers still in operation will receive the workload automatically. When the down computer is ready to rejoin the cluster it comes back online and will regain its share of the workload. This allows the rest of the computers in the cluster to handle less traffic.

NLB is beneficial in that stateless applications (for example, web servers) are available with little downtime and it allows for scalability.

Scalability is the capability of a system, network, or process to handle a growing amount of work, or its potential to be enlarged in order to accommodate growth. Scalability, when used for NLB clusters, is the ability to add one or more systems to an existing cluster when the need arises. An administrator can do the following with NLB to support scalability:

- A single cluster can support up to 32 computers.

- Handle multiple server load requests from across multiple hosts in a cluster.

- For single TCP/IP services, balance load requests across the NLB cluster.

- As the workload grows, be able to add hosts to the NLB cluster without failure.

- When the workload declines, be able to remove hosts from the cluster.

- Allow higher performance and lower overhead by utilizing a pipelined implementation. Pipelining allows requests to be sent to the NLB cluster without waiting for a response.

- Use NLB Manager or Windows PowerShell cmdlets to manage and configure NLB clusters and hosts from a single computer.

- Determine port rules for each website. Port rules allow you to configure which ports are going to be enabled or disabled. Ports are doorways that applications can use to access resources. For example, DNS traffic uses port 53 for all DNS traffic. Here are some of the more common port numbers:

  - FTP uses ports 20/21

  - Secure Shell uses port 22

  - SMTP (mail) uses port 25

  - DNS uses port 53

  - HTTP uses port 80

  - POPv3 uses port 110

  - HTTPS uses port 443

- Determine load balancing behavior using port management rules for an IP port or group of ports.

- Use an optional, single-host rule that will direct all client requests to a single host. NLB will route client requests to a specific host that is running particular applications.

- Allow certain IP ports to block unwanted network access.

- When operating in multicast mode, enable Internet Group Management Protocol (IGMP) support on the cluster host. This will control switch port flooding (when all incoming network packets are sent to all ports on the switch).

- Use Windows PowerShell to start, stop and control NLB actions remotely.
- Check NLB events using Windows Event Log. All NLB actions and cluster changes are logged in the Event Log.

NLB Requirements

NLB cluster hardware requirements:

- All hosts must be on the same subnet.
- For each host, there is no limitation to the number of network adapters.
- All network adapters must be multicast or unicast within the cluster. Mixed environments, within a single cluster, are NOT supported.
- If using unicast mode, the network adapter used to handle client-to-cluster traffic must support media access control (MAC) address changing.

   NLB cluster software requirements:

- The adapter on which NLB is enabled can only support TCP/IP.
- Must have a static IP address on the servers in the cluster.

Installing NLB Nodes

You can install NLB nodes like any other server build. Administrators can install NLB by using either Server Manager or the Windows PowerShell commands for NLB.

   Administrators should first make sure that all NLB servers have the most current updates, provisioned with appropriate resources (typically with multiple network interface cards for capacity and responsiveness), and monitored for health and reliability. In Exercise 7.1, I will walk you through the installation of your NLB nodes.

EXERCISE 7.1

Installing NLB Nodes

1. Once you have multiple hosts ready for the installation of NLB, simply run the Add Roles and Features Wizard and select Network Load Balancing in the Features area of the wizard. If the Add Features dialog box appears, click the Add Features button.

2. Click the Next button. At the Confirmation screen, click the Install button. After the installation is finished, click the Close button and then close Server Manager.

3. This wizard places a new application in your Start menu under Windows Administrative Tools, the Network Load Balancing Manager (see Figure 7.1).

FIGURE 7.1 Network Load Balancing

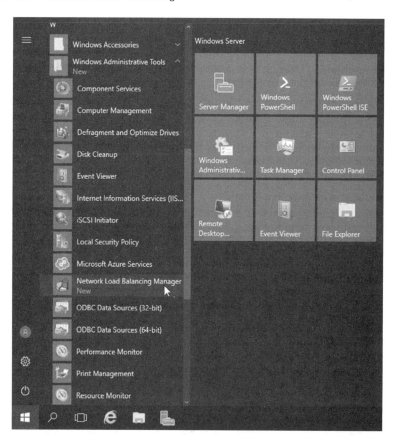

4. Right-click Network Load Balancing Clusters and select New Cluster (see Figure 7.2).

5. You are then presented with the New Cluster: Connect wizard where you can specify the name of one of your hosts. Type in the name of one of your cluster nodes and hit connect (see Figure 7.3). After the connection is made the TCP/IP address will be shown. Click Next.

6. If you get a DHCP dialog box, you will want to disable DHCP on this adapter. Click OK.

FIGURE 7.2   New Cluster

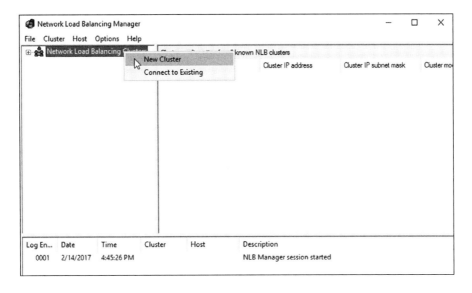

FIGURE 7.3   Host Name setup

7.   The next screen reveals a prompt to add any additional IPs and assign a priority level.
     You can do all this later, so hit Next. If you get a dialog box about No Dedicated IP
     Addresses, click Yes.

8. The next wizard screen is where you specify the cluster IP address. This is the address that the endpoints or clients or users of the NLB cluster will contact. Typically the network team will assign a cluster IP address for this use (see Figure 7.4). Click OK. Then Click Next.

FIGURE 7.4   Add IP address

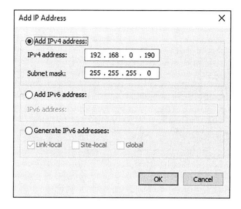

9. On the next screen, you configure the Cluster operation mode (see Figure 7.5) and specify a Full Internet name.

FIGURE 7.5   Cluster Parameters

With regard to the cluster operation modes, the differences between them are as follows:

Unicast

The cluster adapters for all nodes are assigned the same MAC address.

The outgoing MAC address for each packet is modified based on priority to prevent upstream switches from discovering that all nodes have the same MAC address.

Communication between cluster nodes (other than heartbeat and other administrative NLB traffic) is not possible unless there are additional adapters (because all nodes have the same MAC address).

Depending on load, this configuration can cause switch flooding since all inbound packets are sent to all ports on the switch.

Multicast

The cluster adapters for all nodes are assigned their own MAC unicast address.

The cluster adapters for all nodes are assigned a multicast MAC address (derived from the IP of the cluster).

Non-NLB network traffic between cluster nodes works fine since they all have their own MAC address.

IGMP Multicast

This is much like multicast, but the MAC traffic goes only to the switch ports of the NLB cluster, preventing switch flooding.

10. After selecting the appropriate settings, the next page is where port rules (see Figure 7.6) are configured. By default, it is set up to be wide open. Most implementations will limit NLB ports to just the ports needed for the application. For example, a web server would need port 80 enabled. It is also in this area where you can configure filtering mode.

FIGURE 7.6 Port Rules

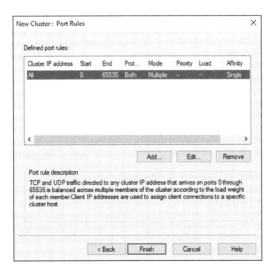

The affinity sets a client's preference to a particular NLB host. It is not recommended to set affinity to None when UDP is an expected traffic type.

11. Click the Finish button. Close the NLB Manager.

If you decide that you want to install NLB using Windows PowerShell commands, you would open an elevated Windows PowerShell prompt and type in the following command:

```
Install-WindowsFeature NLB -IncludeManagementTools
```

Upgrading an NLB Cluster

Upgrading an NLB cluster is a fairly straightforward process. The first thing that you have to do is stop the NLB cluster. There are two ways to stop a NLB cluster: stop or drainstop.

If an administrator decides to use the stop command, the cluster stops immediately. This also means that any current connections to the NLB cluster are killed.

If an administrator decides to use the drainstop command, the cluster stops after answering all of the current NLB connections. So the current NLB connections are finished but no new connections to that node are accepted.

So to do your upgrade, you should execute a stop or drainstop on the NLB cluster node that you want to upgrade or remove existing connections to the application on the local host. After the NLB cluster is stopped you then perform an in-place upgrade in a rolling manner.

If you want to stop the entire cluster from running, while in the NLB manager (type **NLBmgr** in Run command), you would right-click on the cluster, point to Control Hosts, and then choose Stop.

If you want to stop a single node in the cluster from running, while in the NLB manager (type **NLBmgr** in Run command), you would right-click on the node, point to Control Hoss, and then choose Stop.

Setting the Affinity

NLB allows an administrator to configure three types of affinity settings to help response times between NLB clients. Each affinity setting determines a method of distributing NLB client requests. There are three different affinity settings: None, Single, and Class C. The New Cluster Wizard sets the default affinity to Single.

No Affinity (None)   When setting the affinity to No Affinity (None), NLB will not assign a NLB client with any specific member. When a request is sent to the NLB, the requests are balanced among all of the nodes. The No Affinity provides greater performance but there may be issues with clients establishing sessions. This happens because the request may be load balanced between NLB nodes and session information may not be present.

Single Affinity   Setting the cluster affinity to Single will send all traffic from a specific IP address to a single cluster node. This will keep a client on a specific node where the client should not have to authenticate again. Setting the affinity mode to Single would remove the authentication problem but would not distribute the load to other servers unless the initial server was down. Setting the affinity to Single allows a client's IP address to always connect to the same NLB node. This setting allows clients using an intranet to get the best performance.

Class C Affinity   When setting the affinity to Class C, NLB links clients with a specific member based on the Class C part of the client's IP address. This allows an administrator to setup NLB so that clients from the same Class C address range can access the same NLB member. This affinity is best for NLB clusters using the Internet.

PowerShell Commands for a NLB Cluster

In Table 7.2, I will show you some of the different PowerShell commands that you can use to manage the NLB cluster.

TABLE 7.2   PowerShell Commands for NLB

PowerShell Command	Description
Add-NlbClusterNode	This command adds a new node to the NLB cluster.
Add-NlbClusterNodeDip	This command will add a dedicated IP address to a cluster.
Add-NlbClusterPortRule	This command adds a new port rule to a cluster.
Add-NlbClusterVip	This command adds a virtual IP address to a cluster.
Disable-NlbClusterPortRule	This command disables a port rule on a Network Load Balancing (NLB) cluster.
Enable-NlbClusterPortRule	This command enables a port rule on a cluster.
Get-NlbCluster	This command allows you to view information about the Network Load Balancing (NLB) cluster.
Get-NlbClusterDriverInfo	This command allows you to see information about the NLB drivers on a machine.
Get-NlbClusterNode	This command gets the information about the cluster object.
Get-NlbClusterPortRule	This command gets the port rule objects.

TABLE 7.2 PowerShell Commands for NLB *(continued)*

PowerShell Command	Description
New-NlbCluster	This command creates a cluster on the specified interface.
New-NlbClusterIpv6Address	This command generates IPv6 addresses to create cluster virtual IP addresses.
Remove-NlbCluster	This command deletes a cluster.
Remove-NlbClusterNode	This command removes a node from a cluster.
Remove-NlbClusterPortRule	This command deletes a port rule from a cluster.
Resume-NlbCluster	This command resumes all nodes in the cluster.
Set-NlbCluster	This command allows you to edit the configuration of a NLB cluster.
Set-NlbClusterNode	This command allows an administrator to edit the NLB cluster node settings.
Set-NlbClusterPortRule	This command allows you to edit the NLB port rules.
Start-NlbCluster	This command will start all of the nodes in a cluster.
Start-NlbClusterNode	This command will start one of the nodes in a cluster.
Stop-NlbCluster	This command stops all nodes in the cluster.
Stop-NlbClusterNode	This command will stop one of the nodes in a cluster.

Achieving High Availability with Failover Clustering

Taking high availability to the next level for enterprise services often means creating a failover cluster. In a failover cluster, all of the clustered application or service resources are assigned to one node or server in the cluster. Commonly clustered applications are SQL Server and Exchange Server; commonly clustered services are File and Print. Since the differences between a clustered application and a clustered service are primarily related to the number of functions or features, for simplicity's sake I will refer to both as *clustered applications*. Another, more frequently, clustered resource is a Hyper-V virtual machine.

If there is a failure of the primary node or if the primary node is taken offline for maintenance, the clustered application is started on another cluster node. The client requests are then automatically redirected to the new cluster node to minimize the impact of the failure.

How does Failover Clustering improve availability? By increasing the number of server nodes available on which the application or virtual machine can run, you can move the application or virtual machine to a healthy server if there is a problem, if maintenance needs to be completed on the hardware or the operating system, or if patches need to be applied. The clustered application being moved will have to restart on the new server regardless of whether the move was intentional. This is why the term *highly available* is used instead of *fault tolerant*. Virtual machines, however, can be moved from one node to another node using a process known as *live migration*. Live migration is where one or more virtual machines are intentionally moved from one node to another with their current memory state intact through the cluster network with no indicators to the virtual machine consumer that the virtual machine has moved from one server to another. However, in the event of a cluster node or virtual machine failure, the virtual machine will still fail and will then be brought online again on another healthy cluster node.

Figure 7.7 shows an example of SQL Server running on the first node of a Windows Server 2016 failover cluster.

FIGURE 7.7 Using Failover Clustering to cluster SQL Server

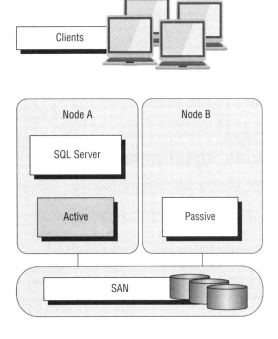

The clustered SQL Server in Figure 7.8 can be failed over to another node in the cluster and still service database requests. However, the database will be restarted.

FIGURE 7.8   Failing the SQL Server service to another node

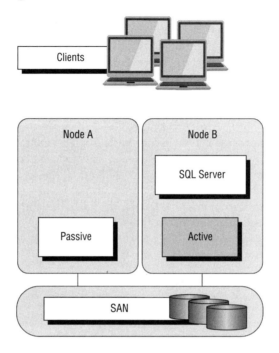

Failover clustering is notorious for being complicated and expensive. Windows Server 2016 makes strides in removing both of these concerns. Troubleshooting and other advanced concepts are outside of the scope of the Microsoft MCSA exams and thus this book, so I will cover only the basic requirements and concepts needed to configure a failover cluster.

Failover Clustering Requirements

The Failover Clustering feature is available in the Datacenter, Standard, and Hyper-V editions of Windows Server 2016.

To be able to configure a failover cluster, you must have the required components. A single failover cluster can have up to 64 nodes when using Windows Server 2016, however, and the clustered service or application must support that number of nodes.

To create a failover cluster, an administrator must make sure that all the hardware involved meets the cluster requirements. To be supported by Microsoft, all hardware must be certified for Windows Server 2016, and the complete failover cluster solution must pass all tests in the Validate a Configuration Wizard. Although the exact hardware will depend on the clustered application, a few requirements are standard:

- Server components must be marked with the "Certified for Windows Server 2016" logo.
- Although not explicitly required, server hardware should match and contain the same or similar components.
- All of the Validate a Configuration Wizard tests must pass.

The requirements for Failover Clustering storage have changed from previous versions of Windows. For example, Parallel SCSI is no longer a supported storage technology for any of the clustered disks. There are, however, additional requirements that need to be met for the storage components:

- Disks available for the cluster must be Fibre Channel, iSCSI, or Serial Attached SCSI.
- Each cluster node must have a dedicated network interface card for iSCSI connectivity. The network interface card you use for iSCSI should not be used for network communication.
- Multipath software must be based on Microsoft's Multipath I/O (MPIO).
- Storage drivers must be based on `storport.sys`.
- Drivers and firmware for the storage controllers on each server node in the cluster should be identical.
- Storage components must be marked with the "Certified for Windows Server 2016" logo.

In addition, there are network requirements that must be met for Failover Clustering:

- Cluster nodes should be connected to multiple networks for communication redundancy.
- Network adapters should be the same make, use the same driver, and have the firmware version in each cluster node.
- Network components must be marked with the "Certified for Windows Server 2016" logo.

There are two types of network connections in a failover cluster. These should have adequate redundancy because total failure of either could cause loss of functionality of the cluster. The two types are as follows:

Public Network   This is the network through which clients are able to connect to the clustered service application.

Private Network   This is the network used by the nodes to communicate with each other.

To provide redundancy for these two network types, additional network adapters would need to be added to the node and configured to connect to the networks.

In previous versions of Windows Server, support was given only when the entire cluster configuration was tested and listed on the Hardware Compatibility List. The tested configuration listed the server and storage configuration down to the firmware and driver versions. This proved to be difficult and expensive from both a vendor and a consumer perspective to deploy supported Windows clusters.

When problems did arise and Microsoft support was needed, it caused undue troubleshooting complexity as well. With Windows Server 2016 Failover Clustering and simplified requirements, including the "Certified for Windows Server 2016" logo program and the Validate a Configuration Wizard, it all but eliminates the guesswork of getting the cluster components configured in a way that follows best practices and allows Microsoft support to assist you easily when needed.

Workgroup and Multi-Domain Clusters

One nice new advantage of using Windows Server 2016 is the ability to set up a cluster on systems not part of the same domain. In Window Server 2012 R2 and previous versions, clusters could only be created on machines that were part of the same domain. Windows Server 2016 allows you to set up a cluster without using Active Directory dependencies. Administrators can create clusters in the following situations:

Single-Domain Cluster   All nodes in a cluster are part of the same domain.

Multi-Domain Cluster   Nodes in a cluster are part of a different domain.

Workgroup Cluster   Nodes are member servers and part of a workgroup.

Site-Aware, Stretched, or Geographically Dispersed Clusters (Geoclustering)

One nice advantage of Windows Server 2016 clustering is that you can set up site-aware failover clusters. Site-aware clustering allows an administrator to expand clustered nodes to different geographic locations (sites). Site-aware failover clusters allow you to set up clusters in remote locations for failover, placement policies, Cross-Site Heartbeating, and for quorum placement.

One of the issues with previous clusters was the heartbeat. The cluster heartbeat is a signal sent between servers so that they know that the machines are up and running. Servers send heartbeats and if after 5 non-responsive heartbeats, the cluster would assume that the node was offline. So if you had nodes in remote locations, the heartbeats would not get the response they needed.

But now Windows Server 2016 includes Cross-Site Heartbeating and it allows you to setup delays so that remote nodes can answer the heartbeat within time. The following two PowerShell commands allow you to setup the delay necessary for Cross-Site Heartbeating.

```
(Get-Cluster).CrossSiteDelay = <value>
(Get-Cluster).CrossSiteThreshold = <value>
```

The first PowerShell command (`CrossSiteDelay`) is what is used to set the amount of time between each heartbeat sent to nodes. This value is done in milliseconds (default is 1000).

The second PowerShell command (`CrossSiteThreshold`) is the value that you set for the number of missed heartbeats (default is 20) before the node is considered offline.

One issue you may face is if you have multiple sites or if the cluster is geographically dispersed. If the failover cluster does not have a shared common disk, data replication between nodes might not pass the cluster validation "storage" tests.

Setting up a cluster in a site-aware, stretched, or geocluster (these terms can be used interchangeably) configuration is a common practice. As long as the cluster solution does not require external storage to fail over, it will not need to pass the storage test to function properly.

Cluster Quorum

When a group of people sets out to accomplish a single task or goal, a method for settling disagreements and for making decisions is required. In the case of a cluster, the goal is to provide a highly available service in spite of failures. When a problem occurs and a cluster node loses communication with the other nodes because of a network error, the functioning nodes are supposed to try to bring the redundant service back online.

How, though, is it determined which node should bring the clustered service back online? If all the nodes are functional despite the network communications issue, each one might try. Just like a group of people with their own ideas, a method must be put in place to determine which idea, or node, to grant control of the cluster. Windows Server 2016 Failover Clustering, like other clustering technologies, requires that a quorum exist between the cluster nodes before a cluster becomes available.

A *quorum* is a consensus of the status of each of the nodes in the cluster. Quorum must be achieved in order for a clustered application to come online by obtaining a majority of the votes available (see Figure 7.9). Windows Server 2016 has four quorum models, or methods, for determining a quorum and for adjusting the number and types of votes available:

- Node majority (no witness)
- Node majority with witness (disk or file share)
- Node and file share majority
- No majority (disk witness only)

Witness Configuration

Most administrators follow some basic rules. For example, when you configure a quorum, the voting components in the cluster should be an odd number. For example, if I set up a quorum for five elements and I lose one element, I continue to work. If I lose two elements, I continue to work. If I lose three elements, the cluster stops—as soon as it hits half plus 1, the cluster stops. This works well with an odd number.

FIGURE 7.9 Majority needed

When a majority of the nodes are communicating, the cluster is functional.

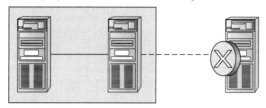

When a majority of the nodes are not communicating, the cluster stops.

If the cluster contains an even number of voting elements, an administrator should then configure a disk witness or a file share witness. The advantage of using a witness (disk or file share) is that the cluster will continue to run even if half of the cluster nodes simultaneously go down or are disconnected. The ability to configure a disk witness is possible only if the storage vendor supports read-write access from all sites to the replicated storage.

One of the advantages of Windows Server 2016 is the advanced quorum configuration option. This option allows you to assign or remove quorum votes on a per-node basis. Administrators now have the ability to remove votes from nodes in certain configurations. For example, if your organization uses a site-aware cluster, you may choose to remove votes from the nodes in the backup site. This way, those backup nodes would not affect your quorum calculations.

There are different ways that you can setup quorum witnesses. Here are some of the options that you can choose from:

Configure a Disk Witness Choosing the quorum disk witness is normally setup if all nodes can see the disks. To set this disk witness up, the cluster must be able to see the Dedicated LUN. The LUN needs to store a copy of the cluster database and it's most useful for clusters that are using shared storage. The following list is just some of the requirements when setting up a Disk Witness:

- LUN needs to be at least 512 MB minimum.
- The disk must be dedicated to cluster use only.
- Must pass disk storage validation tests.
- The disk can't be used in a Cluster Shared Volume (CSV).
- You must use a single volume for Basic disks.

- No drive letter needed.
- Drive must be formatted using NTFS or ReFS.
- Can be used with hardware RAID.
- Should not be used with Antivirus or backup software

Configure a File Share Witness   Administrators should choose to use the File Share Witness when you need to think about multi-site disaster recovery and the file server must be using the SMB file share.

The following list is just some of the requirements when setting up a File Share Witness:

- Minimum of 5 MB of free space required.
- File share must be dedicated to the cluster and not used to store user data or application data.

Configure a Cloud Witness   Windows Server 2016 Cloud Witness is a new type of Failover Cluster quorum witness that leverages Microsoft Azure as the intercession point. The Cloud Witness gets a vote just like any other quorum witness. Administrators can setup the cloud witness as a quorum witness using the Configure a Cluster Quorum Wizard.

Dynamic Quorum Management

Another advantage in Windows Server 2016 is dynamic quorum management. *Dynamic quorum management* automatically manages the vote assignment to nodes. With this feature enabled, votes are automatically added or removed from nodes when that node either joins or leaves a cluster. In Windows Server 2016, dynamic quorum management is enabled by default.

Validating a Cluster Configuration

Configuring a failover cluster in Windows Server 2016 is much simpler than in previous versions of Windows Server. Before a cluster can be configured, the Validate a Configuration Wizard should be run to verify that the hardware is configured in a fashion that is supportable. Before you can run the Validate a Configuration Wizard, however, the Failover Clustering feature needs to be installed using Server Manager. The account that is used to create a cluster must have administrative rights on each of the cluster nodes and have permissions to create a cluster name object in Active Directory (if using Active Directory). Follow these steps:

1. Prepare the hardware and software perquisites.
2. Install the Failover Clustering feature on each server.
3. Log in with the appropriate user ID and run the Validate a Configuration Wizard.
4. Create a cluster.
5. Install and cluster applications and services.

To install the Failover Clustering feature on a cluster node, follow the steps outlined in Exercise 7.2.

EXERCISE 7.2

Installing the Failover Cluster Feature

1. Press the Windows key and select Administrative Tools ➢ Server Manager.

2. Select number 2, Add Roles And Features.

3. At the Select Installation Type screen, choose a role-based or feature-based installation.

4. At the Select Destination Server screen, choose Select A Server From The Server Pool and click Next.

5. At the Select Server Roles screen, click Next.

6. At the Select Features screen, click the Failover Clustering (see Figure 7.10) check box. If the Add Features dialog box appears, click the Add Features button. Click Next.

FIGURE 7.10   Failover Cluster Feature

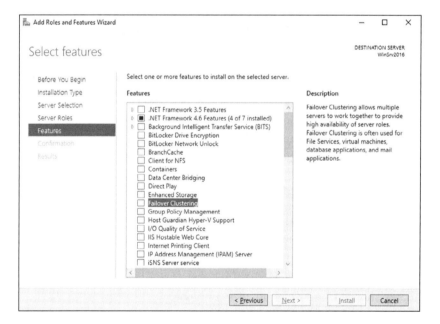

7. At the Confirmation screen (see Figure 7.11), click the Install button.

FIGURE 7.11 Confirmation Screen

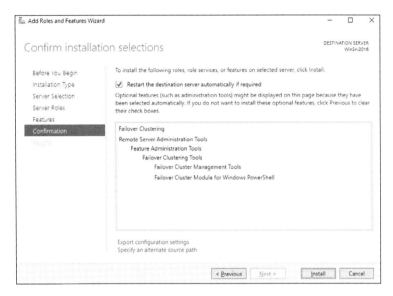

8. Once the installation is complete, click the Close button.

9. Close Server Manager.

Using the Validate a Configuration Wizard before creating a cluster is highly recommended. This wizard validates that the hardware configuration and the software configuration for the potential cluster nodes are in a supported configuration. Even if the configuration passes the tests, take care to review all warnings and informational messages so that they can be addressed or documented before the cluster is created.

Running the Validate a Configuration Wizard does the following:

- Conducts four types of tests (software and hardware inventory, network, storage, and system configuration)

- Confirms that the hardware and software settings are supportable by Microsoft support staff

You should run the Validate a Configuration Wizard before creating a cluster or after making any major hardware or software changes to the cluster. Doing this will help you identify any misconfigurations that could cause problems with the failover cluster.

Running the Validate a Configuration Wizard

The Validate a Configuration Wizard, shown in Figure 7.12, is simple and straightforward to use, as its "wizard" name would suggest. It should be run after the Failover Clustering feature has been installed on each of the cluster nodes, and it can be run as many times as required.

FIGURE 7.12   The Validate a Configuration Wizard

 When you are troubleshooting cluster problems or have changed the configuration of the cluster hardware, it is a good idea to run the Validate a Configuration Wizard again to help pinpoint potential cluster configuration problems.

If you already have a cluster configured and want to run the Validate a Configuration Wizard, you can do so; however, you will not be able to run all of the storage tests without taking the clustered resources offline. You will be prompted either to skip the disruptive tests or to take the clustered resources offline so that the tests can complete.

Exercise 7.3 shows the exact steps to follow to run the Validate a Configuration Wizard successfully on clusters named NODEA and NODEB, which are not yet clustered.

 I am using NODEA and NODEB in the exercises. You need to replace these two nodes with your own two servers to complete these exercises.

EXERCISE 7.3

Running the Validate a Configuration Wizard

1. Press the Windows key and select Administrative Tools ≻ Failover Cluster Management.

2. In the Actions pane (right side of screen), click Validate Configuration.

3. At the Before You Begin screen, click Next.

4. Type **First Server Name** (this is your server's name) in the Enter Name field and click Add.

5. Type **Second Server Name** (this is the second server's name) in the Enter Name field and click Add.

6. Click Next.

7. Leave Run All Tests (Recommended) selected and click Next.

8. You will see tests being run (see Figure 7.13). Let the test complete, review the report in the Summary window, and then click Finish.

FIGURE 7.13   Cluster Tests

9. Close the Failover Cluster Wizard.

Addressing Problems Reported by the Validate a Configuration Wizard

After the Validate a Configuration Wizard has been run, it will show the results, as shown in Figure 7.14. This report can also be viewed in detail later using a web browser. The report is named with the date and time the wizard was run, and it is stored in %windir%\cluster\Reports.

FIGURE 7.14 Validate a Configuration Wizard results

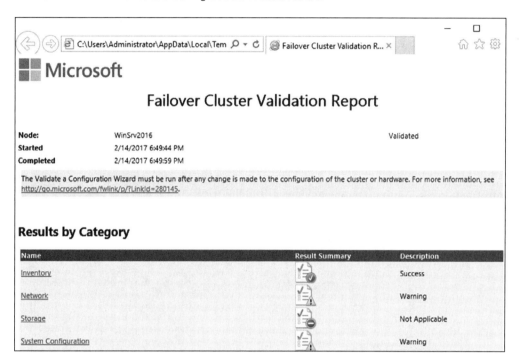

How should errors listed in the report be addressed? Often, the errors reported by the Validate a Configuration Wizard are self-explanatory; however, sometimes additional help is required. The following three guidelines should help troubleshoot the errors:

- Read all of the errors because multiple errors may be related.

- Use the checklists available in the Windows Server help files to ensure that all the steps have been completed.

- Contact the hardware vendor for updated drivers, firmware, and guidance for using the hardware in a cluster.

Creating a Cluster

After you have successfully validated a configuration and the cluster hardware is in a supportable state, you can create a cluster. The process for creating a cluster is straightforward and similar to the process of running the Validate a Configuration Wizard. To create a cluster with two servers, follow the instructions in Exercise 7.4.

EXERCISE 7.4

Creating a Cluster

1. Open the Failover Cluster Management MMC.

2. In the Management section of the center pane, select Create A Cluster.

3. Read the Before You Begin information and click Next.

4. In the Enter Server Name box, type **Your Server** and then click Add.

5. Again, in the Enter Server Name box, type **Your Second Server** and then click Add.
    Click Next.

6. At the Validation screen, choose No for this exercise and then click Next.

7. In the Access Point For Administering The Cluster section, enter **Cluster1** for the
    cluster name.

8. Type an IP address and then click Next. This IP address will be the IP address of
    the cluster.

9. In the Confirmation dialog box, verify the information and then click Next.

10. On the Summary page, click Finish.

Working with Cluster Nodes

Once a cluster is created, a couple of actions are available. First you can add another node to
the cluster by using the Add Node Wizard from the Failover Cluster Management Actions pane.

At this point, you also have the option to pause a node, which prevents resources from
being failed over or moved to the node. You typically would pause a node when the node is
involved in maintenance or troubleshooting. After a node is paused, it must be resumed to
allow resources to be run on it again.

Another action available to perform on a node at this time is *evict*. Eviction is an irre-
versible process. Once you evict the node, it must be re-added to the cluster. You would
evict a node when it is damaged beyond repair or is no longer needed in the cluster. If you
evict a damaged node, you can repair or rebuild it and then add it back to the cluster using
the Add Node Wizard.

Clustering Roles, Services, and Applications

Once the cluster is created, applications, services, and roles can be clustered. Windows Server
2016 includes a number of built-in roles and features that can be clustered.

The following roles and features can be clustered in Windows Server 2016 (see Figure 7.15):

▪ DFS Namespace Server

▪ DHCP Server

▪ Distributed Transaction Coordinator (DTC)

- File Server
- Generic Application
- Generic Script
- Generic Service
- Hyper-V Replica Broker
- iSCSI Target Server
- iSNS Server
- Message Queuing
- Other Server
- Virtual Machine

FIGURE 7.15 High availability roles

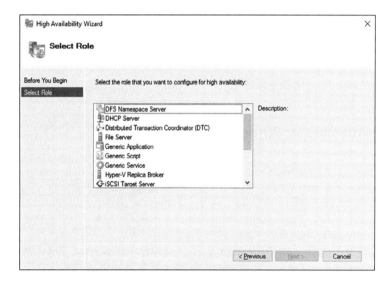

In addition, other common services and applications can be clustered on Windows Server 2016 clusters:

- Enterprise database services, such as Microsoft SQL Server
- Enterprise messaging services, such as Microsoft Exchange Server

To cluster a role or feature such as Print Services, the first step is to install the role or feature on each node of the cluster. The next step is to use the Configure a Service or Application Wizard in the Failover Cluster Management tool. Exercise 7.5 shows you how to cluster the Print Services role once an appropriate disk has been presented to the cluster. To complete this exercise, you must have a cluster created.

EXERCISE 7.5

Clustering the Print Services Role

1. Open the Failover Cluster Management MMC.

2. In the console tree, click the arrow next to the cluster name to expand the items underneath it.

3. Right-click Roles and choose Configure Role.

4. Click Next on the Before You Begin page.

5. Click Other Server on the Select Role screen and then click Next.

6. Type the name of the print server, such as **Print1**, and type in the IP address that will be used to access the print service, such as **80.0.0.34**. Then click Next.

7. At the Select Storage page, just click Next.

8. Click Next at the Confirmation page.

9. After the wizard runs and the Summary page appears, you can view a report of the tasks the wizard performed by clicking View Report.

10. Close the report and click Finish.

The built-in roles and features all are configured in a similar fashion. Other applications, such as Microsoft Exchange Server 2016, have specialized cluster configuration routines that are outside the scope of this exam. Applications that are not developed to be clustered can also be clustered using the Generic Application, Generic Script, or Generic Service option in the Configure a Service or Application Wizard, as shown in Figure 7.16.

FIGURE 7.16   Configuring a generic application

Clustered Application Settings

Windows Server 2016 has options that allow an administrator to fine-tune the failover process to meet the needs of their business. These options will be covered in the next few sections.

Failover occurs when a clustered application or service moves from one node to another. The process can be triggered automatically because of a failure or server maintenance or can be done manually by an administrator. The failover process works as follows:

1. The cluster service takes all of the resources in the application offline in the order set in the dependency hierarchy.

2. The cluster service transfers the application to the node that is listed next on the application's list of preferred host nodes.

3. The cluster service attempts to bring all of the application's resources online, starting at the bottom of the dependency hierarchy.

These steps can change depending on the use of Live Migration.

In a cluster that is hosting multiple applications, it may be important to set specific nodes to be primarily responsible for each clustered application. This can be helpful from a troubleshooting perspective since a specific node is targeted for a hosting service. To set a preferred node and an order of preference for failover, use the General tab in the Properties dialog box of the clustered application.

Also, the order of failover is set in this same dialog box by moving the order in which the nodes are listed. If NODEA should be the primary node and NODEB should be the server that the application fails to first, NODEA should be listed first and selected as the preferred owner. NODEB should be listed second, and the remaining cluster nodes should be listed after NODEB.

A number of failover settings can be configured for the clustered service. The failover settings control the number of times a clustered application can fail in a period of time before the cluster stops trying to restart it. Typically, if a clustered application fails a number of times, some sort of manual intervention will be required to return the application to a stable state.

Specifying the maximum number of failures will keep the application from trying to restart until it is manually brought back online after the problem has been resolved. This is beneficial because if the application continues to be brought online and then fails, it may show as being functional to the monitoring system, even though it continues to fail. After the application is put in a failed state, the monitoring system will not be able to contact the application and should report it as being offline.

Failback settings control whether and when a clustered application would fail back to the preferred cluster node once it becomes available. The default setting is Prevent Failback. If failback is allowed, two additional options are available, either to fail back immediately after the preferred node is available or to fail back within a specified time.

The time is specified in the 24-hour format. If you want to allow failback between 10 p.m. and 11 p.m., you would set the failback time to be between 22 and 23. Setting a failback time to off-hours is an excellent way to ensure that your clustered applications are running on the designated nodes and automatically scheduling the failover process for a time when it will impact the fewest users.

One tool that is valuable in determining how resources affect other resources is the dependency viewer. The *dependency viewer* visualizes the dependency hierarchy created for an application or service. Using this tool can help when troubleshooting why specific resources are causing failures and allow an administrator to visualize the current configuration better and adjust it to meet business needs. Exercise 7.6 will show you how to run the dependency viewer.

EXERCISE 7.6

Using the Dependency Viewer

1. Open the Failover Cluster Management MMC.

2. In the console tree, click the arrow to expand the cluster.

3. Click Roles.

4. Under the Roles section in the center of the screen, click one of the roles (such as Print1).

5. Right-click the role and under More Actions click Show Dependency Report.

6. Review the dependency report.

7. Close the Dependency Report and close the Failover Cluster Manager.

Exercise 7.6 generated a dependency report that shows how the print service is dependent on a network name and a clustered disk resource. The network name is then dependent on an IP address.

Resource Properties

Resources are physical or logical objects, such as a file share or IP address, which the failover cluster manages. They may be services or applications available to clients, or they may be part of the cluster. Resources include physical hardware devices such as disks and logical items such as network names. They are the smallest configurable unit in a cluster and can run on only a single node in a cluster at a time.

Like clustered applications, resources have a number of properties available for meeting business requirements for high availability. This section covers resource dependencies and policies.

Dependencies can be set on individual resources and control how resources are brought online and offline. Simply put, a dependent resource is brought online after the resources that it depends on, and it is taken offline before those resources. As shown in Figure 7.17, dependencies can be set on a specific resource, such as the Generic Application.

FIGURE 7.17   Resource dependencies

Resource policies are settings that control how resources respond when a failure occurs and how resources are monitored for failures. Figure 7.18 shows the Policies tab of a resource's Properties dialog box.

FIGURE 7.18   Resource policies

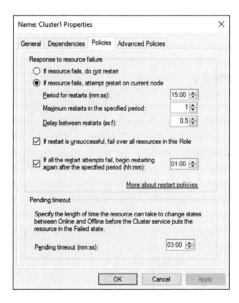

The Policies tab sets configuration options for how a resource should respond in the event of a failure. The options available are as follows:

If Resource Fails, Do Not Restart   This option, as it would lead you to believe, leaves the failed resource offline.

If Resource Fails, Attempt Restart On Current Node   With this option set, the resource tries to restart if it fails on the node on which it is currently running. There are two additional options if this is selected so that the number of restarts can be limited. They set the number of times the resource should restart on the current node in a specified length of time. For example, if you specify 5 for Maximum Restarts In The Specified Period and 10:00 (mm:ss) for Period For Restarts, the cluster service will try to restart the resource five times during that 10-minute period. After the fifth restart, the cluster service will no longer attempt to restart the service on the active node.

If Restart Is Unsuccessful, Fail Over All Resources In This Service Or Application   If this option is selected, when the cluster service is no longer trying to restart the resource on the active node, it will fail the entire service or application to another cluster node. If you wanted to leave the application or service with a failed resource on the current node, you would clear this check box.

If All The Restart Attempts Fail, Begin Restarting Again After The Specified Period (hh:mm)   If this option is selected, the cluster service will restart the resource at a specified interval if all previous attempts have failed.

Pending Timeout   This option is used to set the amount of time in minutes and seconds that the cluster service should wait for this resource to respond to a change in states. If a resource takes longer than the cluster expects to change states, the cluster will mark it as having failed. If a resource consistently takes longer than this and the problem cannot be resolved, you may need to increase this value. Figure 7.19 shows the Advanced Policies tab.

FIGURE 7.19   Resource Advanced Policies

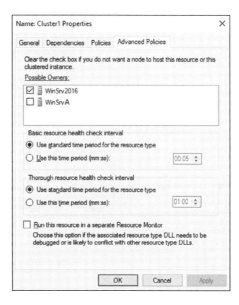

The options available on the Advanced Policies tab are as follows:

Possible Owners   This option allows an administrator to remove specific cluster nodes from running this resource. Using this option is valuable when there are issues with a resource on a particular node and the administrator wants to keep the applications from failing over to that node until the problem can be repaired.

Basic Resource Health Check Interval   This option allows an administrator to customize the health check interval for this resource.

Thorough Resource Health Check Interval   This option allows an administrator to customize the thorough health check interval for this resource.

Run This Resource In A Separate Resource Monitor   If the resource needs to be debugged by a support engineer or if the resource conflicts with other resources, this option may need to be used.

Windows Server 2016 Clustering Features

Many new features are included in the Windows Server 2016 release for clustering. It is a rich feature set of high availability with greatly improved flexibility based on the needs of IT organizations. The new features relate to quorum behavior, virtual machine hosting, Active Directory–detached clusters, and a new dashboard.

Windows PowerShell Cmdlets for Failover Clusters   As I have explained throughout this book, Windows PowerShell is a command-line shell and scripting tool. Windows Server 2016 clustering has new cmdlets that provide powerful ways to script cluster configuration and management tasks. Windows PowerShell cmdlets have now replaced the Cluster.exe command-line interface.

Cluster Shared Volumes   *Cluster Shared Volumes (CSV)* allows for the configuration of clustered virtual machines. CSV allows you to do the following:

- Reduce the number of LUNs (disks) required for your virtual machines.
- Make better use of disk space. Any VHD file on that LUN can use the free space on a CSV volume.
- More easily track the paths to VHD files and other files used by virtual machines.
- Use a few CSV volumes to create a configuration that supports many clustered virtual machines.

CSV volumes also are utilized for the Scale-Out-File-Server cluster role.

Management of Large-Scale Clusters   One advantage of Windows Server 2016 clusters is the ability for Server Manager to discover and manage the nodes in a cluster. By starting the

Failover Cluster Manager from Server Manager, you can do remote multiserver management and role and feature installation. Administrators now have the ability to manage a cluster from one convenient location.

Management and Mobility of Clustered Virtual Machines   Microsoft, as well as the industry as a whole, is moving toward the cloud and virtualization. With that in mind, administrators can now configure settings such as prioritizing the starting or placement of virtual machines in the clustered workloads. This allows administrators to allocate resources efficiently to your cluster.

Cluster-Aware Updating   One issue that every administrator has dealt with is updating a system or application while it is running. For example, if you are running Microsoft Exchange and you want to do an Exchange update, when do you take the server offline to do the update? It always seems that someone is on the system 24 hours a day. Well, Windows Server 2016 clustering has a solution. *Cluster-Aware Updating (CAU)* is a new automated feature that allows system updates to be applied automatically while the cluster remains available during the entire update process.

Cluster Node Fairness   Virtual Machine Load Balancing feature is new to Windows Server 2016. This new load balancing feature helps optimize the nodes in a cluster. When an organization builds a virtual machine cluster, there will be times when that cluster needs to have maintenance and certain virtual machines will be taken offline. When this happens, an unbalanced cluster (this is when some nodes are hosting VMs more often than others) may occur. This is where the VM Load Balancing feature (Node Fairness) helps the cluster. The Balancer will re-distribute VMs from an over balance node to an under balanced node. To setup Node Fairness, you would use the PowerShell command `AutoBalancerLevel` (shown below). The value input is a 1, 2, or 3. 1 is equivalent to the Low setting (move the host when showing more than 80% loaded), 2 is equivalent to Medium (move the host when more than 70% loaded) and 3 is equivalent to High (average nodes and move the host when showing more than 5% above the average).

```
(Get-Cluster).AutoBalancerLevel = <value>
```

Cluster Operating System Rolling Upgrade   One of the problems that many IT people face is the issue with downtime while their servers get upgraded to a new operating system. Windows Server 2016 includes a new feature called Cluster Operating System Rolling Upgrade. This new feature allows an administrator to upgrade a Hyper-V or Scale-Out File Server cluster from Windows Server 2012 R2 to Windows Server 2016 without stopping the servers.

Scale-Out File Server for Application Data   By utilizing *Microsoft Storage Spaces*, you can create a highly available clustered file share that utilizes SMB 3.0 and CSV to provide scalable access to data.

Scale-out file servers are useful for storing the following application data:

- Hyper-V virtual machine storage
- SQL Server database files

Be aware that scale-out file servers are not useful at all for typical file share data because they benefit only from applications that require a persistent connection to their storage.

Shared Virtual Hard Disks   In the previous versions of Windows, Failover Cluster nodes running as virtual machines had to use iSCSI or virtual HBAs to connect directly to SAN-based storage. With Windows Server 2016, you can set your Hyper-V virtualized cluster to use a shared VHDX virtual disk. Shared virtual hard disks can reside on the following:

- A scale-out file server failover cluster
- Cluster CSV volumes

Shared virtual hard disks are extremely useful in providing highly available shared storage for the following virtualized workloads:

- SQL Server
- Virtual Machine Manager
- Exchange Server

Virtual Machine Drain on Shutdown   When needing to perform maintenance on a Hyper-V failover cluster, you may have a lot of virtual machines on one node of a cluster. Inevitably, you will need to restart a cluster node for updates or shut it down for maintenance.

In previous versions of Windows, virtual machines running on the cluster would save their state, and then the cluster node would shut down. Windows Server 2016 helps alleviate this issue by automatically draining the virtual machines running on a node before it shuts down or restarts. Windows does this by attempting to live migrate all virtual machines on the cluster node to other nodes in the cluster when at all possible.

This feature is turned on by default, but it can be disabled through PowerShell.

Active Directory–Detached Clusters   Previous versions of Windows Failover Clustering have depended on Active Directory to provide computer objects for the cluster name object as well as virtual computer objects. With Active Directory–detached failover clusters, communication to the cluster-form clients will use NTLM authentication rather than the normal Kerberos authentication. This is useful in maintaining high availability should a person accidently delete a virtual computer object in Active Directory that a clustered resource depends on for Kerberos authentication.

Dynamic Witness   Earlier in this chapter, I mentioned the Dynamic Quorum model and how votes were dynamically adjusted based on the number of nodes in a cluster. In Windows Server 2016, there is a new feature called *dynamic witness* that is enabled by default when the cluster is configured to use a dynamic quorum. Since it is preferred to have an odd number of votes at any one time in a cluster, the dynamic witness will turn on or off the witness vote in order to ensure that there are an odd number of votes in the cluster.

Tie Breaker For 50% Node Split   Like the *dynamic witness* feature just described, the Tie Breaker For 50% Node Split option in Windows Server 2016 dynamically adjusts cluster node votes in order to maintain an odd number of votes in a cluster where no witness is being used.

This is useful for a cluster in a site-aware, stretched, or geocluster configuration.

Global Update Manager Mode   Since the first release of Microsoft Cluster Services appearing in Windows NT 4.0 Enterprise, all nodes in a cluster maintain a local database that keeps a copy of the cluster configuration. The *Global Update Manager (GUM)* is a component of the cluster that ensures that before a change is marked as being committed for the entire cluster, all nodes have received and committed that change to their local cluster database. If one or more nodes do not report back or commit a change, the cluster node is kicked out of being a member of the cluster. Another issue that can occur is that for various clustered applications, such as SQL and Exchange, their performance can be negatively impacted by the time it takes the GUM to coordinate with all the nodes of a cluster for any changes. The GUM is only as fast as the slowest node in the cluster.

With Windows Server 2016, a new feature was added to Failover Clustering called *Global Update Manager mode*. This feature allows you to configure the GUM read-write modes manually in order to greatly speed up the processing of changes by the GUM and to improve the performance of certain clustered resources.

Turn Off IPsec Encryption for Inter-Node Cluster Communications   In network environments where IPsec is used, slow Group Policy updates and other issues can cause Active Directory Domain Services to be temporarily unavailable to cluster nodes. If the cluster intracluster communications protocol uses IPsec encryption, then these delays could cause cluster nodes to drop out of the cluster for failure to communicate in a timely manner with the rest of the nodes in the cluster. Windows Server 2016 now provides a way to turn off IPsec encryption on the cluster communication network.

Cluster Dashboard   Starting with Windows Server 2012, Failover Clustering supports up to 64 nodes in a cluster. Keeping track of the status and resources on all of these nodes can be an administrative headache! Managing more than one failover cluster and determining what a certain cluster hosts can be painful as well. Fortunately, in Windows Server 2016, the *Failover Cluster Manager*'s main dashboard has been updated to make it easier to see the status and health of multiple clusters.

Hyper-V Replica Broker   Starting with Windows Server 2012, Hyper-V supported continuous replication of virtual machines to another server or cluster for disaster recovery purposes. The Hyper-V Recovery Broker allows for virtual machines in a cluster to be replicated. The Hyper-V Recovery Broker keeps track of which cluster nodes virtual machines are residing on and ensures that replication is maintained.

Hyper-V Manager Integration into Failover Cluster Manager   In Windows Server 2016, the Hyper-V Management Console is integrated with Failover Cluster Manager for managing virtual machines that are clustered. Normal Hyper-V operations such as configuring, exporting, importing, configuring replication, stopping, starting, and live migrating virtual machines are supported directly through Failover Cluster Manager.

Virtual Machine Monitoring   Starting with Windows Server 2012, Failover Clustering supports Virtual Machine Monitoring for Windows Server virtual machines. Virtual Machine Monitoring monitors administrator-selected Windows services running within a virtual machine and will automatically restart a service if it should fail. If the service does not start for the configured number of restart attempts, the virtual machine will fail over to another node and then restart. For example, you can configure Failover Clustering to monitor the Print Spooler service on a Windows Server 2016 virtual machine. If the Print Spooler service goes offline, then the cluster will attempt to restart the Print Spooler service within the virtual machine. If the service still fails, Failover Clustering will move the virtual machine to another node.

PowerShell Commands for Clustering

The following table (Table 7.3) is just some of the PowerShell commands that you can use to configure and manage Windows Server 2016 clustering.

TABLE 7.3   Clustering PowerShell Commands

PowerShell Command	Description
Add-ClusterDisk	This command allows an admin to add a new disk to a failover cluster. The disk's logical unit number (LUN) must be visible to all cluster nodes.
Add-ClusterFileServerRole	This command allows an admin to create a clustered file server.
Add-ClusterGenericApplicationRole	This command allows you to configure high availability for an application that is normally not designed for clustering.
Add-ClusterGroup	This command allows an admin to add a resource group to the failover cluster.
Add-ClusterNode	This command allows an admin to add a node to a failover cluster.
Add-ClusterResource	This command allows an admin to add a resource to a failover cluster.
Add-ClusterResourceDependency	This command allows an admin to add a resource dependency to a failover cluster.
Add-ClusterServerRole	This command allows you to add the cluster server role to a server.
Block-ClusterAccess	This command allows an admin to block the specified users from accessing a cluster.

PowerShell Command	Description
Get-Cluster	This command shows you the information about a failover clusters.
Get-ClusterAccess	This command shows you the permissions for a failover clusters.
Get-ClusterNode	This command shows you the information about the servers in a failover clusters.
Get-ClusterQuorum	This command shows you the information about the cluster quorum in a clusters.
New-Cluster	This command allows you to create a new failover cluster.
Remove-Cluster	This command allows you to remove a failover cluster.
Remove-ClusterAccess	This command allows an admin to remove a user's access from the cluster.
Remove-ClusterNode	This command allows you to remove a node from a failover cluster.
Start-Cluster	This command allows an admin to start the Cluster service on all nodes.
Stop-Cluster	This command allows an admin to stop the Cluster service on all nodes.
Stop-ClusterNode	This command stops the Cluster service on a node.
Test-Cluster	This command allows an admin to complete validation tests for a cluster.

Implementing Storage Spaces Direct

Storage Spaces Direct uses local-attached drives on servers to create highly available storage at a minimal cost of traditional storage devices (SAN or NAS). Storage Spaces Direct uses regular hard drives that are connected to a single node of the failover cluster and these disks can be used as storage for the cluster.

To understand how Storage Spaces Direct truly works, I think it is better to first understand some other technology terms for Windows Server 2016. When an IT administrator takes a bunch of physical disks and puts them together it is called a storage pool. Storage spaces are virtual disks that are created from storage pools. Storage Spaces Direct is the evolution of Storage Spaces.

Many of the same features are used in Windows Server 2016 like Failover Clustering, Cluster Shared Volumes, and SMB.

Storage Spaces Direct utilizes disks that are connected to one node of a failover cluster and allows for the creation of pools using those disks by Storage Spaces. Storage Spaces Direct streamlines deployment by using converged or hyper-converged architecture.

Virtual Disks (Spaces) that are constructed on a pool will have their mirrors or parity (redundant data) span across the disks using different nodes of the cluster. Since replicas of the data are spread across the disks, this allows for access to data in the event a node fails or is going down for maintenance.

You can implement Storage Spaces Direct in virtual machines with each VM configured with two or more virtual disks connected to the VM's SCSI Controller. Each node of the cluster running inside the virtual machine can connect to its own disks, but utilizing Storage Spaces Direct allows all the disks to be part of the Storage Pool that spans the entire cluster node.

For the redundant data (mirror or parity spaces) to be spread across the nodes, Storage Spaces Direct uses SMB3 as the protocol transport.

Networking Hardware   To communicate between servers Storage Spaces Direct uses SMB3, including SMB Direct and SMB Multichannel over Ethernet. It is recommended to use 10+Gbe with Remote-Direct Memory Access (RDMA), or either Internet Wide Area RDMA Protocol (iWARP) or RDMA over Converged Ethernet (RoCE).

Storage Hardware

- 2 – 16 servers with locally-attached SATA, SAS, or NVMe (non-volatile memory express) drives
- Must have at least 2 solid-state drives on each server and at least 4 additional drives.
- SATA and SAS device should be following a Host-Bus Adapter (HBA) and SAS expander.

Failover Clustering   To connect the servers, Windows Server 2016 uses the built-in clustering feature.

Software Storage Bus   Storage Spaces Direct has a new feature called Software Storage Bus. This allows all the servers to see all of each other's local drives by spanning the cluster and establishing a software-defined storage structure.

Storage Bus Layer Cache   The Software Storage Bus joins the fastest drives available to the slower drives to provide server-side read/write caching that speeds up the IO and boosts data.

Storage Pool   The storage pool is the collection of drives that form the Storage Space. It is created automatically and all qualified drives are discovered and added. It is recommended that an administrator use the default settings on one pool per cluster.

Storage Spaces Storage Spaces offers fault tolerance to a virtual disk using mirroring, erasure coding, or both. It is thought of as distributed, software-defined RAID utilizing the drives in the pool. These virtual disks normally have resiliency when two synchronized drives or servers fail.

Resilient File System (ReFS) The Resilient File System (ReFS) is Microsoft's latest file system which was designed to maximize data availability, efficiently scale to large data sets across varied workloads, and provide data integrity. It includes hastening the .vhdx file operations such as creating, expanding, checkpoint merging, and built-in checksums to distinguish and fix bit errors. ReFS also introduced real-time tiers, based on usage, which will rotate data between "hot" and "cold" storage-tiers.

Cluster Shared Volumes The Cluster Shared Volumes (CSV) file system unites all the ReFS volumes into a single namespace available through any server. This namespace allows every server and every volume to look and act like it's mounted locally.

Scale-Out File Server In converged deployments only is this necessary. It offers remote file access by using the SMB3 protocol to clients over the network. This essentially turns Storage Spaces Direct into Network-Attached Storage (NAS).

 To see step-by-step instructions on configuring and deploying Storage Spaces Direct, visit Microsoft's website at:

```
https://technet.microsoft.com/en-us/windows-server-docs/
storage/storage-spaces/
hyper-converged-solution-using-storage-spaces-direct
```

The Benefits of Storage Spaces Direct

The following are just some of the benefits of using Storage Spaces Direct with Windows Server 2016:

Simplicity In less than 15 minutes, an administrator can go from a standard server running Windows Server 2016 to creating a Storage Spaces Direct cluster. It's just the click of a check box if an administrator is using System Center.

Unrivaled Performance Storage Spaces Direct exceeds 150,000 mixed 4k random IOPS per server with reliability, low latency, built-in read/write cache, and support for NVMe drives that are mounted directly on the PCIe bus.

Fault Tolerance Constantly available built-in resiliency that will handle drives, servers, or component failures. Chassis and rack fault tolerance can also be configured for larger deployments. There are no complex management steps needed when hardware fails. Simply change it out for another one and the software will fix itself.

Resource Efficiency   Greater resource efficiency with Erasure coding delivering up to 2.4x more storage. Using Local Reconstruction Codes and ReFS, real-time tiers extend to hard disk drives and mixed hot/cold workloads, all while reducing CPU usage to give the resources back to the virtual machines where they are needed.

Manageability   Keep excessively active virtual machines in order by using Storage QoS Controls with minimum and maximum per-VM IOPS limits. Continuously monitor and alert by using the built-in Health Service. There are also new APIs that make it easier to collect cluster-wide performance statistics and capacity metrics.

Scalability   For multiple petabytes of storage per cluster, an administrator can increase up to 16 servers and add over 400 drives. To scale out, an administrator will just need to add drives or add more servers. Storage Spaces Direct will automatically add the new drives and begin to utilize them.

Deployment Options

When using Windows Server 2016 and installing Storage Spaces Direct, there are two deployment options that you can choose from:

Converged

In converged, there are separate clusters for each storage and compute. The converged deployment option, also called "disaggregated," puts a Scale-Out File Server (SoFS) on top of Storage Spaces Direct to provide Network-Attached Storage (NAS) over SMB3 file shares. This allows for scaling computer/workloads separately from the storage cluster. This is essential when working with large-scale deployments such as Hyper-V Infrastructure as a Service (IaaS).

Hyper-Converged

In hyper-converged, there is only one cluster for storage and compute. The hyper-converged deployment option runs the Hyper-V virtual machines or SQL Server databases directly on the servers delivering the storage, storing files all on the local volumes. This removes the need to configure file server access and permissions. It also reduces the hardware costs associated for small-to-medium business or remote office/branch office deployments.

Requirements to Setup Storage Spaces Direct

To setup Storage Spaces Direct properly, you must make sure that all of your hardware components meet the minimum requirements. Table 7.4 was taken directly from Microsoft's website for the requirements needed and also what is actually recommended by Microsoft for proper configuration of Storage Spaces Direct.

TABLE 7.4 Storage Space Direct Requirements

Component	Requirements
Servers	Minimum of 2 servers, maximum of 16 servers
	All servers should be the same make and model.
CPU	Minimum of Intel Nehalem or later compatible processor
Memory	4 GB of RAM per terabyte (TB) of cache drive capacity on each server, to store Storage Spaces Direct metadata.
	Any memory used by Windows Server, VMs, and other apps or workloads.
Networking	Minimum of 10 Gbps network interface for intra-cluster communication.
	Recommended: Two NICs for redundancy and performance
	Recommended: NICS that are remote-direct memory access (RDMA) capable, iWARP or RoCE
Drives	Use local-attached SATA, SAS, or NVMe drives.
	Every drive must be physically connected to only one server.
	All servers must have the same drive types.
	Recommended: All servers have the same drive configuration.
	SSDs must have power-loss protection, i.e. they are "enterprise-grade."
	Recommended: SSDs used for cache have high endurance, providing a minimum of 5 drive-writes-per-day (DWPD).
	Add capacity drives in multiples of the number of NVMe or SSD cache devices.
	Not supported: Multi-path IO (MPIO) or physically connecting drives via multiple paths.
Host-bus adapter (HBA)	Simple pass-through SAS HBA for both SAS and SATA drives.
	SCSI Enclosure Services (SES) for SAS and SATA drives.
	Any direct-attached storage enclosures must present Unique ID.
	Not Supported: RAID HBA controllers or SAN (Fibre Channel, iSCSI, FCoE) devices.

Storage Spaces Direct Using Windows PowerShell

The following table (Table 7.5) is just some of the PowerShell commands that you can use to configure and manage Storage Spaces Direct.

TABLE 7.5 Storage Spaces Direct PowerShell commands

PowerShell Command	Description
Disable-NetQosFlowControl	This command allows an administrator to turn off flow control.
Enable-ClusterStorageSpacesDirect	This command enables Storage Spaces Direct.
Enable-NetAdapterQos	This command allows an administrator to apply network QoS policies to the target adapters.
Enable-NetAdapterRDMA	This command allows an administrator to enable remote direct memory access (RDMA) on a network adapter.
Enable-NetQosFlowControl	This command allows an administrator to turn on flow control.
Get-NetAdapter	This command will retrieve a list of the network adapters.
Get-StoragePool	This command allows you to see a specific storage pool, or a set of StoragePool objects.
Get-StorageTier	This command allows you to see storage tiers on Windows Storage subsystems. Use this command to see Storage Spaces Direct default tier templates called Performance and Capacity.
New-Cluster	This command creates a new cluster.
New-NetQosPolicy	This command allows an admin to create a new network QoS policy.
New-NetQosTrafficClass	This command allows you to create a traffic class (like SMB).
New-Volume	This command creates a new volume.
Set-Item	This command allows an administrator to configure the trusted hosts to all hosts.
Test-Cluster	This command allows an administrator to test a set of servers for use as a Storage Spaces Direct cluster.
Update-StorageProviderCache	This command allows you to update the cache of the service for a particular provider and associated child objects.

Achieving High Availability with Hyper-V

One of the nice advantages of using Hyper-V is the ability to run an operating server within another server. Virtualization allows you to run multiple servers on top of a single Hyper-V server. But we need to make sure that these servers stay up and running.

That is where Hyper-V high availability comes into play. Having the ability to ensure that your Hyper-V servers are going to continue to run even if there is a hardware issue is an important step in guaranteeing the success of your network.

There are many ways that you can ensure that your virtual machines will continue to operate. One is to set up clustering and another is to set up Hyper-V high availability without clustering.

To set up reliability without clustering requires that your Hyper-V servers have replica copies that can automatically start up if the virtual machine errors out. This is referred to as Live Migration and replica servers.

Implementing a Hyper-V Replica

Hyper-V Replica is an important part of the Hyper-V role. It replicates the Hyper-V virtual machines from the primary site to the replica secondary sites simultaneously.

Once an administrator enables Hyper-V Replica for a particular virtual machine on the primary Hyper-V host server, the Hyper-V replica will begin to create an exact copy of the virtual machine for the secondary site. After this replication, Hyper-V Replica creates a log file for the virtual machine VHDs. This log file is rerun in reverse order to the replica VHD. This is done using replication frequency. The log files and reverse order helps ensure that the latest changes are stored and copied asynchronously. If there is an issue with the replication frequency, then the administrator will receive an alert.

On the virtual machine, an administrator can establish resynchronization settings. This can be setup to be done manually, automatically, or automatically on an explicit schedule. To fix constant synchronization issues an administrator may choose to set up automatic resynchronization.

Hyper-V Replica will aid in a disaster recovery strategy by replicating virtual machines from one host to another while keeping workloads accessible. Hyper-V Replica can create a copy of a running virtual machine to a replica offline virtual machine.

Hyper-V Hosts

With replication over a WAN link the primary and secondary host servers can be located in the same physical location or at different geographical locations. Hyper-V hosts can be standalone, clustered, or a combination of both. Hyper-V Hosts are not dependent upon Active Directory and there is no need to be domain members.

Replication and Change Tracking

When an administrator enables Hyper-V Replica on a particular virtual machine an identical copy of the virtual machine is created on a secondary host server. Once this happens, the Hyper-V Replica will create a log file that will track changes made on a virtual machine VHD. The log file is rerun in reverse order to the replica VHD. This is based on the replication frequency settings. This ensures that the latest changes are created and replicated asynchronously. This can be done over HTTP or HTTPS.

Extended (Chained) Replication

Extended (chained) Replication allows an administrator to replicate a virtual machine from a primary host to a secondary host and then replicate the secondary host to a third host. It is not possible to replicate from the primary host directly to the second and third hosts.

Extended (Chained) Replication aids in disaster recovery in that an administrator can recover from both the primary and extended replica. Extended Replication will also aid if the primary and secondary locations go offline. It must be noted that the extended replica does not support application-consistent replication and it must use the same VHD that the secondary replica uses.

Failover

If the primary or the secondary (extended) host server locations go offline, an administrator can manually initiate failover. Failover is not automatic. There are several different types of manually initiating failover:

Test Failover   Use Test Failover to verify that the replica virtual machine can successfully start in the secondary site. It will create a copy test virtual machine during failover and does not affect standard replication. After the test failover, if the administrator selects Failover on the replica test virtual machine the test failover will be deleted.

Planned Failover   Use Planned Failover during scheduled downtime. The administrator will have to turn off the primary machine before performing a planned failover. Once the machine fails over, the Hyper-V Replica will start replicating changes back to the primary server. The changes are tracked and sent to ensure that there is no data lost. Once the planned failover is complete, the reverse replication begins so that the primary virtual machine becomes the secondary and vice versa. This ensures that the hosts are synchronized.

Unplanned Failover   Use Unplanned Failover during unforeseen outages. Unplanned failover is started on the replica virtual machine. This should only be used if the primary machine goes offline. A check will confirm whether the primary machine is running. If the administrator has recovery history enabled, then it is possible to recover to an earlier point in time. During failover an administrator should ensure that the recovery point is acceptable and then finish the failover to ensure that recovery points are combined.

Virtual Machine Advanced Features

One nice feature of virtual machines is the ability to setup advanced features. In the Advanced Features section (see Figure 7.20), there are multiple settings that you can configure.

FIGURE 7.20 VM Advanced Features

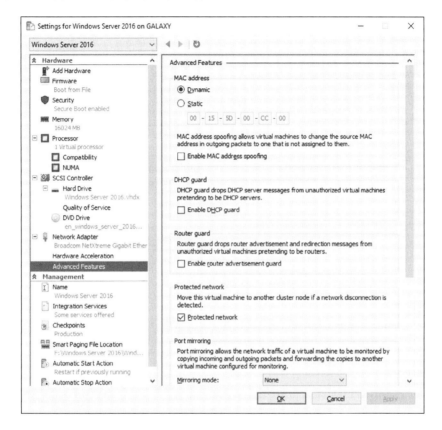

MAC Addressing

The first thing that you can configure in the Advanced Features section is setting a MAC address. The MAC address is a physical address that is associated to the NIC adapter. Administrators have the ability to set the MAC address to Dynamic (creates its own MAC addresses) or Static (this is where you can set a MAC address).

You also have the ability to do MAC spoofing. This is where a VM can change the source MAC address in outgoing packets to one that is not assigned to the NIC adapters.

DHCP Guard

DHCP guard drops DHCP server messages from unauthorized virtual machines pretending to be a DHCP server. So what does this mean to you? If a server tries to pretend to be a DHCP server, your virtual machine will drop any messages that are sent by that DHCP server.

Router Guard

Router guard drops router advertisement and redirection messages from unauthorized virtual machines pretending to be routers. It almost works the same way DHCP guard works. If an unauthorized router tries to send messages to a virtual machine, that VM will not accept those messages.

Protected Network

Administrators have the ability to set Network Health Detection at the virtual machine level for a Hyper-V host cluster. This is configured as a Protected Network. By setting the Protected Network checkbox, the virtual machine will be moved to another cluster node if a network disconnection is detected. If the health of a network connection is showing as disconnected, the VM will be automatically moved.

Port Mirroring

Port mirroring allows the network traffic of a virtual machine to be monitored by copying incoming and outgoing packets and forwarding the copies to another virtual machine configured for monitoring.

Single Root I/O Virtualization

The single root I/O virtualization (SR-IOV) interface is a continuation of the PCI Express (PCIe) interface specification. SR-IOV allows a device (like a network adapter) to separate its resources between multiple PCIe hardware functions.

Device Naming

Device naming causes the name of the network adapter to be propagated into supported guest operating systems.

NIC Teaming

NIC Teaming, also known as load balancing and failover (LBFO), gives an administrator the ability to allow multiple network adapters on a system to be placed into a team. Independent hardware vendors (IHVs) have required NIC Teaming, but until Windows Server 2012, NIC Teaming was *not* part of the Windows Server operating system.

To be able to use NIC Teaming, the computer system must have at least one Ethernet adapter. If you want to provide fault protection, an administrator must have a minimum of two Ethernet adapters. One advantage of Windows Server 2016 is that an administrator can set up 32 network adapters in a NIC team.

NIC Teaming is a common practice when setting up virtualization. This is one way that you can have load balancing with Hyper-V.

NIC Teaming gives an administrator the ability to allow a virtual machine to use virtual network adapters in Hyper-V. The advantage of using NIC Teaming in Hyper-V is that the administrator can use NIC Teaming to connect to more than one Hyper-V switch. This allows Hyper-V still to have connectivity even if the network adapter under the Hyper-V switch gets disconnected.

An administrator can configure NIC Teaming in either Server Manager or PowerShell. NIC teaming can be configured in different configuration models including Switch Independent or Switch Dependent. Switch Independent means that each NIC adapter is connected into a different switch. Switch Dependent means that all NIC adapters are connected into the same switch. If you use Switch Independent NIC Teaming, then you must connect your NICs to different switches, but both switches must be on the same subnet.

Remote Direct Memory Access

When most of us think of Hyper-V, we think of a group of virtual machines sharing access to a systems resource. With Windows Server 2016, Hyper-V includes Remote Direct Memory Access (RDMA).

RDMA allows one computer to directly access memory from the memory of another computer without the need of interfacing with either one's operating system. This gives systems the ability to have high throughput and low-latency networking. This is very useful when it comes to clustering systems (including Hyper-V).

Windows Server 2012 R2 RDMA services couldn't be bound to a Hyper-V Virtual Switch and because of this, Remote Direct Memory Access and Hyper-V had to be on the same computer as the network adapters. Because of this, there was a need for a higher number of physical network adapters that were required to be installed on the Hyper-V host.

Because of the improvements of RDMA on Windows Server 2016, administrators can use less network adapters while using RDMA.

Switch Embedded Teaming

Earlier we discussed NIC Teaming but we also have the ability to do Switch Embedded Teaming (SET). SET can be an alternative to using NIC Teaming in environments that include Hyper-V and the Software Defined Networking (SDN) stack in Windows Server 2016.

SET does use some of the functionality of NIC Teaming in the Hyper-V Virtual Switch, but SET allows an administrator to combine a group of physical adapters (minimum of 1 adapter and a maximum of 8 adapters) into software based virtual adapters.

By using virtual adapters, you get better performance and greater fault tolerance in the event of a network adapter going bad. For SET to be enabled, all of the physical network adapters must be installed on the same physical Hyper-V host.

One of the requirements of SET is that all network adapters that are members of the SET group be identical adapters. This means that they need to be the same adapter types from the same manufacturer.

One main difference between NIC Teaming and Set is that SET only supports Switch Independent mode setups. Again this means that the NIC adapters are connected to different switches.

Administrators need to create a SET team at the same time that they create the Hyper-V Virtual Switch. Administrators can do this by using the Windows PowerShell command `New-VMSwitch`.

At the time an administrator creates a Hyper-V Virtual Switch, the administrator needs to include the EnableEmbeddedTeaming parameter in their command syntax. The following example shows a Hyper-V switch named StormSwitch:

```
New-VMSwitch -Name StormSwitch -NetAdapterName "NIC 1","NIC 2"
-EnableEmbeddedTeaming $true
```

Administrators also have the ability to remove a SET team by using the following PowerShell command. This example removes a Virtual Switch named StormSwitch.

```
Remove-VMSwitch "StormSwitch
```

Virtual Machine Queue

Windows Server 2016 Hyper-V includes a feature called Virtual machine queue (VMQ) as long as the hardware is VMQ compatible network hardware. VMQ uses packet filtering to provide data from an external virtual machine network directly to virtual machines. This helps reduce the overhead of routing packets from the management operating system to the virtual machine.

Once VMQ is enabled on Hyper-V, a dedicated queue is created on the physical network adapter for each virtual network adapter to use. When data arrives for the virtual network adapter, the physical network adapter places that data in a queue and once the system is available, all of the data in the queue is delivered to the virtual network adapter.

To enable the virtual machine queue on a specific virtual machine, enter the settings for the virtual machine and expand Network Adapter. Click on Hardware Acceleration and on the right hand window; check the box for Enable virtual machine queue.

To enable VMQ on a physical network adapter:

1. Open Device Manager.

2. Expand the Network adapters section and right-click the name of the network adapter. Choose Properties.

3. On the Advanced tab in the properties, locate the setting for virtual machine queues and make sure it is enabled. If the setting is not available, the adapter does not support VMQ.

Receive Side Scaling

Receive Side Scaling (RSS) allows a system's network adapter to spread the network processing between multiple processor cores in systems that have a multi-core processor. Due to the fact that RSS can distribute the networking load across multiple processors, the system can handle more network traffic.

RSS has the ability to work with systems that have more than sixty four (64) processors. RSS can do this because it spreads the load across all of the processors. Because RSS can spread the network load, you end up with TCP load balancing. RSS also has the ability to load balance non-TCP traffic like UDP and multicast messages. RSS also allows an administrator to have better auditing and management capabilities.

With the release of Windows Server 2012, RSS started working with load balancing across Non-Uniform Memory Access (NUMA) systems. RSS also includes some of the following capabilities:

▪ Event tracing for RSS logs

▪ RSS configuration information

▪ Windows Management Instrumentation (WMI) for RSS

- PowerShell for RSS
- Dynamic load balancing
- RSS profiles
- Benefits for working with low latency

If you want to enable or disable RSS, you would complete the following steps.

1. Open an elevated Command prompt by right clicking Command Prompt, and then choosing Run as administrator.

2. At the Command Prompt, type the following command and hit Enter.

   netsh interface tcp set global rss=enabled

3. Close the Command Prompt window.

4. Open Device Manager (right click Start and then click Device Manager).

5. Expand Network adapters, right-click the network adapter you want to work with, and then click Properties.

6. In the network adapter properties, click on the Advanced tab. On the Receive-side scaling setting, make sure it is enabled or disabled (depending on what you need to do).

Virtual Receive-Side Scaling

Virtual Receive-side scaling (VRSS) is the virtual equivalent of RSS. VRSS is a Windows Server 2016 feature that allows a virtual network adapter to distribute the load across multiple virtual processors in a virtual machine.

VRSS works with many different types of technologies including:

- IPv4 and IPv6
- TCP and UDP
- LBFO (NIC Teaming)
- Live Migration
- Network Virtualization using Generic Routing Encapsulation (NVGRE)

VRSS is not enabled by default. VRSS is easily enabled or disabled inside of the virtual machine or on a physical host by using PowerShell cmdlets. If you are going to enable VRSS in a virtual machine, the Windows operating system of the virtual machine must be one of the following:

- Windows 8.1
- Windows 8.1 with integration components installed.
- Windows 10
- Windows Server 2012 R2
- Windows Server 2012 R2 with integration components installed.
- Windows Server 2016.

To enable VRSS using PowerShell, you would need to run one of the following commands from PowerShell. Either PowerShell command will enable VRSS.

```
Enable-NetAdapterRSS -Name "AdapterName"
Set-NetAdapterRSS -Name "AdapterName" -Enabled $True
```

To disable VRSS using PowerShell, you would need to run one of the following commands from PowerShell. Either PowerShell command will disable VRSS.

```
Disable-NetAdapterRSS -Name "AdapterName"
Set-NetAdapterRSS -Name "AdapterName" -Enabled $False
```

Virtual Machine Multi-Queue

Windows Server 2016 Hyper-V includes a new feature called Virtual Machine Multi-Queue (VMMQ). VMMQ was created using previous versions of RSS and VMQ.

Today's network adapters have more queues than the virtual machines they work with. In previous versions of virtualization (before Windows Server 2012 R2) a single virtual machine could be assigned to a single virtual machine queue. This single queue would have a set affinity to a single processor. So what this means is that even though network adapters can handle multiple queues, the virtual machines could only send traffic using a single queue.

VMMQ helps resolve this issue. VMMQ allocates multiple queues to a single virtual machine and each queue will have its own affinity settings to a core. For this to operate properly, the virtual machine must have the ability to work with multiple virtual CPUs (vCPUs).

Virtual Machine Quality of Service

There may be times when you want to control the traffic that is generated by a virtual machine. Virtual Machine Quality of Service (vmQoS) is a Hyper-V features that does just that.

Virtual Machine Quality of Service allows an administrator to set the bandwidth limits generated by a virtual machine. Administrators can also use vmQoS to set a bandwidth reserve on an external network connection. This helps stop a single virtual machine from chocking the bandwidth of another virtual machine. Administrators have the ability to set minimum and maximum bandwidth limits.

Administrators that have the ability to set performance levels can use these features when service level agreements (SLAs) need to be enforced between your organization and your clients. This allows you to guarantee certain bandwidth levels for your customers and it makes sure that no other customer's bandwidth is compromised. Hyper-V QoS gives an administrator the ability to:

- Enforce minimum and maximum bandwidth limits for traffic flow. This is identified with a port number in the Hyper-V Virtual Switch.

- Configure Hyper-V virtual switch port minimum and maximum bandwidth by using either PowerShell cmdlets or Windows Management Instrumentation (WMI).

- Configure multiple Hyper-V virtual network adapters and specify the QoS on each virtual network adapter independently.

Windows Server 2016 Hyper-V QoS also allows an administrator to use compatible hardware for Data Center Bridging (DCB).

DCB is a suite of Institute of Electrical and Electronics Engineers (IEEE) standards that allow multiple infrastructure technologies (i.e. storage, data networking, Inter-Process Communication (IPC), and management traffic) to all share the same Ethernet network infrastructure. To enable DCB, you would use the following PowerShell cmdlet:

```
Install-WindowsFeature -Name Data-Center-Bridging -IncludeManagementTools
```

By using DCB, administrators can unite multiple types of network traffic onto a single network adapter. This allows administrators to have a guaranteed level of service for every type of network traffic.

To enable the vmQoS features, an administrator can use Windows PowerShell. Administrators can configure these features manually or by writing a script to automate the installation.

VM Checkpoints

One thing that you may want to setup on your Hyper-V server is recovery points or checkpoints. A checkpoint is a snap shot in time from when an administrator can recover a virtual machine. It's like taking a picture of the virtual machine and using that picture to recover the VM. Administrators can create multiple checkpoints of a VM and then recover back to any of those checkpoints if there is an issue. Using a more recent recovery point will result in less data lost. Checkpoints can be accessed from up to 24 hours ago.

If you want to enable these checkpoints in time for Hyper-V, you just need to follow the steps below:

1. In Hyper-V Manager, right-click on the virtual machine and then click Settings.

2. Under the Management section, choose Checkpoints.

3. To enable checkpoints for a VM, check the box Enable checkpoints. If you want to disable checkpoints, just clear the box.

4. Once finished, Click Apply. Once you are finished, click OK and close the Hyper-V Manager.

Understanding Live Migration

Before we can implement Live Migration, first you need to understand what Live Migration does for Hyper-V. Hyper-V live migration transfers a running virtual machine from one physical server to another. The real nice advantage of Live Migration is that during the move of the virtual machine, there is no impact on the network's users. The virtual machine will continue to operate even during the move. This is different from using Quick Migrations. Quick Migrations require a pause in the Hyper-V VM while it's being moved.

Live Migrations allow administrators to move virtual machines between servers. This is very useful when a Hyper-V server starts having issues. For example, if a Hyper-V machine is starting to have hardware issues, you can move the virtual machines from that Hyper-V server to another server that is running properly.

When setting up VM migrations, you have a few options. You can Live Migrate a VM, Quick Migrate a VM, or just move a VM. As stated before, Live Migration requires no interruption of the VM. Quick Migration requires that you first pause the VM, then save the VM, then move the VM and finally re-start the VM. Moving a virtual machine means that you are going to copy a VM from one Hyper-V server to another while the virtual machine is turned off.

So if you decide to setup and use Live Migrations, there are a few things that you should understand before setting it up. So let's take a look at some of the configuration settings that you can configure.

Configure CredSSP or Kerberos authentication

When choosing to setup Live Migrations, one of the settings that you get to manipulate is the type of authentication you can use. Choosing the authentication type is a feature listed under the Advanced Features of Live Migration. Administrators can choose two types of authentication (as shown in Figure 7.21): Kerberos or Credential Security Support Provider (CredSSP).

FIGURE 7.21 Live Migration Advanced Features

Authentication is choosing which protocol you will use to guarantee that live migration traffic between the source and destination servers are verified. Let's take a look at both options.

- Use Credential Security Support Provider (CredSSP):
  - This option allows an administrator to setup better security but requires constrained delegation for Live Migration. Administrators have the ability to sign in to the source server. Administrators can sign in to the source server by using a local console session, a Remote Desktop session, or a remote Windows PowerShell session.

- Use Kerberos:
  - This option allows an administrator to avoid having to sign in to the server, but requires constrained delegation to be set up.

Another section that you setup in the Advanced Features of Live Migrations is the Performance options. This section allows you to choose how the network traffic for Live Migrations will be configured. There are three options that you can choose from:

TCP/IP   The memory of the virtual machine being migrated is copied over the network to the destination server over a TCP/IP connection.

Compression   The memory of the virtual machine being migrated is compressed and then copied over the network to the destination server over a TCP/IP connection.

SMB   The memory of the virtual machine is copied over the network to the destination server over a SMB (Server Message Block) connection. SMB Direct will be used if the network adapters of both the source and destination server have Remote Direct Memory Access (RDMA) capabilities enabled.

Implementing Live Migration

You will need the following to set up non-clustered hosts for live migration:

- A user account in the local Hyper-V Administrators group or the Administrators group on both the source and destination computers. Membership in the Domain Administrators group (if using a domain).

- The Hyper-V role in Windows Server 2016 or Windows Server 2012 R2 installed on both the source and destination servers. Live migration can be done if the virtual machine is at least version 5.

- The source and destination computers must belong to the same Workgroup or Active Directory domain or belong to trusted domains.

- The Hyper-V management tools installed on the server. Computer must be running Windows Server 2016 or Windows 10.

If an administrator wants to setup the source and destination of the live migration, they would need to use the following steps in Hyper-V Manager:

1. Open Hyper-V Manager. (Click Start ➤ Administrative Tools ➤ Hyper-V Manager.)

2. In the navigation pane, click on one of the servers. Right click on the server ➤ Hyper-V Settings ➤ Live Migrations.

3. Click on the Live Migrations pane. Check the box Enable incoming and outgoing live migrations.

4. Under the section Simultaneous live migrations, specify the number of Simultaneous live migrations (the default is 2).

5. Under Incoming live migrations, administrators can choose to accept any network for live migrations or specifically the IP address you want to use for live migration. If you want to use an IP address, click the Add button and type in the IP address information. Click OK once you're finished.

6. For Kerberos and performance options, expand Live Migrations (click the plus sign next to Live Migrations) and then select Advanced Features.

    ▪ Under Authentication protocol, select either Use CredSSP or Use Kerberos.

    ▪ Under Performance options, Select performance configuration options (either TCP/IP, Compression, or SMB).

7. Click OK.

8. If you have any other servers that you want to setup for Live Migrations, select the server and repeat the steps.

Implement Shared Nothing Live Migration

Administrators can now Live Migrate virtual machines even if the Hyper-V host is not part of a cluster. Before using Live Migrate without a Windows Cluster an administrator will need to configure the servers. Either choose Kerberos or Credential Security Support Provider (CredSSP) to authenticate the Live Migration.

To trigger a Shared Nothing Live Migration remotely, the administrator will need to enable Kerberos constrained delegation.

Constrained delegation is configured through Active Directory Users and Computers in the Delegation tab for each computer taking part in the Shared Nothing Live Migration.

Implementing Storage Migration

Hyper-V supports moving virtual machine storage without downtime by allowing the administrator to move storage while the virtual machine is running. This can be performed by using Hyper-V Manager or Windows PowerShell.

An administrator can add storage to a Hyper-V cluster or a standalone computer, and then move virtual machines to the new storage while the virtual machines continue to run.

An administrator can move virtual machine storage between physical storage devices to respond to a decrease in performance that results from bottlenecks.

Storage Migration Requirements

The following will be needed to utilize Hyper-V functionality of moving virtual machine storage:

- One or more installations of Windows Server 2016 with the Hyper-V role installed.
- A server that is capable of running Hyper-V.
- Virtual machines that are configured to use only virtual hard disks for storage.

Storage Migration allows administrators to move the virtual hard disks of a virtual machine while the virtual hard disks are still able to be used by the running virtual machine (see Figure 7.22). When an administrator moves a running virtual machine's virtual hard disks, Hyper-V performs the following steps:

1. Disk reads and writes utilize the source virtual hard disk.

2. When reads and writes occur on the source virtual hard disk, the disk data is copied to the new destination virtual hard disk.

3. Once the initial disk copy is complete, the disk writes are mirrored to both the source and destination virtual hard disks, while outstanding disk changes are replicated.

4. After the source and destination virtual hard disks are entirely synchronized, the virtual machine changes over to using the destination virtual hard disk.

5. The source virtual hard disk is deleted.

FIGURE 7.22   Storage Migration Settings

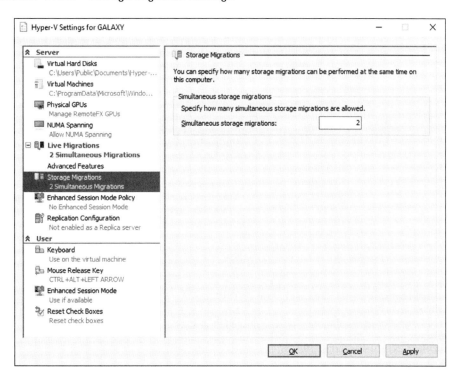

PowerShell Commands for Hyper-V High Availability

When configuring Hyper-V high availability, you may want to setup some of the components using PowerShell. Table 7.6 shows you some of the available PowerShell commands available for setting up Hyper-V high availability.

TABLE 7.6   PowerShell Commands for High Availability

PowerShell Command	Description
Complete-VMFailover	This command helps finish a virtual machine's failover process on the replica server.
Disable-VMMigration	This command allows an administrator to disable virtual machine migration on a virtual machine host.
Enable-VMMigration	This command allows an administrator to enable virtual machine migration on a virtual machine host.
Enable-VMReplication	This command allows an administrator to enable replication of a virtual machine.
Get-VMMigrationNetwork	This command shows you the virtual machine networks used for migration.
Get-VMReplication	This command shows an administrator the replication settings for a virtual machine.
Get-VMReplicationAuthorizationEntry	This command shows an administrator the authorization entries of a replica server.
Get-VMReplicationServer	This command shows an administrator the replication and authentication settings of a replica server.
Import-VMInitialReplication	This command imports initial replication files for a replica virtual machine when using external media.
Measure-VMReplication	This command shows an administrator the replication statistics and information associated with a virtual machine.
New-VMReplicationAuthorizationEntry	This command allows you to create an authorization entry to replicate data to a specified replica server.

PowerShell Command	Description
Remove-VMMigrationNetwork	This command allows an administrator to remove a network from use in migration.
Remove-VMReplication	This command removes the replication from a specific virtual machine.
Reset-VMReplicationStatistics	This command allows an administrator to reset the replication statistics of a virtual machine.
Resume-VMReplication	This command allows an administrator to resume virtual machine replication after an error, a pause, a suspension, or a resynchronization is required.
Set-VMProcessor	This command allows an administrator to configure which processors are used for a virtual machine.
Set-VMReplication	This command allows an administrator to modify the replication settings of a virtual machine.
Set-VMReplicationServer	This command allows an admin to configure a host as a replica server.
Start-VMInitialReplication	This command starts replication of a virtual machine.
Stop-VMReplication	This command stops replication of a virtual machine.
Suspend-VMReplication	This command suspends replication of a virtual machine.
Test-VMReplicationConnection	This command allows an administrator to test the connection of a primary server and a replica server.

Summary

High availability is more than just clustering. It is achieved through improved hardware, software, and processes. This chapter focused on how to configure Failover Clustering and Network Load Balancing in order to achieve high availability and scalability.

High availability should be approached through proper hardware configuration, training, and operational discipline. Failover clustering provides a highly available base for many applications, such as databases and mail servers.

Network load-balanced clusters are used to provide high availability and scalability for network-based applications, such as VPNs and web servers. Network load-balanced clusters can be configured with any edition of Windows Server 2016 except for the Windows Server 2016 Hyper-V Edition.

Windows Server 2016 Hyper-V can also have high availability set up on it without using clustering. Administrators have the ability to setup Live Migrations on Hyper-V virtual machines.

Live Migration allows you to move a virtual machine from one server to another without any impact on the users. This can be very useful if you have a Hyper-V server that is starting to show hardware issues. Administrators can move the virtual machine from the server with issues to a server without any issues.

Exam Essentials

Know how to modify failover and failback settings.   These settings are set on the clustered service or application, but they can be modified by settings on the resources.

Know the hardware requirements for Network Load Balancing.   Network Load Balancing has distinct hardware requirements. Know the requirements for NLB.

Know the PowerShell commands for NLB.   Make sure you know the different PowerShell commands for Network Load Balancing. Understand which command is used to create, manage, and stop NLB clusters.

Understand Live Migration.   Understand how Live Migrations work and why we use them. Understand that Live Migrations allow an administrator to move a virtual machine from one server to another without any impact on the users.

Know PowerShell for VM Replication.   Make sure you know the different PowerShell commands for Virtual Machine Replication. Understand which commands are used to create, manage, and stop VM Replication.

Video Resources

There are videos available for the following exercises:

Exercise 7.2

Exercise 7.5

You can access the videos at http://sybextestbanks.wiley.com on the Other Study Tools tab.

Review Questions

1. You are the administrator for a mid-size organization. You have been asked by the owner to set up a NLB cluster. You want to use PowerShell to set up the cluster. What command would you use?

   A. `New-NlbCluster`

   B. `Create-NlbCluster`

   C. `Setup-NlbCluster`

   D. `Set-NlbCluster`

2. Which of the following editions of Windows Server 2016 can be configured in a Network Load Balancing cluster? (Choose all that apply.)

   A. Windows Server 2016 Virtual Edition

   B. Windows Server 2016 Standard Edition

   C. Windows Server 2016 Small Business Server

   D. Windows Server 2016 Datacenter Edition

3. What is the maximum number of nodes that can participate in a Windows Server 2016 NLB single cluster?

   A. 32

   B. 4

   C. 16

   D. 64

4. Which of the following actions should be performed against an NLB cluster node if maintenance needs to be performed while not terminating current connections?

   A. Evict

   B. Drainstop

   C. Pause

   D. Stop

5. Which of the following actions should be performed against an NLB cluster node if maintenance needs to be performed and all connections must be terminated immediately?

   A. Evict

   B. Drainstop

   C. Pause

   D. Stop

6. You are the network administrator for your organization and you want to stop virtual machine replication. What PowerShell command would you use?

    A. Stop-VMReplication

    B. Terminate-VMReplication

    C. Kill-VMReplication

    D. Drainstop-VMReplication

7. Which of the following applications would be better suited on a Network Load Balancing cluster instead of a failover cluster? (Choose all that apply.)

    A. SQL Server

    B. Website

    C. Database servers

    D. Terminal Services

8. To configure an NLB cluster with unicast, what is the minimum number of network adapters required in each node?

    A. One

    B. Two

    C. Three

    D. Six

9. Users who are connecting to an NLB cluster have been complaining that after using the site for a few minutes they are prompted to log in using their username. What should you do to fix the problem and retain scalability?

    A. Create a port rule to allow only ports 80 and 443.

    B. Set the cluster affinity to None.

    C. Set the filtering mode to Single Host.

    D. Set the cluster affinity to Single.

10. Users who are connecting to an NLB cluster through the Internet are complaining that they keep connecting to different NLB nodes in different locations. You want to keep Internet users connecting to the same NLB members each time they connect. What should you do to fix the problem?

    A. Create a port rule to allow only ports 80 and 443.

    B. Set the cluster affinity to None.

    C. Set the cluster affinity to Class C.

    D. Set the cluster affinity to Single.

Chapter

8

Implementing Software Defined Networking

THE FOLLOWING 70-741 EXAM OBJECTIVES ARE COVERED IN THIS CHAPTER:

✓ **Determine scenarios and requirements for implementing Software Defined Networking (SDN)**

> ▪ This objective may include but is not limited to: Determine deployment scenarios and network requirements for deploying SDN; determine requirements and scenarios for implementing Hyper-V Network Virtualization (HNV) using Network Virtualization Generic Route Encapsulation (NVGRE) encapsulation or Virtual Extensible LAN (VXLAN) encapsulation; determine scenarios for implementation of Software Load Balancer (SLB) for North-South and East-West load balancing; determine implementation scenarios for various types of Windows Server Gateways, including L3, GRE, and S2S, and their use; determine requirements and scenarios for distributed firewall policies and network security groups.

One of the greatest improvements to Microsoft's servers over the past few versions is its implementation of their Virtual Server called Hyper-V.

Hyper-V is a server role in Windows Server 2016 that allows you to virtualize your environment and therefore run multiple virtual operating system instances simultaneously on a physical server. This not only helps you to improve server utilization but also helps you to create a more cost-effective and dynamic system.

Hyper-V allows an organization of any size to act and compete with other organizations of any size. A small company can buy a single server and then virtualize that server into multiple servers. Hyper-V gives a small company the ability to run multiple servers on a single box and compete with a company of any size.

For the large organizations, an administrator can consolidate multiple servers onto Hyper-V servers thus saving an organization time and money by using less physical boxes but still having all the servers needed to run the business.

In Windows Server 2016, Microsoft has taken virtualization to the next level with Software Defined Networking. This allows you to use virtualization and also create a virtual network (including virtual routers, switches, etc.).

In this chapter, you will learn the basic concepts and features of Software Defined Networking and Hyper-V. You will also get a solid understanding of what is important in virtualization and in what areas of your work life you can use it.

Understanding Software Defined Networking

Software Defined Networking (SDN) allows an administrator to centrally manage and control all of your virtual and physical network devices. These devices include things like datacenter switches, routers, and gateways. SDN also allows administrators to manage virtual elements like Hyper-V virtual switches and gateways. Administrators can easily manage their entire networks centrally.

Administrators that want to run Hyper-V and virtual machines using SDN servers, like Network Controllers and Software Load Balancing systems, need to use Windows Server 2016 Datacenter. Administrators can use Windows Server 2016 Standard edition if they want to run SDN controlled networks components like tenant VMs.

One of the nice advantages of using SDN is the ability to still use your current network hardware components like switches, routers, and other types of network hardware devices. SDN gives an administrator the ability to merge both virtual and physical networks together.

To understand SDN, you must first understand some of the components that SDN uses. So let's take a look at some of the available SDN components.

Network Controllers

Network Controllers are new to Windows Server 2016. Network Controllers allow an administrator to have a centralized virtual and physical datacenter infrastructure. This allows administrators to manage, configure, and troubleshoot all of their infrastructure components from one location. Administrators no longer need to manually configure each network component separately.

Network Controllers use three different application programming interface (API) languages to control all of the different hardware on your network. The Southbound API allows Network Controllers to communicate with the network and the Northbound API allows you to communicate with the Network Controller.

Administrators can use Windows PowerShell to communicate with the Representational State Transfer (REST) API (this is the management application) to manage their network infrastructure components. These components include the:

- Physical switches
- Physical routers
- Hyper-V switches and Virtual Machines (VMs)
- Datacenter Firewalls
- VPN Gateways
- Load Balancing components

If you would like to setup a Network Controller using Windows PowerShell, you would use the `New-NetworkControllerNodeObject` command as shown:

```
New-NetworkControllerNodeObject -Name <String> -Server <String> -FaultDomain
<String> -RestInterface <String>  [-NodeCertificate <X509Certificate2>]
[-WhatIf] [-Confirm] [<CommonParameters>]
```

The following is an example of the `New-NetworkControllerNodeObject` command. The name of the Network Controller Node Object is Node1. The server name is NCServer1. StormWind.com and the ethernet adapter is being used.

```
New-NetworkControllerNodeObject -Name "Node1" -Server "NCNode1.StormWind.com"
-FaultDomain "fd:/rack1/host1" -RestInterface "Ethernet"
```

Internal DNS Service (iDNS)

The Domain Name System (DNS) is a service that allows you to resolve a hostname to an Internet Protocol (IP) address. As stated in Chapter 2 "Configuring DNS", an easy way to understand DNS is to think about making a telephone call. If you wanted to call Microsoft and did not know the phone number, you could call information, tell the operator the name (Microsoft), and get the telephone number. You would then make the call.

Now think about trying to connect to Server1. You don't know the TCP/IP number (the computer's telephone number), so your computer asks DNS (information) for the number of Server1. DNS returns the number, and your system makes the connection (call). DNS is your network's 411, or information, and it returns the TCP/IP data for your network.

Organizations that work with Cloud Service Providers (CSP) or enterprise networks that use Windows Server 2016 SDNs, administrators can use DNS for their hosted virtual machines by using Internal DNS (iDNS). Windows Server 2016 SDN automatically integrates iDNS. This can provide virtual machines with DNS name resolution services for their isolated local name space and for their Internet resources.

Since the iDNS service is not available from the tenant's Virtual Network, unless it goes through the iDNS proxy, this stops the server from being vulnerable from malicious activities on tenant networks. The iDNS service includes both the iDNS server and the iDNS proxy.

iDNS Servers   The iDNS service contains DNS servers that host tenant specific data (i.e., virtual machine Resource Records). iDNS servers are the authoritative zone for the hosted virtual machines and also the resolver for external resources.

iDNS Proxy   The iDNS proxy is a Windows Server 2016 service that runs on your host server. The iDNS proxy forwards virtual network DNS traffic to the iDNS Server.

Software Load Balancer (SLB) and Network Address Translation (NAT)

Organizations that work with Cloud Service Providers (CSP) or enterprise networks that use Windows Server 2016 SDNs can use Software Load Balancing (SLB) to evenly distribute network traffic for tenants and/or tenant customers between the virtual network resources.

SLB allows an administrator to setup multiple servers that can host the same workload. This gives an organization the ability to have high availability and scalability between the server's workload.

When it comes to SLB and NAT, you may hear the terms north-south or east-west. These terms just refer to the way that your application traffic patterns go in context of your datacenter. Now it's not as simple as direction. North-south and east-west layer 4 (L4) load balancing and NAT improves your company's data by using Direct Server Return. Direct Server Return allows the return network traffic to be bypassed by the Load Balancing multiplexer.

Applications can be designed using many tiers when residing in your datacenter. Most developers use Three-tier application architecture. Three-tier architecture is the most common architecture used by developers today and it is just the way that applications talk to other applications and servers.

For example: Applications that send data to other applications within the same data center or between datacenters has an east-west traffic pattern. If your organization has an older data center where clients simply requested data from a single server, it is more likely to have a north-south data pattern.

Windows Server 2016 SLB includes some of the following capabilities.

- Layer 4 load balancing services for north-south and east-west traffic patterns.

- Load balancing for internal and public network traffic.

- Supports dynamic IP addresses (DIPs) on virtual networks.

- Support for health probes.

- Scalability for multiplexers and Host Agents.

Windows Server 2016 SLB is scalable and it supports tens of gigabytes of data per cluster along with easy provisioning models. SLB is possible because it maps virtual IP addresses (VIPs) to dynamic IP addresses (DIPs). When an administrator sets up load balancing of virtual machines, users can gain access to these VMs by using a single IP address setup by the VIPs. VIPs are IP addresses on the Internet that allows users to connect to the cloud resources. DIPs are the IP addresses that sit behind the VIPs. The DIPs are the actual IP addresses of the load balancing servers.

The easiest way to configure your SLB and NAT setup is by using System Center 2016 Virtual Machine Manager or by using Windows PowerShell commands.

 To see all of the steps needed to configure SLB, please visit Microsoft's website at:

https://docs.microsoft.com/en-us/windows-server/networking/sdn/manage/configure-slb-and-nat

Datacenter Firewall

Firewalls allow an administrator to set up policies on who or what can be allowed past the firewall. For example, if you want to allow DNS traffic to pass through the firewall, you would enable port 53. If you want the traffic to leave the firewall, you would configure port 53 outbound. If you want to have the traffic enter into the company, you would configure inbound.

Datacenter Firewalls are new Windows Server 2016 network layer, Stateful, multitenant firewalls. Network administrators that work with virtual network tenants can install and then configure firewall policies. These firewall policies can help protect their virtual networks from unwanted traffic from Internet and intranet networks.

The Datacenter Firewall allows you to setup granular access control lists (ACLs) and this allows you to apply firewall policies at the VM interface level or at the subnet level. To create ACLs on the Datacenter Firewall, an administrator can use Windows PowerShell.

The following is an example of the PowerShell command that is used to assign the ACL to the AccessControlList property of the network interface.

```
$nic.properties.ipconfigurations[0].properties.AccessControlList = $acl
```

Windows Server 2016 Datacenter Firewalls give you the following tenant benefits:

- Administrators have the ability to define firewall rules that help protect Internet facing workloads on virtual networks.

- Administrators have the ability to define firewall rules to protect data between virtual machines on the same layer 2 or different layer 2 virtual subnets.

- Administrators have the ability to define firewall rules to protect and isolate network traffic between tenants on a virtual network from a service provider.

RAS Gateway

Administrators can setup Remote Access Server (RAS) gateways that you can use for bridging traffic between virtual and non-virtual networks. Gateways are used so traffic can be transferred from one type of system to another. This is very useful when you are setting up site-to-site (S2S) VPNs, forwarding gateways, and Generic Routing Encapsulation (GRE) gateways.

RAS Gateways are software-based, multitenant, and Border Gateway Protocol (BGP) capable routers available in Windows Server 2016.

One nice advantage to using Windows Server 2016 gateways is that N+M redundancy of gateways is supported. N+M is an industry standard for setting up clusters. There may be times when a single cluster is managing many services and having only one dedicated failover server may not be enough. In these situations more than one (M) standby server is needed. This is the N+M redundancy standard and Windows Server 2016 supports this type of setup.

RAS Gateways for routing traffic between virtual networks and physical networks can be deployed using Internet Key Exchange version 2 (IKEv2) site-to-site VPNs, Layer 3 (L3) VPNs, or Generic Routing Encapsulation (GRE) gateways.

RAS Gateways can be setup one of two ways: single tenant mode or multitenant mode.

Single Tenant Mode   Single tenant mode is used for organizations of any size that want to deploy RAS Gateways. In single tenant mode, the RAS Gateway is used as the exterior or Internet facing VPN or DirectAccess edge server. In single tenant mode, administrators will deploy the RAS Gateway on a Windows Server 2016 physical server or virtual machine.

Multitenant Mode   Multitenant mode is used for Cloud Service Providers (CSPs) or enterprise networks to allow datacenter or cloud network traffic routing between virtual and physical networks. This includes traffic that goes over the Internet. In multitenant mode, administrators will deploy the RAS Gateway on a Windows Server 2016 virtual machine.

Remote Direct Memory Access and Switch Embedded Teaming

If you are using any Windows version prior to Windows Server 2016, configuring RDMA on network adapters, bound to NIC teaming or Hyper-V switches, was not available. Windows Server 2016 has changed that.

Windows Server 2016 allows an administrator to enable Remote Direct Memory Access (RDMA) on the bound Hyper-V network adapters. Administrators have the ability to enable RDMA with or without using Switch Embedded Teaming (SET). Administrators can now use less network adapters when RDMA and SET are used at the same time.

Remote Direct Memory Access (RDMA) allows nodes in your network to interchange data in RAM without involving the processor, cache, or operating system. RDMA allows a system to run better because it doesn't use any of the other resources.

Before an administrator can enable RDMA it is recommended that they first enable Data Center Bridging (DCB). DCB is not required for Internet Wide Area RDMA Protocol (iWARP) networks but ethernet based RDMA networks have shown better performance when working with DCB. To enable DCB and RDMS, you would run the following PowerShell commands:

```
Install-WindowsFeature Data-Center-Bridging
Add-VMNetworkAdapter -SwitchName RDMAswitch -Name SMB_1
Enable-NetAdapterRDMA "vEthernet (SMB_1)"
```

Switch Embedded Teaming is another option to NIC teaming. SET has the ability to be used in multiple environments including Hyper-V and SDN networks in Windows Server 2016. Administrators have the ability to group physical network adapters together when using SET. SET also integrates many of the NIC Teaming functionality into the Hyper-V Virtual Switch. SET gives you the ability to group between one and eight network adapters into software based virtual adapters.

Virtual adapters allow you to have faster performance while also providing fault tolerance in the event of any of your network adapters failing. One requirement to setting up SET is that all SET group adapters need to be installed on the same physical Hyper-V host server.

Administrators have the ability to connect their teamed NICs to either the same physical switch or to different physical switches. If you decide to connect your NICs to different switches, both switches must be part of the same subnet. To setup SET using PowerShell, you would run the following command:

```
New-VMSwitch -Name SETswitch -NetAdapterName "SLOT 2","SLOT 3"
-EnableEmbeddedTeaming $true
```

 To learn more about Remote Direct Memory Access and Switch Embedded Teaming, visit Microsoft's website at https://technet.microsoft.com/en-us/library/mt403349.aspx.

Windows Server Containers

Windows Containers are independent and isolated environments that run an operating system. These isolated environments allow an administrator to place an application into its own container thus not affecting any other applications or containers.

Think of containers as virtual environments that are used to run independent applications. They load much faster than virtual machines and you can run as many containers as needed for all of the different applications that you run.

Administrators can use containers to separate applications or services from other services that are running on the same host. This is possible because each container has its own operating system, processes, file system, registry, and IP address. With Windows Server 2016, you can now connect Windows Server containers to virtual networks.

One of the nice advantages of using Windows Containers is that the containers can be managed the same way an administrator can manage an operating system. A container works the same way as a newly installed physical or virtual machine. So once you know how to configure these containers, management is much easier than configuring a physical machine.

There are two different types of containers that the Windows Container can use:

Windows Server Containers   This container allows an administrator to isolate applications so applications can run in their own space and not affect other applications. The question that you may be asking is why not use a virtual machine? Well the advantage of Windows Server Containers is that they are already pre-built and you don't need all of the other services that a virtual machine would need to run. So Windows Containers are smaller, faster, and more efficient when isolating applications. In a Windows Server Container, the kernel is shared between all of the different Windows Containers.

Hyper-V Containers   Hyper-V Containers and Windows Containers work the same way. The difference between the two is that Hyper-V Containers run within a virtual machine and the Windows Containers don't need to run in a Hyper-V environment. In a Hyper-V Container the container host's kernel is not shared between the other Hyper-V Containers.

As with any new technology, it is important to understand the terminology that goes along with that new technology. The first thing that you may have noticed is that a container works a lot like a virtual machine. Just like a virtual machine, the container has a running operating system within the container.

The container has a file system and the container can also be accessed through the network the same way a virtual machine does. The advantage is that a container is a more efficient operating system. But to truly understand how containers work, you need to understand all of the different components that allow containers to function properly.

Container Host   This component can be on a physical or virtual machine and it's the component that is configured with the Windows Container feature. So the Windows Container sits on top of the Container Host.

Container OS Image   This component provides the operating system to the container. Containers are made up from multiple images that are stacked on top of each other within the container.

Container Image   This is the component that contains all of the layers of the container. So the Container Image contains the operating system, the application, and all of the services required to make that application function properly.

Container Registry   This component is the heart and brain of the container. The container images are kept within the container's registry. The advantage of doing containers this way is that you can download other registries to automatically add other applications or services quickly.

Docker Daemon   This is the component that runs the docker application. The docker daemon is automatically installed after you complete the installation of the docker application.

Dockerfile   This component is used to create the container images. The advantage of using the Dockerfile is that you can automate how containers are created. Dockerfiles are batches of instructions (within a txt file) and commands that are called on when an image is assembled.

Docker Hub Repositories   This component is a location where all of your images are stored. By having a central location for stored images, the images can be used among co-workers, customers, or for the entire IT community. There are docker hub repositories on the internet and these locations allow you to grab and use images for your organization.

To learn more about Windows Containers, Please read William Panek's Windows Server 2016 book "MCSA Windows Server 2016 Study Guide: Exam 70-740" published by Sybex, 2017.

Hyper-V Components

One of the nice advantages of SDN is the ability to work with Hyper-V components. Administrators setup a virtual network and then you configure SDN services. So to truly understand how this works, you must understand Hyper-V. So let's take a look at Windows Server 2016 Hyper-V.

Hyper-V Overview

In the following sections, I'll introduce you to Hyper-V. To begin, you'll take a look at virtualization and what types of virtualization exist. I will then discuss Hyper-V features and the Hyper-V architecture before finishing up with the Hyper-V requirements for software and hardware.

What Is Virtualization?

Virtualization is a method for abstracting physical resources from the way that they interact with other resources. For example, if you abstract the physical hardware from the operating system, you get the benefit of being able to move the operating system between different physical systems.

This is called *server virtualization*. But there are also other forms of virtualization available, such as presentation virtualization, desktop virtualization, and application virtualization. I will now briefly explain the differences between these forms of virtualization:

Server Virtualization   This basically enables multiple servers to run on the same physical server. Hyper-V is a server virtualization tool that allows you to move physical machines to virtual machines and manage them on a few physical servers. Thus, you will be able to consolidate physical servers.

Presentation Virtualization   When you use *presentation virtualization*, your applications run on a different computer, and only the screen information is transferred to your computer. An example of presentation virtualization is Microsoft Remote Desktop Services in Windows Server 2016.

Desktop Virtualization   *Desktop virtualization* provides you with a virtual machine on your desktop, comparable to server virtualization. You run your complete operating system and applications in a virtual machine so that your local physical machine just needs to run a very basic operating system. An example of this form of virtualization is Microsoft Virtual PC or Windows 10 with Hyper-V.

Application Virtualization   *Application virtualization* helps prevent conflicts between applications on the same PC. Thus, it helps you to isolate the application running environment from the operating system installation requirements by creating application-specific copies of all shared resources. It also helps reduce application-to-application incompatibility and testing needs. An example of an application virtualization tool is Microsoft Application Virtualization (App-V).

Hyper-V Features

As a lead-in to the virtualization topic and Hyper-V, I will start with a list of key features, followed by a list of supported guest operating systems. This should provide you with a quick, high-level view of this feature before you dig deeper into the technology.

Key Features of Hyper-V

The following are the key features of Hyper-V:

Architecture   The hypervisor-based architecture, which has a 64-bit micro-kernel, provides a new array of device support as well as performance and security improvements.

Operating System Support   Both 32-bit and 64-bit operating systems can run simultaneously in Hyper-V. Also, different platforms like Windows, Linux, and others are supported.

Support for Symmetric Multiprocessors   Support for up to 64 processors in a virtual machine environment provides you with the ability to run applications as well as multiple virtual machines faster.

Network Load Balancing   Hyper-V provides support for *Windows Network Load Balancing (NLB)* to balance the network load across virtual machines on different servers.

Hardware Architecture   Hyper-V's architecture provides improved utilization of resources such as networking, memory, and disks.

Quick Migration   Hyper-V's *quick migration* feature provides you with the functionality to run virtual machines in a clustered environment with switchover capabilities when there is a failure. Thus, you can reduce downtime and achieve higher availability of your virtual machines.

Virtual Machine Checkpoints   You can take checkpoints of running virtual machines, which provides you with the capability to recover to any previous virtual machine checkpoints state quickly and easily.

Resource Metering   Hyper-V *resource metering* allows an organization to track usage within the businesses departments. It allows an organization to create a usage-based billing solution that adjusts to the provider's business model and strategy.

Scripting   Using the Windows Management Instrumentation (WMI) interfaces and APIs, you can easily build custom scripts to automate processes in your virtual machines.

RemoteFX   Windows Server 2016 Hyper-V RemoteFX allows for an enhanced user experience for RemoteFX desktops by providing a 3D virtual adapter, intelligent codecs, and the ability to redirect USB devices in virtual machines.

Fibre Channel   The virtual Fibre Channel feature allows you to connect to the Fibre Channel storage unit from within the virtual machine. *Virtual Fibre Channel* allows an administrator to use their existing Fibre Channel to support virtualized workloads. Hyper-V users have the ability to use Fibre Channel storage area networks (SANs) to virtualize the workloads that require direct access to SAN logical unit numbers (LUNs).

Enhanced Session Mode   *Enhanced Session Mode* enhances the interactive session of the Virtual Machine Connection for Hyper-V administrators who want to connect to their virtual machines. It gives administrators the same functionality as a remote desktop connection when the administrator is interacting with a virtual machine.

In previous versions of Hyper-V, the virtual machine connection gave you limited functionality while you connected to the virtual machine screen, keyboard, and mouse. An administrator could use an RDP connection to get full redirection abilities, but that would require a network connection to the virtual machine host.

Enhanced Session Mode gives administrators the following benefits for local resource redirection:

- Display configuration
- Audio
- Printers
- Clipboard
- Smart cards

- ▪ Drives
- ▪ USB devices
- ▪ Supported Plug and Play devices

Shared Virtual Hard Disk   Windows Server 2016 Hyper-V has a feature called Shared Virtual Hard Disk. Shared Virtual Hard Disk allows an administrator to cluster virtual machines by using shared virtual hard disk (VHDX) files.

Shared virtual hard disks allow an administrator to build a high availability infrastructure, which is important if you are setting up either a private cloud deployment or a cloud-hosted environment for managing large workloads. Shared virtual hard disks allow two or more virtual machines to access the same virtual hard disk (VHDX) file.

Automatic Virtual Machine Activation (AVMA)   *Automatic Virtual Machine Activation (AVMA)* is a feature that allows administrators to install virtual machines on a properly activated Windows Server 2016 system without the need to manage individual product keys for each virtual machine. When using AVMA, virtual machines get bound to the licensed Hyper-V server as soon as the virtual machine starts.

Network Isolation   One nice feature of using Microsoft Hyper-V network virtualization is the ability of Hyper-V to keep virtual networks isolated from the physical network infrastructure of the hosted system. Because administrators can set up Hyper-V software–defined virtualization policies, you are no longer limited by the IP address assignment or VLAN isolation requirements of the physical network. Hyper-V allows for built-in network isolation to keep the virtual network separated from the virtual network.

Discrete Device Assignment   One feature of Windows Server 2016 is the ability to use Discrete Device Assignment (DDA). DDA allows an administrator to take full advantage of performance and application compatibility improvements in the user experience by allowing the system's graphic cards to be directly assigned to a virtual machine. This allows the graphic card processor to be fully available to the virtual desktops that are utilizing the native driver of the graphics card processor.

Non-Uniform Memory Access   Non-Uniform Memory Access (NUMA) is a multiprocessor memory architecture that allows a processor to access its local memory quicker than memory located on another processor. NUMA allows a system to access memory quickly by providing separate memory on each processor. Processors can access their local assigned memory thus speeding the system performance. Normally a multi-processor system runs into performance issues when multiple processors access the same memory at the same time. NUMA helps prevent this by allowing processors to access their own memory. Memory that is dedicated to a processor is referred to as a NUMA node.

Dynamic Memory   *Dynamic Memory* is a feature of Hyper-V that allows it to balance memory automatically among running virtual machines. Dynamic Memory allows Hyper-V to adjust the amount of memory available to the virtual machines in response to the needs of the virtual machines. It is currently available for Hyper-V in Windows Server 2016.

Virtual Machine Queue   Windows Server 2016 Hyper-V includes a feature called Virtual machine queue (VMQ) as long as the hardware is VMQ compatible network hardware. VMQ uses packet filtering to provide data from an external virtual machine network directly to virtual machines. This helps reduce the overhead of routing packets from the management operating system to the virtual machine.

Once VMQ is enabled on Hyper-V, a dedicated queue is created on the physical network adapter for each virtual network adapter to use. When data arrives for the virtual network adapter, the physical network adapter places that data in a queue and once the system is available, all of the data in the queue is delivered to the virtual network adapter.

To enable the virtual machine queue on a specific virtual machine, enter the settings for the virtual machine and expand Network Adapter. Click on Hardware Acceleration and on the right hand window; check the box for Enable virtual machine queue.

Network Virtualization using Generic Routing Encapsulation   Windows Server 2016 now supports Hyper-V Network Virtualization using Generic Routing Encapsulation (NVGRE). NVGRE is a tool that allows you to virtualize IP addresses and the virtual machine's packets are then encapsulated inside of other packets. The NVGRE header packet will then have the correct source and destination provider area (PA) IP addresses along with a 24-bit Virtual Subnet ID (VSID).

Virtual Extensible LAN   Virtual Extensible LAN (VXLAN) is an industry technology for network virtualization. VXLAN uses a VLAN compatible encapsulation method to help encapsulate MAC-based OSI layer 2 Ethernet frames within layer 4 UDP packets. The UDP packets use the default IANA-assigned destination UDP port number 4789.

Hyper-V Nesting   Windows Server 2016 has introduced a new feature of Hyper-V called Hyper-V nesting. Hyper-V nesting allows you to run a virtual machine in a virtual machine. So let's say that you build a new 2016 Hyper-V server. You install Windows Server 2016 into a virtual machine. Then in that virtual machine, you can install Hyper-V and build other virtual machines within the first virtual machine. This is new to Windows Server 2016 and can be very useful in training situations. You can install a Windows Server 2016 virtual machine and still show others how to install and create virtual machines in the original virtual machine. To enable Hyper-V nesting, you would run the following PowerShell command on the Hyper-V Host. The virtual machines must be in the OFF State when this command is run (this means the virtual machines must be turned off):

```
Set-VMProcessor -VMName <VMName> -ExposeVirtualizationExtensions $true
```

Supported Guest Operating Systems

The following guest operating systems have been successfully tested on Hyper-V and are hypervisor-aware. Table 8.1 shows all of the guest server operating systems and the maximum number of virtual processors. Table 8.2 shows all of the guest client operating systems and the maximum number of virtual processors.

TABLE 8.1 Hyper-V guest server operating systems

Guest Operating System (Server)	Maximum Number of Virtual Processors
Windows Server 2016	64
Windows Server 2012 and Server 2012 R2	64
Windows Server 2008 R2 with Service Pack 1 (SP1)	64
Windows Server 2008 R2	64
Windows Server 2008 with Service Pack 2 (SP2)	8
Windows Home Server 2011	4
Windows Small Business Server 2011	Essentials edition: 2 Standard edition: 4
Windows Server 2003 R2 with Service Pack 2 (SP2)	2
Windows Server 2003 with Service Pack 2 (SP2)	2
Red Hat Enterprise Linux 5.7 and 5.8	64
Red Hat Enterprise Linux 6.0–6.3	64
SUSE Linux Enterprise Server 11 SP2	64
Open SUSE 12.1	64
Ubuntu 12.04	64

TABLE 8.2 Hyper-V guest client operating systems

Guest Operating System (Client)	Maximum Number of Virtual Processors
Windows 10	32
Windows 8	32
Windows 7 with Service Pack 1 (SP1)	4

Guest Operating System (Client)	Maximum Number of Virtual Processors
Windows 7	4
Windows Vista with Service Pack 2 (SP2)	2
Windows XP with Service Pack 3 (SP3)	2
Windows XP x64 Edition with Service Pack 2 (SP2)	2
CentOS 5.7 and 5.8	64
CentOS 6.0–6.3	64
Red Hat Enterprise Linux 5.7 and 5.8	64
Red Hat Enterprise Linux 6.0–6.3	64
SUSE Linux Enterprise Server 11 SP2	64
Open SUSE 12.1	64
Ubuntu 12.04	64

 The list of supported guest operating systems may always be extended. Please check the official Microsoft Hyper-V site to obtain a current list of supported operating systems: www.microsoft.com/virtualization.

Hyper-V Architecture

This section will provide you with an overview of the Hyper-V architecture (see Figure 8.1). I'll explain the differences between a hypervisor-aware and a non-hypervisor-aware child partition.

As you can see, Hyper-V is based on the microkernel architecture. Hyper-V provides a virtualization layer called a *hypervisor* that runs directly on the system hardware. You can see that the hypervisor is similar to what the kernel is to Windows. It is a software layer responsible for the interaction with the core hardware and works in conjunction with an optimized instance of Windows Server 2016 that allows running multiple operating systems on a physical server simultaneously. The Hyper-V architecture consists of the hypervisor and parent and child partitions.

FIGURE 8.1   Hyper-V architecture

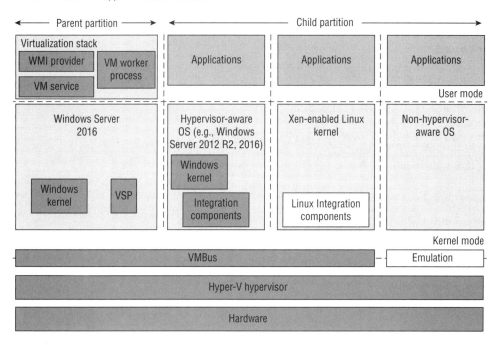

The Windows Server 2016 operating system runs in the parent partition, and it delivers the WMI provider for scripting as well as the VM service.

Virtual machines each run in their own child partitions. Child partitions do not have direct access to hardware resources; instead, they have a virtual view of the resources, which are called *virtual devices*.

If you're running a hypervisor-aware operating system like Windows Server 2003, Windows Server 2008, Windows Server 2008 R2, Windows Server 2012, or Windows Server 2016 in your virtual machine, any request to the virtual devices is redirected via the high-speed bus to the devices in the parent partition, which will manage the requests.

By default, only Windows Server 2008 R2, Server 2012, and Server 2012 R2 are hypervisor-aware operating systems. Once you install Hyper-V Integration Components on an operating system other than Windows Server 2008 R2 and newer, it will be hypervisor-aware. Microsoft provides a hypervisor adapter to make Linux hypervisor aware.

Non-hypervisor-aware operating systems (for example, Windows NT 4.0) use an emulator to communicate with the Windows hypervisor, which is slower than molasses in the winter.

Hyper-V Requirements

The following sections will describe the hardware and software requirements for installing the Hyper-V server role. It is important to understand these requirements for obtaining your software license as well as for planning for server hardware. When you understand the requirements, you can design and configure a Hyper-V solution that will meet the needs of your applications.

Hardware Requirements

In addition to the basic hardware requirements for Windows Server 2016, there are requirements for running the Hyper-V server role on your Windows server. They are listed in Table 8.3.

TABLE 8.3 Hardware requirements for Hyper-V

Requirement Area	Definition
CPU	x64-compatible processor with Intel VT or AMD-V technology enabled. Hardware Data Execution Prevention (DEP), specifically Intel XD bit (execute disable bit) or AMD NX bit (no execute bit), must be available and enabled. Minimum: 1.4 GHz. Recommended: 2 GHz or faster.
Memory	Minimum: 1 GB RAM. Recommended: 2 GB RAM or greater. (Additional RAM is required for each running guest operating system.) Maximum: 1 TB.
Hard disk	Minimum: 8 GB. Recommended: 20 GB or greater. (Additional disk space needed for each guest operating system.)

The Add Roles Wizard in Server Manager additionally verifies the hardware requirements. A good starting point is to check your hardware against the Microsoft hardware list to make sure that Windows Server 2016 supports your hardware. If you try to install the Hyper-V server role on a computer that does not meet the CPU requirements, you'll get a warning window that looks like Figure 8.2.

FIGURE 8.2 Warning window that Hyper-V cannot be installed

Software Requirements

To use virtualization in Windows Server 2016, you need to consider the basic software requirements for Hyper-V. Hyper-V runs only on the following editions of the Windows Server 2016 operating system:

- Windows Server 2016 Standard edition
- Windows Server 2016 Datacenter edition
- Microsoft Hyper-V Server 2016 edition

Hyper-V Installation and Configuration

The following sections explain how to install the Hyper-V role using Server Manager in Windows Server 2016 Full installation mode or the command-line mode in Windows Server 2016 Server Core. We will then take a look at Hyper-V as part of Server Manager before discussing how to use the Hyper-V Manager. Finally, we will look at the Hyper-V server settings and then cover two important areas for Hyper-V: virtual networks and virtual hard disks.

Install the Hyper-V Role

Now it's time to see how to install the Hyper-V server role on the two installation options of Windows Server 2016, namely, a Full installation and a Server Core installation.

Installing Hyper-V in Full Installation Mode

You can install the Hyper-V server role on any Windows Server 2016 installation for which the Full option was chosen. In addition, the server must meet both the hardware and software requirements. The installation process is simple, as Exercise 8.1 demonstrates.

EXERCISE 8.1

Installing Hyper-V in Full Installation Mode

1. Open Server Manager.

2. In Server Manager, choose option 2, Add Roles And Features.

3. At the Select Installation Type page, choose the role-based or feature-based installation. Click Next.

4. On the Select Destination Server screen, choose Select A Server From The Server Pool and choose the server to which you want to add this role. Click Next.

5. On the Select Server Roles screen, click the check box next to Hyper-V (see Figure 8.3). When the Add Features dialog box appears, click the Add Features button. Then click Next.

FIGURE 8.3 Server Manager Add Features

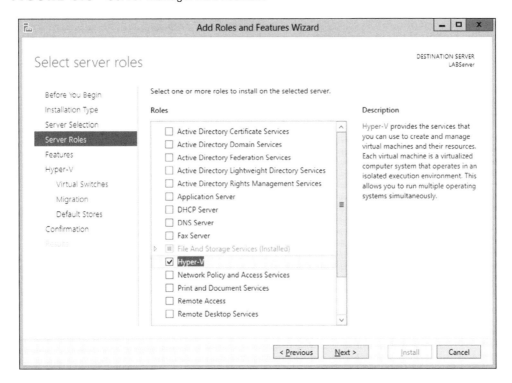

6. At the Select Features screen, click Next.

7. At the Hyper-V introduction screen, click Next.

8. At the Create Virtual Switches screen, choose your adapter (see Figure 8.4) and click Next.

9. At the Virtual Machine Migration screen, click Next. You want to use migration only if you have multiple Hyper-V servers. Since we will have only one for this exercise, just skip this screen.

FIGURE 8.4   Virtual Switch Screen

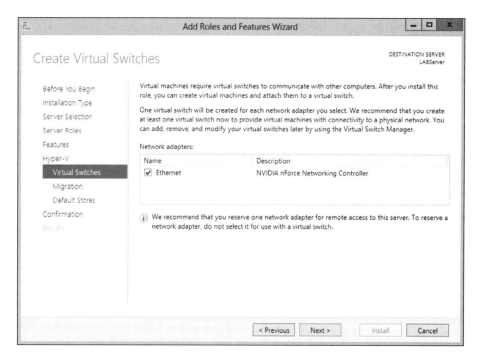

10. At the Default Stores screen, accept the defaults and click Next.

11. At the Confirmation screen, click the Install button.

12. After the installation is complete, click the Close button.

13. Restart your server.

Installing Hyper-V in Server Core

The Server Core installation option is introduced in Windows Server 2016. It creates an operating system installation without a GUI shell. You can either manage the server remotely from another system or use the Server Core's command-line interface.

This installation option provides the following benefits:

▪ Reduces attack surface (because fewer applications are running on the server)

▪ Reduces maintenance and management (because only the required options are installed)

- Requires less disk space and produces less processor utilization
- Provides a minimal parent partition
- Reduces system resources required by the operating system as well as the attack surface

By using Hyper-V on a Server Core installation, you can fundamentally improve availability because the attack surface is reduced and the downtime required for installing patches is optimized. It will thus be more secure and reliable with less management.

To install Hyper-V for a Windows Server 2016 installation, you must execute the following command in the command-line interface:

```
Dism /online /enable-feature /featurename:Microsoft-Hyper-V
```

Hyper-V in Server Manager

As with all of the other Windows Server 2016 roles, the Hyper-V role neatly integrates into Server Manager. Server Manager filters the information just for the specific role and thus displays only the required information. As you can see in Figure 8.5, the Hyper-V Summary page shows related event log entries, the state of the system services for Hyper-V, and useful resources and support.

FIGURE 8.5   Hyper-V in Server Manager

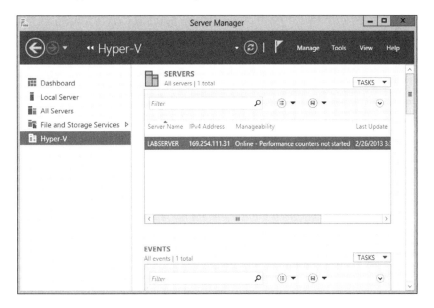

Using Hyper-V Manager

Hyper-V Manager is the central management console to configure your server and create and manage your virtual machines, virtual networks, and virtual hard disks. Unlike some other virtual servers where you managed all virtual machines through a web interface, Hyper-V Manager is managed through a Microsoft Management Console (MMC) snap-in. You can access it either in Server Manager or by using Administrative Tools ➤ Hyper-V Manager. Figure 8.6 shows how Hyper-V Manager looks once you start it.

FIGURE 8.6 Hyper-V Manager

Hyper-V Manager is available for the following operating systems:

- Windows Server 2016
- Windows Server 2012 R2
- Windows Server 2012
- Windows Server 2008 R2
- Windows Server 2008
- Windows 10
- Windows 8
- Windows 7
- Windows Vista with Service Pack 1 (SP1)

Hyper-V Manager is installed on a Windows Server 2016 machine only when you install Hyper-V on it. On Windows Server 2012 R2/2012/2008/2008 R2/ 2003, Windows 10/8/7, or Windows Vista, you will need to install the Hyper-V Manager MMC.

You can use Hyper-V Manager to connect to any Full or Server Core installation remotely. Besides Hyper-V Manager, you can use the WMI interface for scripting Hyper-V.

Configure Hyper-V Settings

In this section, you will get an overview of the available Hyper-V settings for the server. You configure all server-side default configuration settings like default locations of your configuration files or the release key. You can open the Hyper-V Settings page (see Figure 8.7) in Hyper-V Manager by clicking Hyper-V Settings in the Action pane.

FIGURE 8.7   Hyper-V Settings

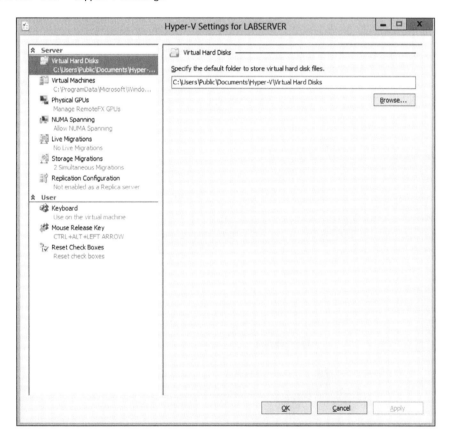

The Hyper-V Settings page includes the following settings:

Virtual Hard Disks   Specifies the default location of your virtual hard disk files (`.vhd` and `.vdhx`).

Virtual Machines   Specifies the default location of your virtual machine configuration files. It includes the Virtual Machine XML configuration files (part of the `Virtual Machines` folder) as well as related snapshots (part of the `Snapshot` folder).

Physical GPUs   This feature allows for graphical processing unit (GPU) accelerated video within a virtual machine. The GPU will allow you to support 3D GPU accelerated graphics.

NUMA Spanning   An administrator can configure Hyper-V to allow virtual machines to span nonuniform memory architecture (NUMA) nodes. When the physical computer has NUMA nodes, this setting provides virtual machines with additional computing resources. Spanning NUMA nodes can help you run more virtual machines at the same time. However, using NUMA can decrease overall performance.

Live Migrations   *Live Migration* allows a Hyper-V administrator to relocate running virtual machines easily from one node of the failover cluster to another node in the same cluster.

Storage Migrations   *Storage Migration* allows an administrator to move their virtual machine storage from one location to another. This setting allows you to specify how many storage migrations can be performed at the same time on this system.

Replication Configuration   This setting allows you to configure this computer as a Replica Server to another Hyper-V server. Hyper-V Replica allows administrators to replicate their Hyper-V virtual machines from one Hyper-V host at a primary site to another Hyper-V host at the Replica site.

Each node of the failover cluster that is involved in Replica must have the Hyper-V server role installed. One of the servers in the Hyper-V replication needs to be set up as a Replica Broker to allow the replication to work properly.

Keyboard   Defines how to use Windows key combinations. Options are Physical Computer, Virtual Machine, and Virtual Machine Only When Running Full Screen.

Mouse Release Key   Specifies the key combination to release the mouse in your virtual machine. Options are Ctrl+Alt+left arrow, Ctrl+Alt+right arrow, Ctrl+Alt+space, and Ctrl+Alt+Shift.

Reset Check Boxes   Resets any check boxes that hide pages and messages when checked. This will bring any window up again on which you checked the Do Not Show This Window Again check box.

Manage Virtual Switches

A *virtual network* provides the virtual links between nodes in either a virtual or physical network. Virtual networking in Hyper-V is provided in a secure and dynamic way because you can granularly define virtual network switches for their required usage. For example, you can define a private or internal virtual network if you don't want to allow your virtual machines to send packages to the physical network.

To allow your virtual machines to communicate with each other, you need virtual networks. Just like normal networks, virtual networks exist only on the host computer and allow you to configure how virtual machines communicate with each other, with the host, and with the network or the Internet. You manage virtual networks in Hyper-V using Virtual Switch Manager, as shown in Figure 8.8.

FIGURE 8.8   Virtual Network Manager

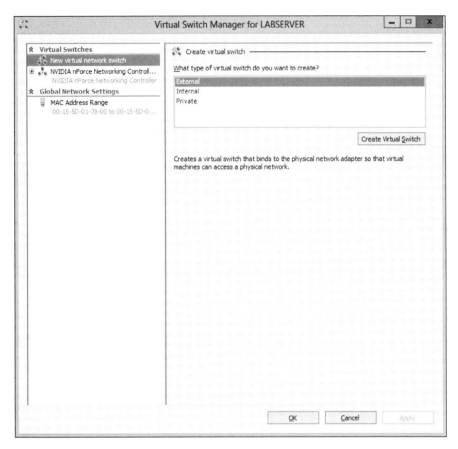

Hyper-V virtual switches are layer-2 software-based ethernet switches available in Hyper-V Manager. These switches are available as soon as you have installed the Hyper-V server role. Windows Server 2016 Hyper-V virtual switches allow you to deploy Switch Embedded Teaming (SET) and Remote Direct Memory Access (RDMA).

Using *Virtual Switch Manager*, you can create, manage, and delete virtual switches. You can define the network type as external, internal only, or private.

External   Any virtual machine connected to this virtual switch can access the physical network. You would use this option if you want to allow your virtual machines to access, for example, other servers on the network or the Internet. This option is used in production environments where your clients connect directly to the virtual machines.

Internal   This option allows virtual machines to communicate with each other as well as the host system but not with the physical network. When you create an internal network, it also creates a local area connection in Network Connections that allows the host machine to communicate with the virtual machines. You can use this if you want to separate your host's network from your virtual networks.

Private   When you use this option, virtual machines can communicate with each other but not with the host system or the physical network; thus, no network packets are hitting the wire. You can use this to define internal virtual networks for test environments or labs, for example.

On the external and internal-only virtual networks, you also can enable virtual LAN (VLAN) identification. You can use VLANs to partition your network into multiple subnets using a VLAN ID. When you enable virtual LAN identification, the NIC that is connected to the switch will never see packets tagged with VLAN IDs. Instead, all packets traveling from the NIC to the switch will be tagged with the access mode VLAN ID as they leave the switch port. All packets traveling from the switch port to the NIC will have their VLAN tags removed. You can use this if you are already logically segmenting your physical machines and also use it for your virtual ones.

Exercise 8.2 explains how to create an internal-only virtual switch.

EXERCISE 8.2

Creating an Internal Virtual Network

1. Click the Windows Key ➢ Administrative Tools ➢ Hyper-V Manager.

2. In Hyper-V Manager, in the Action pane, choose Virtual Switch Manager.

3. On the Virtual Switch page, select Private and click the Create Virtual Switch button.

4. On the New Virtual Switch page, enter Private Virtual Network in the Name field.

5. Click OK.

When you create the internal virtual switch, a network device is created in Network Connections, as shown in Figure 8.9.

This is also the case when you create an external virtual network because it will replace the physical network card of the host machine to give the parent partition a virtual network card that is also used in the child partitions.

Hyper-V binds the virtual network service to a physical network adapter only when an external virtual network is created. The benefit of this is that the performance is better if you do not use the external virtual network option. The downside, however, is that there will be a network disruption when you create or delete an external virtual network.

 Communication between the virtual machine and the local host computer is not configured automatically. Once you install a virtual machine, you need to make sure that the TCP/IP settings are in agreement with the settings you define in the virtual network card. Start with a ping from your host machine to the virtual machines to verify that communication is working.

FIGURE 8.9 Virtual Switch Manager

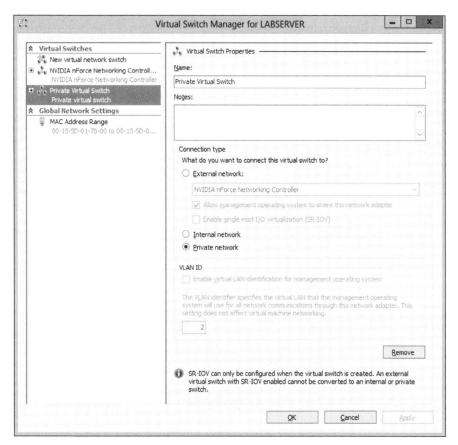

Managing Virtual Hard Disks

In addition to virtual networks, you need to manage virtual hard disks that you attach to your virtual machines. A virtual hard disk in Hyper-V, apart from a pass-through disk, is a VHD or VHDX file that basically simulates a hard drive on your virtual machine.

The following sections will first show you what types of virtual hard disks are available and then show you how to create them. You will also learn about what options are available to manage virtual hard disks.

Types of Hard Disks

Depending on how you want to use the disk, Hyper-V offers various types, as described in Table 8.4.

TABLE 8.4   Virtual hard disks in Hyper-V

Type of Disk	Description	When to Use It
Dynamically expanding	This disk starts with a small VHD file and expands it on demand once an installation takes place. It can grow to the maximum size you defined during creation. You can use this type of disk to clone a local hard drive during creation.	This option is effective when you don't know the exact space needed on the disk and when you want to preserve hard disk space on the host machine. Unfortunately, it is the slowest disk type.
Fixed size	The size of the VHD file is fixed to the size specified when the disk is created. This option is faster than a dynamically expanding disk. However, a fixed-size disk uses up the maximum defined space immediately. This type is ideal for cloning a local hard drive.	A fixed-size disk provides faster access than dynamically expanding or differencing disks, but it is slower than a physical disk.
Differencing	This type of disk is associated in a parent-child relationship with another disk. The differencing disk is the child, and the associated virtual disk is the parent. Differencing disks include only the differences to the parent disk. By using this type, you can save a lot of disk space in similar virtual machines. This option is suitable if you have multiple virtual machines with similar operating systems.	Differencing disks are most commonly found in test environments and should not be used in production environments.
Physical (or pass-through disk)	The virtual machine receives direct pass-through access to the physical disk for exclusive use. This type provides the highest performance of all disk types and thus should be used for production servers where performance is the top priority. The drive is not available for other guest systems.	This type is used in high-end datacenters to provide optimum performance for VMs. It's also used in failover cluster environments.

Creating Virtual Hard Disks

To help you gain practice in creating virtual hard disks, the following three exercises will teach you how to create a differencing hard disk, how to clone an existing disk by creating a new disk, and how to configure a physical or pass-through disk to your virtual machine. First, in Exercise 8.3, you will learn how to create a differencing virtual hard disk.

EXERCISE 8.3

Creating a Differencing Hard Disk

1. Open Hyper-V Manager.

2. In Hyper-V Manager, on the Action pane, choose New ➢ Hard Disk.

3. In the New Virtual Hard Disk Wizard, click Next on the Before You Begin page.

4. At the Choose Disk Format screen, choose VHDX and click Next. The size of your VHDs depends on which format you choose. If you're going to have a VHD larger than 2,040 GB, use VHDX. If your VHD is less than 2,040 GB, then you should use VHD.

5. On the Choose Disk Type page, select Fixed Size and click Next.

6. On the Specify Name And Location page, enter the new name of the child disk (for example, **newvirtualharddisk.vhd**). You can also modify the default location of the new VHD file if you want. Click Next to continue.

7. Next, on the Configure Disk page, you need to specify the size of the VHD file. Choose a size based on your hard disk and then click Next to continue. I used 60 GB as our test size.

8. On the Completing The New Virtual Hard Disk Wizard page, verify that all settings are correct and click Finish to create the hard disk.

The process to add a physical or pass-through disk to a virtual machine is quite different. For this, first you need to create the virtual machine, and then you open the virtual machine settings to configure the physical disk. If you want to add a physical disk to a virtual machine, the physical disk must be set as Offline in Disk Management, as shown in Figure 8.10.

To access Disk Management, click the Windows key, choose Administrative Tools ➢ Computer Management, expand Storage in the left pane, and click Disk Management.

 You cannot share a physical disk among multiple virtual machines or with the host system.

Physical or pass-through disks might not be that important if your use of virtualization is based on test environments, but they become crucial when you need to plan for highly available virtual datacenters. This is especially true if you consider using failover clusters to provide the Quick Migration feature, which is when you should consider matching one logical unit number (LUN) from your enterprise storage system or storage area network (SAN) as one physical disk. This provides you with the optimum performance you need in such an environment.

FIGURE 8.10   In Disk Management, you can set disks as Offline.

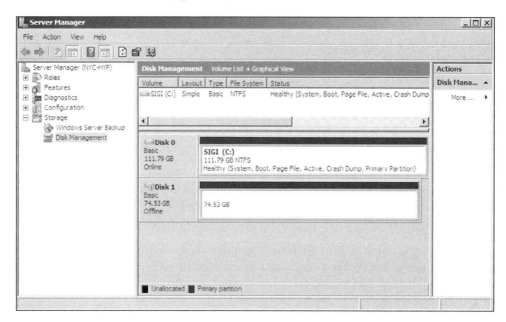

Managing Virtual Hard Disks

Hyper-V also provides two tools to manage virtual hard disks: Inspect Disk and Edit Disk. These tools are available on the Action pane in Hyper-V Manager.

Inspect Disk   This provides you with information about the virtual hard disk. It shows you not only the type of the disk but also information such as the maximum size for dynamically expanding disks and the parent VHD for differencing disks.

Edit Disk   This provides you with the Edit Virtual Hard Disk Wizard, which you can use to compact, convert, expand, merge, or reconnect hard disks. Figure 8.11 shows you the wizard's options when you select a dynamically expanding disk.

Table 8.5 provides you with an overview of what you can do with the wizard.

Generation 1 vs. Generation 2 VHDs

Previous versions of Hyper-V had some pretty major drawbacks. One big drawback was that Hyper-V could not boot a virtual machine from a virtual hard drive that was SCSI. Believe it or not, SCSI controllers were not even recognized by Hyper-V unless you installed the Integration Services component.

Another issue that the previous versions of Hyper-V had was the inability to copy files from the Hyper-V host to the virtual machines without the use of a network connection in the virtual machine. The older versions of Hyper-V, prior to Windows Server 2012, are now considered generation 1 versions. Why is it so important to know which generations of Hyper-V you should use or need to use?

FIGURE 8.11   The Edit Virtual Hard Disk Wizard

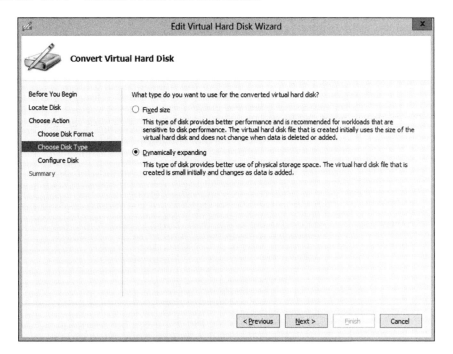

TABLE 8.5   Edit Disk overview

Action	Description
Compact	Reduces the size of a dynamically expanding or differencing disk by removing blank space from deleted files.
Convert	Converts a dynamically expanding disk to a fixed disk or vice versa.
Expand	Increases the storage capacity of a dynamically expanding disk or a fixed virtual hard disk.
Merge	Merges the changes from a differencing disk into either the parent disk or another disk (applies to differencing disks only!).
Reconnect	If a differencing disk no longer finds its referring parent disk, this option can reconnect the parent to the disk.

Hyper-V generations help determine what functionality and what virtual hardware you can use in your virtual machine. Windows Server 2016 Hyper-V now supports two different virtual machine generations: generation 1 and generation 2.

As already explained, previous versions of Hyper-V are considered generation 1, and this provides the same virtual hardware to the virtual machine as in previous versions of Hyper-V.

Generation 2 is included with Windows Server 2016, and it provides better functionality on the virtual machines including secure boot (which is enabled by default), the ability to boot from a SCSI virtual hard disk or boot from a SCSI virtual DVD, the ability to use a standard network adapter to PXE boot, and Unified Extensible Firmware Interface (UEFI) firmware support. Generation 2 now gives you the ability to support UEFI firmware instead of BIOS-based firmware. On a virtual machine that is Generation 2, you can configure Secure Boot, Enable TPM, and set security policies by clicking on the Security section of the virtual machines properties.

So when you create VHDs in Windows Server 2016, one of your choices will be the ability to create the VHDs as a generation 1 or generation 2 VHD. If you need the ability to have your VHDs run on older versions of Hyper-V, make them a generation 1 VHD. If they are going to run only on Windows Server 2016, make your VHDs generation 2 and take advantage of all the new features and functionality.

Configuring Virtual Machines

The following sections cover the topics of creating and managing virtual machines as well as how to back up and restore virtual machines using features such as Import and Export and Checkpoints. You'll also briefly look at Hyper-V's Live Migration feature.

Creating and Managing Virtual Machines

It is important to learn how to create a virtual machine, how to change its configuration, and how to delete it. You will take a look at the Virtual Machine Connection tool and install the Hyper-V Integration Components onto a virtual machine.

Virtual Machines

Virtual machines define the child partitions in which you run operating system instances. Each virtual machine is separate and can communicate with the others only by using a virtual network. You can assign hard drives, virtual networks, DVD drives, and other system components to it. A virtual machine is similar to an existing physical server, but it no longer runs on dedicated hardware—it shares the hardware of the host system with the other virtual machines that run on the host.

Exercise 8.4 shows you how to create a new virtual machine. Before completing this exercise, download an eval copy of Windows Server from Microsoft's website (www.microsoft.com/downloads). Make sure the file downloaded is an image file (.iso). You will use this image to install the operating system into the virtual machine.

EXERCISE 8.4

Creating a New Virtual Machine

1. Open Hyper-V Manager (see Figure 8.12).

FIGURE 8.12   Hyper-V Manager

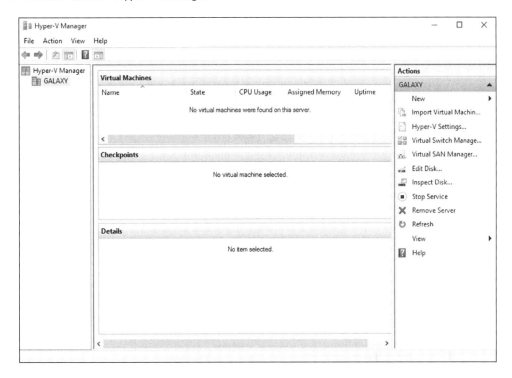

2. In Hyper-V Manager, on the Action pane, choose New ➢ Virtual Machine.

3. In the New Virtual Machine Wizard, click Next on the Before You Begin page.

4. On the Specify Name And Location page, give your virtual machine a name and change the default location of the virtual machine configuration files. Click Next to continue.

5. The Specify Generation screen is next. Choose Generation 2 (see Figure 8.13) and click Next.

6. On the Assign Memory page (see Figure 8.14), define how much of your host computer's memory you want to assign to this virtual machine. Remember that once your virtual machine uses up all of your physical memory, it will start swapping to disk, thus reducing the performance of all virtual machines. Click Next to continue.

FIGURE 8.13   Specify Generation Screen

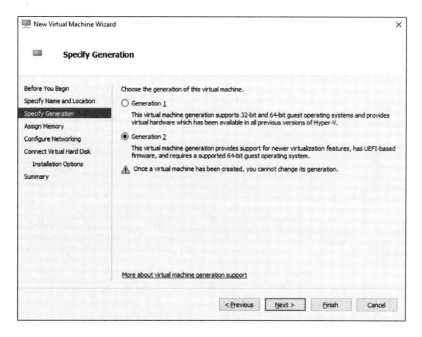

FIGURE 8.14   VM RAM

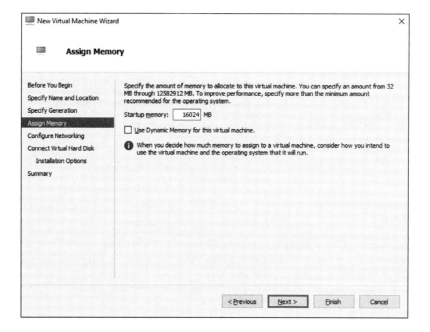

7. On the Configure Networking page, select the virtual network that you previously configured using Virtual Network Manager (see Figure 8.15). Click Next to continue.

FIGURE 8.15   Networking Page

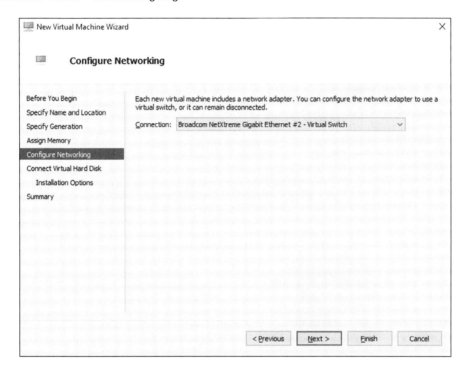

8. On the next page, you configure your virtual hard disk (see Figure 8.16). You can create a new virtual hard disk, select an existing disk, or choose to attach the hard disk later. Be aware that you can create only a dynamically expanding virtual disk on this page; you cannot create a differencing, physical, or fixed virtual hard disk there. However, if you created the virtual hard disk already, you can, of course, select it. Click Next to continue.

9. On the Installation Options page (see Figure 8.17), you can select how you want to install your operating system. You have the option to install an operating system later, install the operating system from a boot CD/DVD-ROM where you can select a physical device or an image file (.iso file), install an operating system from a floppy disk image (VFD file, or a virtual boot floppy disk), or install an operating system from a network-based installation server. The last option will install a legacy network adapter to your virtual machine so that you can boot from the network adapter. Select Install An Operating System from a bootable CD/DVD-ROM and choose Image File (.iso). Then click Next.

EXERCISE 8.4 *(continued)*

FIGURE 8.16 Virtual Hard Disk Page

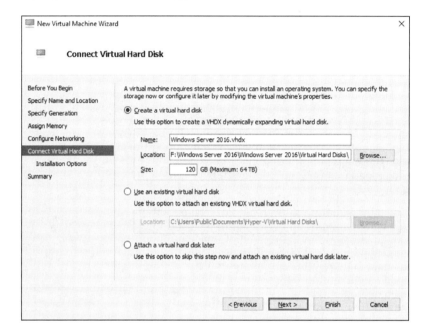

FIGURE 8.17 Installing OS screen

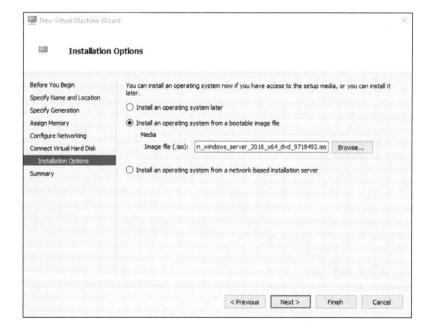

10. On the Completing The New Virtual Machine Wizard summary page, verify that all settings are correct. You also have the option to start the virtual machine immediately after creation (see Figure 8.18). Click Next to create the virtual machine.

FIGURE 8.18   Completing the New Virtual Machine Wizard screen

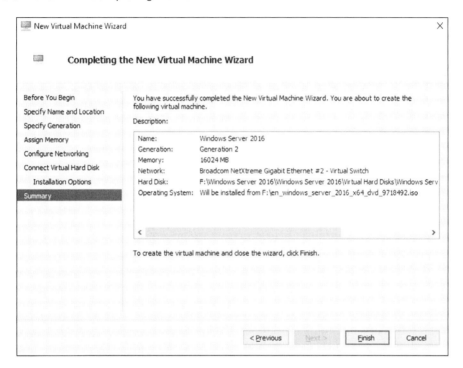

11. Repeat this process and create a few more virtual machines.

After completing Exercise 8.4, you will have a virtual machine available in Hyper-V Manager. Initially, the state of the virtual machine will be Off. Virtual machines can have the following states: Off, Starting, Running, Paused, and Saved. You can change the state of a virtual machine in the Virtual Machines pane by right-clicking the virtual machine's name, as shown in Figure 8.19, or by using the Virtual Machine Connection window.

Here is a list of some of the state options (when the VM is running) available for a virtual machine:

Start   Turn on the virtual machine. This is similar to pressing the power button when the machine is turned off. This option is available when your virtual machine is Off or in Saved state.

Turn Off   Turn off the virtual machine. This is similar to pressing the power-off button on the computer. This option is available when your virtual machine is in Running, Saved, or Paused state.

FIGURE 8.19   Options available when right-clicking a virtual machine

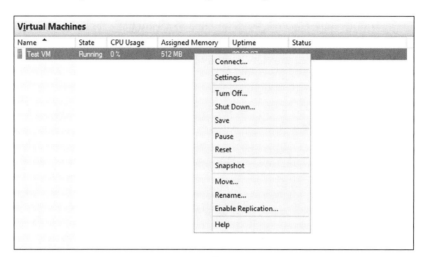

Shut Down   This option shuts down your operating system. You need to have the Hyper-V Integration Components installed on the operating system; otherwise, Hyper-V will not be able to shut down the system.

Save   The virtual machine is saved to disk in its current state. This option is available when your virtual machine is in Running or Paused state.

Pause   Pause the current virtual machine, but do not save the state to disk. You can use this option to release processor utilization quickly from this virtual machine to the host system.

Reset   Reset the virtual machine. This is like pressing the reset button on your computer. You will lose the current state and any unsaved data in the virtual machine. This option is available when your virtual machine is in Running or Paused state.

Resume   When your virtual machine is paused, you can resume it and bring it online again.

Changing Configuration on an Existing Virtual Machine

To change the configuration settings on an existing virtual machine, you right-click your virtual machine's name in the Virtual Machines pane in Hyper-V Manager and choose Settings. You can change settings such as memory allocation and hard drive configuration. All items that you can configure are described in the following list:

Add Hardware   Add devices to your virtual machine, namely, a SCSI controller, a network adapter, or a legacy network adapter. A legacy network adapter is required if you want to perform a network-based installation of an operating system.

BIOS   This is the replacement of the virtual machine's BIOS. Because you can no longer enter the BIOS during startup, you need to configure it with this setting. You can turn Num Lock on or off and change the basic startup order of the devices.

Memory   Change the amount of random access memory (RAM) allocated to the virtual machine.

Processor   Change the number of logical processors this virtual machine can use and define resource control to balance resources among virtual machines by using a relative weight.

IDE Controller   Add/change and remove devices from the IDE controller. You can have hard drives or DVD drives as devices. Every IDE controller can have up to two devices attached, and by default, you have two IDE controllers available.

Hard Drive   Select a controller to attach to this device as well as to specify the media to use with your virtual hard disk. The available options are Virtual Hard Disk File (with additional buttons labeled New, Edit, Inspect, and Browse) and Physical Hard Disk. You can also remove the device here.

DVD Drive   Select a controller to attach to this device and specify the media to use with your virtual CD/DVD drive. The available options are None, Image File (ISO Image), and Physical CD/DVD Drive Connected To The Host Computer. You also can remove the device here.

SCSI Controller   Configure all hard drives that are connected to the SCSI controller. You can add up to 63 hard drives to each SCSI controller, and you can have multiple SCSI controllers available.

Network Adapter   Specify the configuration of the network adapter or remove it. You can also configure the virtual network and MAC address for each adapter and enable virtual LAN identification. The network adapter section also allows you to control Bandwidth Management.

Bandwidth Management allows an administrator to specify how the network adapter will utilize network bandwidth. Administrators have the ability to set a minimum network bandwidth that a network adapter can use and a maximum bandwidth. This gives administrators greater control over how much bandwidth a virtual network adapter can use.

COM1 and COM2   Configure the virtual COM port to communicate with the physical computer through a named pipe. You have COM1 and COM2 available.

Diskette   Specify a virtual floppy disk file to use.

Name   Edit the name of the virtual machine and provide some notes about it.

Integration Services   Define what integration services are available to your virtual machine. Options are Operating System Shutdown, Time Synchronization, Data Exchange, Heartbeat, and Backup (Volume Snapshot).

Snapshot File Location   Define the default file location of your snapshot files.

Smart Paging File Location   This area allows you to set up a paging file for your virtual machine. Windows Server 2016 has a Hyper-V feature called Smart Paging. If you have a virtual machine that has a smaller amount of memory than what it needs for startup memory, when the virtual machine gets restarted, Hyper-V then needs additional memory to restart the virtual machine. Smart Paging is used to bridge the memory gap between minimum memory and startup memory. This allows your virtual machines to restart properly.

Automatic Start   Define what this virtual machine will do when the physical computer starts. Options are Nothing, Automatically Start If The Service Was Running, and Always Start This Virtual Machine. You also can define a start delay here.

Automatic Stop   Define what this virtual machine will do when the physical computer shuts down. Options are Save State, Turn Off, and Shut Down.

Please be aware that only some settings can be changed when the virtual machine's state is Running. It is best practice to shut down the virtual machine before you modify any setting.

Deleting Virtual Machines

You can also delete virtual machines using Hyper-V Manager. This deletes all of the configuration files, as shown in Figure 8.20.

FIGURE 8.20   Delete Virtual Machine warning window

Make sure you manually delete any virtual disks that were part of the virtual machines to free up disk space. Virtual disks are *not* deleted when you delete a virtual machine.

Virtual Machine Connection

Hyper-V comes with Virtual Machine Connection to connect to virtual machines that run on a local or remote server.

You can use it to log into the virtual machine and use your computer's mouse and keyboard to interact with the virtual machine. You can open Virtual Machine Connection in Hyper-V Manager by double-clicking a virtual machine or by right-clicking a virtual machine and selecting Connect. If your virtual machine is turned off, you might see a window similar to the one in Figure 8.21.

Virtual Machine Connection not only provides you with functionality similar to that of Hyper-V Manager, such as being able to change the state of a virtual machine, but it also provides you with additional features that are especially useful when you want to work with a virtual machine.

File Access Settings or Exit Virtual Machine Connection   Change the state of a virtual machine and create or revert a snapshot. Additionally, you have the options to send Ctrl+Alt+Delete to your virtual machine and Insert Integration Services Setup Disk.

FIGURE 8.21   Virtual Machine Connection window when the machine is turned off

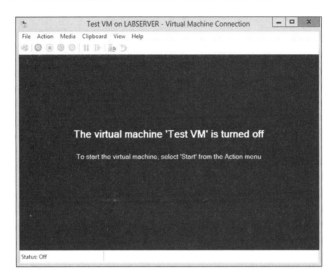

Context-Sensitive Buttons Provide Quick Access to Key Features   These buttons are available under the menu bar to provide you with fast access to the most important features, as you can see in Figure 8.22. It shows the connection of a running VM, but the VM has not had an operating system installed yet, so the figure shows the Windows Server 2016 Setup screen.

FIGURE 8.22   Virtual Machine Connection window showing a running Windows Server 2016 virtual machine

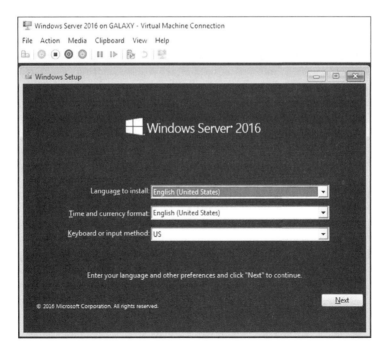

NIC Teaming

NIC Teaming, also known as load balancing and failover (LBFO), gives an administrator the ability to allow multiple network adapters on a system to be placed into a team. Independent hardware vendors (IHVs) have required NIC Teaming, but until Windows Server 2012, NIC Teaming was *not* part of the Windows Server operating system.

To be able to use NIC Teaming, the computer system must have at least one Ethernet adapter. If you want to provide fault protection, an administrator must have a minimum of two Ethernet adapters. One advantage of Windows Server 2016 is that an administrator can set up 32 network adapters in a NIC team.

NIC Teaming is a common practice when setting up virtualization. This is one way that you can have load balancing with Hyper-V.

NIC Teaming gives an administrator the ability to allow a virtual machine to use virtual network adapters in Hyper-V. The advantage of using NIC Teaming in Hyper-V is that the administrator can use NIC Teaming to connect to more than one Hyper-V switch. This allows Hyper-V still to have connectivity even if the network adapter under the Hyper-V switch gets disconnected.

An administrator can configure NIC Teaming in either Server Manager or PowerShell. NIC teaming can be configured in different configuration models including Switch Independent or Switch Dependent. Switch Independent means that each NIC adapter is connected into a different switch. Switch Dependent means that all NIC adapters are connected into the same switch. If you use Switch Independent NIC Teaming, then you must connect your NICs to different switches, but both switches must be on the same subnet.

Remote Direct Memory Access

When most of us think of Hyper-V, we think of a group of virtual machines sharing access to a systems resource. With Windows Server 2016, Hyper-V includes Remote Direct Memory Access (RDMA).

RDMA allows one computer to directly access memory from the memory of another computer without the need of interfacing with either one's operating system. This gives systems the ability to have high throughput and low-latency networking. This is very useful when it comes to clustering systems (including Hyper-V).

Windows Server 2012 R2 RDMA services couldn't be bound to a Hyper-V Virtual Switch and because of this, Remote Direct Memory Access and Hyper-V had to be on the same computer as the network adapters. Because of this, there was a need for a higher number of physical network adapters that were required to be installed on the Hyper-V host.

Because of the improvements of RDMA on Windows Server 2016, administrators can use less network adapters while using RDMA.

Switch Embedded Teaming

Earlier we discussed NIC Teaming but we also have the ability to do Switch Embedded Teaming (SET). SET can be an alternative to using NIC Teaming in environments that include Hyper-V and the Software Defined Networking (SDN) stack in Windows Server 2016. SET is available in all versions of Windows Server 2016 that include Hyper-V and SDN stack.

SET does use some of the functionality of NIC Teaming into the Hyper-V Virtual Switch but SET allows an administrator to combine a group of physical adapters (minimum of 1 adapter and a maximum of 8 adapters) into software based virtual adapters.

By using virtual adapters, you get better performance and greater fault tolerance in the event of a network adapter going bad. For SET to be enabled, all of the physical network adapters must be installed on the same physical Hyper-V host.

One of the requirements of SET is that all network adapters that are members of the SET group be identical adapters. This means that they need to be the same adapter types from the same manufacturers.

One main difference between NIC Teaming and Set is that SET only supports Switch Independent mode setups. Again this means that the NIC adapters are connected to different switches.

Administrators need to create a SET team at the same time that they create the Hyper-V Virtual Switch. Administrators can do this by using the Windows PowerShell command New-VMSwitch.

At the time an administrator creates a Hyper-V Virtual Switch, the administrator needs to include the EnableEmbeddedTeaming parameter in their command syntax. The following example shows a Hyper-V switch named StormSwitch.

```
New-VMSwitch -Name StormSwitch -NetAdapterName "NIC 1","NIC 2"
-EnableEmbeddedTeaming $true
```

Administrators also have the ability to remove a SET team by using the following PowerShell command. This example removes a Virtual Switch named StormSwitch.

```
Remove-VMSwitch "StormSwitch
```

Storage Quality of Service

Windows Server 2016 Hyper-V includes a feature called *Storage Quality of Service (QoS)*. Storage QoS allows a Hyper-V administrator to manage how virtual machines access storage throughput for virtual hard disks.

Storage QoS gives an administrator the ability to guarantee that the storage throughput of a single VHD cannot adversely affect the performance of another VHD on the same host. It does this by giving administrators the ability to specify the maximum and minimum I/O loads based on I/O operations per second (IOPS) for each virtual disk in your virtual machines.

To configure Storage QoS, you would set the maximum IOPS values (or limits) and set the minimum values (or reserves) on virtual hard disks for virtual machines.

 If you are using shared virtual hard disks, Storage QoS will not be available.

Installing Hyper-V Integration Components

Hyper-V *Integration Components*, also called *Integration Services*, are required to make your guest operating system hypervisor-aware. Similar to the VM Additions that were part of Microsoft Virtual Server 2005, these components improve the performance of the guest operating system once they are installed. From an architectural perspective, virtual devices are redirected directly via the VMBus; thus, quicker access to resources and devices is provided.

If you do not install the Hyper-V Integration Components, the guest operating system uses emulation to communicate with the host's devices, which of course makes the guest operating system slower.

Exercise 8.5 shows you how to install Hyper-V Integration Components on one of your virtual machines running Windows Server 2016.

EXERCISE 8.5

Installing Hyper-V Integration Components

1. Open Hyper-V Manager.

2. In Hyper-V Manager, in the Virtual Machines pane, right-click the virtual machine on which you want to install Hyper-V Integration Components and click Start.

3. Right-click the virtual machine again and click Connect. Meanwhile, your virtual machine should already be booting.

4. If you need to log into the operating system of your virtual machine, you should do so.

5. Once the Windows Desktop appears, you need to select Insert Integration Services Setup Disk from the Actions menu of your Virtual Machine Connection window.

6. Once the Hyper-V Integration Components are installed, you are asked to perform a reboot.

After the reboot, Hyper-V Integration Components are installed on your operating system, and you will be able to use them.

Linux and FreeBSD Image Deployments

One of the features of Windows 2016 is the ability for Hyper-V to support Linux and FreeBSD virtual machines. Hyper-V now can support these new virtual machines because Hyper-V has the ability to emulate Linux and FreeBSD devices. Because Hyper-V now has the ability to emulate these two devices, no additional software needs to be installed on Hyper-V.

Unfortunately, because Hyper-V has to emulate these devices, you lose some of the Hyper-V functionality like high performance and full management of the virtual machines. So it's a tradeoff. You get to run Linux and FreeBSD type Hyper-V virtual machines but you lose some of the benefits of Hyper-V.

But wait; there is a way to get your Hyper-V functionality back. This issue can be resolved as long as you install Hyper-V on machines that can support Linux and FreeBSD operating systems. The drivers that are needed on Hyper-V are called Linux Integration Services (LIS) and FreeBSD Integrated Services (FIS). By putting these drivers on a device that can handle Linux and FreeBSD, you can then have Hyper-V with all of the features Microsoft offers.

To get these drivers and make Hyper-V work will all of its functionality, you must make sure that you install a newer release of Linux that includes LIS. To get the most out of FreeBSD you must get a version after 10.0. For FreeBSD versions that are older than 10.0, Microsoft offers ports that work with BIS drivers that need to be installed. Hyper-V will work with Linux and FreeBSD without the need of any additional drivers or equipment. By having drivers and equipment that supports Linux and FreeBSD, you just get all of the Hyper-V features that your organization may need.

In Exercise 8.6, I will show you how to install Linux into a virtual machine. I will then walk you through a full installation of a Linux Server. Before you complete this lab, you must download a copy of Linux. For this exercise, I downloaded a free copy of Linux Ubuntu as an image file (.iso). If you choose a different version of Linux, the installation screens during the exercise may be different.

EXERCISE 8.6

Creating a Linux Virtual Machine

1. Open Hyper-V Manager.

2. In the right hand window under Actions, click New ➤ Virtual Machine (see Figure 8.23).

3. At the Before you Begin screen, just choose Next.

4. At the Specify Name and Location screen, Enter in the name of the Linux virtual machine and the location you would like to store the virtual machine files. Then click Next.

5. At the Generation screen, choose Generation 2 and click Next.

6. At the Assign Memory screen, enter in the amount of memory you want to allocate to this virtual machine. I am using 12 GB (12000 MB). Click Next.

7. Choose which network connection you want to use and click Next.

8. At the Connect Virtual Hard Disk screen, choose Create a virtual hard disk. Set the location of where you want the files to reside and also how much space you want to use (I chose 127 GB). Click Next.

9. At the Installation Options screen, choose Install an Operating system from a bootable image file and point to your Linux .iso download. Click Next.

10. At the Completing the New Virtual Machine Wizard screen, make sure all of the settings are correct and choose Finish.

FIGURE 8.23 New Virtual Machine

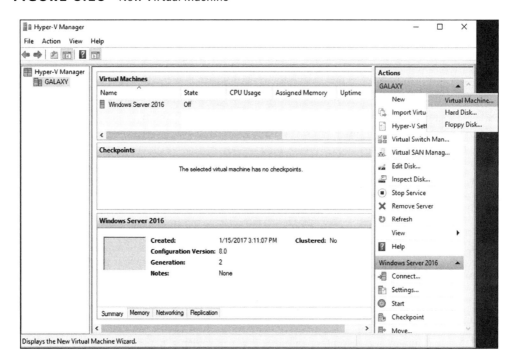

11. After the virtual machine was created, click on the virtual machine and on the right side under Linux, click Start.

12. When the Linux install starts, click your Language.

13. At the Ubuntu menu, choose Install Ubuntu Server.

14. Again, you will need to choose your language for the install.

15. Choose your country.

16. On the detect keyboard layout, choose No. Choose your keyboard (ours is US Normal). The installation will Continue.

17. Next you will choose a hostname. I am keeping the default of Ubuntu. Click Continue.

18. Enter your user account (full name) and click Continue.

19. Enter your username. First name is fine and click Continue.

20. Type in your password and click Continue. Do not choose to show your password in clear text. You will then be asked to re-enter your password and click Continue.

21. When it asks you to encrypt your home directory, choose No.

22. The install will try to figure out your time zone. If it picks correctly, chose Yes. If it doesn't, choose No and enter your time zone.

23. The next screen will ask you about setting up a Partition disk. I am going to allow Linux to configure the disk (Guided) and I will allow it to use the entire drive with a Logical Volume Manager (LVM). So I am choosing Guided - use entire disk and set up LVM.

24. It will then ask about partition type. I am choosing SCSI3.

25. The next screen will verify your choices for partitioning. Choose Yes.

26. It will then verify your disk size and then if you want to continue. Choose the disk size and then choose Yes to continue.

27. The next screen will ask you if you use a Proxy server for Internet access. If you use a Proxy, put it in and if you don't, just click Continue.

28. You will be asked about updates for Linux. Choose how you want to do your updates. Since this is a test virtual machine, I am choosing No automatic updates.

29. At the Software selection screen, choose what software you want installed during this process. I chose DNS, Samba File Server, and standard system utilities. Click Continue.

30. At the GRUB boot screen, click Yes to install the GRUB boot loader. This is OK since we have no other operating system on this virtual machine.

31. Once the installation is complete, choose Continue. At this point, Linux will restart and ask you for your login and password. After you enter them, you will be at a Linux prompt.

32. Type shutdown at the prompt to shut down the virtual machine.

Now that we have installed Linux (or FreeBSD), the next step is to help improve the Hyper-V performance. As I stated earlier, this issue will be resolved as long as we install the drivers that are needed on Hyper-V called Linux Integration Services (LIS) and FreeBSD Integrated Services (FIS). By putting these drivers on a device that can handle Linux and FreeBSD, you can then have Hyper-V with all of the features Microsoft offers.

Depending on what version of Linux or FreeBSD that you installed, you will need to download some additional updates to get the best performance out of Hyper-V. The following Microsoft website has a list of links for the different versions of Linux and FreeBSD updates. https://technet.microsoft.com/windows-server-docs/compute/hyper-v/supported-linux-and-freebsd-virtual-machines-for-hyper-v-on-windows ?f=255&MSPPError=-2147217396.

In Exercise 8.7, I will show you how to install the additional updates needed for the Linux Ubuntu version (16.10) that I installed in Exercise 8.6.

EXERCISE 8.7

Updating Linux Ubuntu 16.10

1. Open Hyper-V Manager.

2. Start the Linux virtual machine by clicking on the Linux virtual machine and clicking Start on the right hand menu.

3. At the Ubuntu login, enter the login and password that you created in Exercise 8.6.

4. Since we are using Ubuntu 16.10, we need to install the latest virtual kernel to have up-to-date Hyper-V capabilities. To install the virtual HWE kernel, run the following commands as root (or sudo):

    ```
    sudo apt-get update
    ```

5. You will be asked for your password. Enter your password.

6. Next type in the following command;

    ```
    sudo apt-get install linux-image-virtual
    ```

7. You will be asked to confirm your choice by typing Y and hit enter.

8. Type in the following command;

    ```
    sudo apt-get install linux-tools-virtual linux-cloud-tools-virtual
    ```

9. You will be asked to confirm your choice by typing Y and hit enter.

10. After everything is installed, you are ready to go. You can clear the screen by typing Clear and hit enter. To shut down the system, type shutdown.

Finally, if you want to setup the Linux or FreeBSD virtual machines to use the advantages of secure boot, you would need to run the following PowerShell command on the Hyper-V server;

```
Set-VMFirmware -VMName "VMname" -EnableSecureBoot Off
```

PowerShell Commands

One of the things that Microsoft has stated is that the exams are going to be more PowerShell intensive. So, I wanted to add a PowerShell section showing the different PowerShell commands that you can use for Hyper-V. This table has been taken directly from Microsoft's websites. Table 8.6 explains just some of the PowerShell commands that you can use with Hyper-V.

This table shows you just some of the PowerShell commands for Hyper-V. To see a more comprehensive list, please visit Microsoft's website at https://technet.microsoft.com/en-us/library/hh848559.aspx.

TABLE 8.6   Hyper-V PowerShell commands

Command	Explanation
Add-VMDvdDrive	Adds a DVD drive to a virtual machine
Add-VMHardDiskDrive	Adds a hard disk drive to a virtual machine
Add-VMMigrationNetwork	Adds a network for virtual machine migration on one or more virtual machine hosts
Add-VMNetworkAdapter	Adds a virtual network adapter to a virtual machine
Add-VMSwitch	Adds a virtual switch to an Ethernet resource pool
Checkpoint-VM	Creates a checkpoint of a virtual machine
Convert-VHD	Converts the format, version type, and block size of a virtual hard disk file
Copy-VMFile	Copies a file to a virtual machine
Debug-VM	Debugs a virtual machine
Disable-VMConsoleSupport	Disables keyboard, video, and mouse for virtual machines
Disable-VMMigration	Disables migration on one or more virtual machine hosts
Dismount-VHD	Dismounts a virtual hard disk
Enable-VMConsoleSupport	Enables keyboard, video, and mouse for virtual machines
Enable-VMMigration	Enables migration on one or more virtual machine hosts
Enable-VMReplication	Enables replication of a virtual machine
Enable-VMResourceMetering	Collects resource utilization data for a virtual machine or resource pool
Export-VM	Exports a virtual machine to disk
Export-VMSnapshot	Exports a virtual machine checkpoint to disk

TABLE 8.6   Hyper-V PowerShell commands *(continued)*

Command	Explanation
Get-VHD	Gets the virtual hard disk object associated with a virtual hard disk
Get-VHDSet	Gets information about a VHD set
Get-VHDSnapshot	Gets information about a checkpoint in a VHD set
Get-VM	Gets the virtual machines from one or more Hyper-V hosts
Get-VMDvdDrive	Gets the DVD drives attached to a virtual machine or snapshot
Get-VMHardDiskDrive	Gets the virtual hard disk drives attached to one or more virtual machines
Get-VMMemory	Gets the memory of a virtual machine or snapshot
Get-VMNetworkAdapter	Gets the virtual network adapters of a virtual machine, snapshot, management operating system or of a virtual machine and management operating system
Get-VMProcessor	Gets the processor of a virtual machine or snapshot
Get-VMReplication	Gets the replication settings for a virtual machine
Get-VMSwitch	Gets virtual switches from one or more virtual Hyper-V hosts
Merge-VHD	Merges virtual hard disks
Mount-VHD	Mounts one or more virtual hard disks
Move-VM	Moves a virtual machine to a new Hyper-V host
New-VHD	Creates one or more new virtual hard disks
New-VM	Creates a new virtual machine
New-VMGroup	Creates a virtual machine group
New-VMSwitch	Creates a new virtual switch on one or more virtual machine hosts
Remove-VHDSnapshot	Removes a snapshot from a VHD set file
Remove-VM	Deletes a virtual machine

Command	Explanation
Remove-VMHardDiskDrive	Deletes one or more virtual hard disks (VHDs) from a virtual machine (VM)
Remove-VMNetworkAdapter	Removes one or more virtual network adapters from a virtual machine
Remove-VMReplication	Removes the replication relationship of a virtual machine
Remove-VMSan	Removes a virtual storage area network (SAN) from a Hyper-V host
Remove-VMSwitch	Deletes a virtual switch
Rename-VM	Renames a virtual machine
Rename-VMGroup	Renames virtual machine groups
Resize-VHD	Resizes a virtual hard disk
Restart-VM	Restarts a virtual machine
Save-VM	Saves a virtual machine
Set-VHD	Sets properties associated with a virtual hard disk
Set-VM	Configures a virtual machine
Set-VMBios	Configures the BIOS of a Generation 1 virtual machine
Set-VMMemory	Configures the memory of a virtual machine
Set-VMNetworkAdapter	Configures features of the virtual network adapter in a virtual machine or the management operating system
Set-VMProcessor	Configures one or more processors of a virtual machine
Set-VMReplicationServer	Configures a host as a Replica server
Set-VMSan	Configures a virtual storage area network (SAN) on one or more Hyper-V hosts
Set-VMSwitch	Configures a virtual switch
Stop-VM	Shuts down, turns off, or saves a virtual machine
Suspend-VM	Suspends, or pauses, a virtual machine

Summary

In this chapter, I started the discussion with Software Defined Networking (SDN). I talked about Software Load Balancing (SLB), Network Controllers, NAT, and RAS Gateways. I explained how SDNs use virtualization to design and create the network.

I then showed you how to configure virtual machines using the Hyper-V environment and how to create your own virtual datacenter on top of your Hyper-V machines. I showed you how to create and manage virtual machines, how to use Virtual Machine Connection to control a virtual machine remotely, and how to install Hyper-V Integration Components. You also learned how to export and import virtual machines as well as how to do snapshots of your virtual machine.

If you have never worked with virtualization software before, the information in this chapter may have been completely new to you. You should now be well prepared to try Hyper-V in your own environment.

Exam Essentials

Understand Software Defined Networking. Know what Software Defined Networking (SDN) is and the different components needed to setup SDN. Some of these components include Software Load Balancing, Network Controllers, NAT, and RAS Gateways.

Know Hyper-V's requirements and how to install it. Know the hardware and software requirements as well as how to install Hyper-V. Hyper-V requires an x64-based processor and Data Execution Protection (DEP). Hardware-assisted virtualization must be enabled—don't forget this! Also remember that you can install Hyper-V two ways: using Server Manager or using the command line in Server Core.

Understand virtual networks and virtual hard disks. Virtual networks and hard disks are the two most tested topics. You definitely should know the types of virtual networks available (that is, external, internal only, and private virtual network) as well as all types of virtual hard disks (namely, dynamically expanding, fixed size, differential, and physical or pass-through). You should be able to apply the correct one when needed. Don't forget the Edit Virtual Hard Disk Wizard, which is also a good source for questions in the exam.

Know how to create and manage virtual machines. You should be able to explain how to create a virtual machine, what options are available to install an operating system in a virtual machine, and how to install the Hyper-V Integration Components on a virtual machine. Don't forget about the virtual machine states and the virtual machine settings!

Review Questions

1. You are the network administrator for a large organization that has decided to start using Network Controllers. What PowerShell command allows you to create a new Network Controller?

    A. `New-NetworkController`

    B. `New-NetworkControllerServerObject`

    C. `New-NetworkControllerObject`

    D. `New-NetworkControllerNodeObject`

2. You are an application developer and network admin. You create an application named App1. App1 is going to be distributed to multiple Hyper-V virtual machines in a multitenant environment for both virtual and non-virtual networks. What should you include in the environment if you need to ensure that the traffic is distributed evenly among the virtual machines that host App1?

    A. Network Controller and Windows Server Network Load Balancing (NLB) nodes.

    B. A RAS Gateway and Windows Server Software Load Balancing (SLB) nodes.

    C. A RAS Gateway and Windows Server Network Load Balancing (NLB) nodes.

    D. Network Controller and Windows Server Software Load Balancing (SLB) nodes.

3. You are the Network Administrator for your company. You have an Active Directory domain that contains multiple Hyper-V hosts that run Windows Server 2016. You plan to deploy network virtualization and to centrally manage Datacenter Firewall policies. What component must be installed for the planned deployment?

    A. Data Center Bridging feature.

    B. Network Controller server role.

    C. Routing role service.

    D. Canary Network Diagnostics feature.

4. You want to make sure the hard disk space for your virtual machines is occupied only when needed. What type of virtual hard disk would you recommend?

    A. Dynamically expanding disk

    B. Fixed-size disk

    C. Differencing disk

    D. Physical or pass-through disk

5. How do you add a physical disk to a virtual machine?

    A. Use the Virtual Hard Disk Wizard.

    B. Use the Edit Virtual Hard Disk Wizard.

    C. Use the virtual machine's settings.

    D. Use the New Virtual Machine Wizard.

6. Rich bought a new server with an Itanium IA-64 processor, 4 GB RAM, and a SAN that provides 1 TB hard disk space. After installing Windows Server 2016 for Itanium-based systems, he wants to install Hyper-V on this server. Can Hyper-V be installed on this system?

A. Yes

B. No

7. What are the minimum CPU requirements for running Hyper-V on a machine? (Choose all that apply.)

A. An x64-based processor (Intel or AMD).

B. Hardware Data Execution Protection (DEP) must be enabled.

C. Hardware-assisted virtualization must be enabled.

D. The processor must at least have a dual core.

8. What is the command to install Hyper-V on a Windows Server 2016 machine that was installed in Server Core?

A. `start /w ocsetup Hyper-V`

B. `start /w ocsetup microsoft-hyper-v`

C. `start /w ocsetup Microsoft-Hyper-V`

D. `start /w ocsetup hyper-v`

9. You are the network administrator for your company. You want to deploy the RAS Gateway as an edge VPN server, an edge DirectAccess server, or both simultaneously. The RAS Gateway will provide remote employees with connectivity to your network by using either VPN or DirectAccess connections. What RAS Gateway Mode type will you be setting up?

A. Multitenant mode

B. Single tenant mode

C. Dual tenant mode

D. Lone tenant mode

10. What statement is correct for an external virtual network?

A. The virtual machines can communicate with each other and with the host machine.

B. The virtual machines can communicate with each other only.

C. The virtual machines can communicate with each other, with the host machine, and with an external network.

D. The virtual machines cannot communicate with each other.

Appendix

Answers to the Review Questions

Chapter 1: Configuring TCP/IP

1. D. To calculate the network mask, you need to figure out which power number (2^x) is greater than or equal to the number you need. Since we are looking for 1000, $2^{10} = 1024$. You then add the power (10) to the current network mask (53 + 10 = 63).

2. A. When you look at an IPv6 address, the first sections tell you the IPv6 address space prefix. Fd00:: /8 is the unique local unicast prefix, and this allows the server to communicate with all local machines within your intranet.

3. C. The unique local address can be FC00 or FD00, and it is used like the private address space of IPv4. Unique local addresses are not expected to be routable on the global Internet, but they are used for private routing within an organization.

4. A. A Class B address with a default subnet mask of 255.255.0.0 will support up to 65,534 hosts. To increase the number of networks that this network will support, you need to subnet the network by borrowing bits from the host portion of the address. The subnet mask 255.255.252.0 uses 6 bits from the host's area, and it will support 64 subnets while leaving enough bits to support 1,022 hosts per subnet. The subnet mask 255.255.248.0 uses 5 bits from the hosts and will support 32 subnetworks while leaving enough bits to support 2,046 hosts per subnet. 255.255.252.0 is the better answer because it leaves quite a bit of room for further growth in the number of networks while still leaving room for more than 1,000 hosts per subnet, which is a fairly large number of devices on one subnet. The subnet mask 255.255.254.0 uses 7 bits from the host's area and will support 126 networks, but it will leave only enough bits to support 500 hosts per subnet. The subnet mask 255.255.240.0 uses 4 bits from the hosts and will support only 16 subnetworks, even though it will leave enough bits to support more than 4,000 hosts per subnet.

5. A. The network mask applied to an address determines which portion of that address reflects the number of hosts available to that network. The balance with subnetting is always between the number of hosts and individual subnetworks that can be uniquely represented within one encompassing address. The number of hosts and networks that are made available depends on the number of bits that can be used to represent them. This scenario requires more than 35 networks and fewer than 1,000 workstations on each network. If you convert the subnet masks as described in the chapter, you will see that the mask in option A allows for 64 networks and more than 1,000 hosts. All of the other options are deficient in either the number of networks or the number of hosts that they represent.

6. A. The subnet mask 255.255.255.192 borrows 2 bits from the hosts, which allows you to build four separate networks that you can route through the Windows server. This will allow you to have 62 hosts on each segment. A mask of 255.255.255.128 would have been even better, with two subnets of 126 hosts each, but that wasn't an option and this solution gives you room for growth in the number of subnets. The subnet mask 255.255.255.224 borrows 3 bits from the hosts. This allows you to create 8 networks, which you don't need, and it leaves only enough bits for 30 hosts. The subnet mask 255.255.255.252 borrows 6 bits from the hosts. This allows you to create 64 networks, which you don't need, and it leaves only enough bits for 2 hosts. The subnet mask 255.255.255.240 borrows 4 bits from the hosts. This allows you to create 16 networks, which you don't need, and it leaves only enough bits for 14 hosts per subnet.

7. B, C, D. When you add up the locations that currently need to be given a network address, the total is 3,150, and the maximum number of hosts at any one of these locations is fewer than 1,000. The subnet masks need to support those requirements. Assuming that you choose the Class A private address space 10.0.0.0/8, the subnet masks given in options B, C, and D will provide the address space to support the outlined requirements. The subnet mask 255.255.240.0 supports 4,096 subnets and more than 4,000 hosts. The subnet mask 255.255.248.0 supports 8,192 subnets and 2,046 hosts. The subnet mask 255.255.252.0 supports more than 16,000 subnets and more than 1,000 hosts. Although each of these subnet masks will work, at the rate that this company is growing, 255.255.252.0 is probably the best mask to prepare for the future. It's unlikely that there will ever be more than 1,000 hosts on any given network. In fact, that number would probably cause performance problems on that subnet. Therefore, it's better to have more subnets available to deploy as the company grows. The subnet mask 255.255.224.0 supports 2,048 subnets—an insufficient number to cover the locations. The subnet mask 255.255.254.0 supports 32,768 subnets, but only 500 hosts per subnet, which are not enough hosts to cover all of the locations.

8. C. The CIDR /27 tells you that 27 1s are turned on in the subnet mask. Twenty-seven 1s equals 11111111.11111111.11111111.11100000. This would then equal 255.255.255.224.

The network address 192.168.11.192 with a subnet mask of 255.255.255.224 is perfect for Subnet A because it supports up to 30 hosts. The network address 192.168.11.128 with a subnet mask of 255.255.255.192 is perfect for Subnet B because it supports up to 62 hosts. The network address 192.168.11.0 with a subnet mask of 255.255.255.128 is perfect for Subnet C because it supports up to 126 hosts.

9. C. You need to configure a subnet mask that can accommodate 3,500 clients. The way to figure it out is to use the formula of $2^x-2=$Mask Number. So 3,500 clients means it is $2^{12}-2=4094$. 4094 (power of 12) is the first Power number that is greater than 3,500. So since it is 2^{12}, that means that our subnet mask has 12 zeros. So it looks like the following; 11111111.11111111.11110000.00000000. This translates into 255.255.240.0.

10. B, D. If the first word of an IPv6 address is FE80 (actually the first 10 bits of the first word yields 1111 1110 10 or FE80:: /10), then the address is a link-local IPv6 address. If it's in EUI-64 format, then the MAC address is also available (unless it's randomly generated). The middle FF:FE is the filler and indicator of the EUI-64 space, with the MAC address being 00:03:FF:11:02:CD. Remember also the 00 of the MAC becomes 02 in the link-local IPv6 address, flipping a bit to call it local.

Chapter 2: Configuring DNS

1. B. Because of the .(root) zone, users will not be able to access the Internet. The DNS forwarding option and DNS root hints will not be configurable. If you want your users to access the Internet, you must remove the .(root) zone.

2. C. Active Directory Integrated zones store their records in Active Directory. Because this company only has one Active Directory forest, it's the same Active Directory that both DNS servers are using. This allows ServerA to see all of the records of ServerB and ServerB to see all the records of ServerA.

3. D. The Secure Only option is for DNS servers that have an Active Directory Integrated zone. When a computer tries to register with DNS dynamically, the DNS server checks Active Directory to verify that the computer has an Active Directory account. If the computer that is trying to register has an account, DNS adds the host record. If the computer trying to register does not have an account, the record gets tossed away and the database is not updated.

4. A. If you need to complete a zone transfer from Microsoft DNS to a BIND (Unix) DNS server, you need to enable BIND secondaries on the Microsoft DNS server.

5. B. Conditional forwarding allows you to send a DNS query to different DNS servers based on the request. Conditional forwarding lets a DNS server on a network forward DNS queries according to the DNS domain name in the query.

6. B. On a Windows Server 2016 DNS machine, debug logging is disabled by default. When it is enabled, you have the ability to log DNS server activity, including inbound and outbound queries, packet type, packet content, and transport protocols.

7. D. Active Directory Integrated zones give you many benefits over using primary and secondary zones, including less network traffic, secure dynamic updates, encryption, and reliability in the event of a DNS server going down. The Secure Only option is for dynamic updates to a DNS database.

8. A. Windows Server 2016 DNS supports two features called DNS Aging and DNS Scavenging. These features are used to clean up and remove stale resource records. DNS zone or DNS server aging and scavenging flags old resource records that have not been updated in a certain amount of time (determined by the scavenging interval). These stale records will be scavenged at the next cleanup interval.

9. C. The dnscmd /zoneexport command creates a file using the zone resource records. This file can then be given to the Compliance department as a copy.

10. D. Stub zones are very useful for slow WAN connections. These zones store only three types of resource records: NS records, glue host (A) records, and SOA records. These three records are used to locate authoritative DNS servers.

Chapter 3: Configuring DHCP

1. C. Out of the possible answers provided, the only DHCP configuration option that would be both fault tolerant and redundant is DHCP failover.

2. C. Admins can use the Set-DhcpServerv4Scope command to configure the settings of an existing IPv4 scope.

3. D. Microsoft recommends the 80/20 rule for redundancy of DHCP services in a network. Implementing the 80/20 rule calls for one DHCP server to make approximately 80 percent of the addresses for a given subnet available through DHCP while another server makes the remaining 20 percent of the addresses available.

4. A. DHCP can become a single point of failure within a network if there is only one DHCP server. If that server becomes unavailable, clients will not be able to obtain new leases or renew existing leases. For this reason, it is recommended that you have more than one DHCP server in the network. However, more than one DHCP server can create problems if they both are configured to use the same scope or set of addresses. Microsoft recommends the 80/20 rule for redundancy of DHCP services in a network. To do this, you run the Configure Failover Wizard.

5. B. DHCP can't be loaded onto a Nano Server. You can load DHCP on a Server Core server (Server with no GUI desktop) or a server with the GUI desktop.

6. A. 003 Router is used to provide a list of available routers or default gateways on the same subnet.

7. D. Admins can use the `Set-DhcpServerv4Scope` command to configure the settings of an existing IPv4 scope.

8. B. 006 DNS is used to provide a list of available DNS servers to your scope settings or to your server settings.

9. B. Reservations are set up by using the machine's network adapter's MAC address. Every network adapter has its own MAC address. So when the network card got replaced, the new MAC address needs to be put into the current reservation.

10. C. Conflict Detection Attempts specifies how many ICMP echo requests (pings) the server sends for an address it is about to offer. The default is 0. Conflict detection is a way to verify that the DHCP server is not issuing IP addresses that are already being used on the network. Since you only have one DHCP server, lower the value to zero (0).

Chapter 4: Implement IP Address Management

1. B. Administrators can use the `Set-IpamBlock` PowerShell command to configure an IP address block in IPAM.

2. C. Administrators can use the `Add-IpamRange` PowerShell command to add an IP address range to an IPAM server.

3. D. Administrators can use the `Set-IpamDiscoveryDomain` PowerShell command to change the IPAM discovery configuration.

4. A. Administrators can use the `Get-IpamDnsZone` PowerShell command to view the DNS zone information from IPAM database.

5. C. Administrators need to create and links IPAM group policies (GPOs) for provisioning. To do this, you can either manually create the GPOs or run the `Invoke-IpamGpoProvisioning` PowerShell command.

6. C. The IPAM ASM Administrators group is specifically designed for the delegation of IPAM Address Space Management. The IPAM Administrators group would give her domain account way too much access within the environment, and the other two possible answers would not provide her with enough permissions to perform her required responsibilities.

7. B. Out of the three real possible deployment methods—Distributed, Centralized, and Hybrid—only the Centralized deployment method allows one primary IPAM server to manage the entire enterprise. The Distributed method places an IPAM server at each site location, and the Hybrid method uses a primary server with an additional IPAM server at each site location within the enterprise.

8. A. The Set-IPAMConfiguration command is used if the GPOs are already created. If you need to create the GPOs, you use the Invoke-IpamGpoProvisioning.

9. C. After you have successfully installed and provisioned your IPAM server, the next logical step in the IPAM deployment configuration is to configure and run server discovery.

10. A. The Move-IpamDatabase command allows an admin to move an IPAM database to a SQL Server database.

Chapter 5: Configuring Network Access

1. B. Using single tenant mode allows you to deploy the RAS Gateway as an edge VPN server, an edge DirectAccess server, or both simultaneously.

2. A. The Get-BgpRouter PowerShell command allows you to see the configuration information for BGP routers.

3. B. Administrators use the Get-DAClient command to see the list of client security groups that are part of the DirectAccess deployment and the client properties.

4. D. Logman creates and manages Event Trace Session and Performance logs and allows an administrator to monitor many different applications through the use of the command line.

5. D. The higher the RADIUS priority number, the less that the RADIUS server gets used. To make sure that RADIUS ServerD is only used when ServerB and ServerC is unavailable, you would set the RADIUS priority from 1 to 10. This way it will only get used when ServerB and ServerC is having issues or is unresponsive.

6. B. SSTP is secure sockets and secure sockets uses port 443.

7. C. The Get-RemoteAccess command shows the configuration of a DirectAccess and VPN server.

8. B. The Set-DAServer command allows an administrator to set the properties specific to the DirectAccess server.

9. C. Administrators use the `Set-VpnAuthType` command to set the authentication type to be used for a VPN connection.

10. D. The `Add-RemoteAccessRadius` command allows an administrator to add a new external RADIUS server for VPN or DirectAccess connectivity.

Chapter 6: Understanding File Services

1. C. You need to publish shares in the directory before they are available to the users of the directory. If NetBIOS is still enabled on the network, the shares will be visible to the NetBIOS tools and clients, but you do not have to enable NetBIOS on shares. Although replication must occur before the shares are available in the directory, it is unlikely that the replication will not have occurred by the next day. If this is the case, then you have other problems with the directory as well.

2. A. The Sharing tab contains a check box that you can use to list the printer in Active Directory.

3. B. The `Get-FsrmQuota` command allows you to view the quotas on the FSRM server.

4. C. The `New-FsrmFileGroup` command allows an administrator to create a file group.

5. A. Administrators can use the `New-FsrmQuotaTemplate` command to create a new quota template on FSRM.

6. C. An administrator can use the `Remove-FsrmClassificationRule` command to delete the FSRM classification rule.

7. B. Offline files give you the opportunity to set up files and folders so that users can work on the data while outside the company walls. Offline files allows a user to work on files while at home without the need to be logged into the network.

8. A, B, C, D. Improved security, quotas, compression, and encryption are all advantages of using NTFS over FAT32. These features are not available in FAT32. The only security you have in FAT32 is shared folder permissions.

9. B. Disk quotas allow you to limit the amount of space on a volume or partition. You can set an umbrella quota for all users and then implement individual users' quotas to bypass the umbrella quota.

10. B. Cipher is a command-line utility that allows you to configure or change EFS files and folders.

Chapter 7: Configuring High Availability

1. A. To create a new NLB cluster, you would use the PowerShell command `New-NlbCluster`.

2. B, D. Answers B and D are the only versions that are real. There is no 2016 Small Business Server or Virtual Edition. The Windows Server 2016 server for virtualization is Hyper-V.

3. A. The maximum number a single cluster can support is 32 computers.

4. B. If an administrator decides to use the drainstop command, the cluster stops after answering all of the current NLB connections. So the current NLB connections are finished but no new connections to that node are accepted.

5. D. If you want to stop the entire cluster from running, while in the NLB manager (type NLBmgr in Run command), you would right click on the cluster, point to Control Hosts, and then choose Stop.

6. A. The PowerShell command `Stop-VMReplication` will stop virtual machine replication from happening.

7. B, D. Websites and Terminal Services are all designed to work with NLB clusters. Database servers like SQL Server do not work on NLB clusters.

8. B. To use unicast communication between NLB cluster nodes, each node must have a minimum of two network adapters.

9. D. Setting the cluster affinity to Single will send all traffic from a specific IP address to a single cluster node. Using this affinity will keep a client on a specific node where the client should not have to authenticate again. Setting the filtering mode to Single would remove the authentication problem but would not distribute the load to other servers unless the initial server was down.

10. C. When setting the affinity to Class C, NLB links clients with a specific member based on the Class C part of the client's IP address. This allows an administrator to setup NLB so that clients from the same Class C address range can access the same NLB member. This affinity is best for NLB clusters using the Internet.

Chapter 8: Implementing Software Defined Networking

1. D. The `New-NetworkControllerNodeObject` command is the PowerShell command that allows you to setup a new Network Controller.

2. B. Remote Access Server (RAS) gateways are used for bridging traffic between virtual and non-virtual networks. Organizations can use Software Load Balancing (SLB) to evenly distribute network traffic between the virtual network resources.

3. B. Network Controllers are new to Windows Server 2016. Network Controllers allow an administrator to have a centralized virtual and physical datacenter infrastructure. This allows administrators to manage, configure, and troubleshoot all of their infrastructure components from one location.

4. A. The only virtual hard disk that increases in size is the dynamically expanding disk. Thus this is the only valid answer to this question. The fixed-size disk creates a disk of the size you specify, the differencing disk is a special disk that stores only the differences between it and a parent disk, and the physical disk uses a physical drive and makes it available to the virtual machine.

5. C. Physical hard disks cannot be configured using the Virtual Hard Disk Wizard, the Edit Virtual Hard Disk Wizard, or the New Virtual Machine Wizard. You can configure and attach a physical disk only by using the virtual machine's settings.

6. B. Hyper-V is not supported on Itanium-based systems, thus he cannot install it.

7. A, B, C. The minimum CPU requirement for running Hyper-V is a x64-based processor (Itanium is not supported), hardware Data Execution Protection must be enabled, and hardware-assisted virtualization must be enabled. There is no minimum requirement for a dual-core processor.

8. C. This question relates to the setup command used to install the Hyper-V server role on a Windows Server 2016 Server Core machine. It's important to remember that these commands are case sensitive, and that the correct command is start /wocsetup Microsoft-Hyper-V, which is option C. All of the other commands will fail to install Hyper-V on a Server Core machine.

9. B. In single tenant mode, the RAS Gateway is used as the exterior or Internet facing VPN or DirectAccess edge server.

10. C. The virtual network type in which the machines communicate with each other and with the host machine is called *internal only*. In a private virtual network, the virtual machines can communicate only with each other, not with the network or the host machine. The external network type defines a network where the virtual machines can communicate with each other, with the host machine, and with an external network like the Internet.

Index

J

N

Comprehensive Online Learning Environment

Register on Sybex.com to gain access to the comprehensive online interactive learning environment and test bank to help you study for your MCSA Windows Server 2016 certification.

The online test bank includes:

- **Assessment Test** to help you focus your study to specific objectives
- **Chapter Tests** to reinforce what you've learned
- **Practice Exams** to test your knowledge of the material
- **Digital Flashcards** to reinforce your learning and provide last-minute test prep before the exam
- **Searchable Glossary** to define the key terms you'll need to know for the exam
- **Videos** created by the author to accompany chapter exercises

Go to http://www.wiley.com/go/sybextestprep to register and gain access to this comprehensive study tool package.